THE IMPROVISING FINGERSTYLE GUITARIST

Gilbert Isbin

I0808789

Online Audio

To access the online audio go to:

WWW.MELBAY.COM/30697MEB

The image of the guitar featured on the cover, a Martin OM-21, is courtesy of Martin Guitar.

© 2020 By Mel Bay Publications, Inc. All Rights Reserved.
WWW.MELBAY.COM

CONTENTS

GILBERT ISBIN

Belgian composer Gilbert Isbin is one of the most interesting, dynamic and poetic composers writing for the guitar today.

Isbin's compositional and performing style defies genre, blending elements for contemporary classical, jazz, early music, world music and improvisation. He has been compared favorably to the likes of Ralph Towner and Egberto Gismonti, his music described as 'oblique, subtle, and hauntingly beautiful'.

Thus far he composed more that 400 compositions for guitar, lute and small ensembles.

He has performed in concert at festivals and major venues throughout Europe and the US.

As a leader and co-leader, he has released an impressive string of recordings for various labels with internationally acclaimed artists such as Cameron Brown, Joe Fonda, Hugh Hopper, Scott Walton, Vinny Golia, Bruce Arnold, Jeff Gauthier, Michel Godard, and Sandro di Stefano.

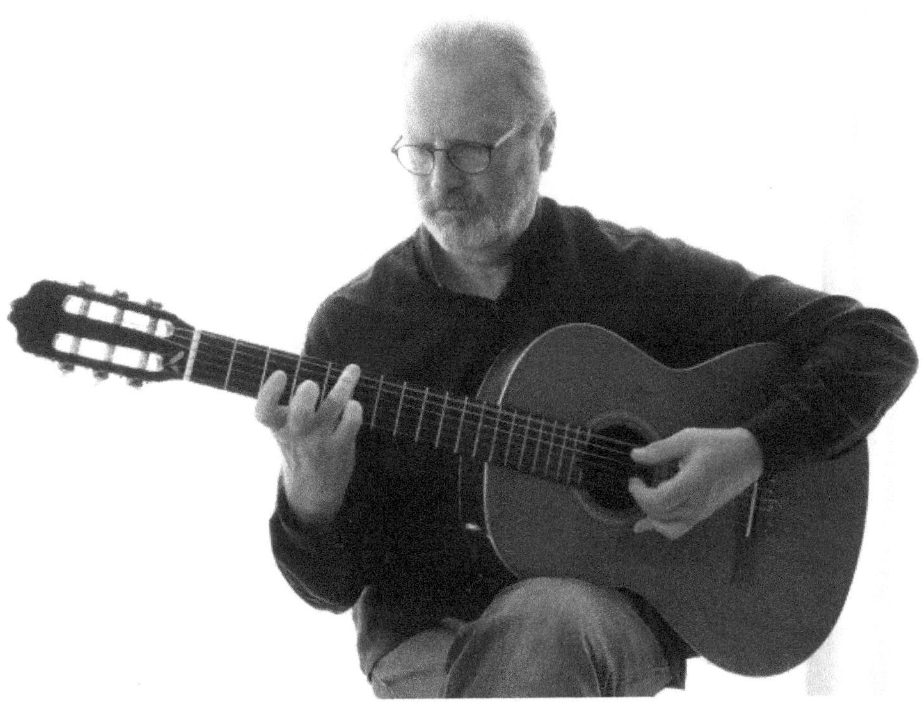

Gilbert Isbin

FOREWORD

Improvising is like composing; no matter how much theoretical knowledge you absorb, imagination is essential.

This book is written to help you improvise in a contemporary way on the guitar. Every musician can learn to improvise. You just need to learn and practice the right tools. Improvisation is not intimidating at all!

Each chapter focuses on a different improvisational approach. Play through the examples at your own tempo but don't feel as though you have to memorize them. This is not necessary nor desirable. When you feel ready, start practicing improvising using the exercises given in the book.

At first, you will probably not play in strict time, but you will be able to maintain a steady tempo as you become more experienced and confident.

In every chapter there is a 'Your turn' section, following the examples. Here you are learning the tools of improvisation and it is important to invest time when it is 'Your turn'.

The aim is always to create your own improvisations, but if this seems too difficult, you could begin by composing some ideas on paper.

The book will not deal in great detail with theoretical aspects. These can be found in thousands of books that have already been published.

The Improvising Fingerstyle Guitarist is written with the guitar at hand and is focused on improvising in a contemporary way on scales and modes, bass and chord progressions.

Thanks to Stuart Walsh for help with proofreading and William Bay for his support of my music.

I have recorded many of the exercises and online access to the audio is included.

I hope this book will be stimulating, rewarding and enjoyable.

Gilbert Isbin

CHAPTER 1

Breaking Down the C Major Scale

In this chapter we will explore the fretboard using the C Major Scale. This scale will function as a basis for all other scales/modes that we will use.
The aim of this book is to help create melodic lines on the spot.
You will be encouraged to use adjacent and non-adjacent strings in your improvisations and in this way (as you will see in the examples) you will discover interesting intervals so you can free yourself from relying on simple, scale-like passages.

Improvisation means playing in the moment, so don't just memorize the examples or play them as licks as this has nothing to do with improvisation. You are free to write down your creations, of course, and use them for composing purposes or as a starting point for further explorations.

The C Major Scale

Notations
do re mi fa sol la si do
C D E F G A B C
♭ before any tone = lower that tone by a half step (one fret's distance).
♯ = raise that tone with a half step.

Rather than just going from C to C, we will be playing the full range of notes available in the 1st position. 1st position means that you have your index finger on the first fret.

Track 1

ascending **descending**

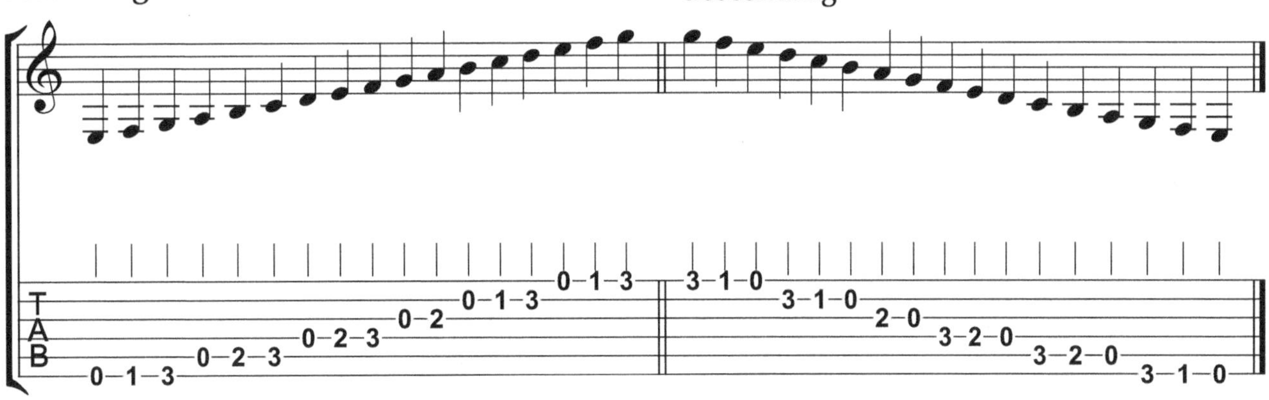

Scale tones

The notes of a scale can be numbered according to their interval.
Look for these intervals on the fretboard and sing them while you are plucking them.

1 2 or 9 3 4 or 11 5 6 or 13 7
C D E F G A B

Intervals greater than an octave are called compound intervals. (9,11,13)
Find the intervals on the fretboard.

Track 2

1 2 or 9 3 4 or 11 5 6 or 13 7

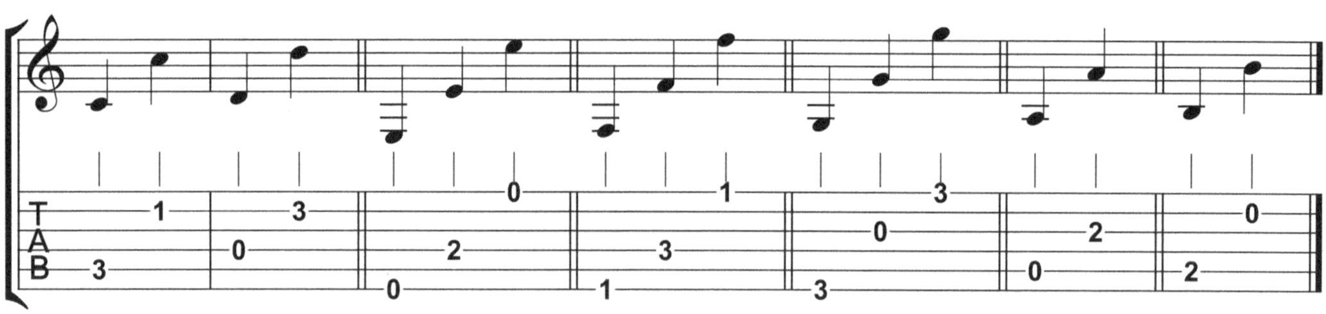

When improvising you should be able to hear the pitches in your mind and find them on the fretboard. To do this you should practice singing (or humming) every scale note. Each note has a unique intervallic relationship to a root note. Simply put : the root note or tonic (1), the major 3rd (3), perfect 4th (4), perfect 5th (5), major 6th (6) are considered as consonant. 'Consonant' is associated with sweetness. The major 2nd (2) and major 7th (7) are considered as 'dissonant' (harsh, less pleasant). It's up to your personal taste which intervals you like or dislike.

Exercise

Play first the tonic (root note) and then sing it. Then pluck a scale note and sing it. You might sing the note's name or you could just hum the sound. Sing first the 1,3 and 5 as they are part of a C major triad. Then we continue with the other consonant intervals to end with the dissonant ones. Listen to the different sonic colors.

Let's start with the tonic or root note.
Sing a C while sustaining the C (as a sort of drone) and listen to its specific tonic color. Then sing the root without plucking it. Then play the C and listen to check if you were singing correctly.

Root or octave **Major 3rd** or or

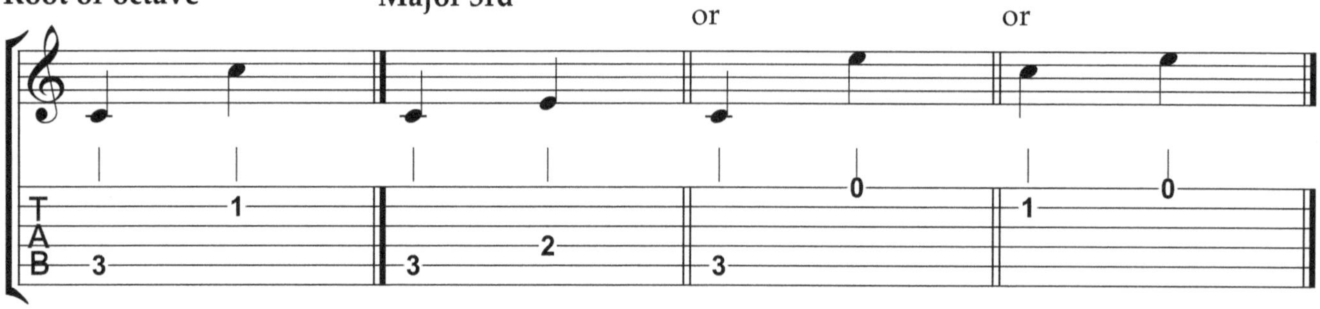

Perfect 5th

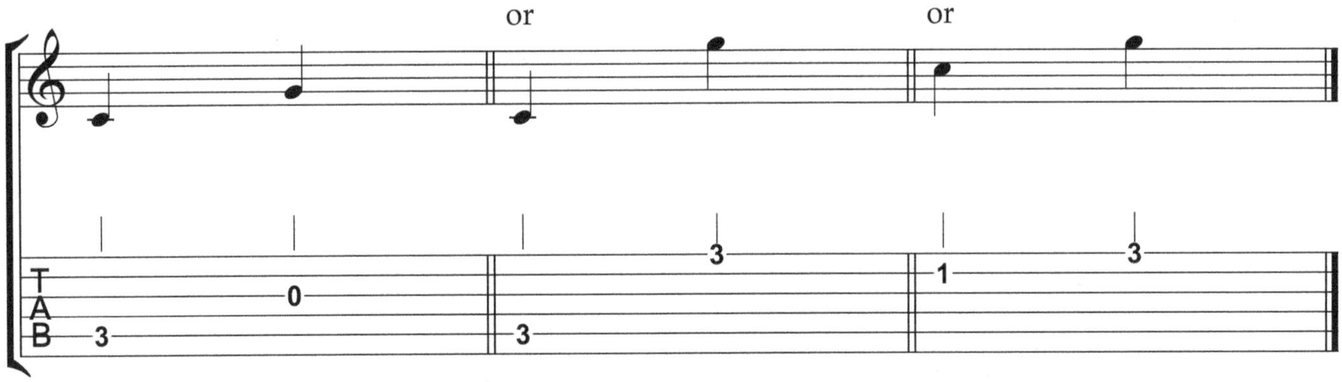

Perfect 4th or 11th

Major 6th

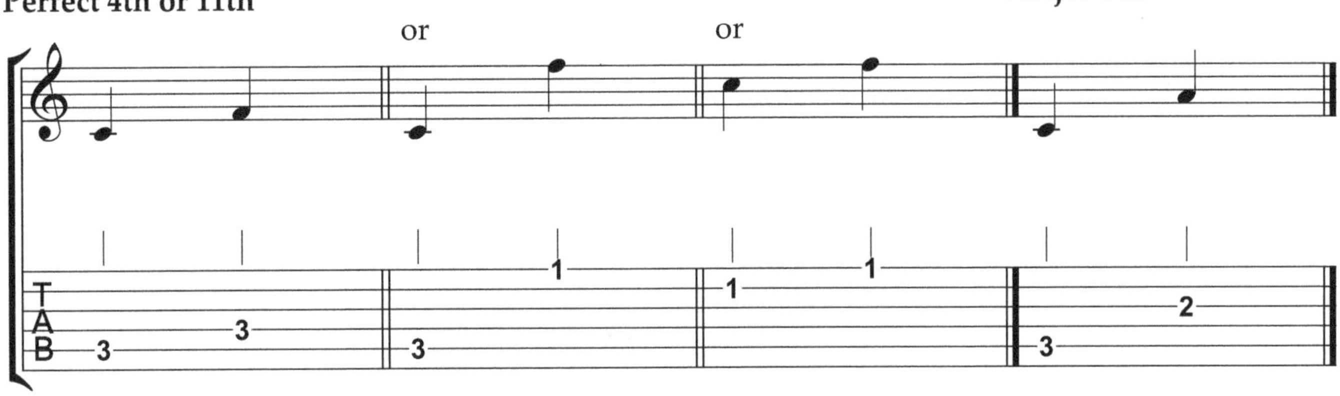

Major 2nd or 9th

Major 7th

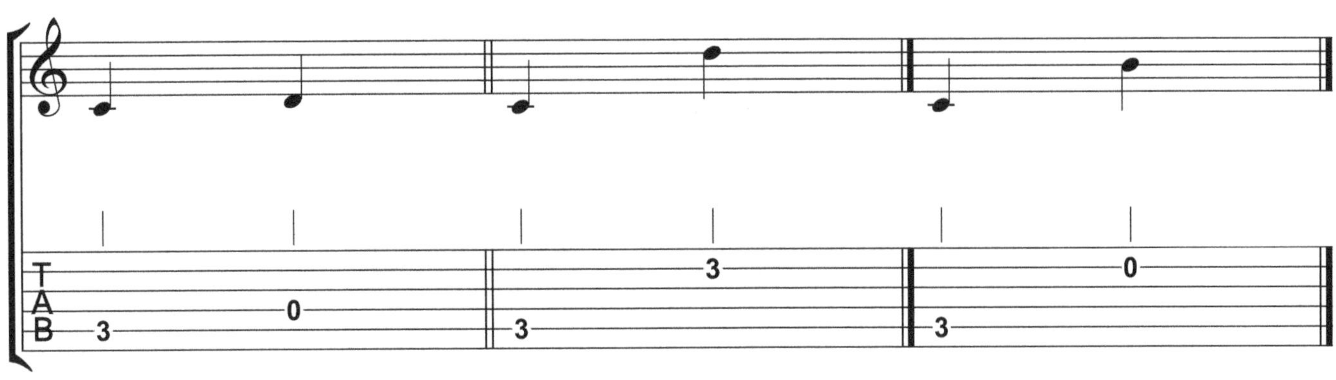

Breaking down the C Major scale

As you become familiar with the available notes on each string try to play interesting melodic phrases that are not just based on stepwise motion. Creating lines from notes on non-adjacent strings will help you develop a personal, colorful vocabulary. Try to sing these notes too. You should, with some practice, be able to play what you hear in your mind. Name the intervals.

①= first string, etc.

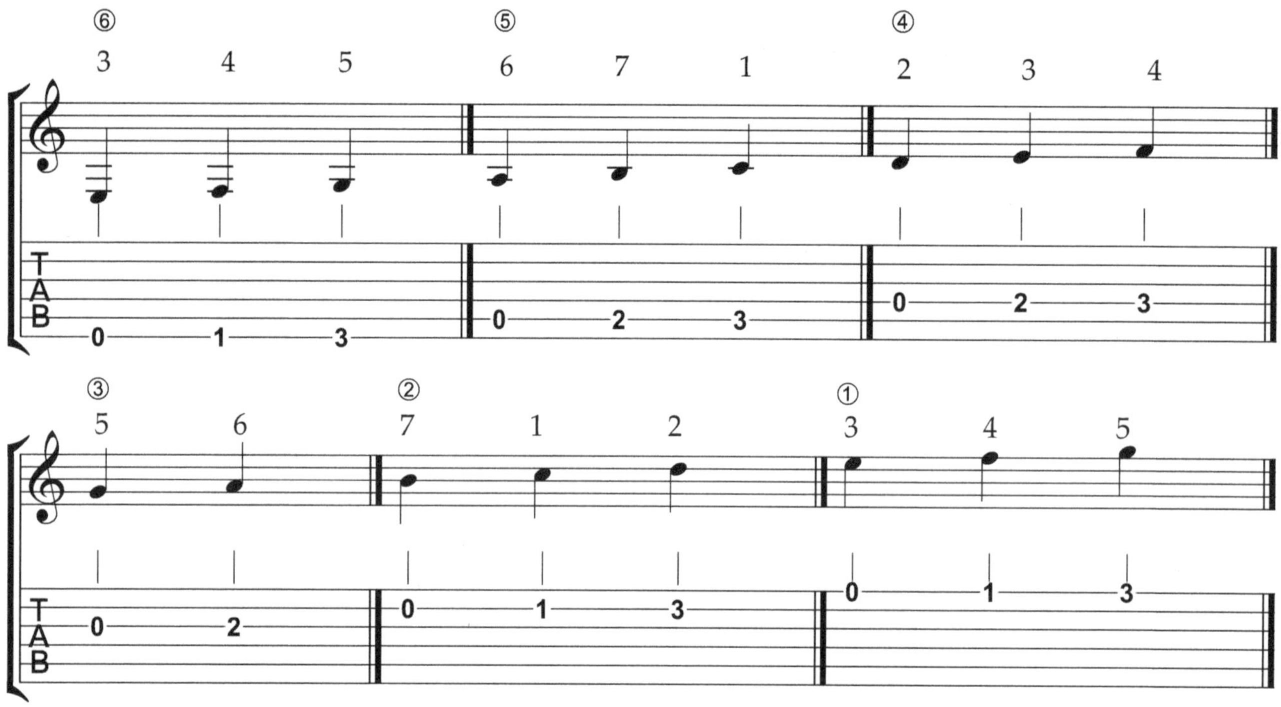

Improvising single note lines on different strings

Try to liberate yourself from a reliance on scale like passages and create interesting melodic lines (and increase your technical ability). All the following lines in the examples came out of my intuitive sense and not from formulas.

It's not a terrible mistake if you hit a note that is not part of the C Major scale. Don't stop, just play on. Perhaps these 'mistakes' might become a part of your improvising approach. To start, use the following rhythms, but if you would like to play a rhythm that is not from the ones specified, feel free to do so.

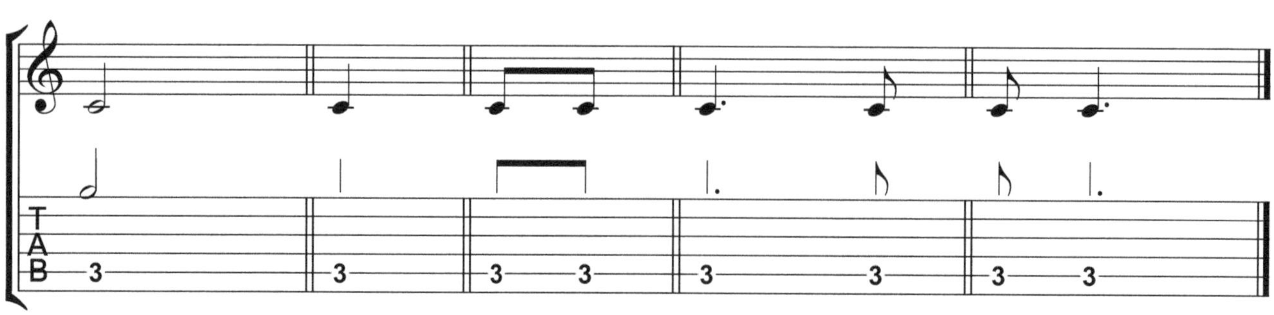

On 1 string

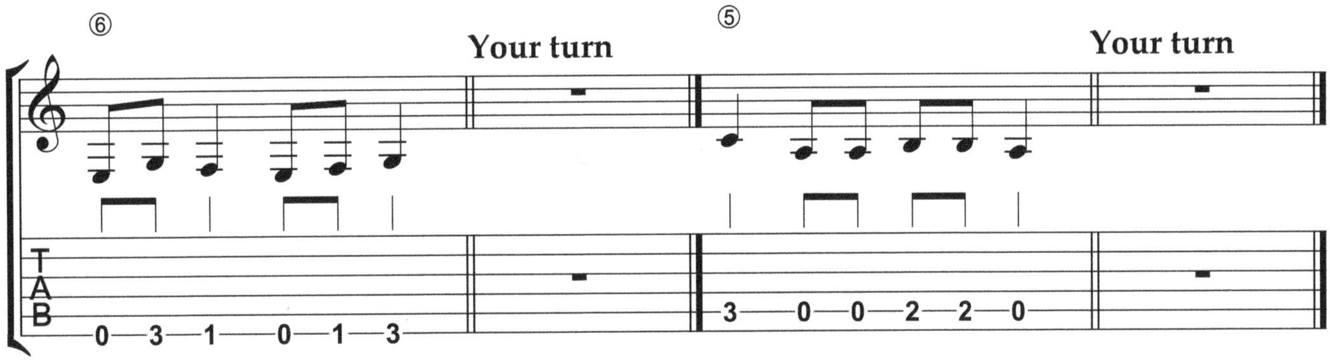

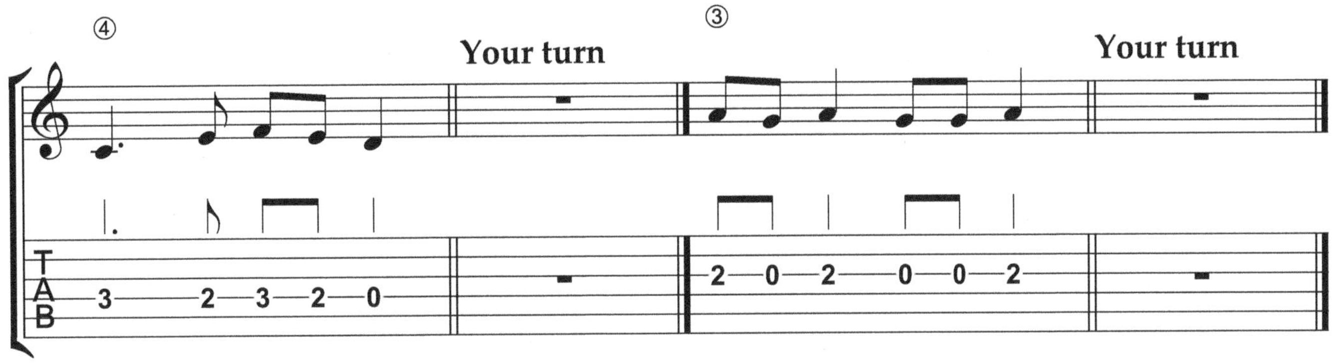

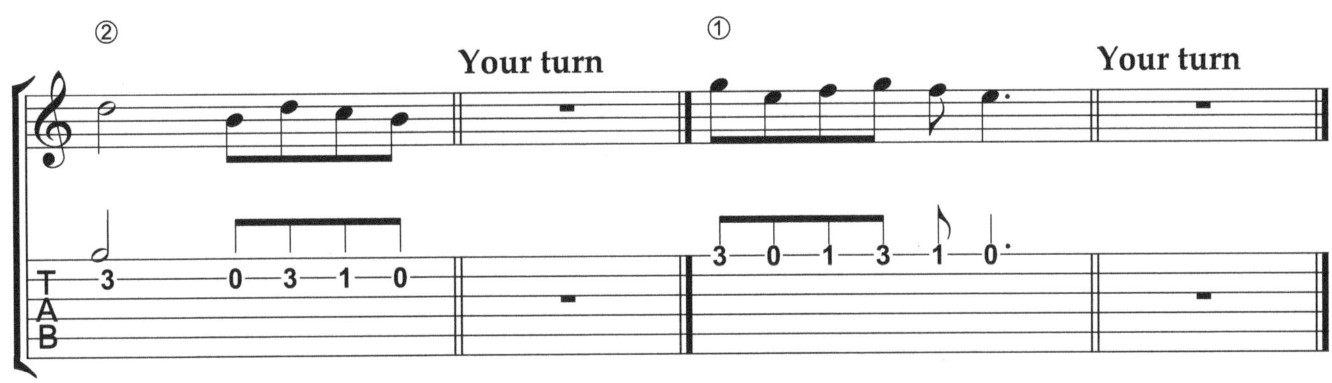

On 2 strings

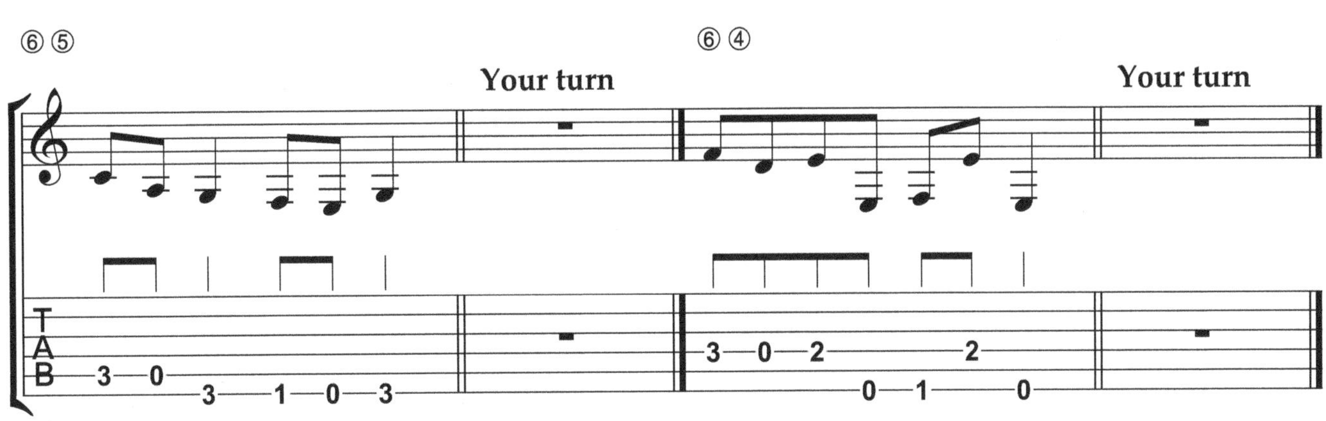

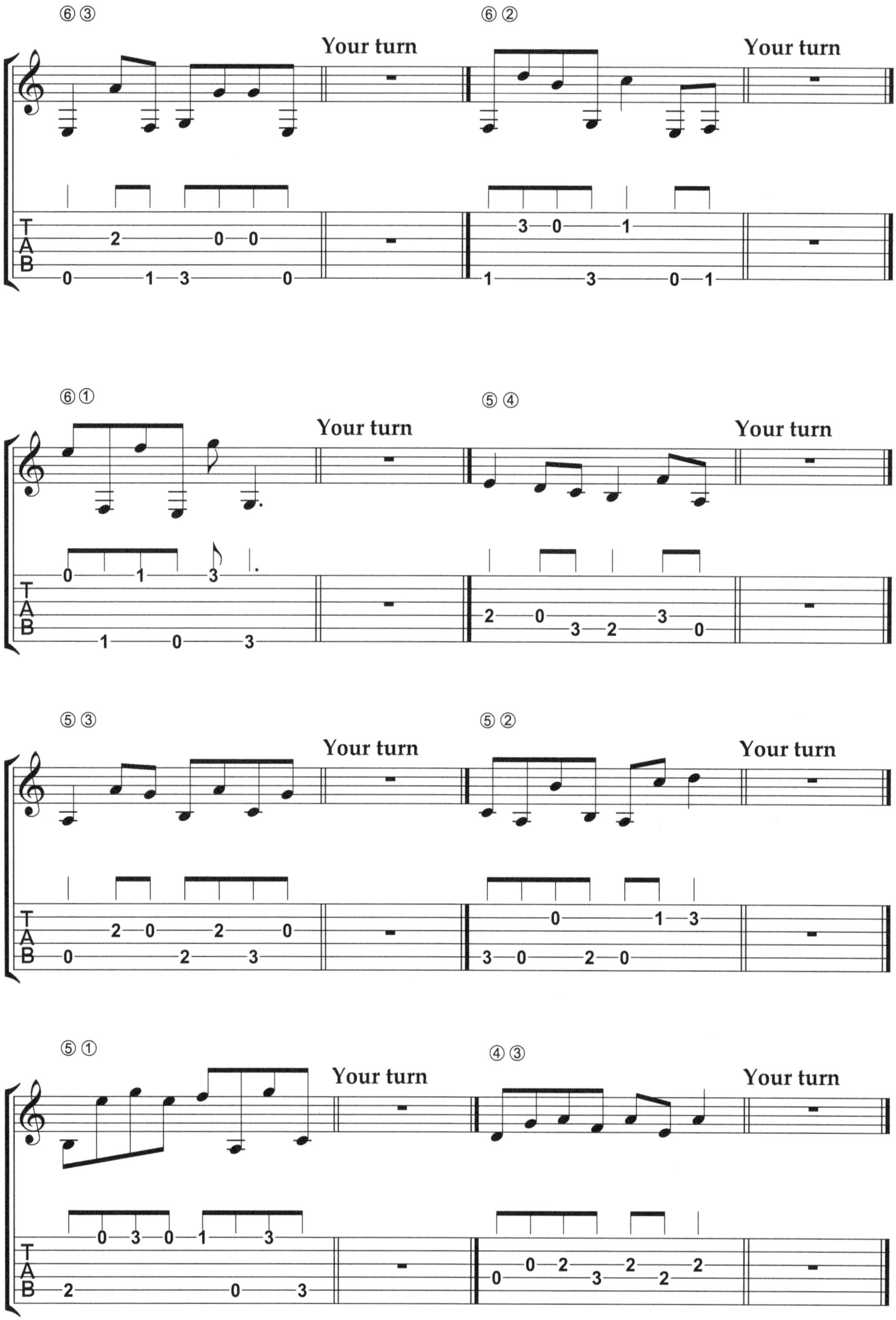
⑥ ③
Your turn
⑥ ②
Your turn
⑥ ①
Your turn
⑤ ④
Your turn
⑤ ③
Your turn
⑤ ②
Your turn
⑤ ①
Your turn
④ ③
Your turn

On 3 Strings

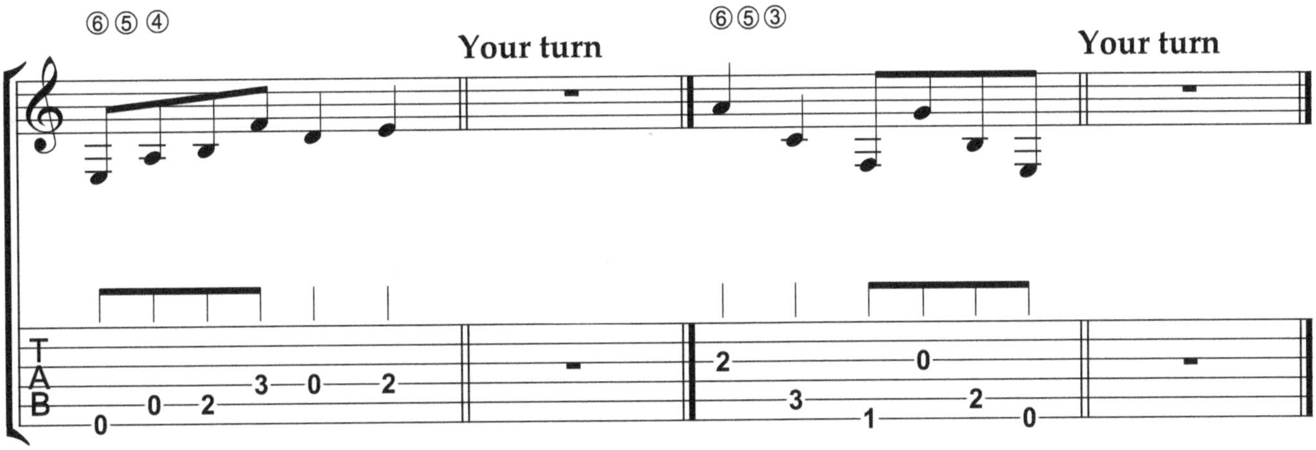
⑥⑤④
Your turn
⑥⑤③
Your turn

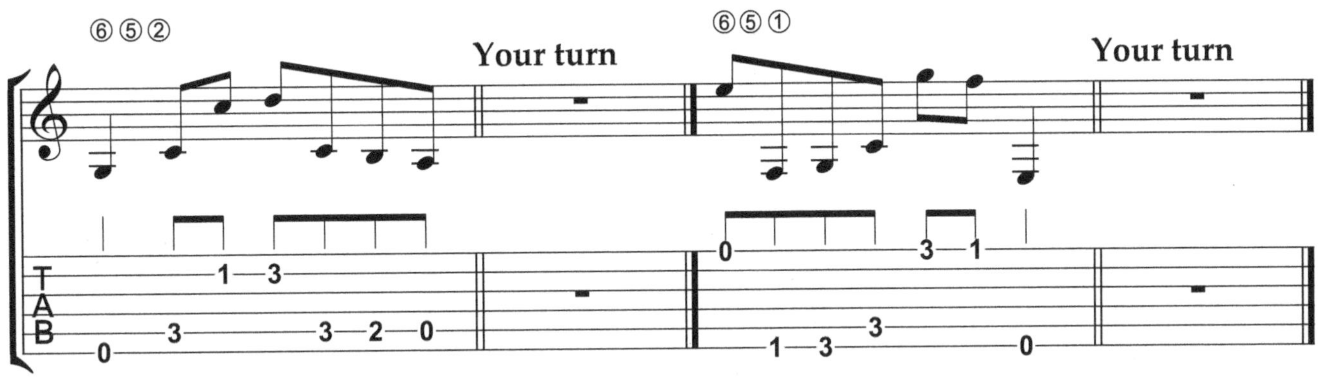
⑥⑤②
Your turn
⑥⑤①
Your turn

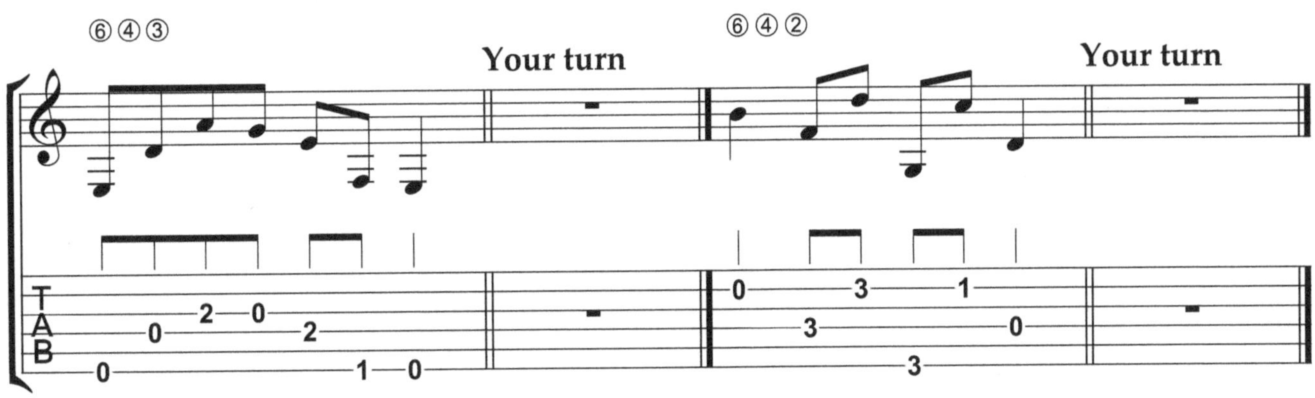
⑥④③
Your turn
⑥④②
Your turn

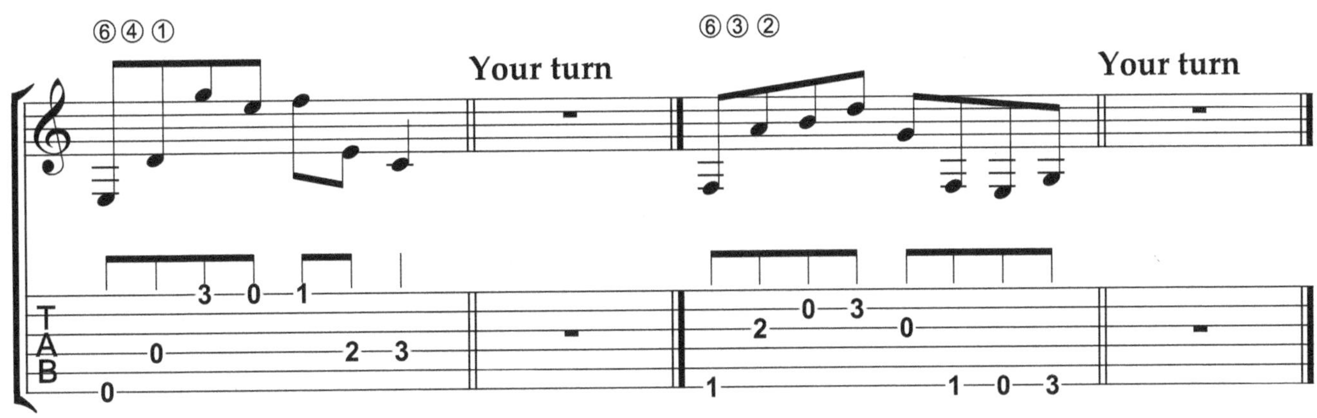
⑥④①
Your turn
⑥③②
Your turn

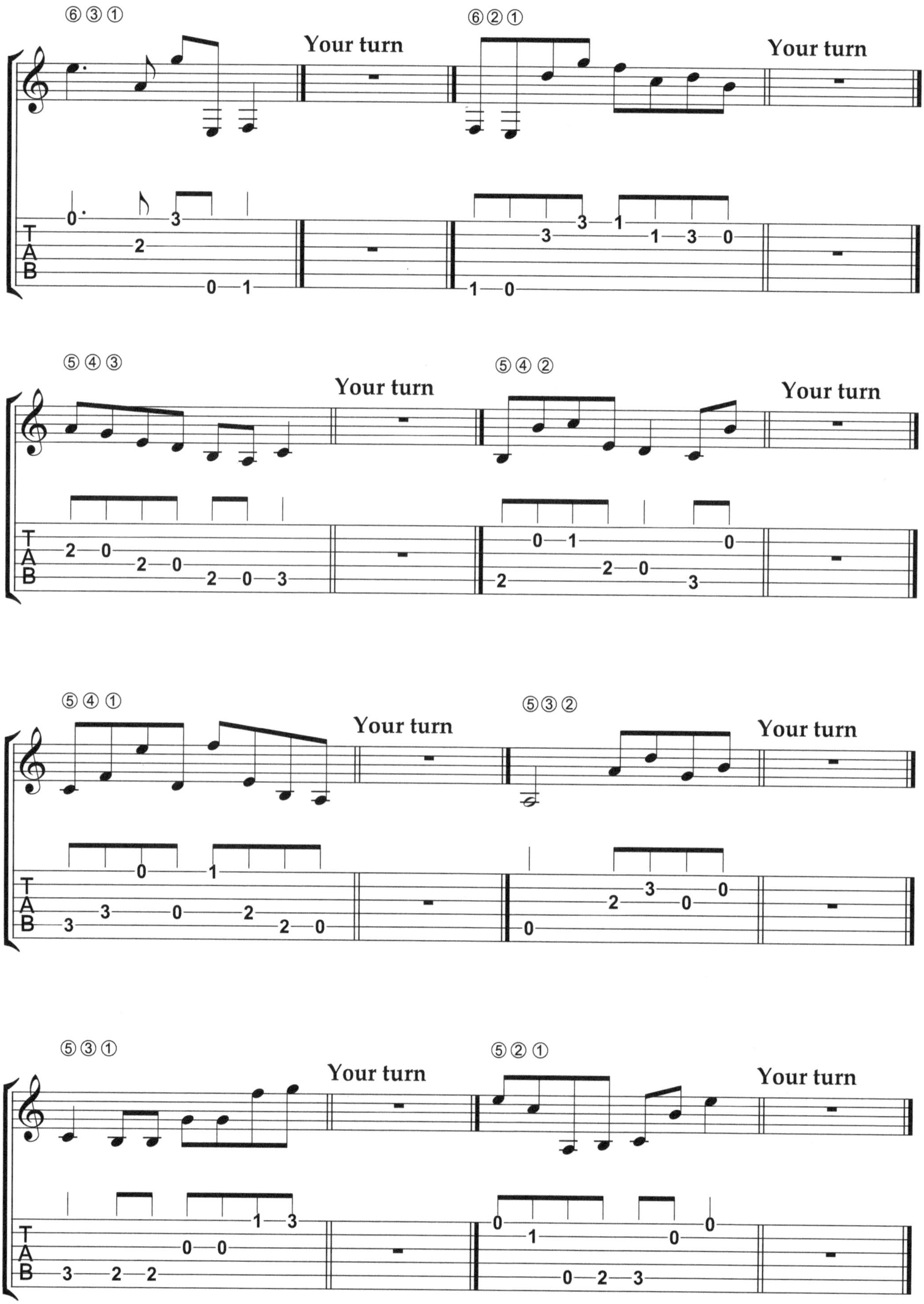
⑥ ③ ①
Your turn
⑥ ② ①
Your turn
⑤ ④ ③
Your turn
⑤ ④ ②
Your turn
⑤ ④ ①
Your turn
⑤ ③ ②
Your turn
⑤ ③ ①
Your turn
⑤ ② ①
Your turn

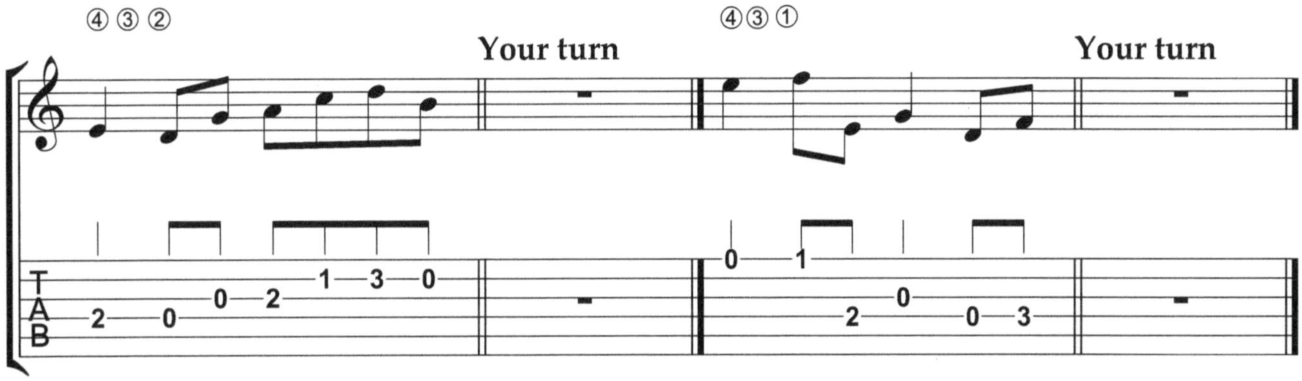
④ ③ ②
Your turn
④③①
Your turn

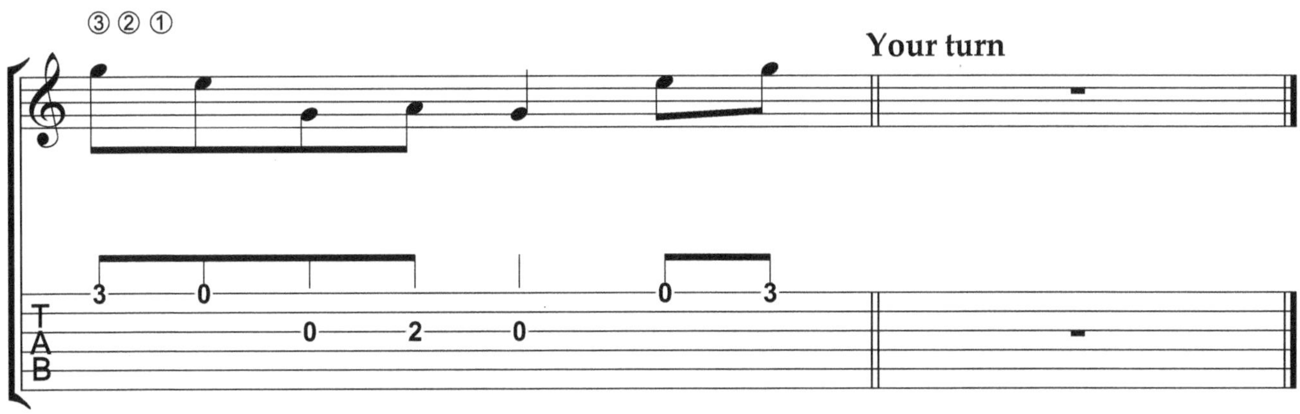
③ ② ①
Your turn

On 4 Strings

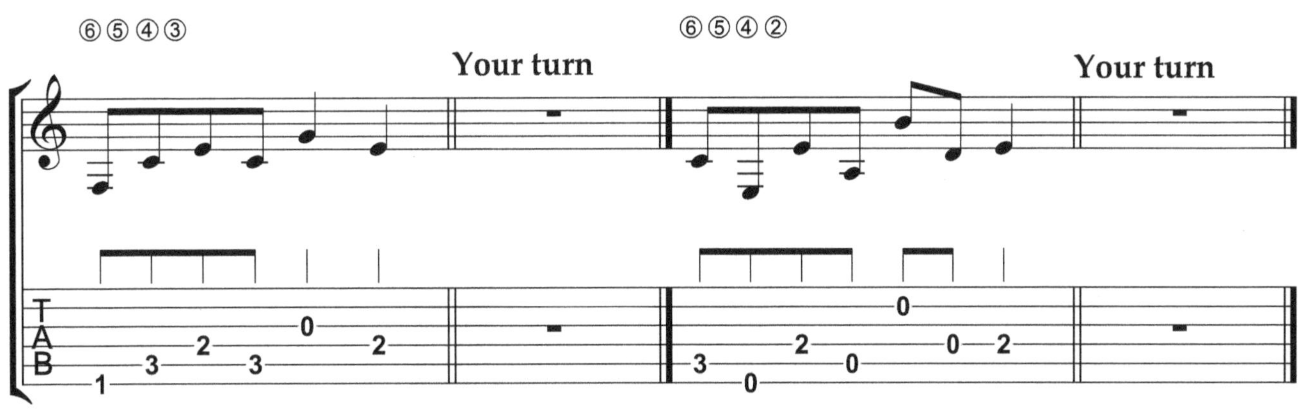
⑥⑤④③
Your turn
⑥⑤④②
Your turn

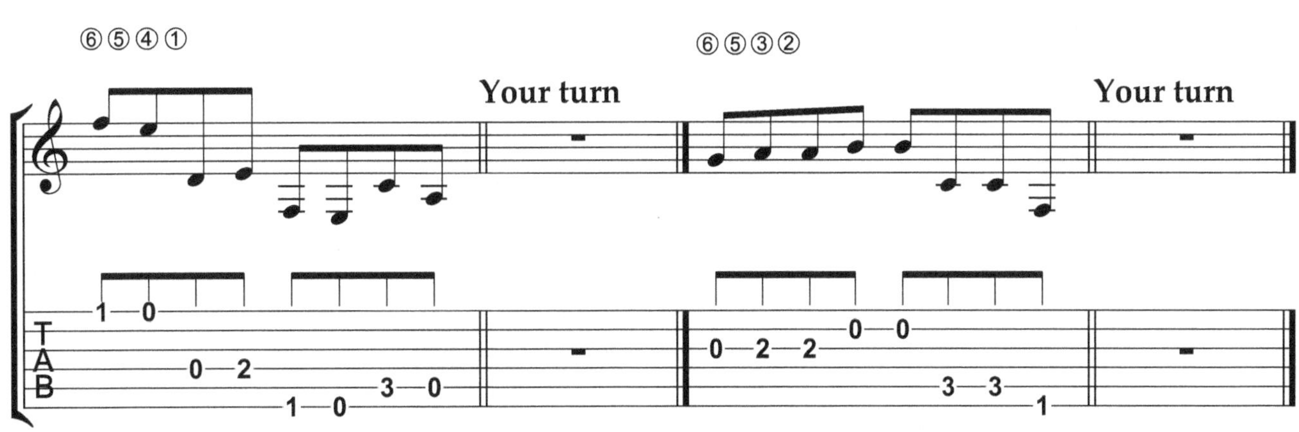
⑥⑤④①
Your turn
⑥⑤③②
Your turn

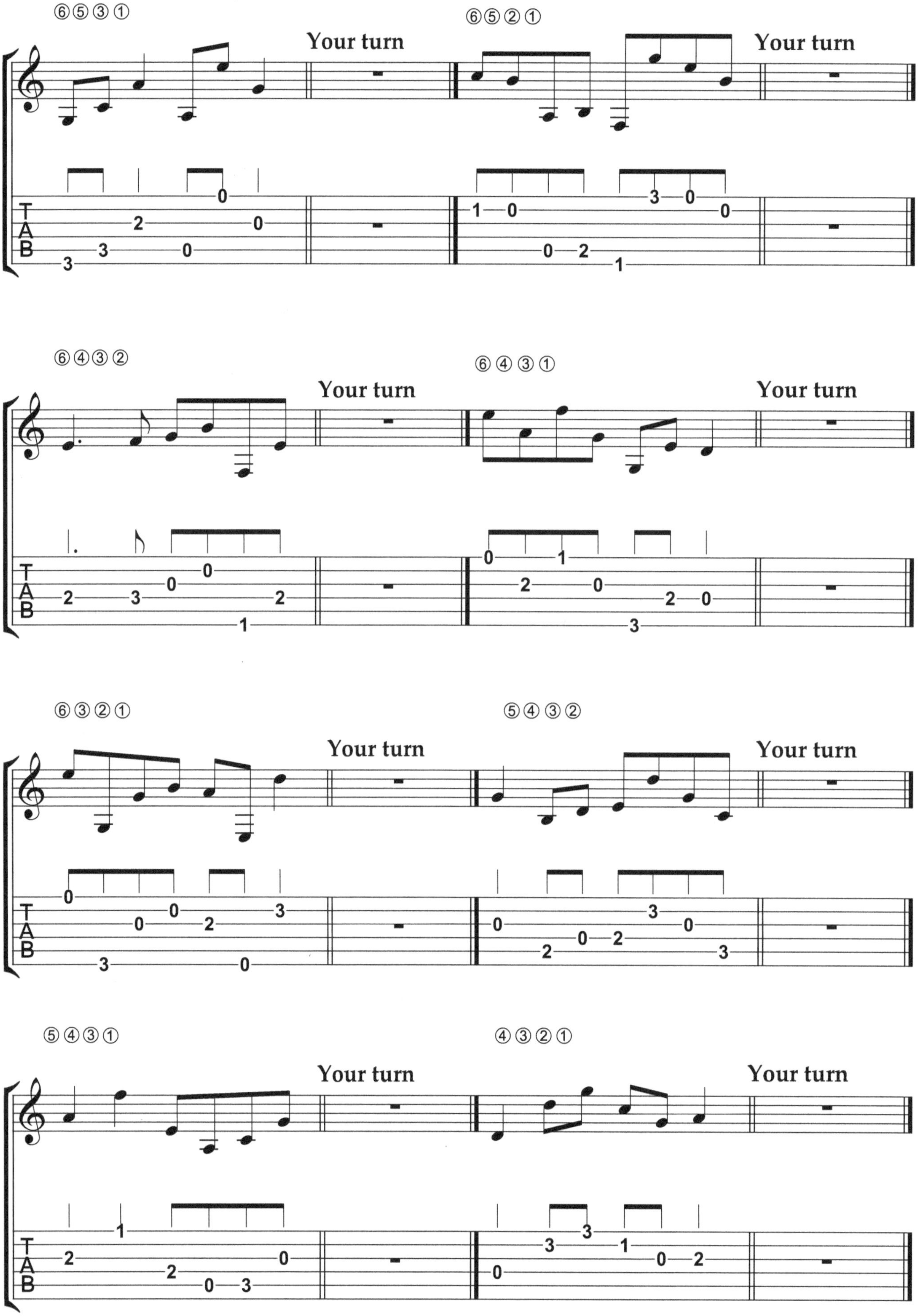
⑥⑤③①
Your turn
⑥⑤②①
Your turn
⑥④③②
Your turn
⑥④③①
Your turn
⑥③②①
Your turn
⑤④③②
Your turn
⑤④③①
Your turn
④③②①
Your turn

On 5 Strings

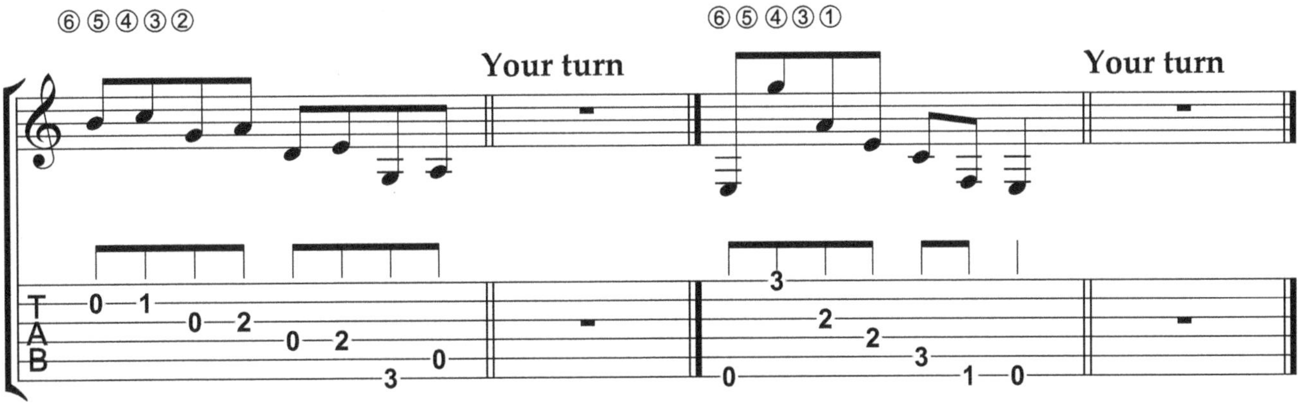

On 6 Strings

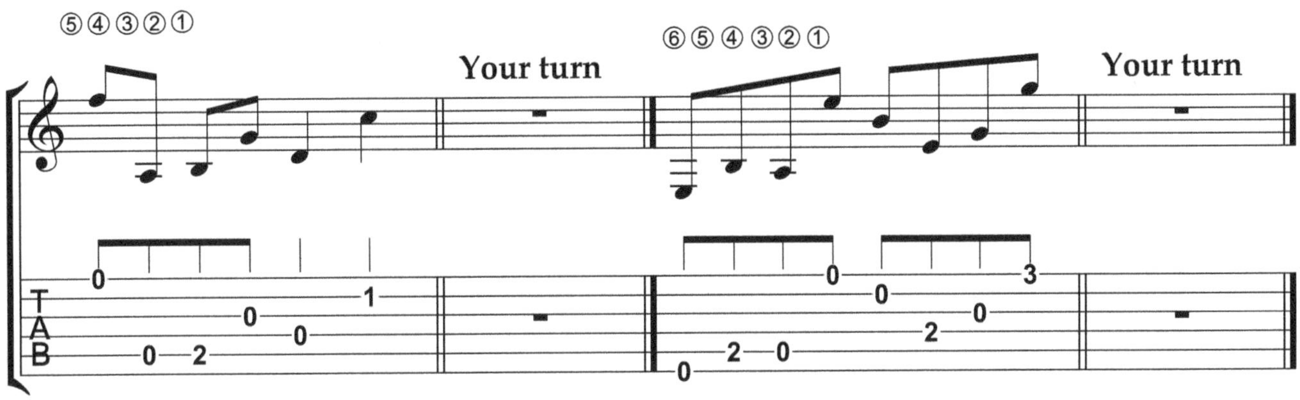

Some examples:

Track 3

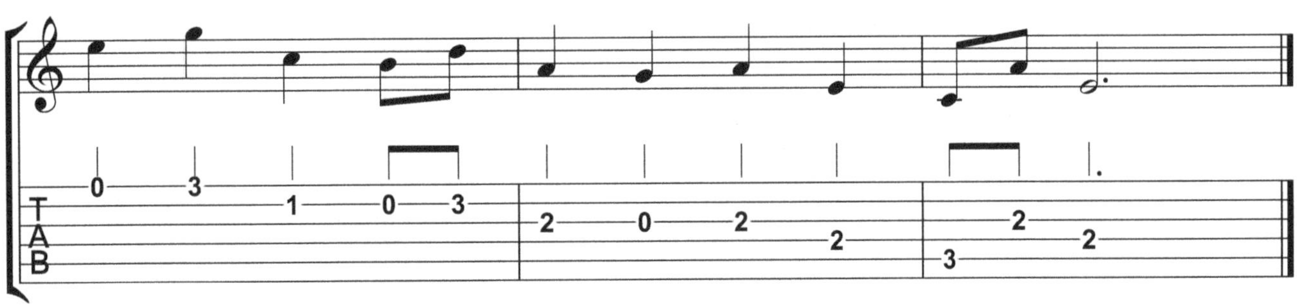

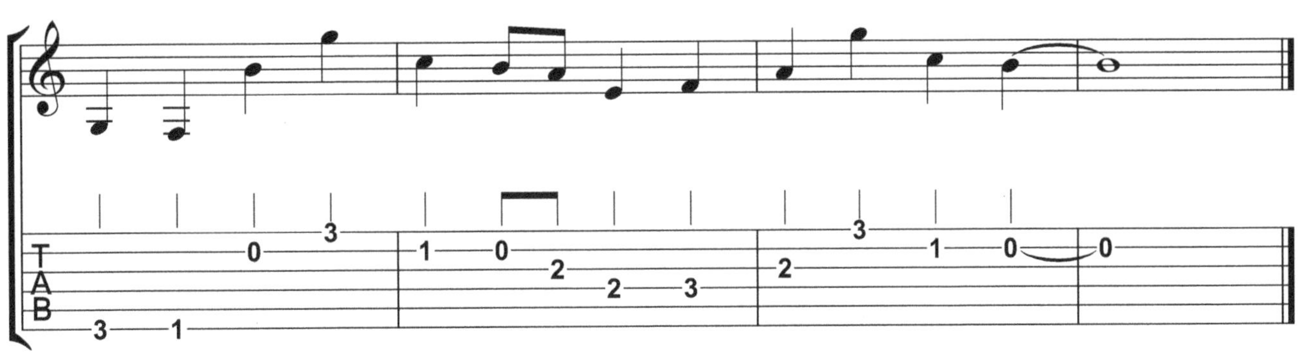

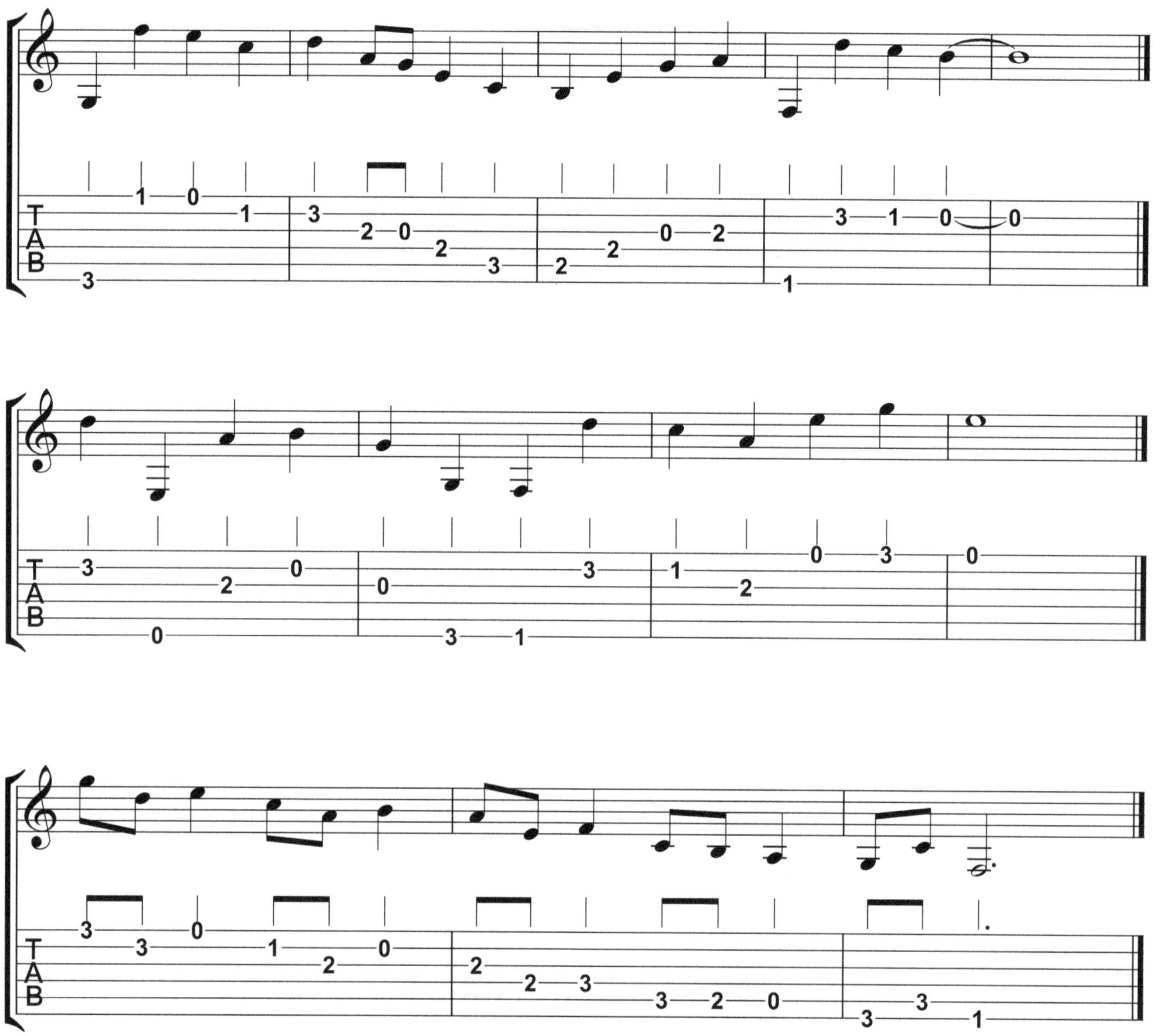
TAB

CHAPTER 2

Single Note Lines Preceded by a Bass Note

As soloists we have to deal with the melody voice, the accompaniment (could be one note, dyads - 2-note groupings - and other chord parts) and the bass voice. Let's concentrate first on the melody voice and the bass voice. Improvise melodic lines on strings 1, 2, 3 and 4 and play the bass notes on strings 4, 5 and 6. Remember you are still playing in the key of C Major. Only the bass notes changed. As a matter of fact, every bass note is the root of a mode. Every scale has as many modes as it has notes in it.

For your convenience, they are listed below. It's good to be aware of them, but they are not essential for our further explorations in improvisation.

Ionian : C D E F G A B C
Dorian : D E F G A B C D
Phrygian : E F G A B C D E
Lydian : F G A B C D E F
Mixolydian : G A B C D E F G
Aeolian : A B C D E F G A
Locrian : B C D E F G A B

No accidentals involved! Play a melodic line preceded by a bass note on the first beat of each bar. Here are some examples.

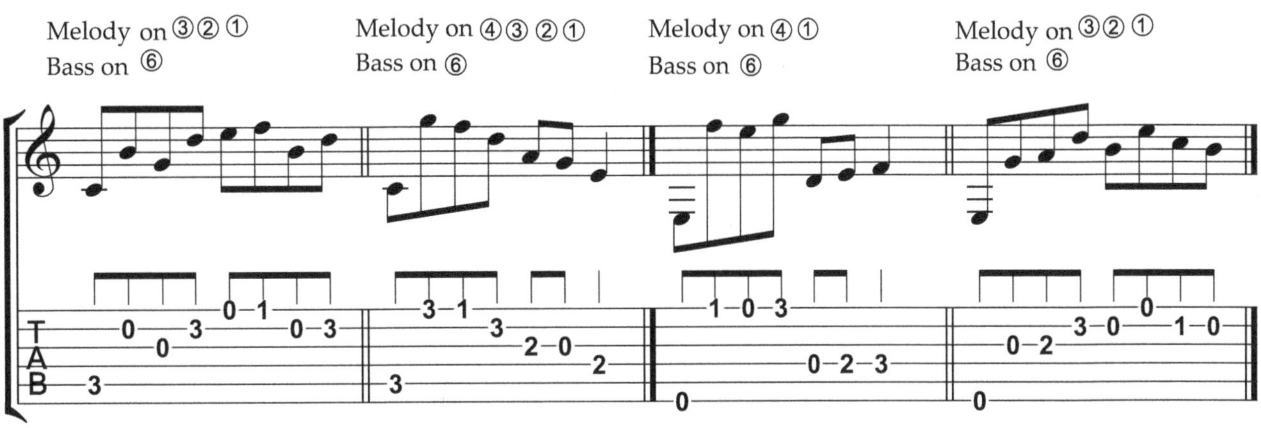

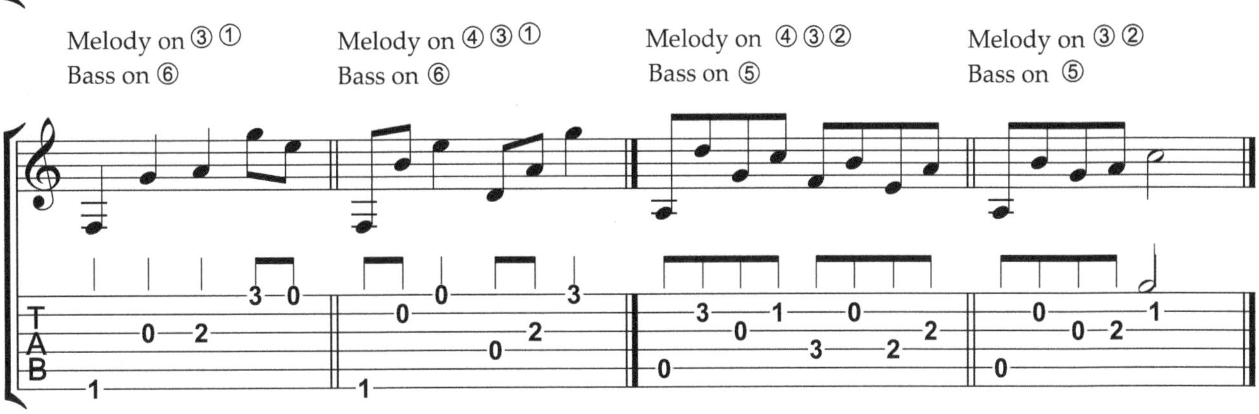

Melody on ③ ② ①
Bass on ⑤

Melody on ④ ③ ②
Bass on ⑤

Melody on ② ①
Bass on ⑤

Melody on ④ ③ ② ①
Bass on ⑤

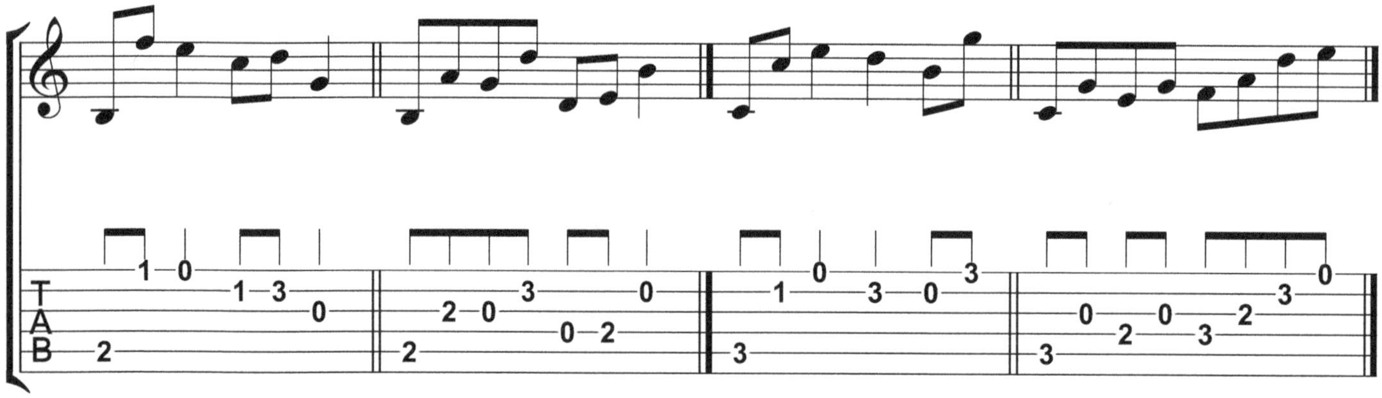

Melody on ③ ② ①
Bass on ④

Melody on ② ①
Bass on ④

Melody on ③ ② ①
Bass on ④

Melody on ③ ②
Bass on ④

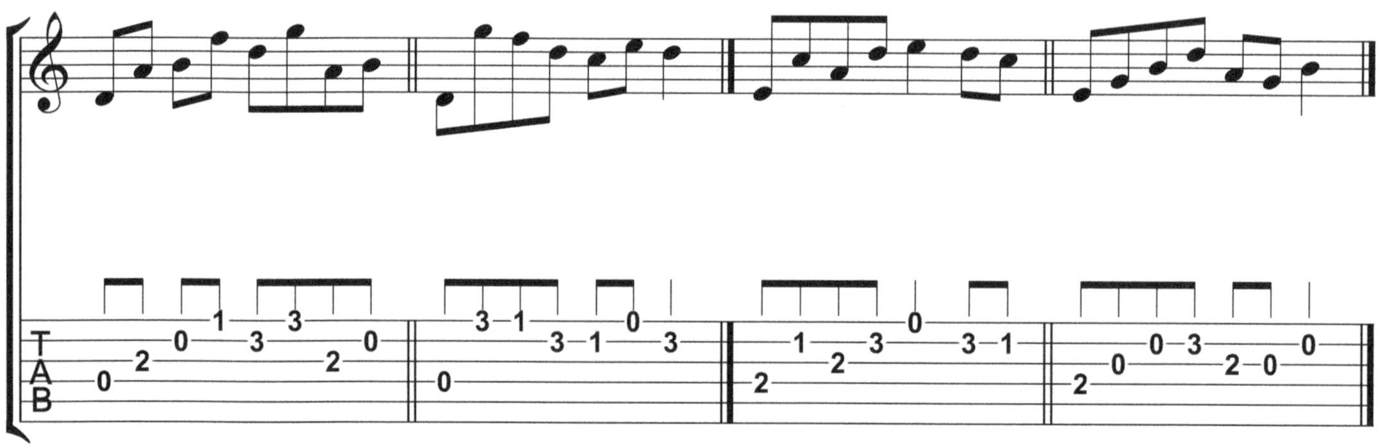

Melody on ③ ② ①
Bass on ④

Melody on ② ①
Bass on ④

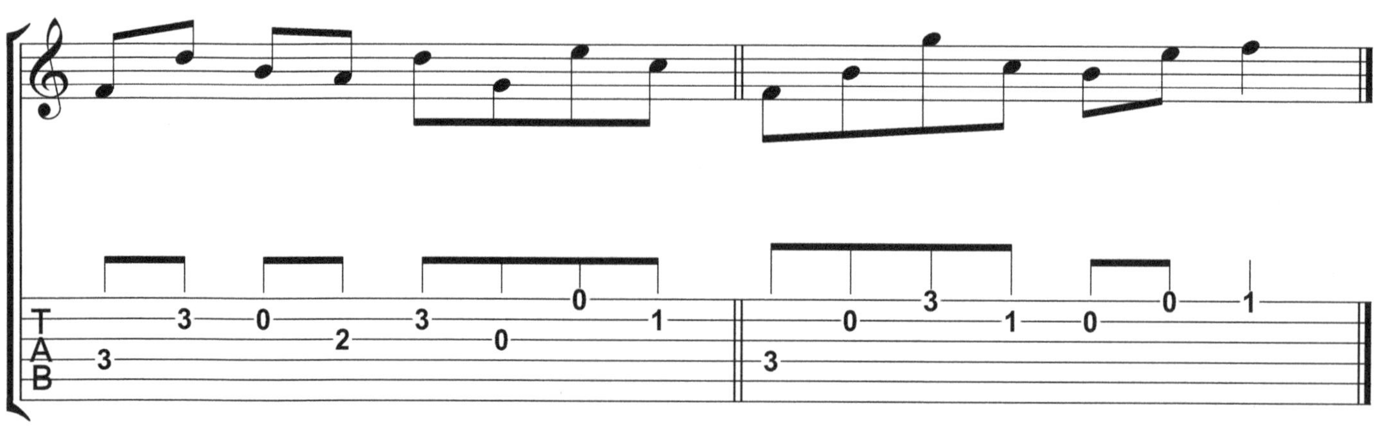

Your turn

Improvise a melodic line preceded by a sustained bass note.

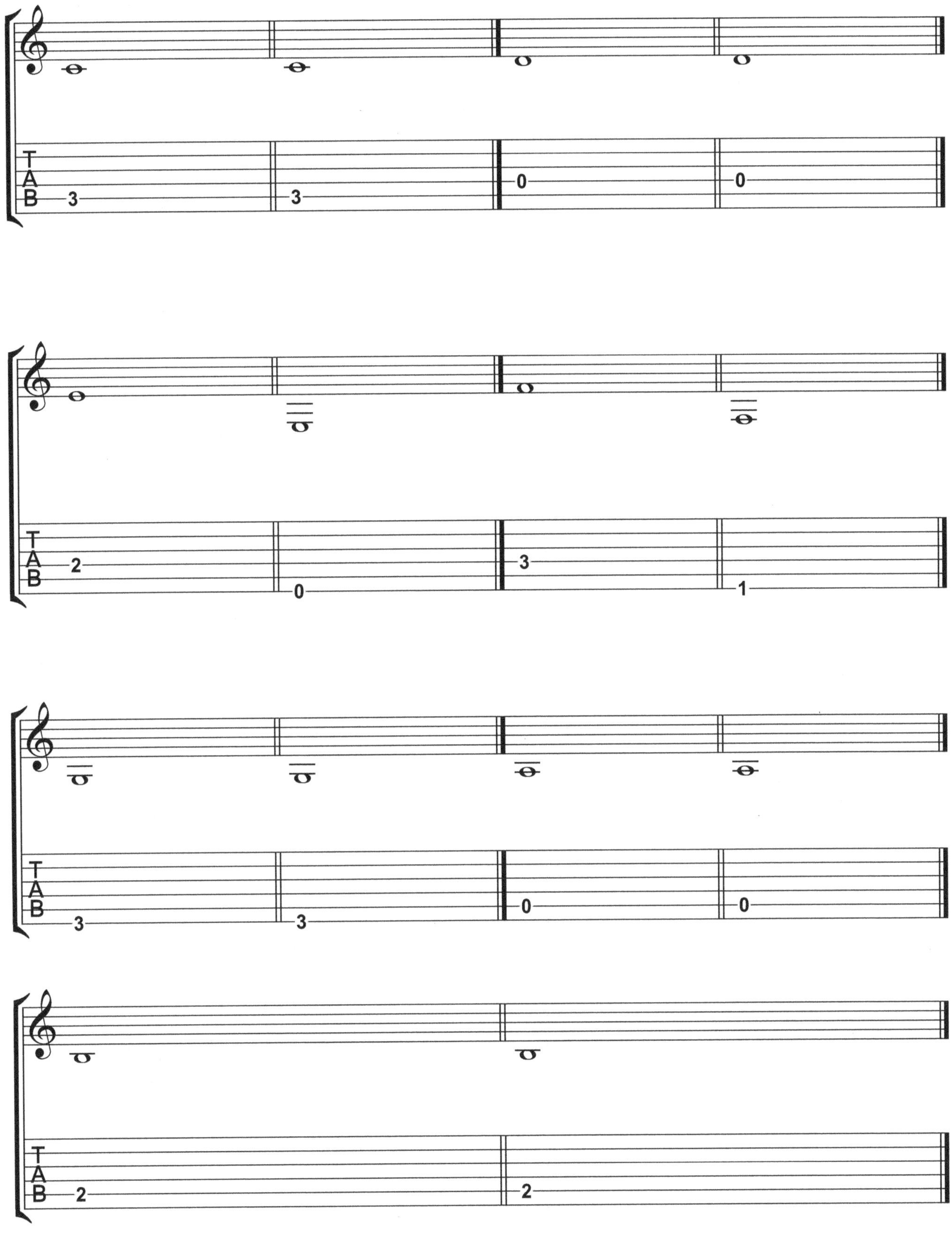

Let's practice on this series of bass notes.

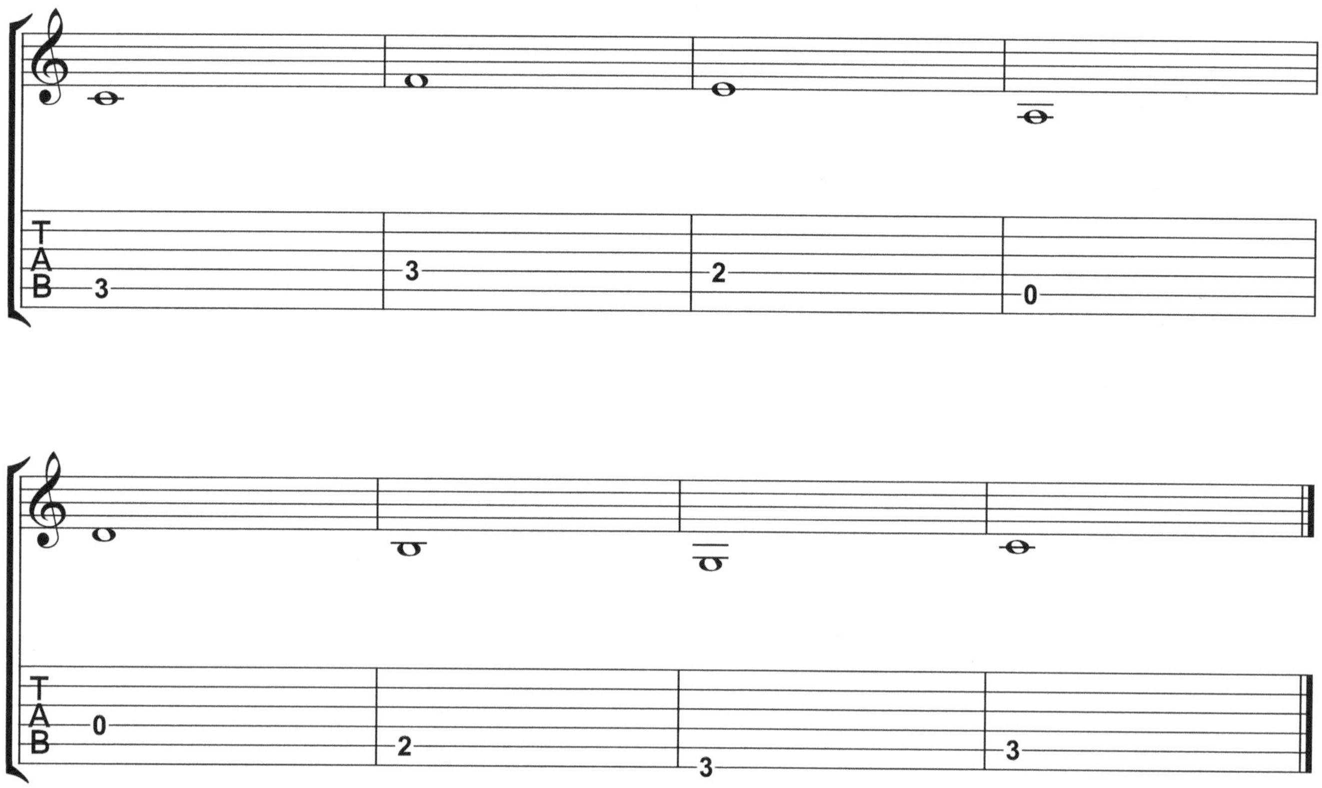

Example

Track 4

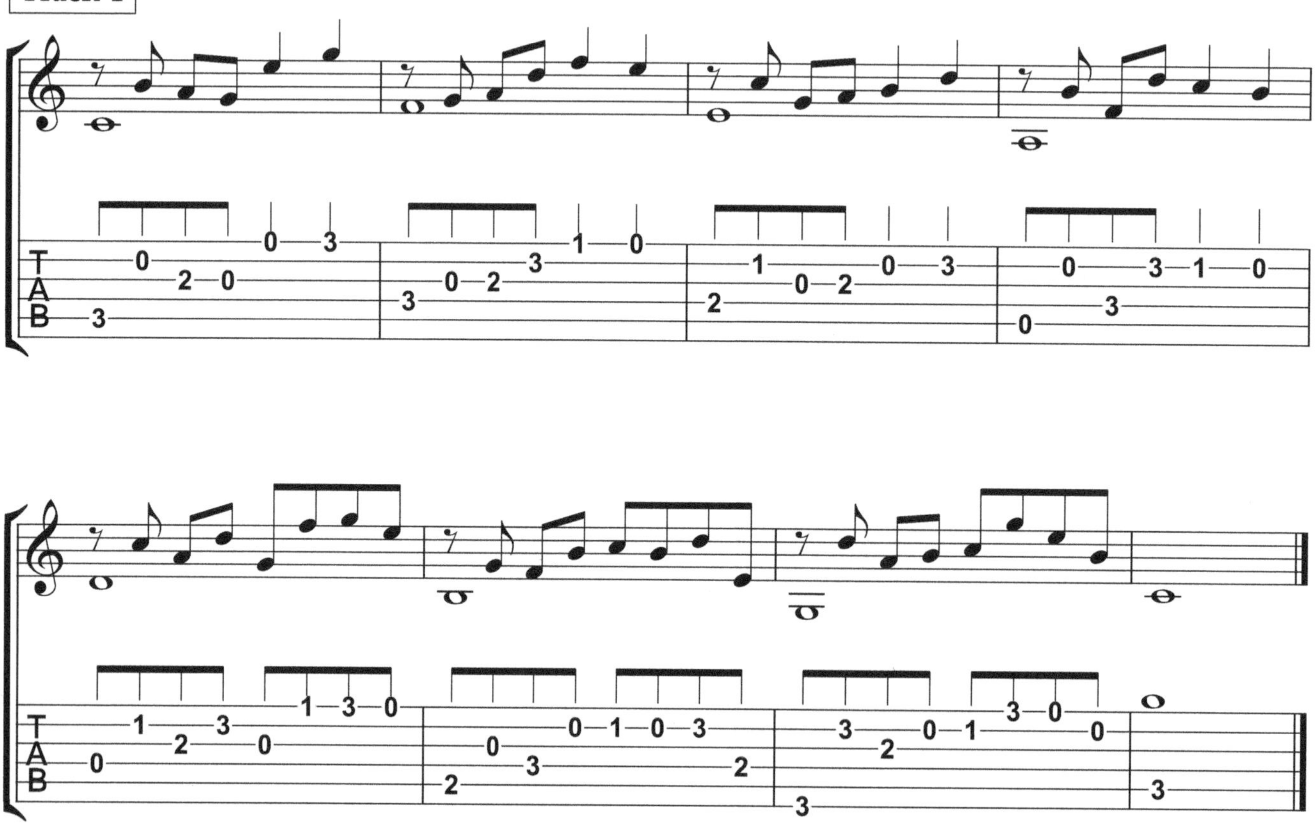

Your turn

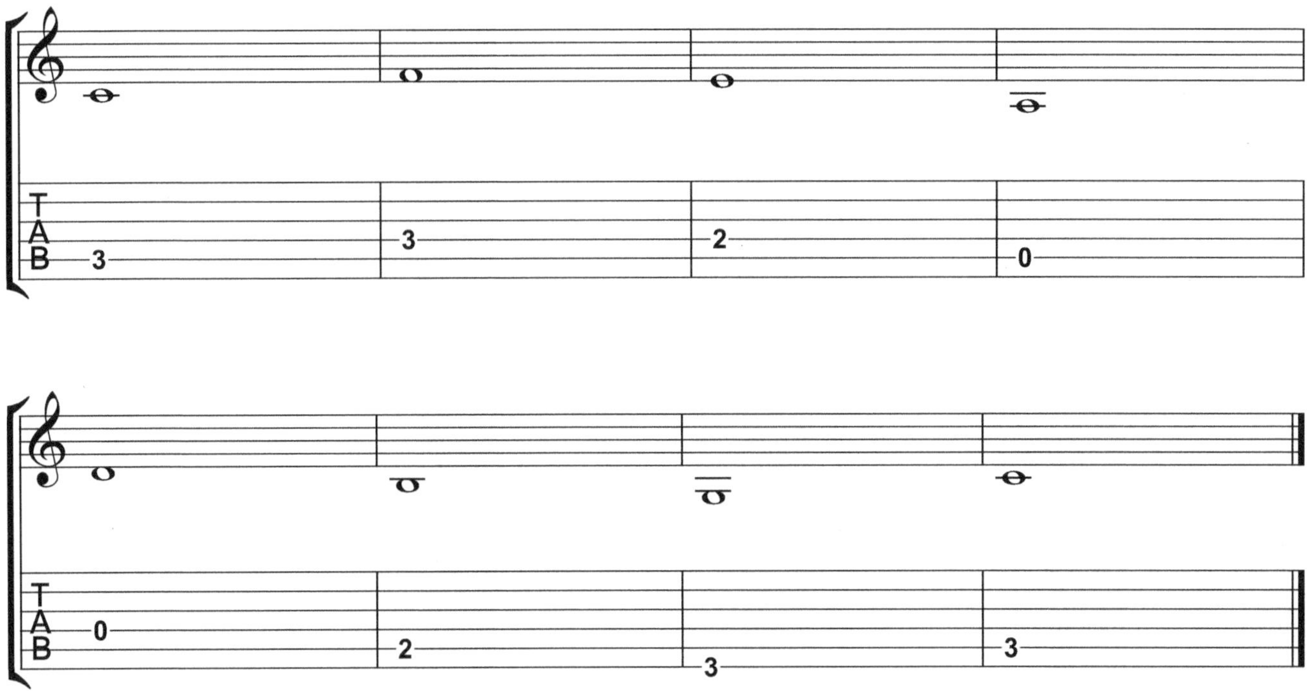

CHAPTER 3

Dyads and Melodic Invention

Dyads or two-part chords are important foundations for two-part counterpoint technique. They also create contrasts to single-note melodic lines and three and four-part chords which we will explore later on. In this chapter, the dyads are root + any scale note.

Play all the available notes of the C Major scale on strings 1, 2, 3 and 4 accompanied by one of the scale notes in the bass on strings 4, 5 and 6.

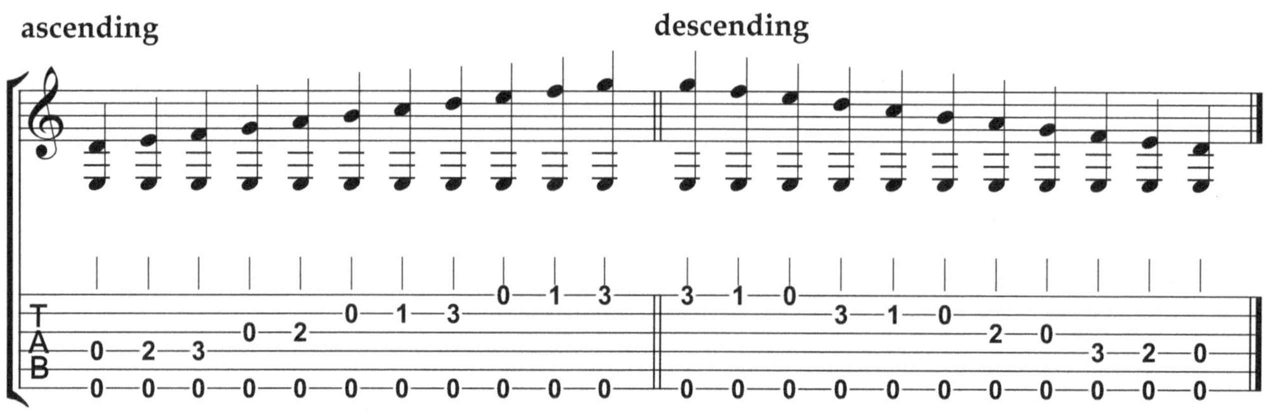

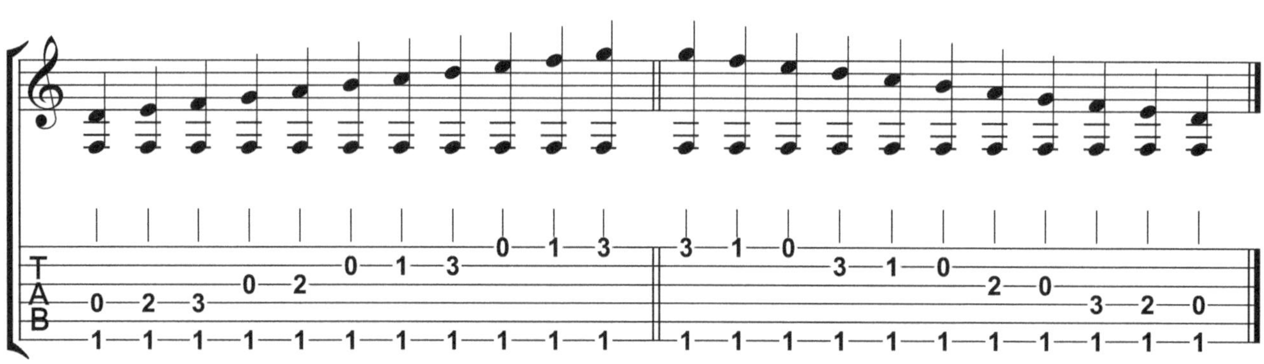

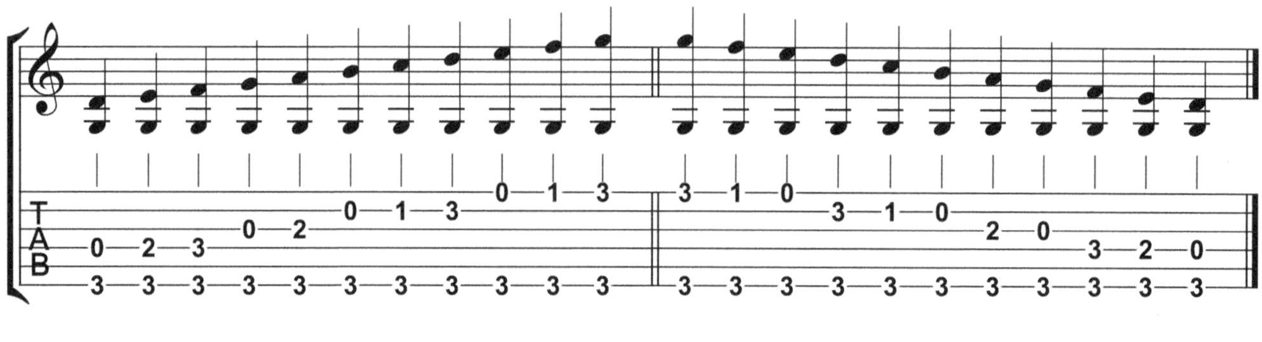

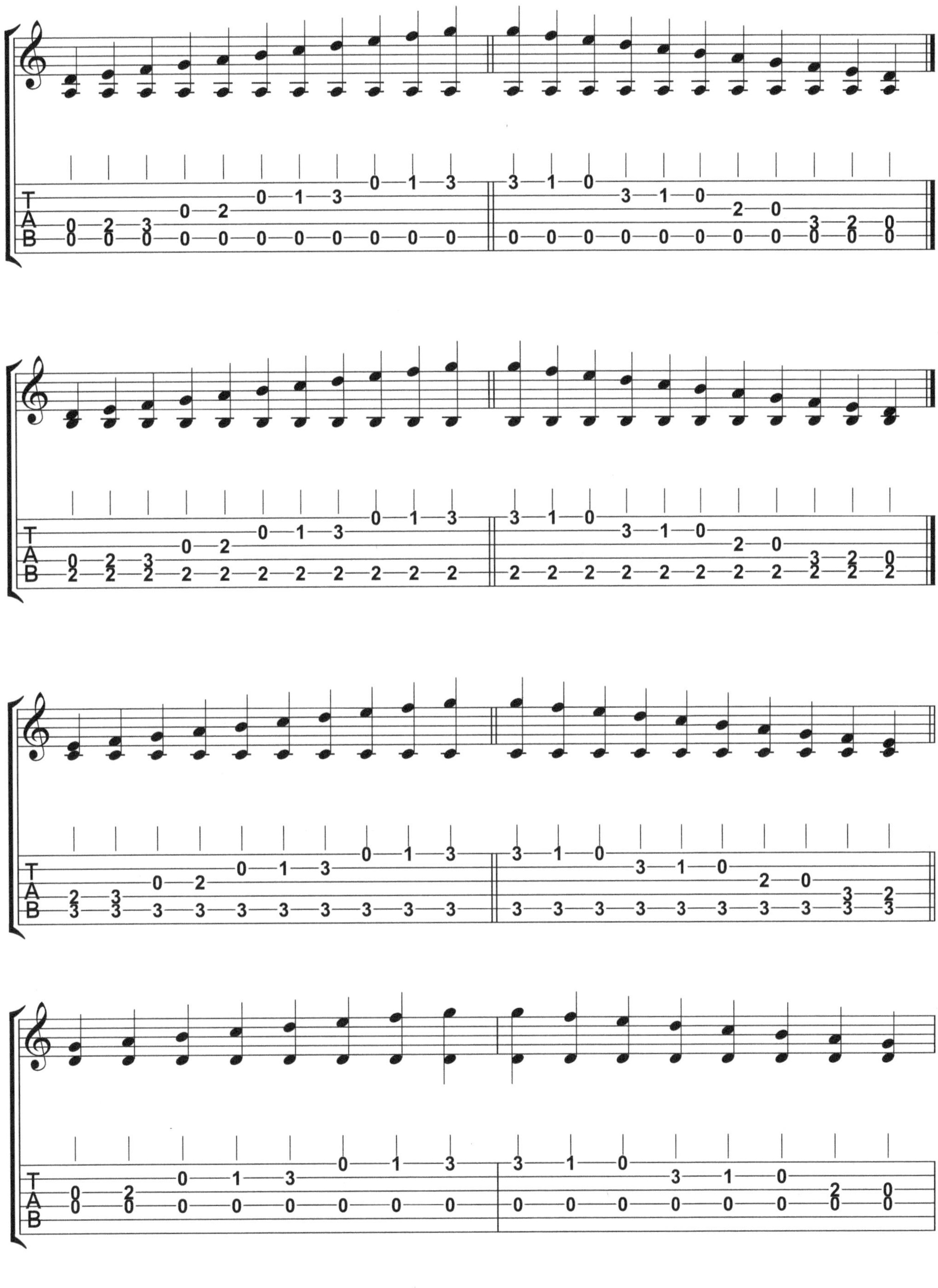

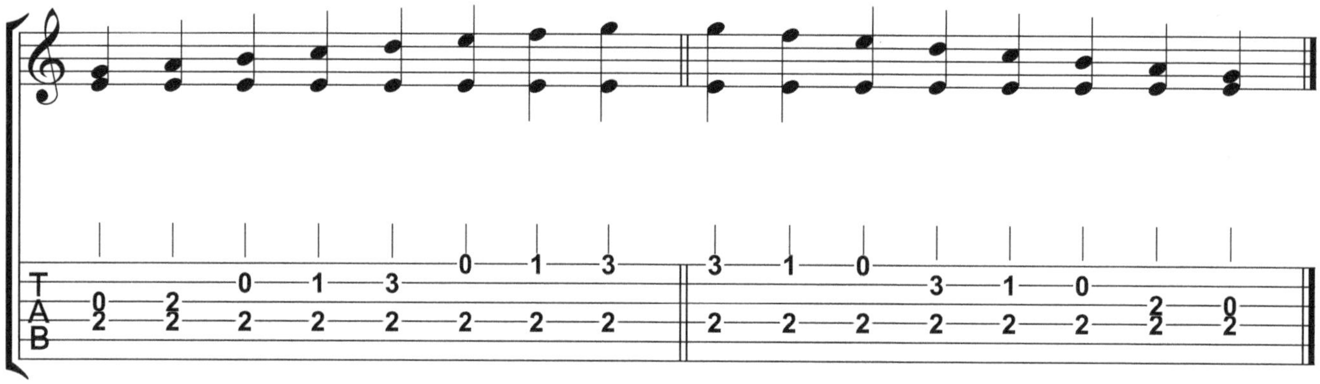

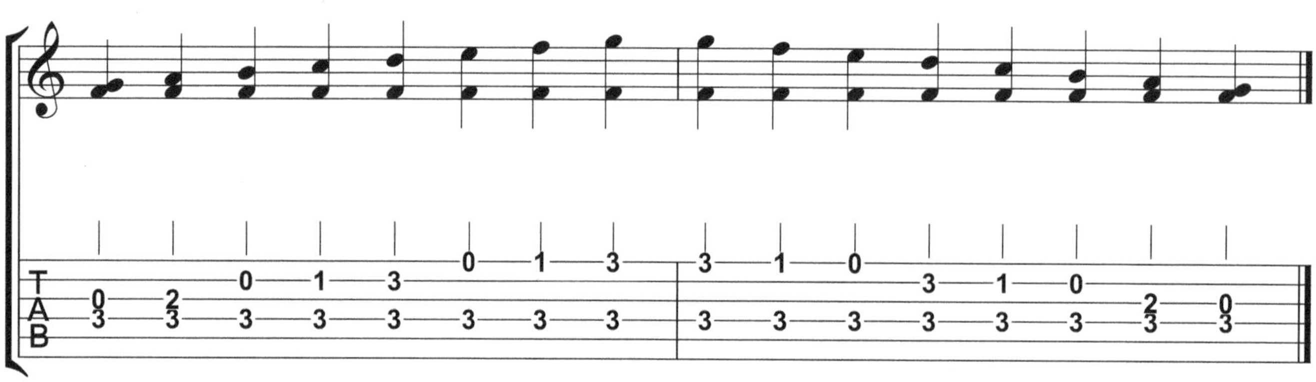

Same root/different dyads

Play through these examples and then improvise your own successions of two-part chords.

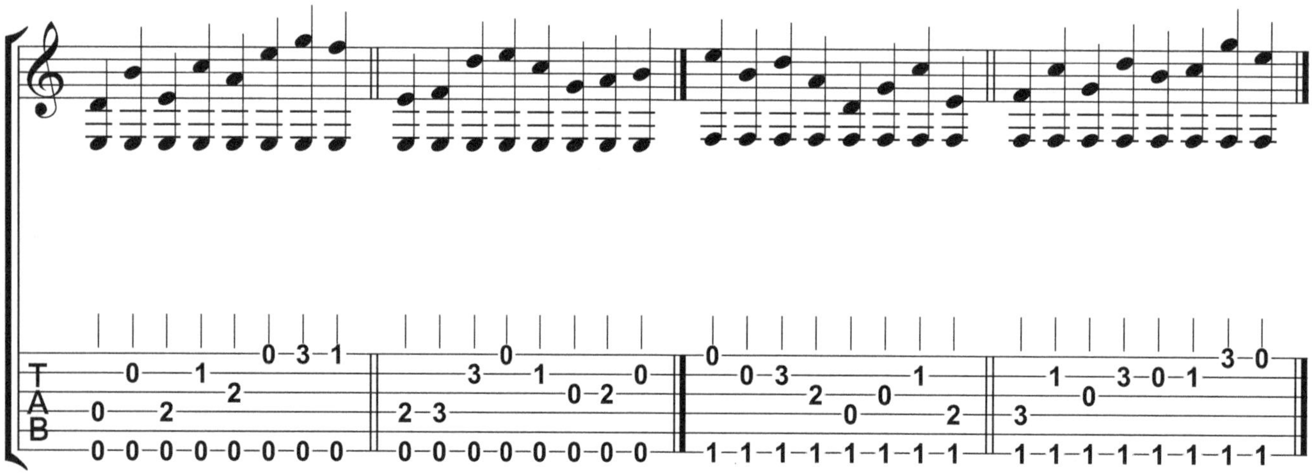

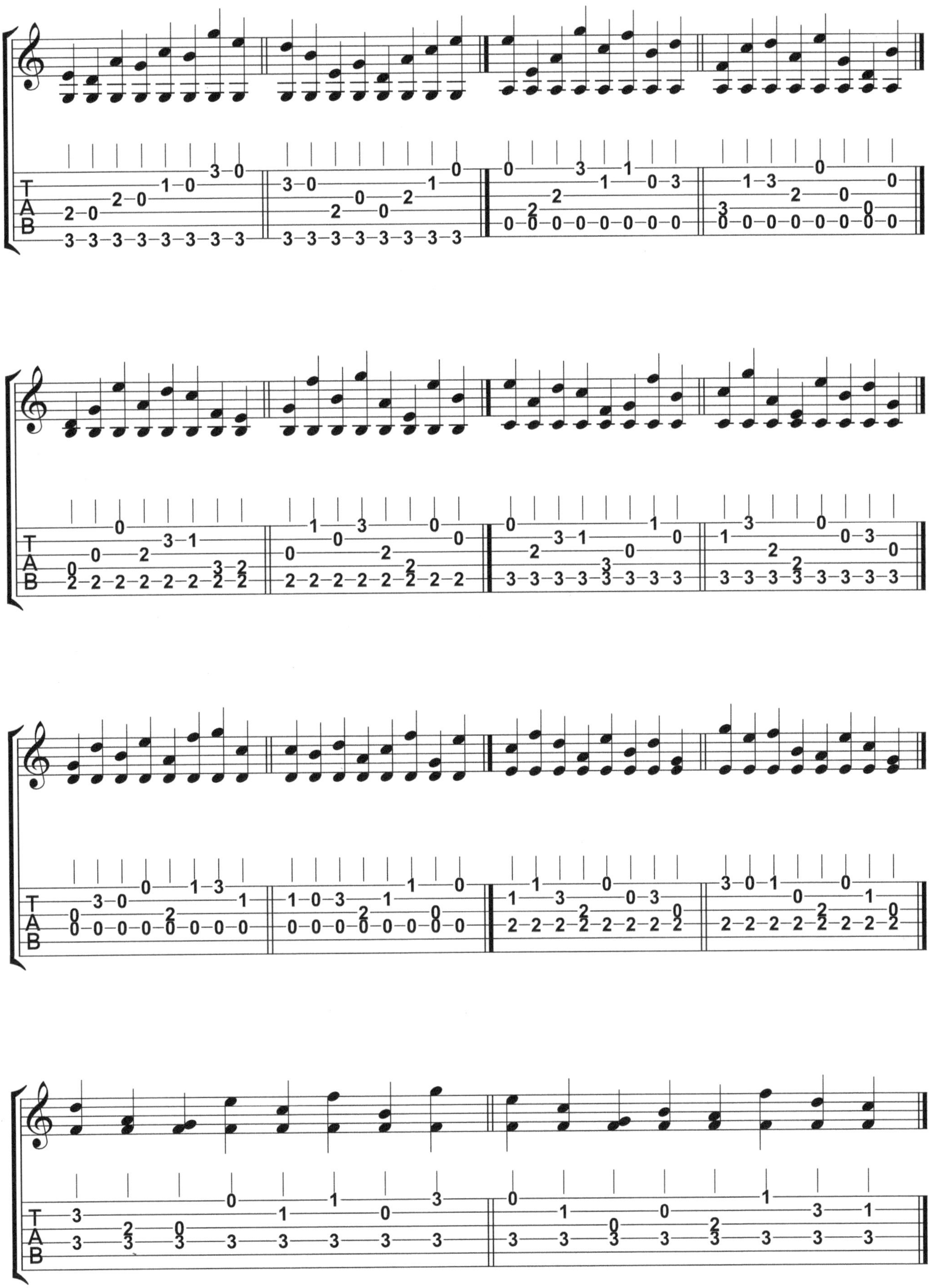

Example

Track 5

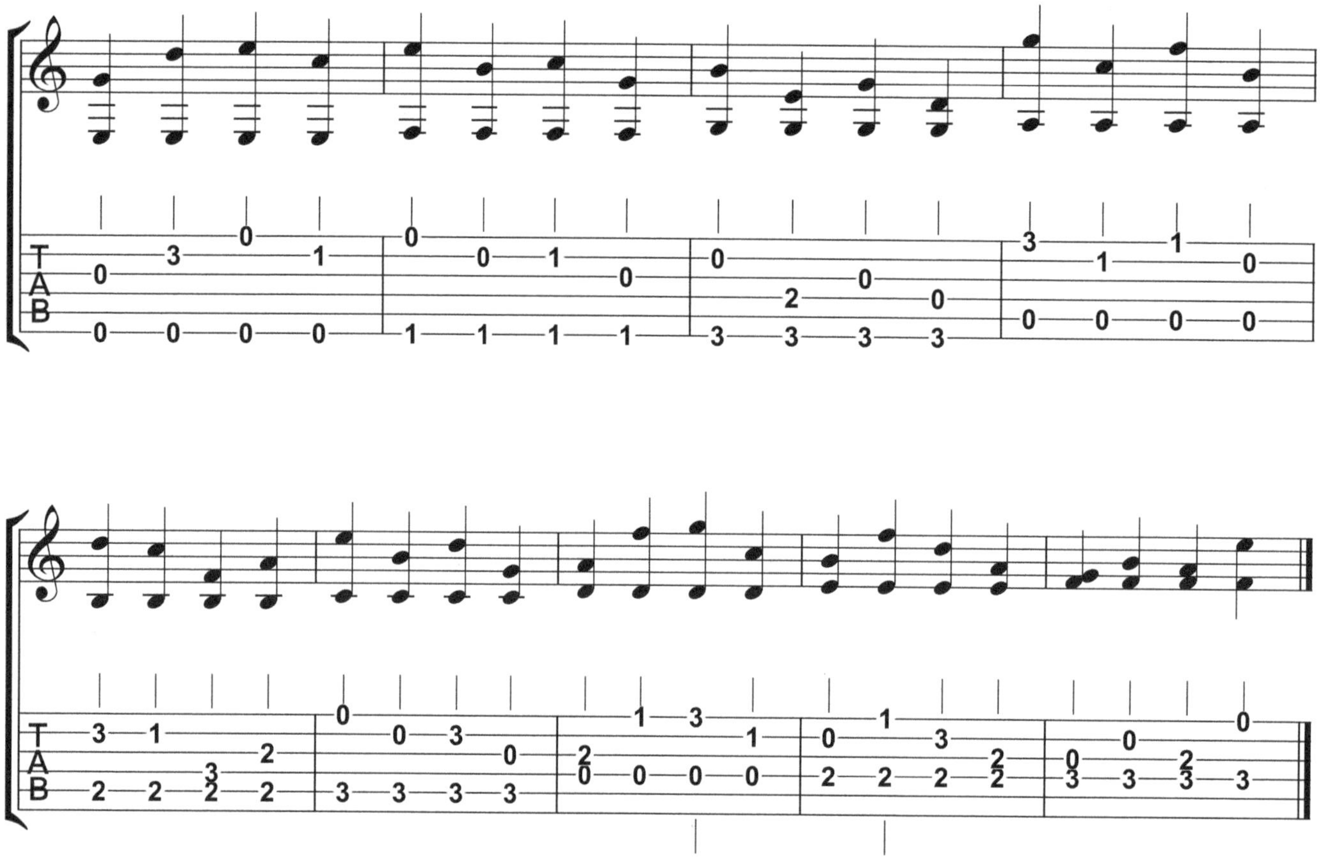

Your turn

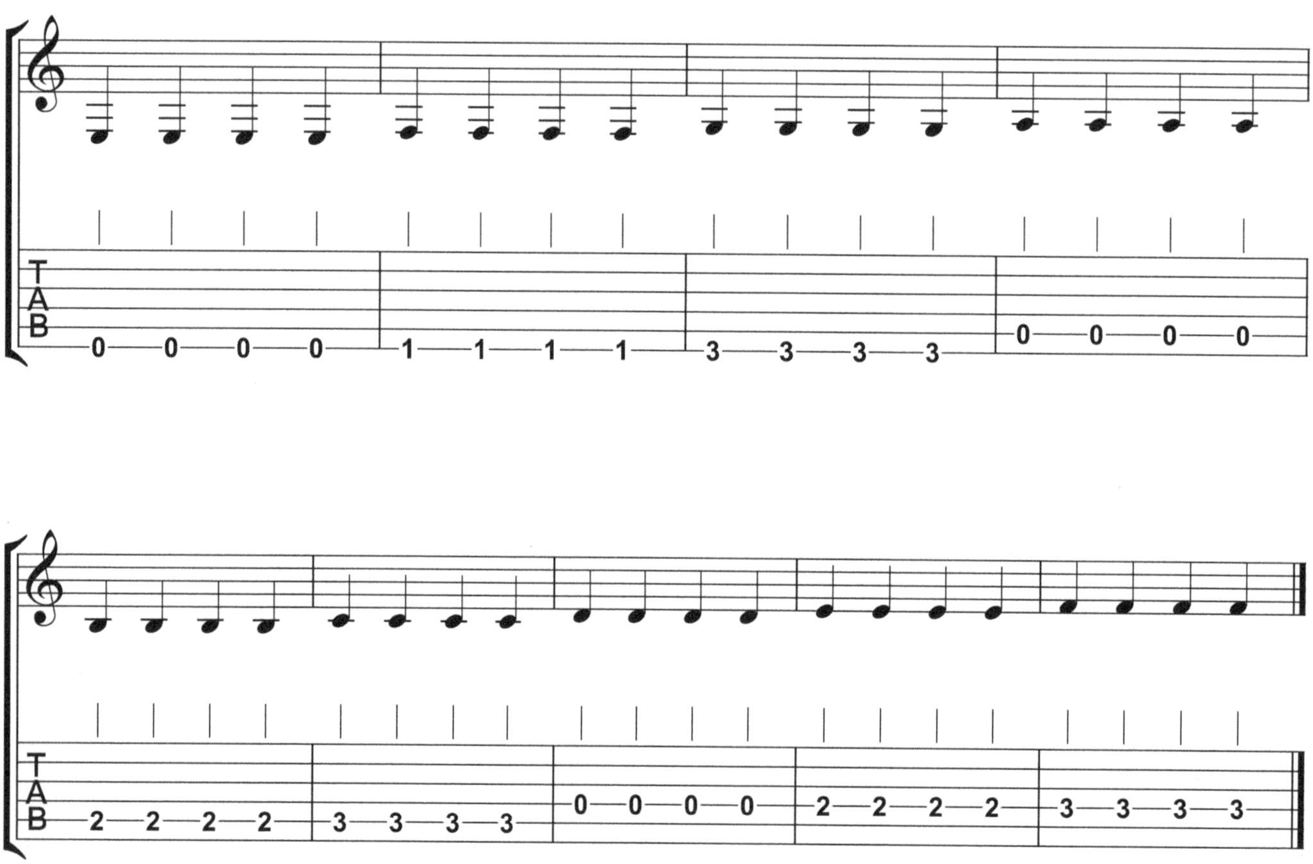

Different roots/different dyads

Track 6

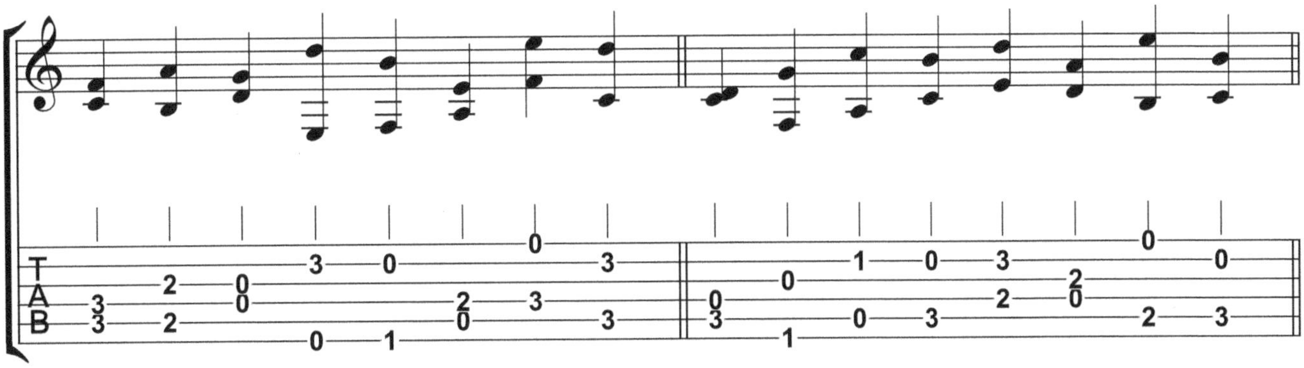

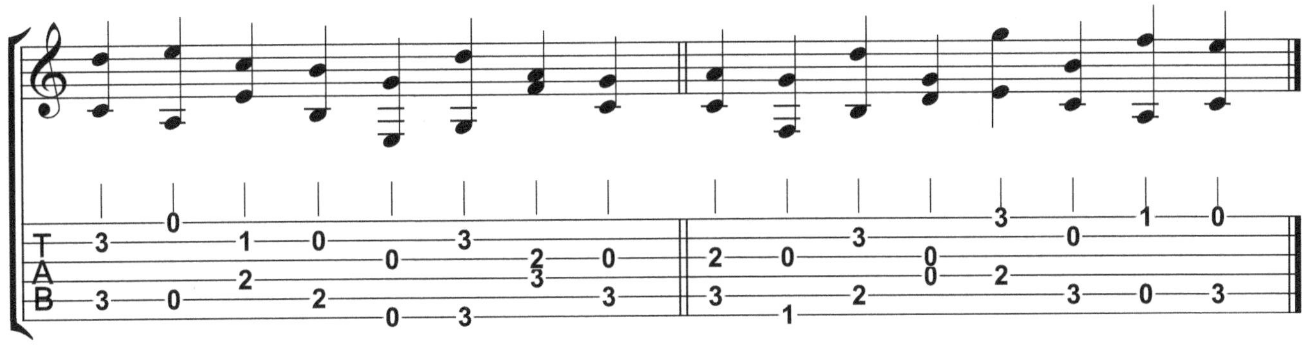

Your turn

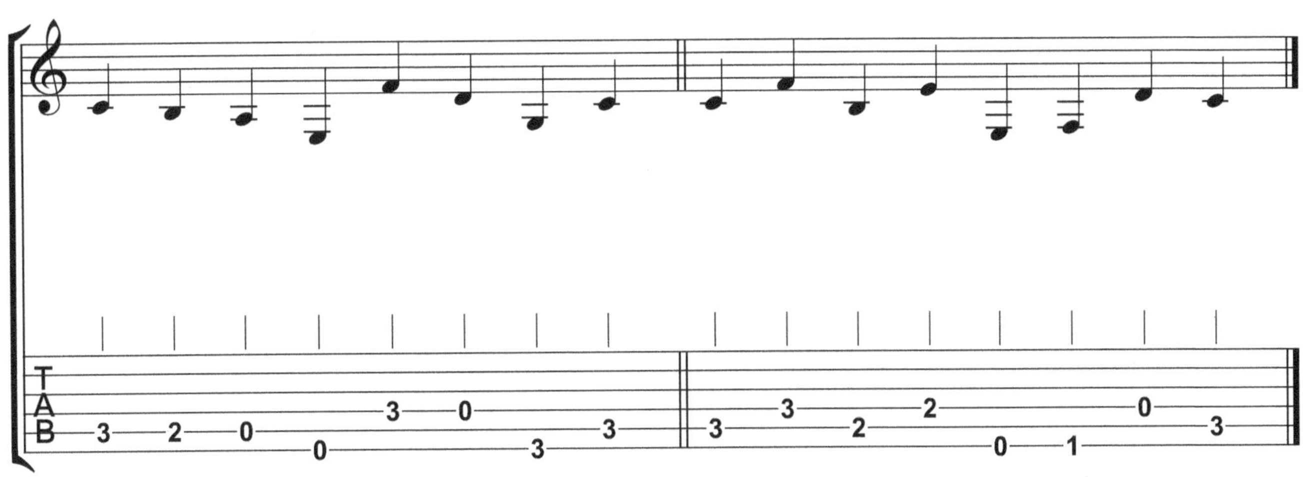

Melodic line preceded by a dyad on a bass progression

Using a dyad as a starting point, start improvising melodic lines on the upper note of the dyad. Keep in mind that every note is equally important and try to sing (hum) your melodic lines. Play through all the examples and then improvise your own lines.

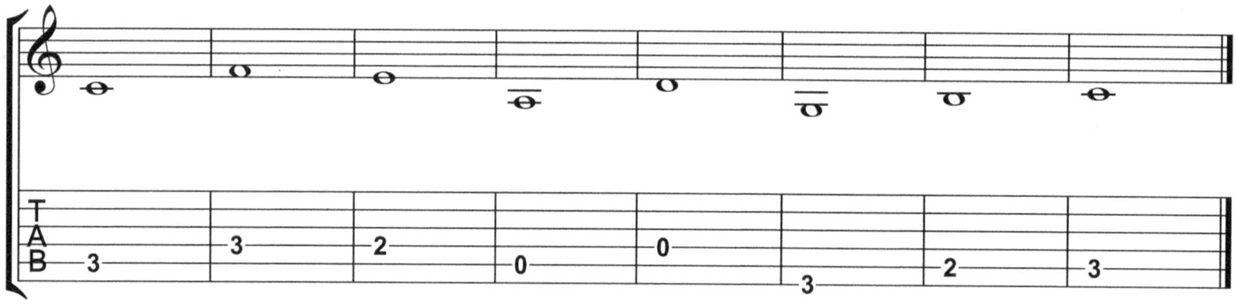

Example 1

Track 7

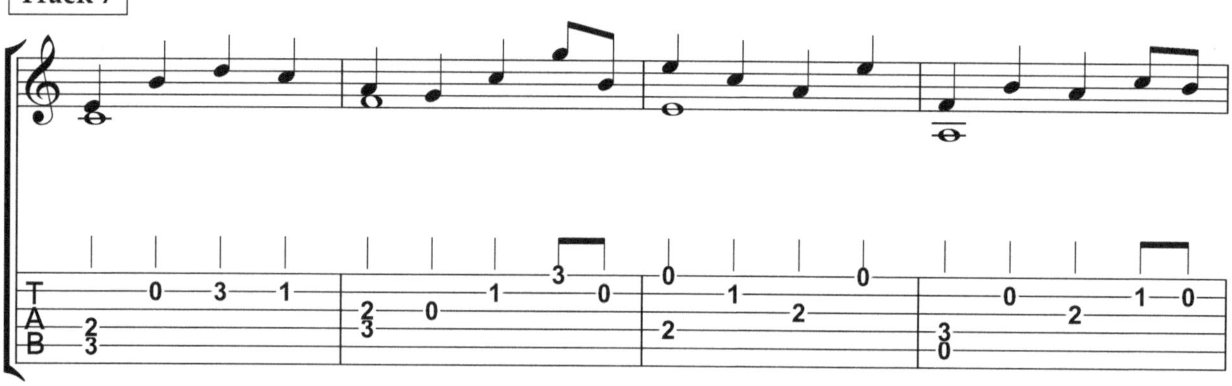

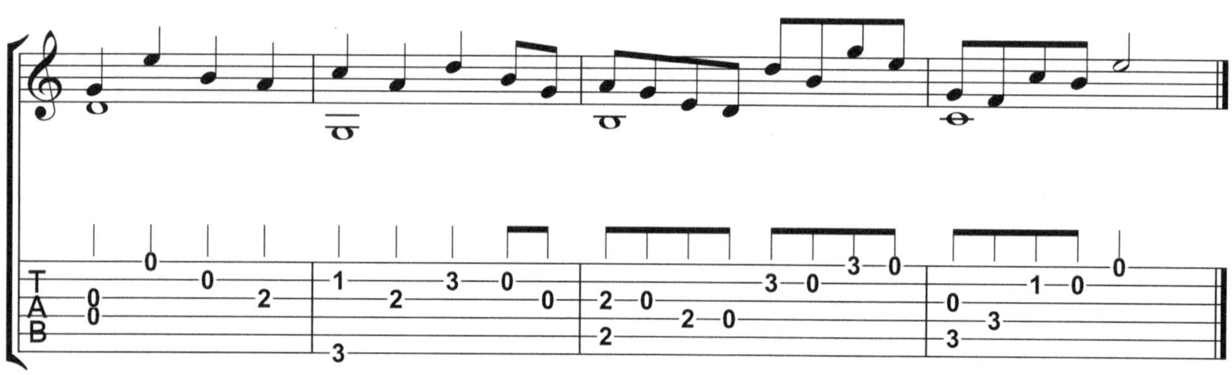

Example 2

Let's add some new rhythmic patterns.

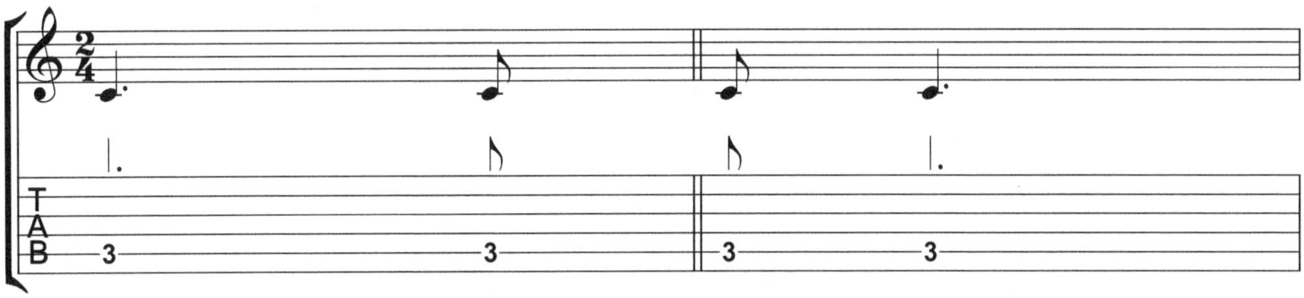

Track 8

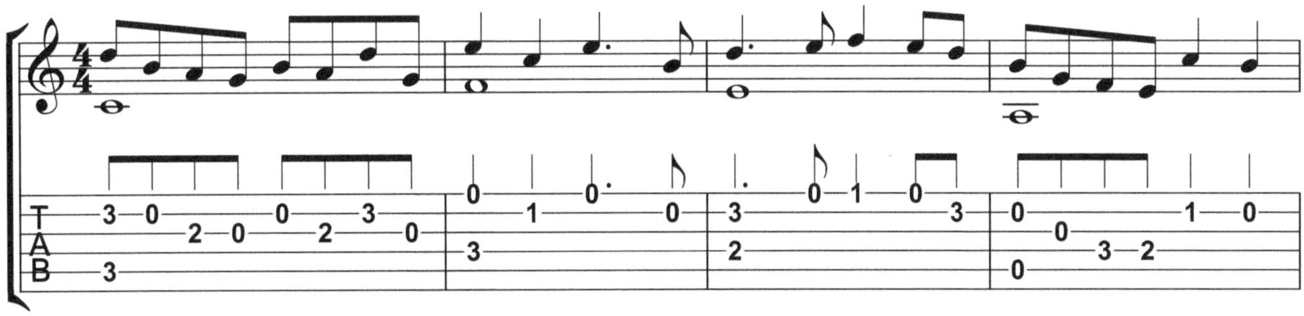

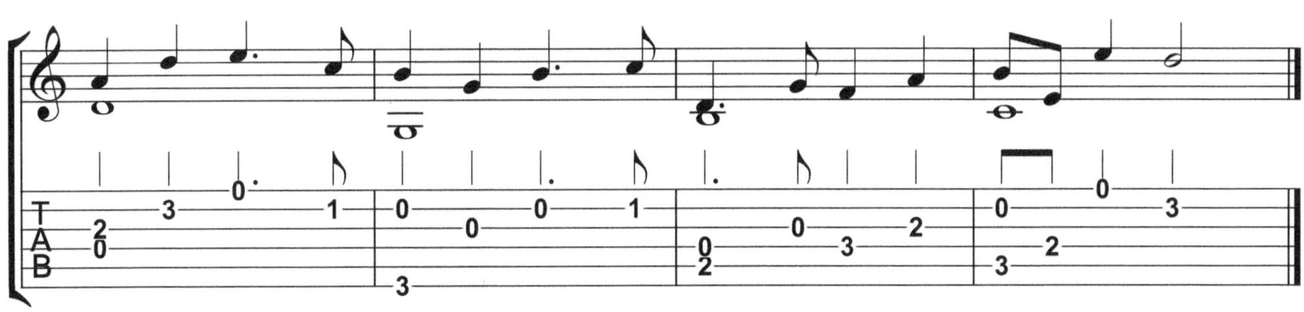

Example 3

Track 9

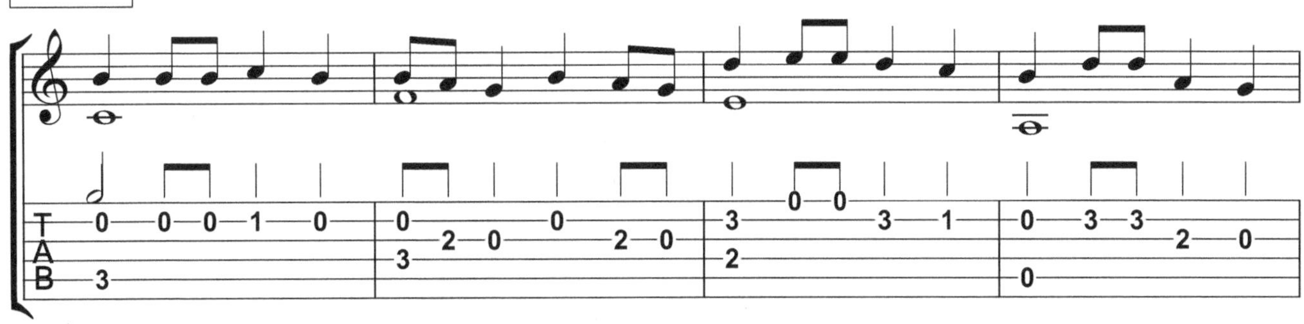

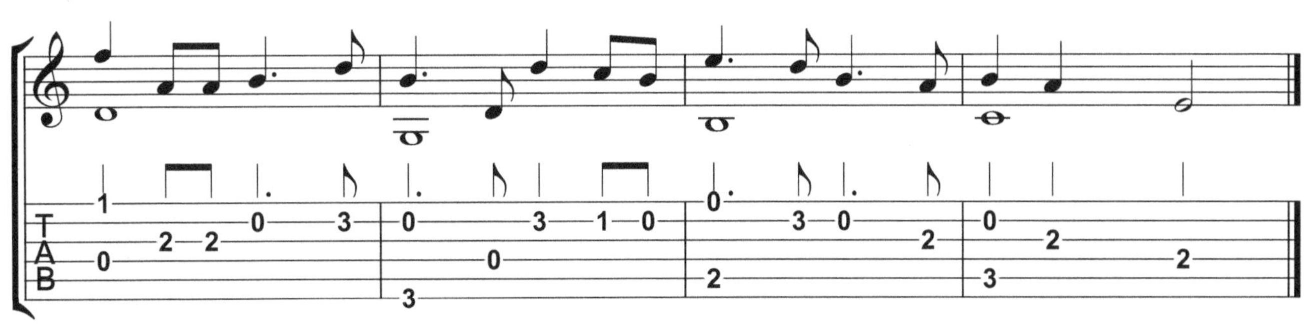

Example 4

Track 10

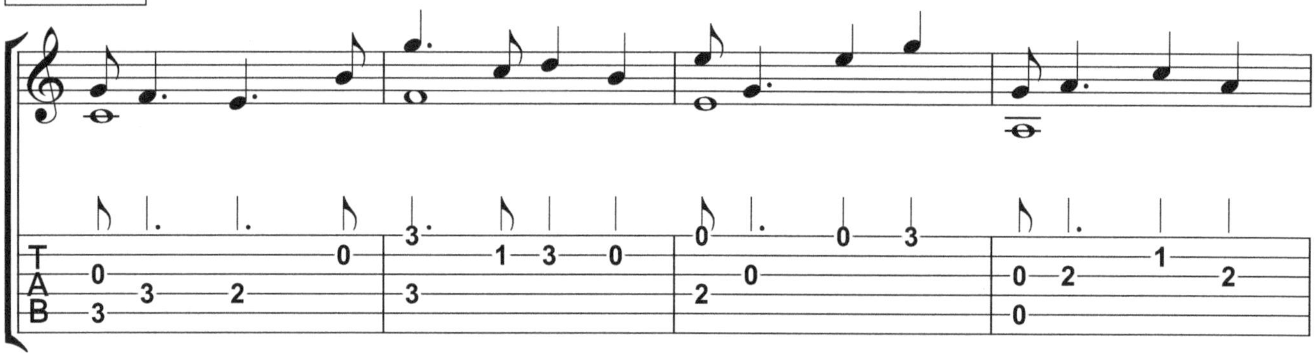

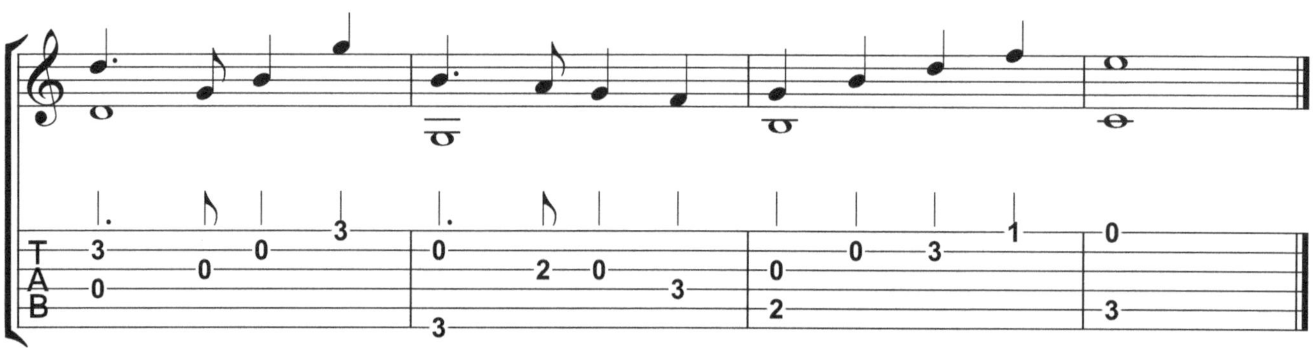

Your turn

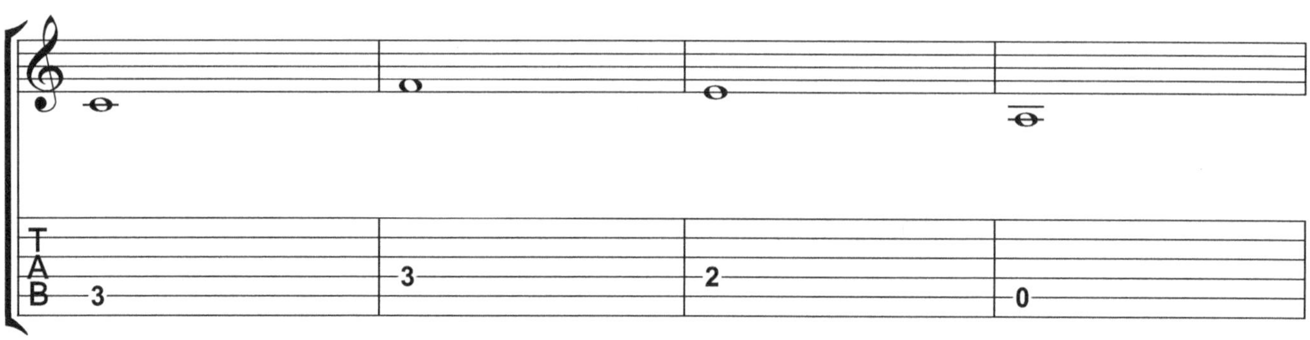

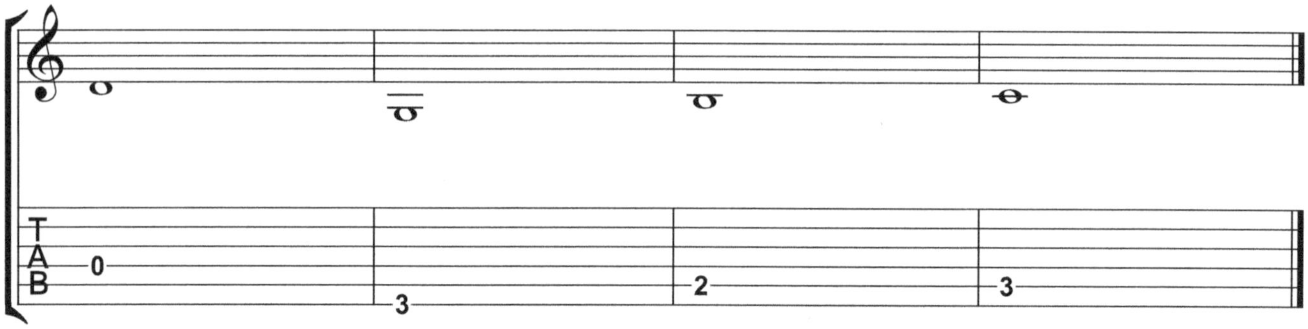

Progression 2

Let's add another new rhythmic pattern.

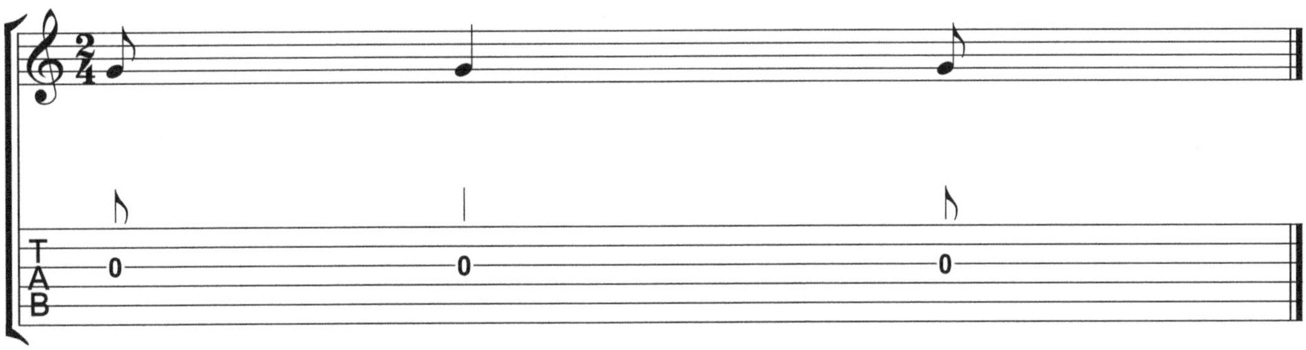

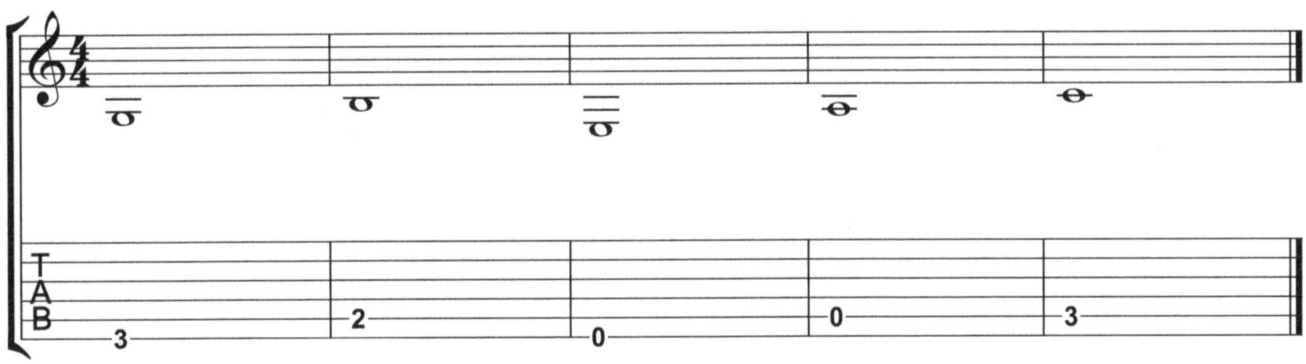

Example

Track 11

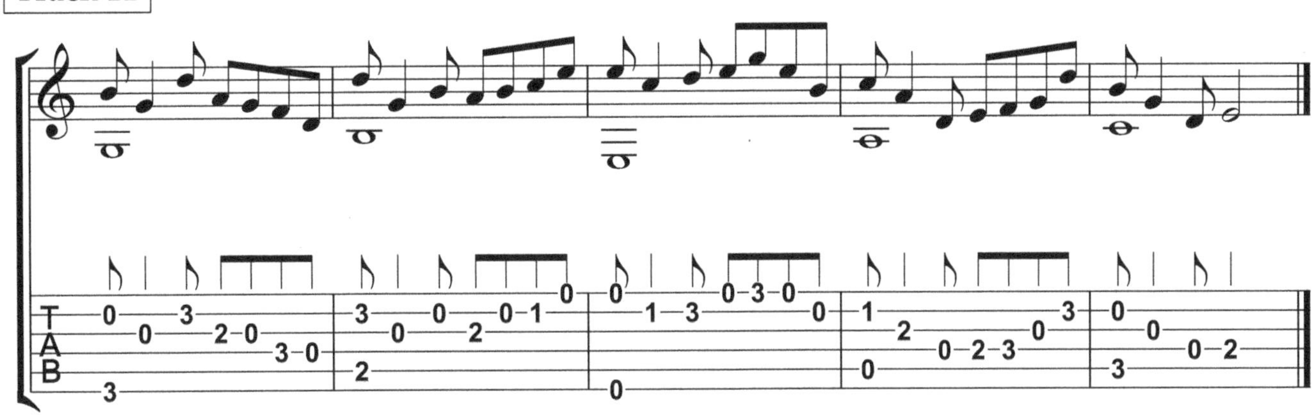

Your turn

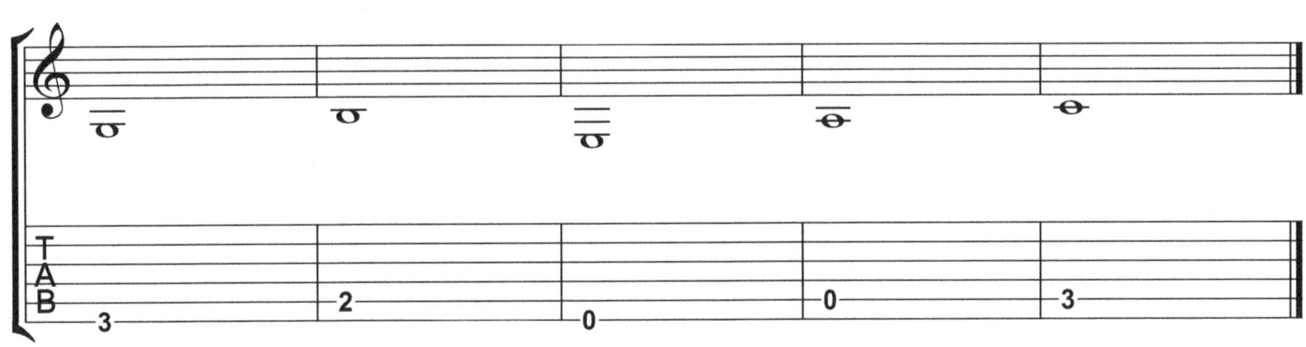

Progression 3

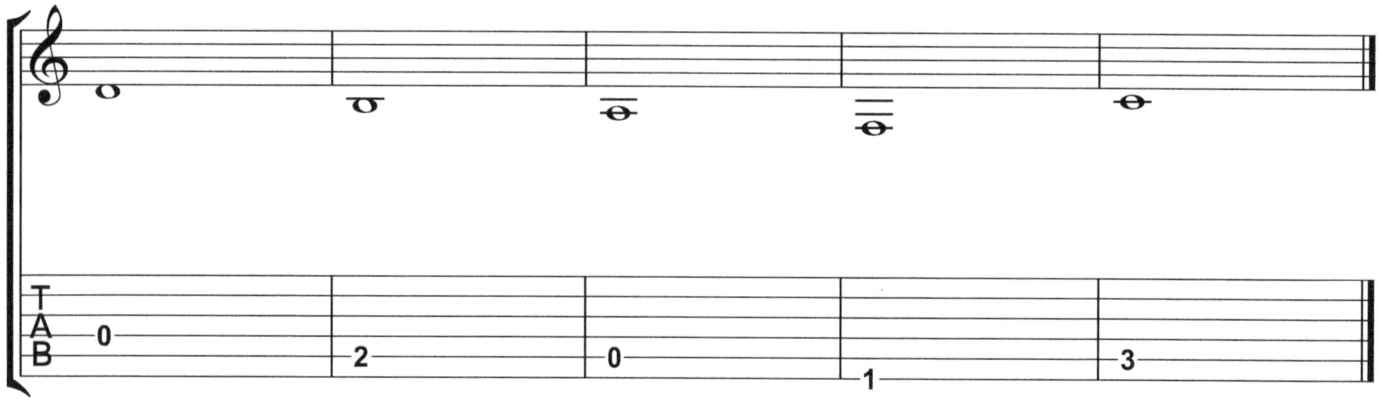

Example

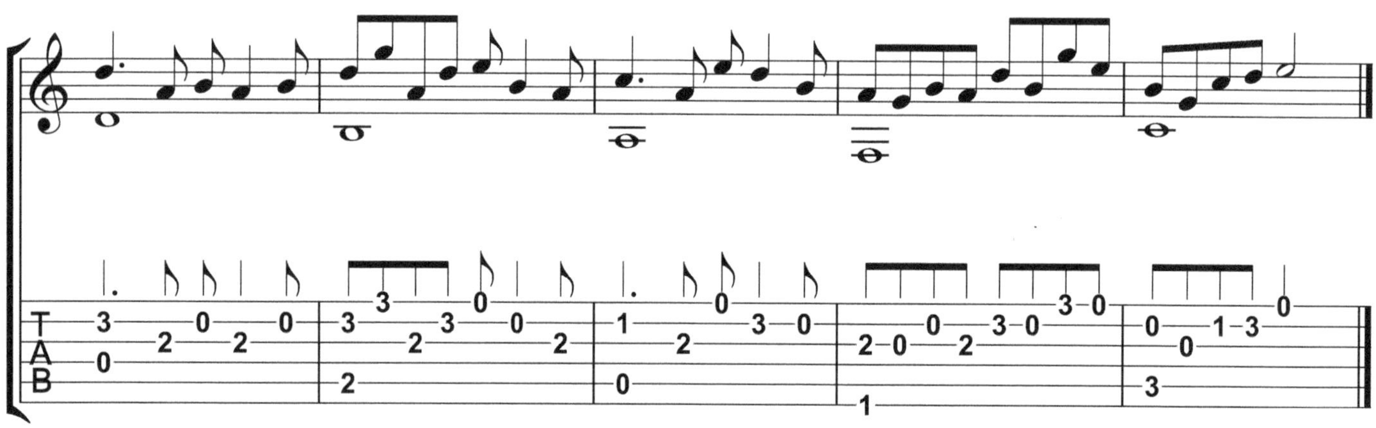

Your turn

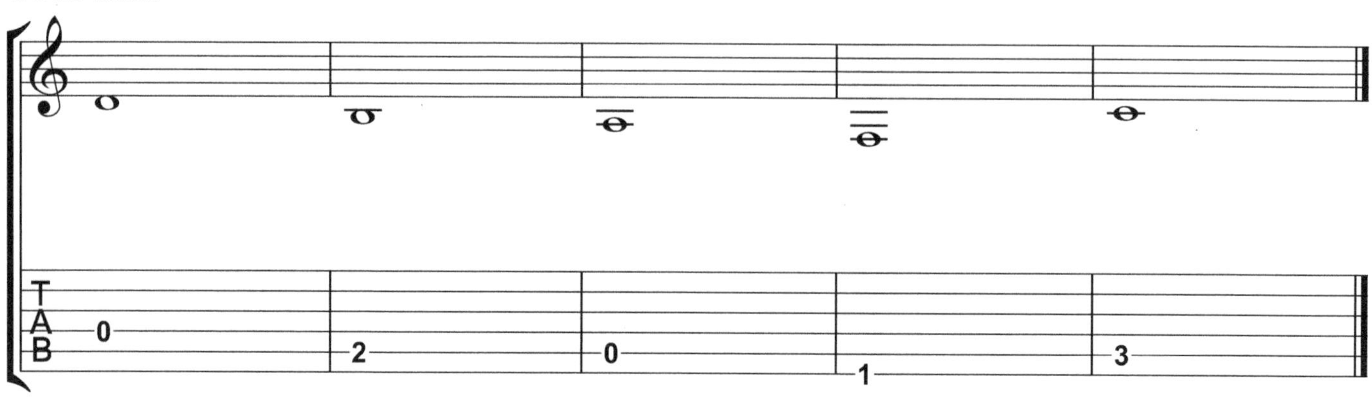

CHAPTER 4

Root-Root Alteration in the Bass

In this chapter a dyad is a root + any scale note. Playing the root-root alteration is a good start to playing and improvising music in two independent parts: melody and bass line. Both parts are moving.

Here are some possibilities.

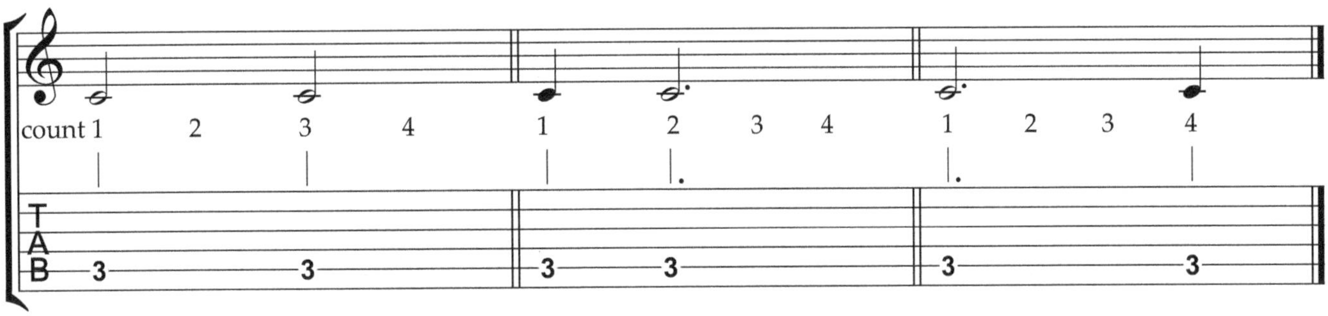

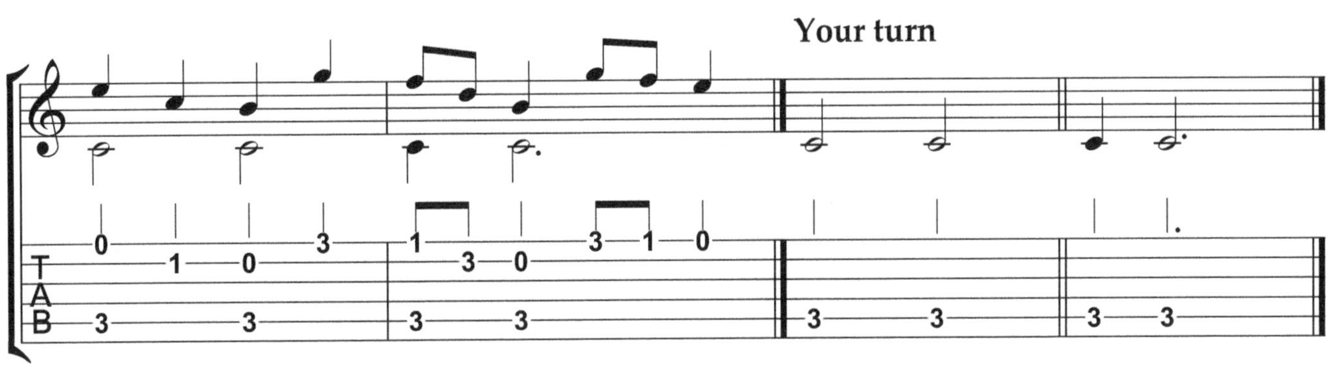

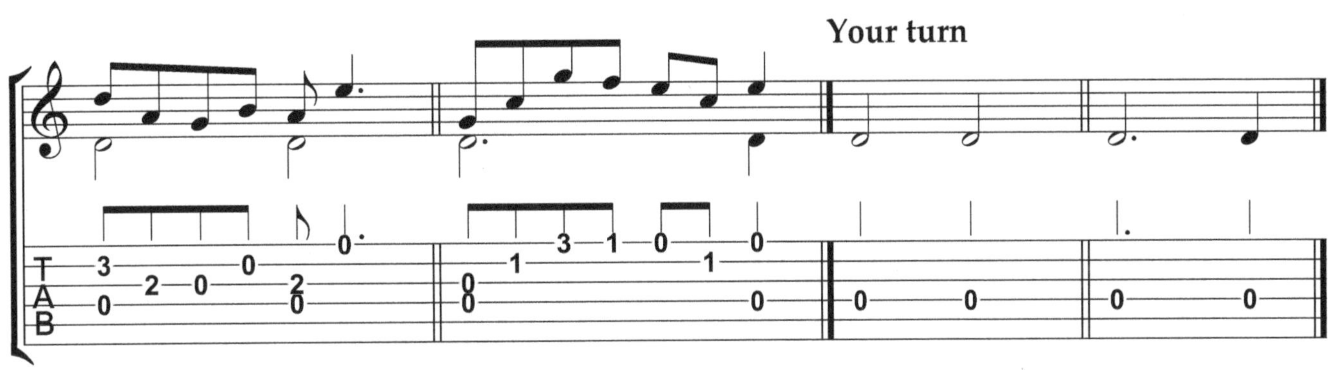

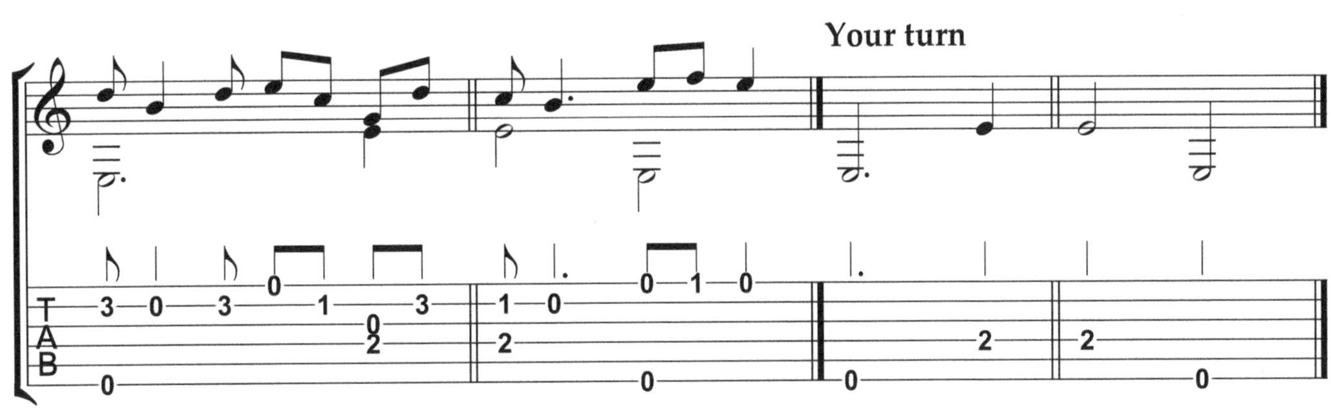

Your turn

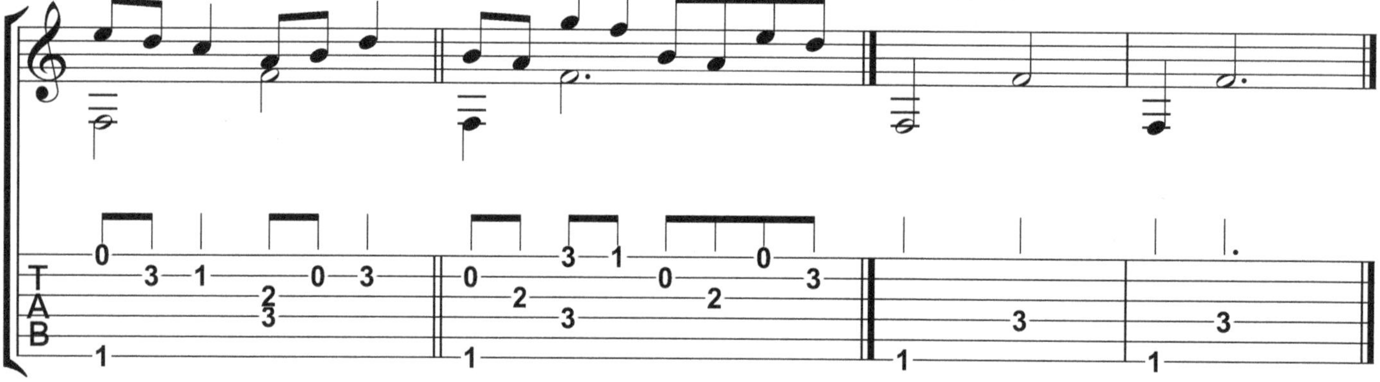

Your turn

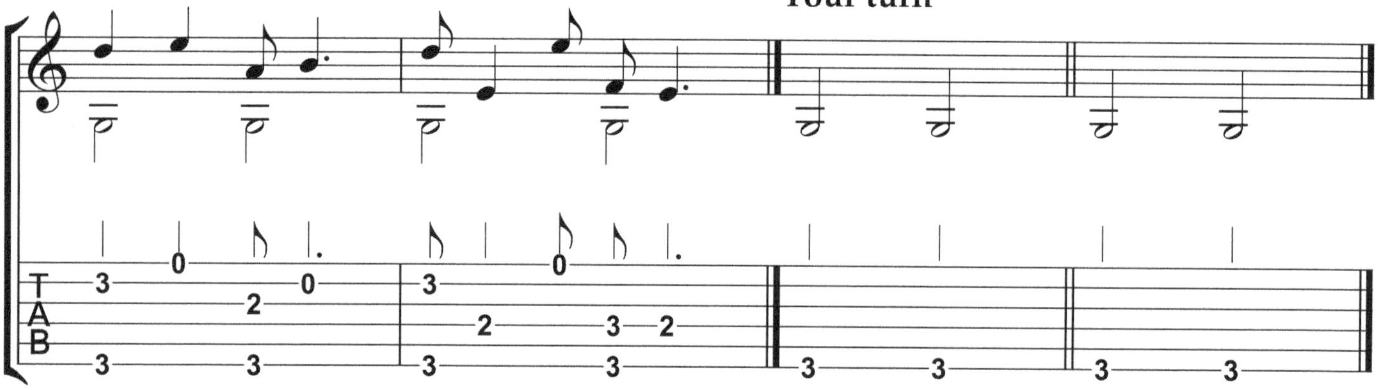

Your turn

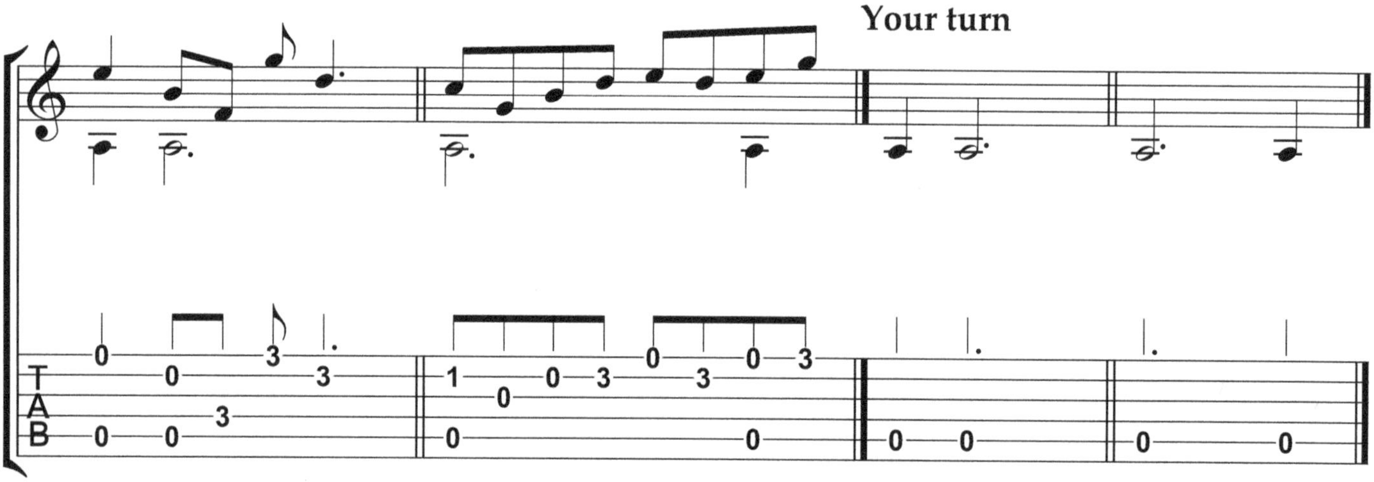

Your turn

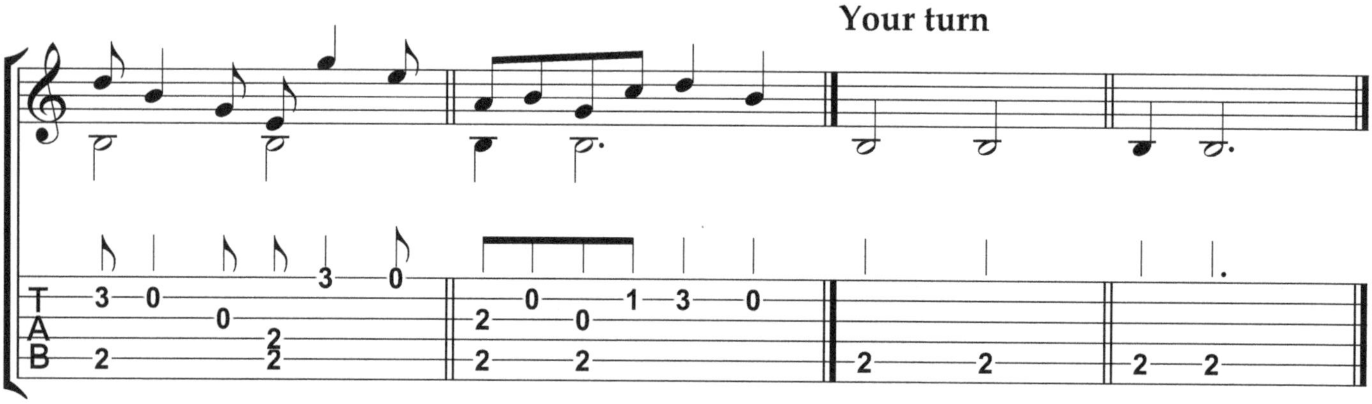

On a progression

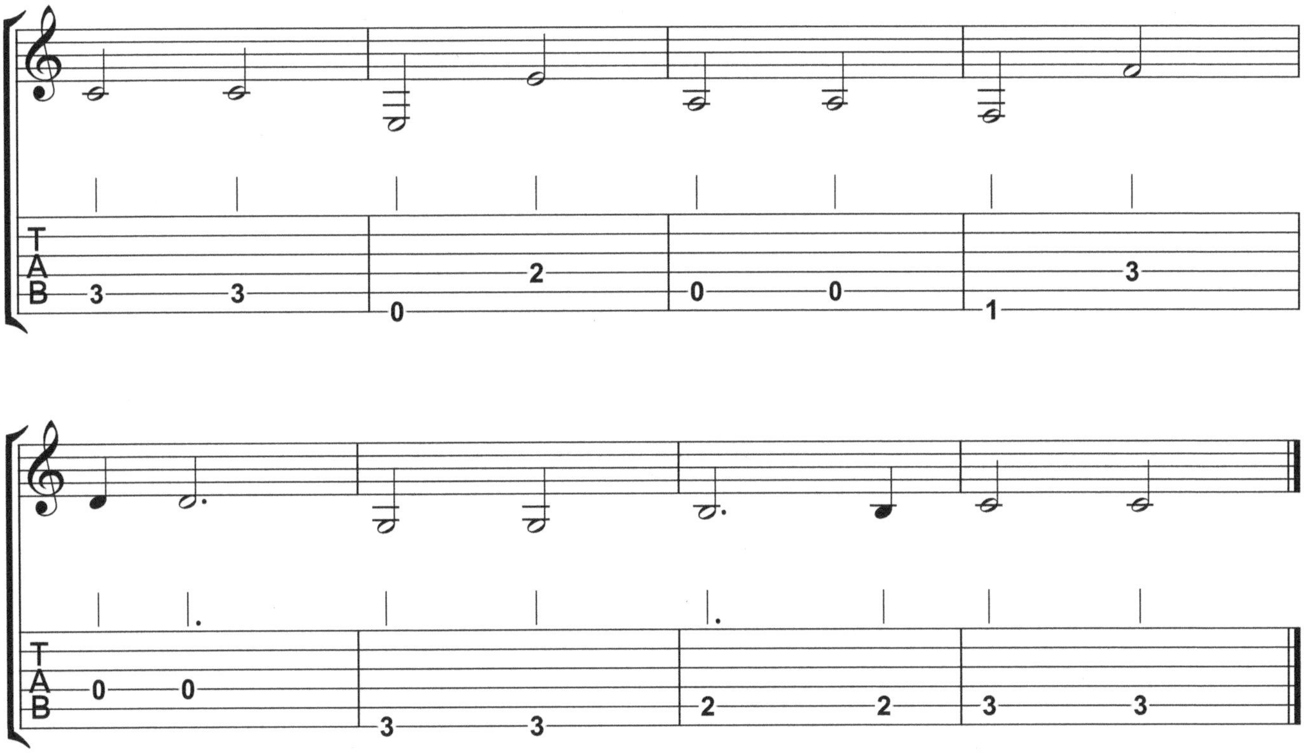

Example 1

Track 12

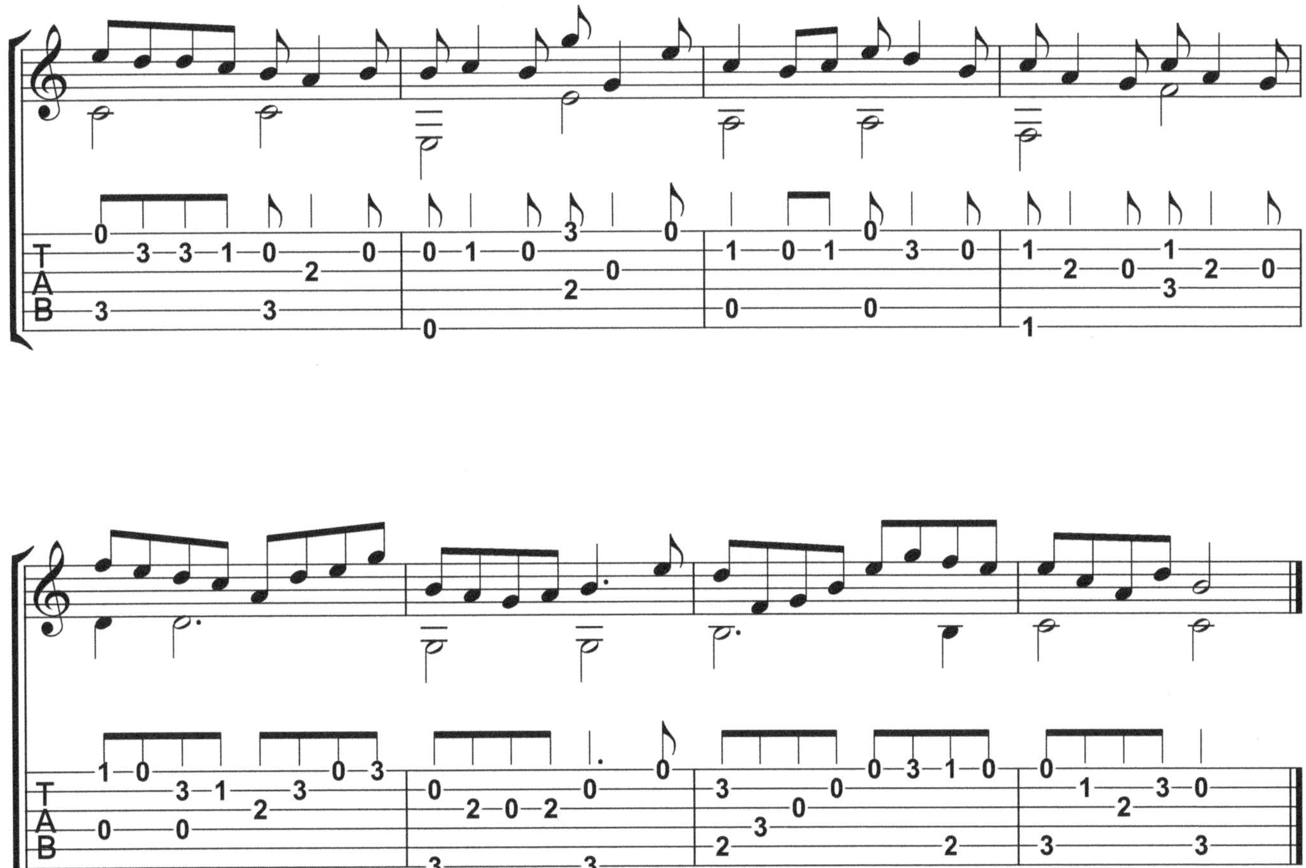

Example 2

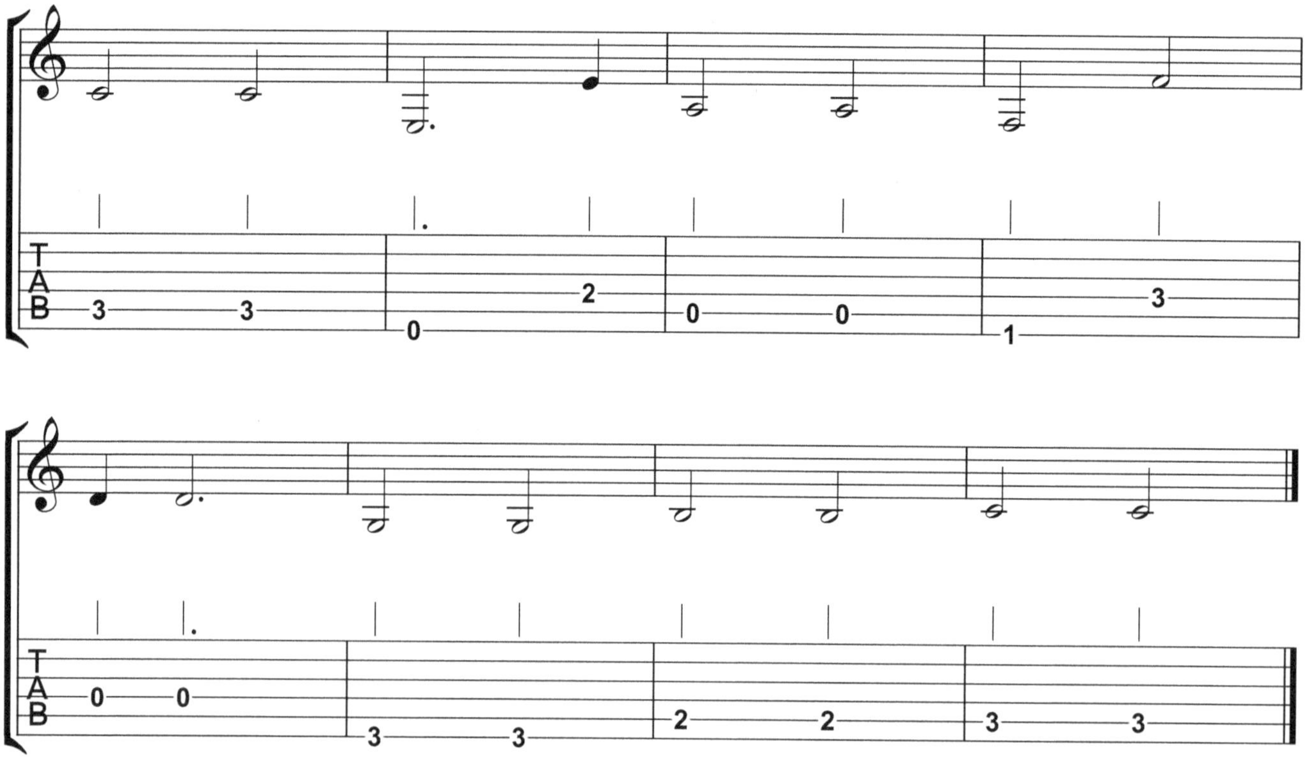

Track 13

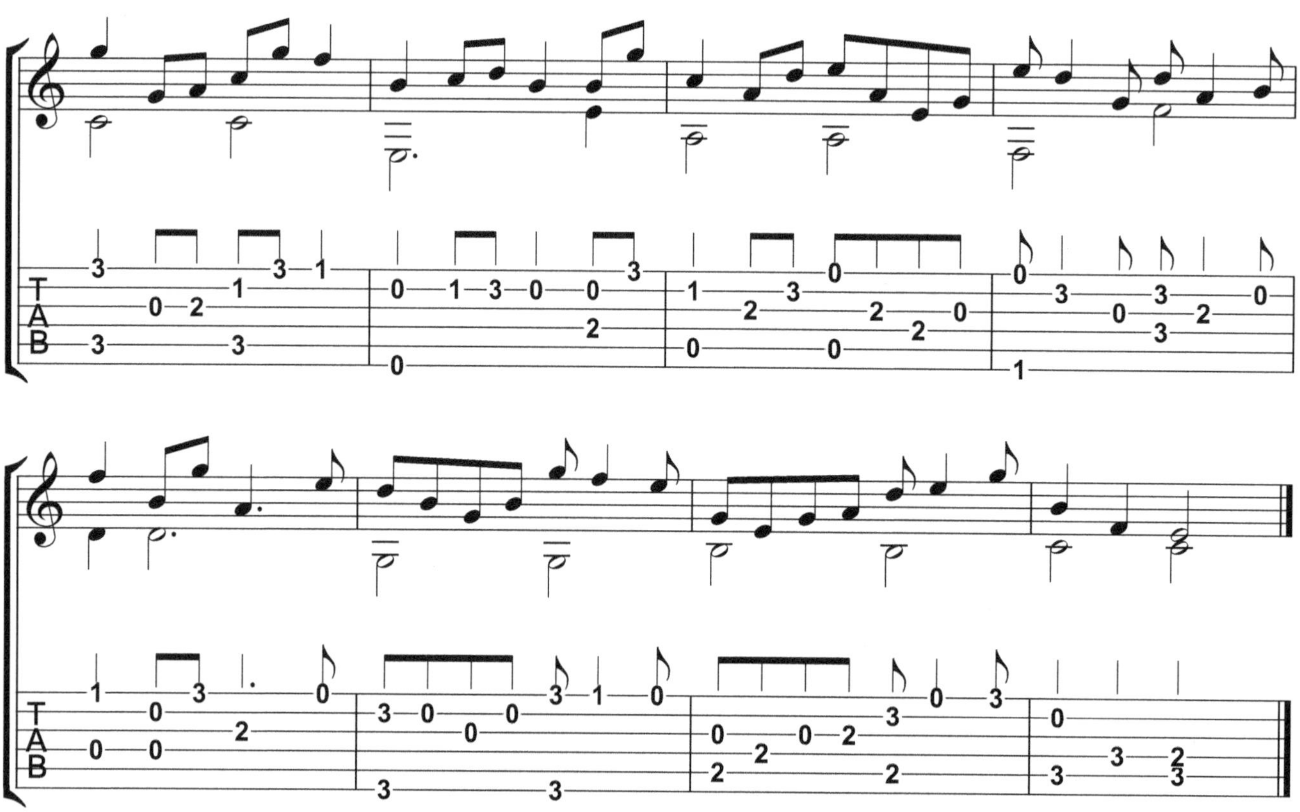

Example 3

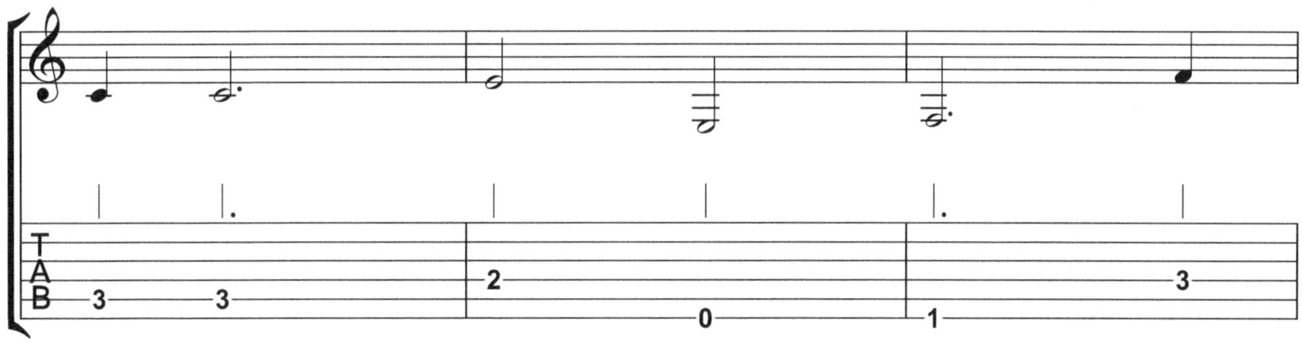

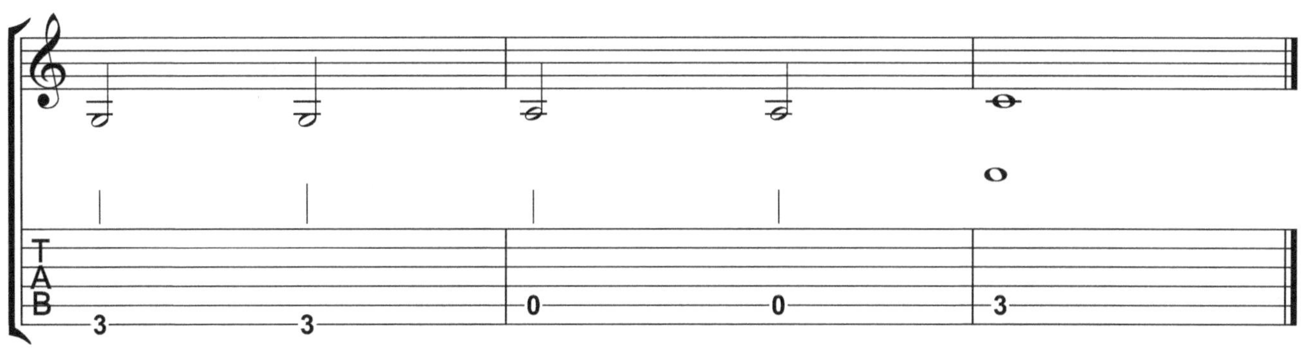

Track 14

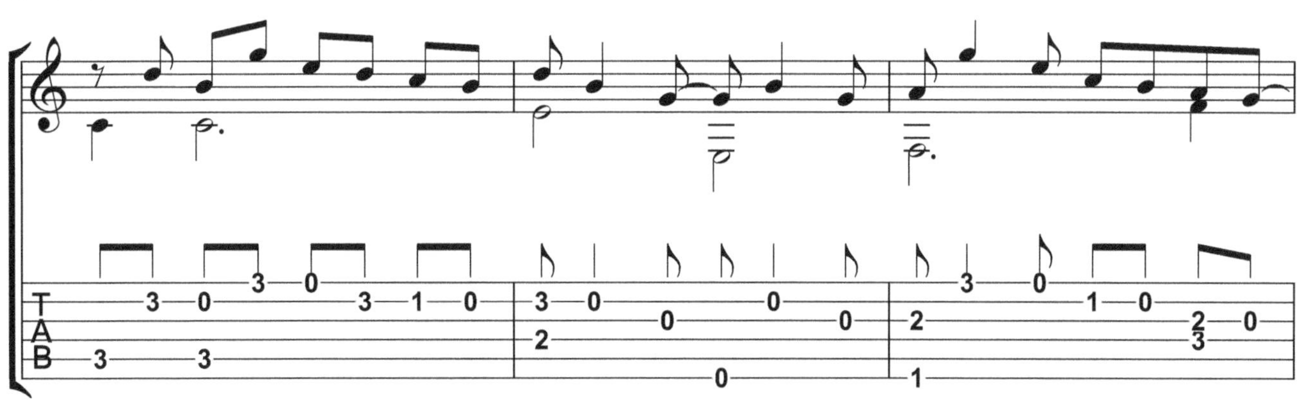

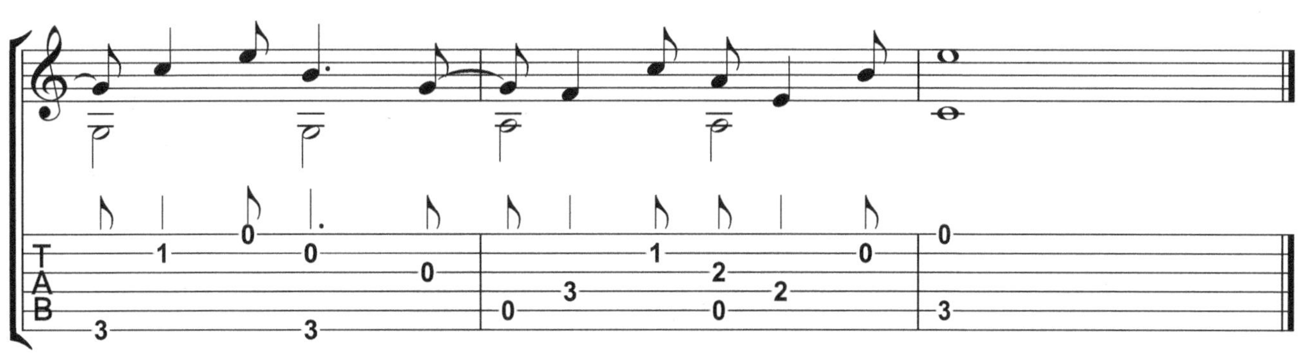

Your turn

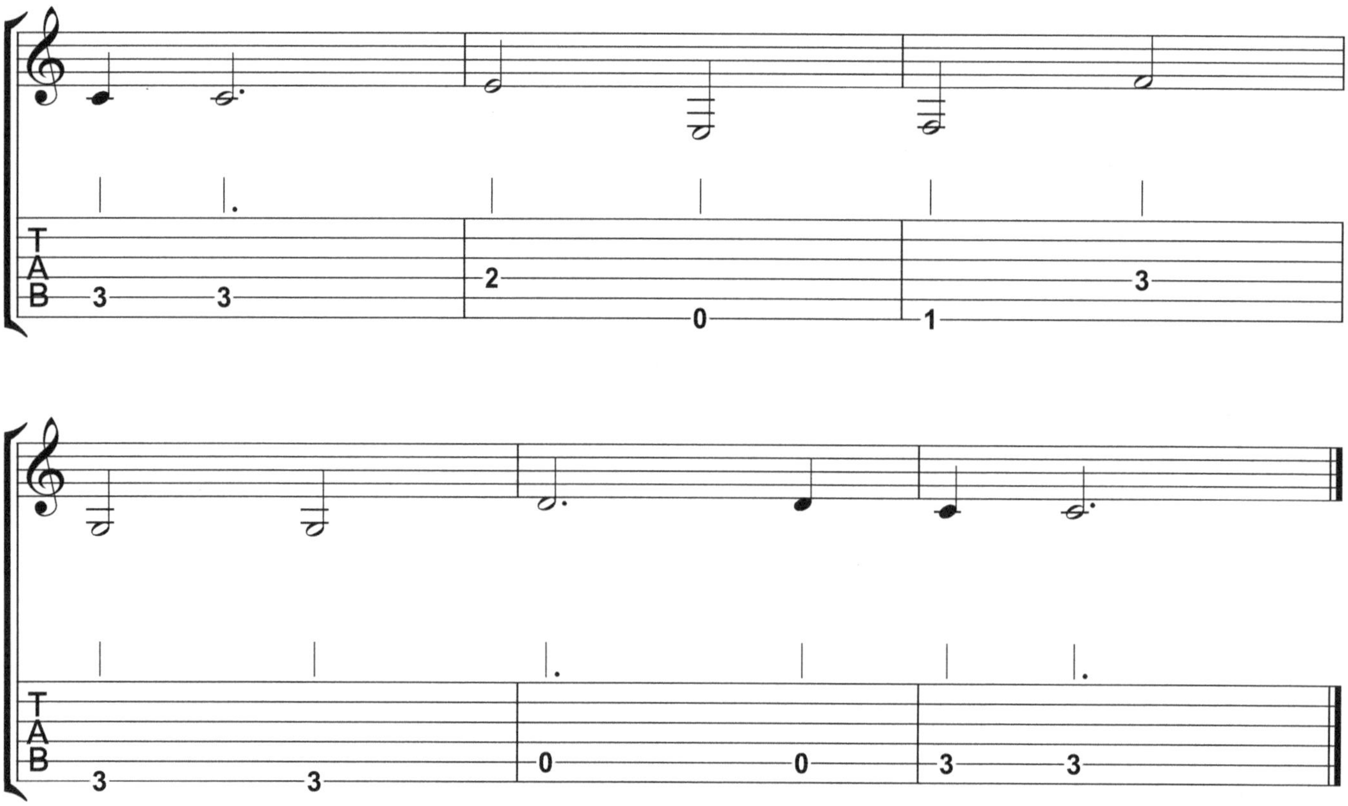

Adding a Middle Voice

Let's practice on the following bass progression.

Three Steps:

1. Create dyads.
2. Add a note on the strings between the upper and bottom voices.
3. Invent melodic lines. Incorporate scalar passages but don't be reliant on them!

These 3 steps should be first practiced separately until you feel comfortable and then try to improvise on-the-spot melodic lines combined with the middle and bottom voices. Be aware of the intervallic relationships!!

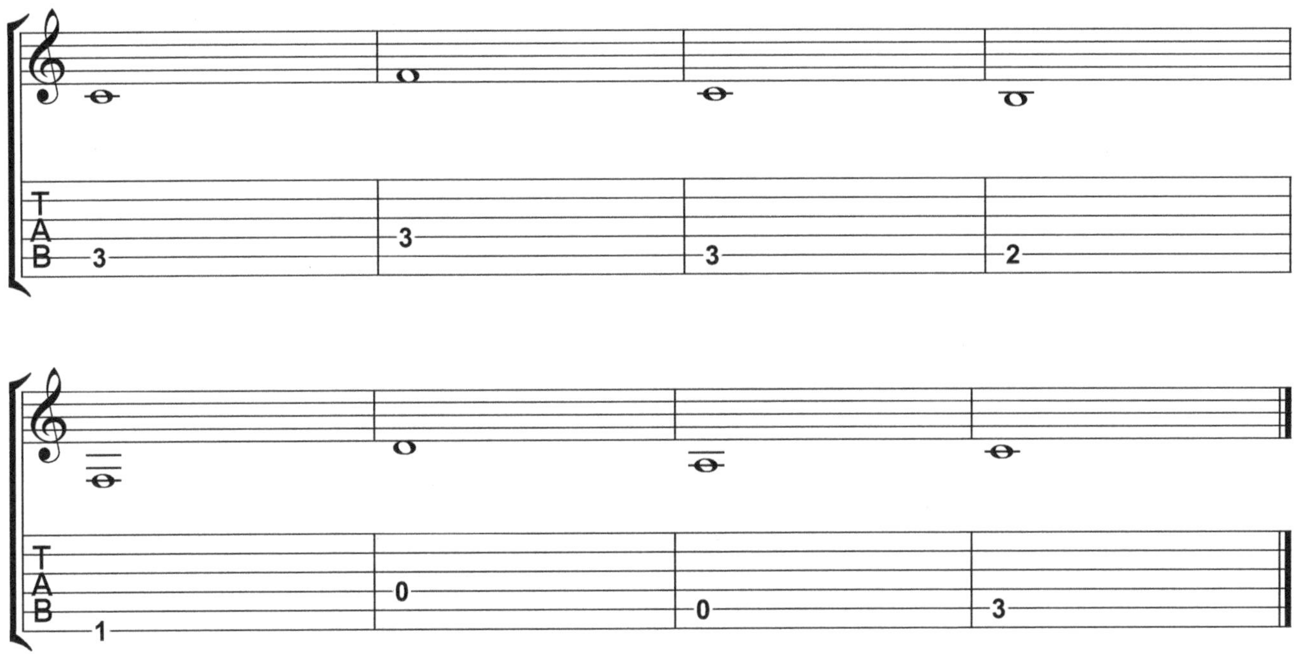

Play a melody note on top of the bass note (dyad).

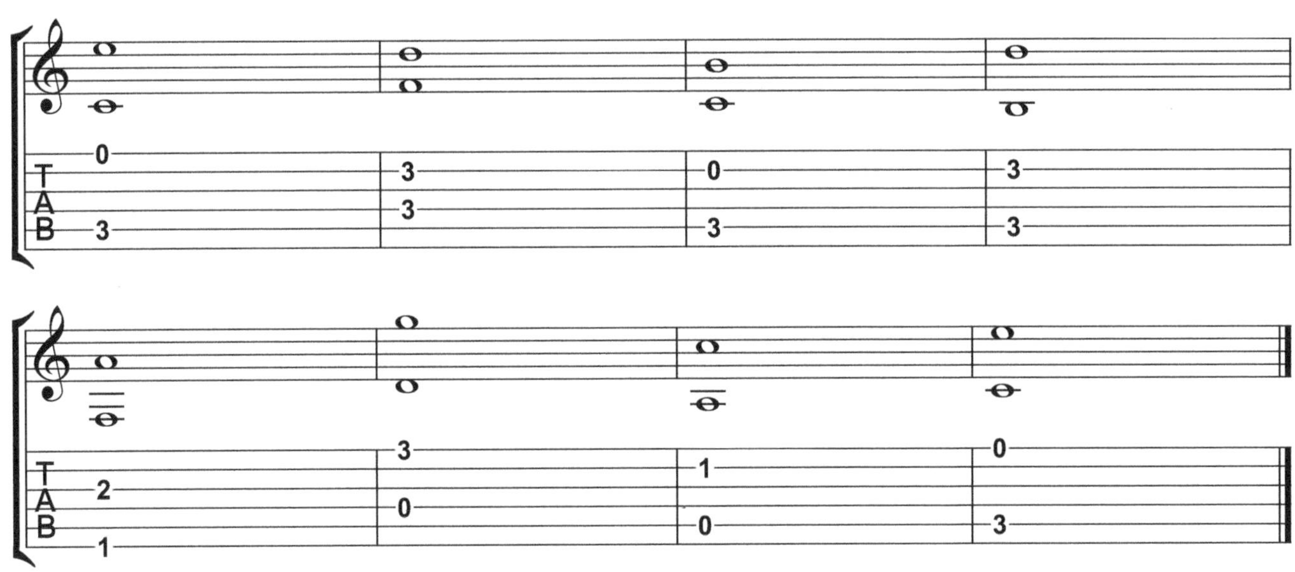

Add a note in the middle voice on the available strings from the C Major scale, between the upper and bottom voices. I like to include open strings along with fretted notes. They can offer your musical palette some surprisingly fresh and original sounds.

Here are the possibilities for the dyads we have created thus far.

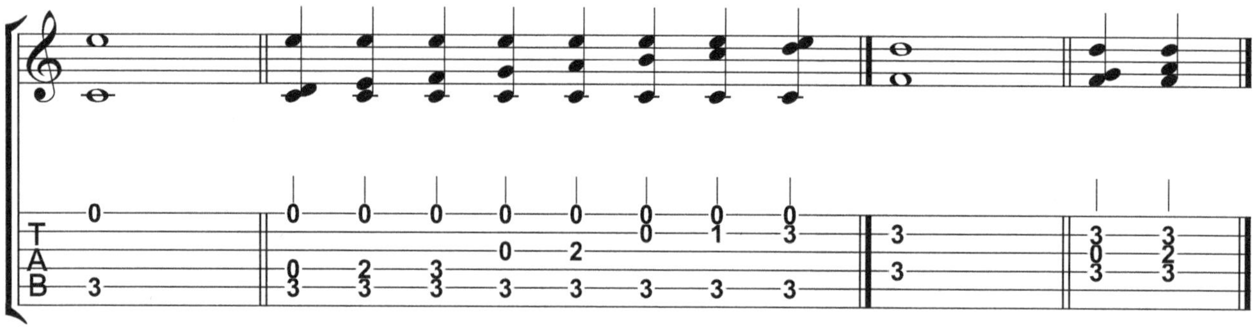

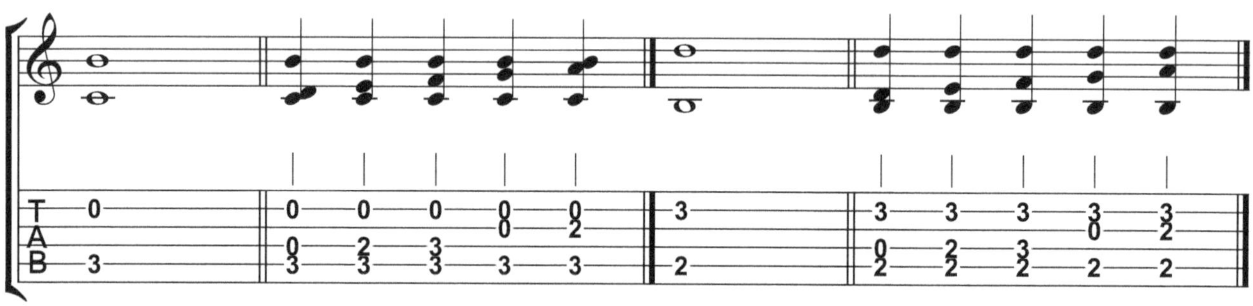

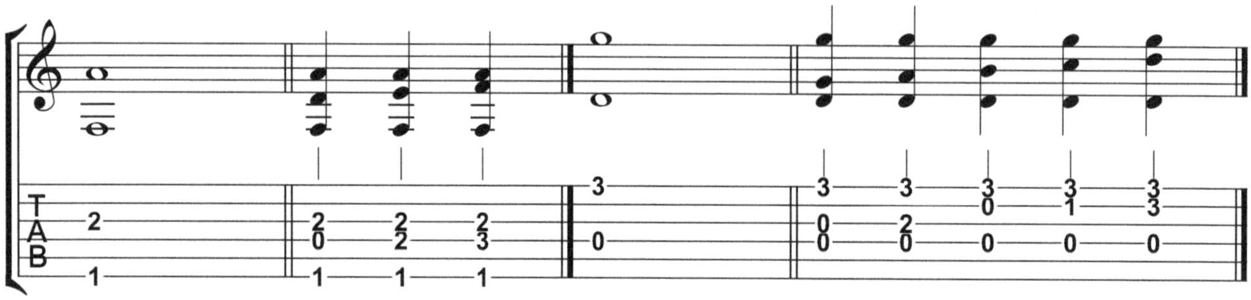

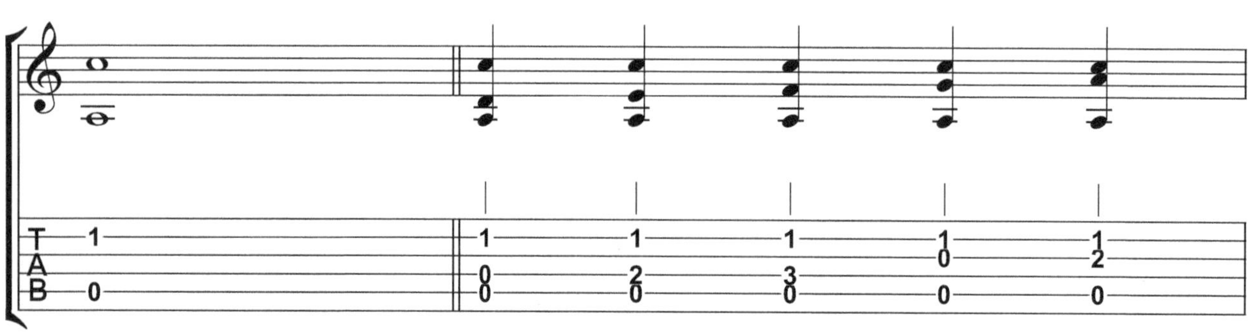

This might be the result on the progression on page 39.

Example 1

Add a middle voice.

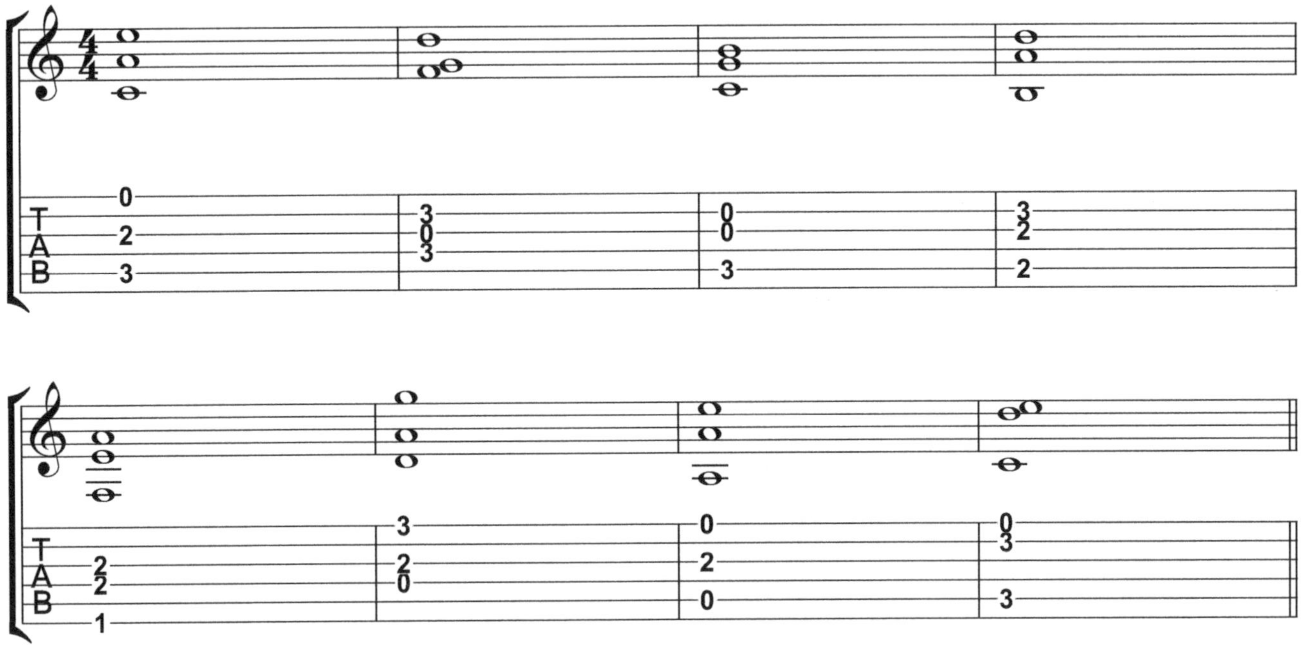

Improvise a melodic line on top.

Track 15

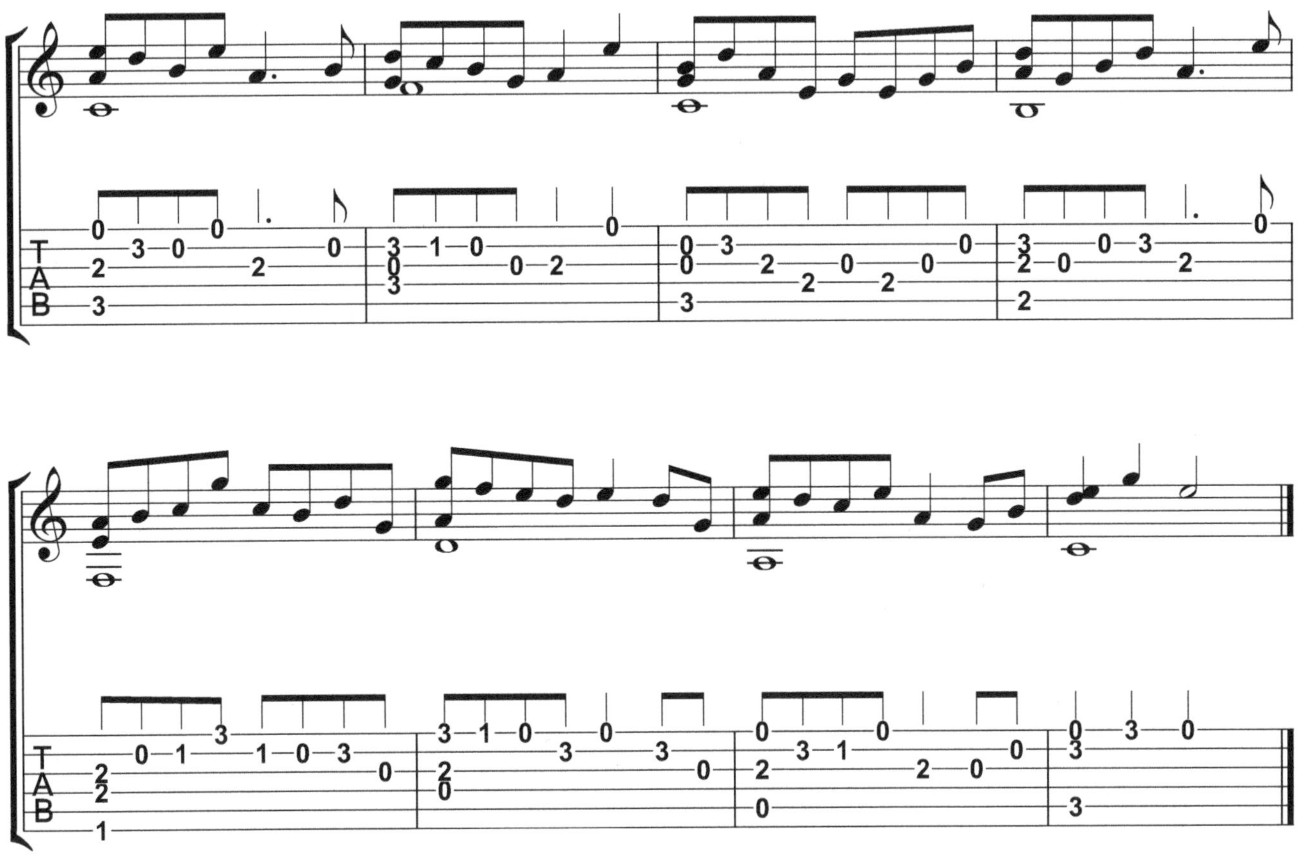

or

Example 2, same progression, different dyads and middle voices.

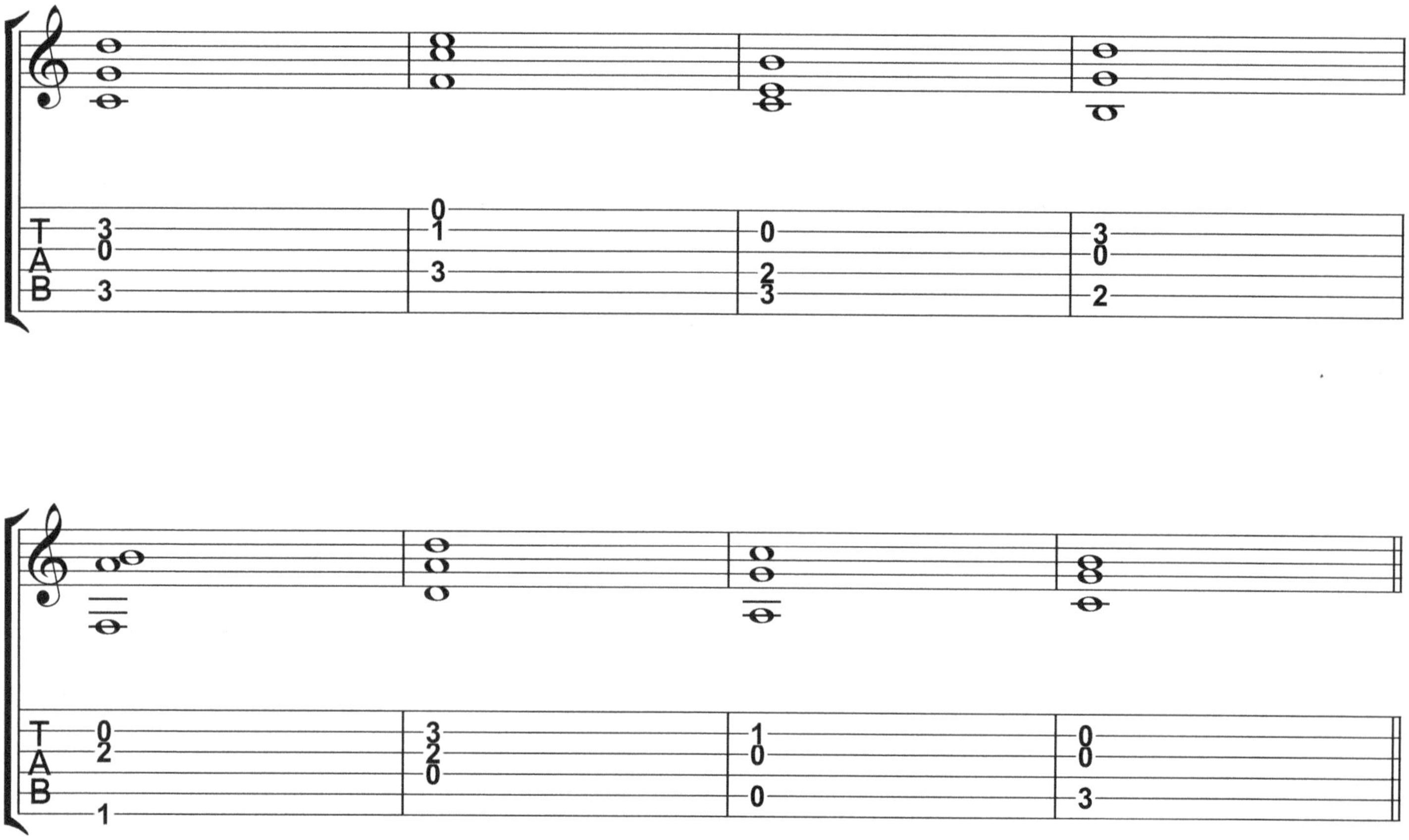

Improvise a melodic line on top.

Track 16

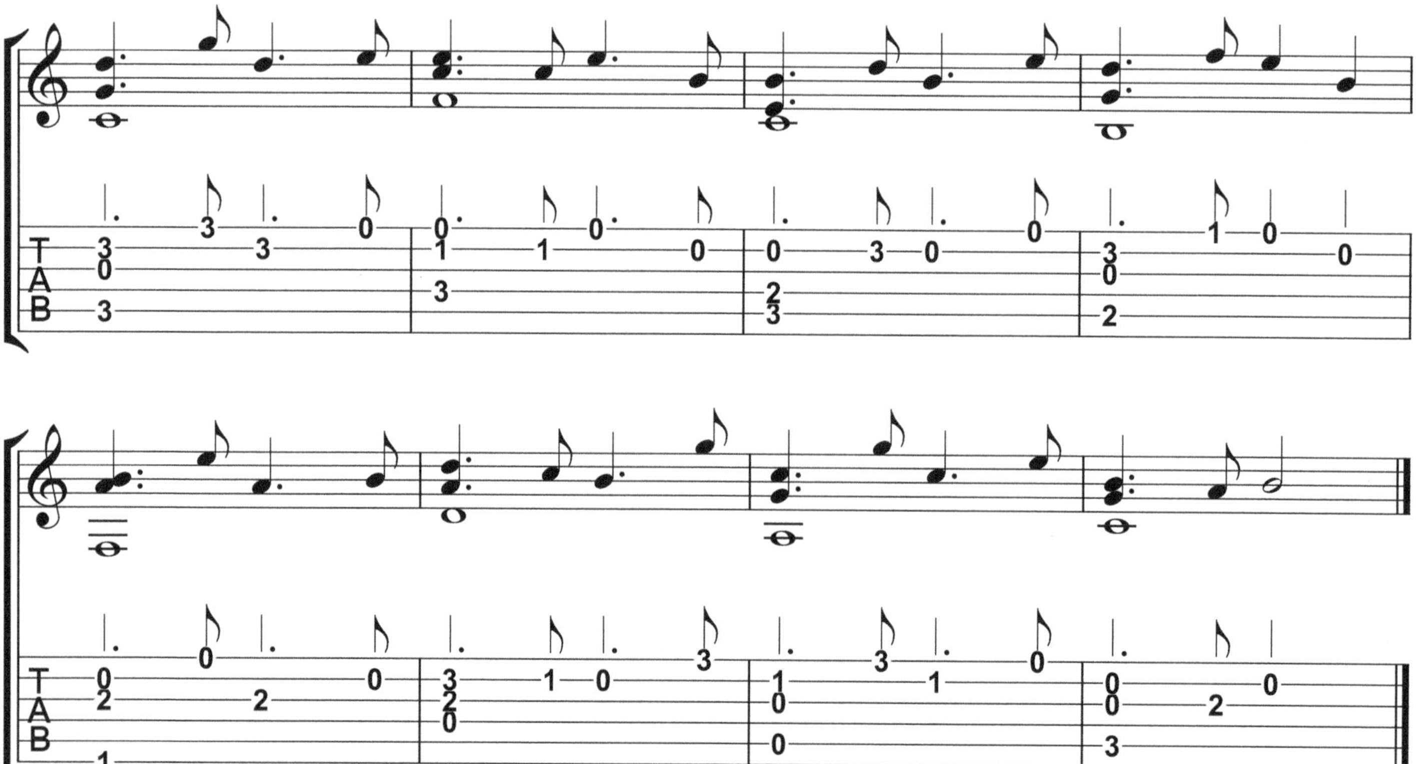

Your turn

1. Create dyads.

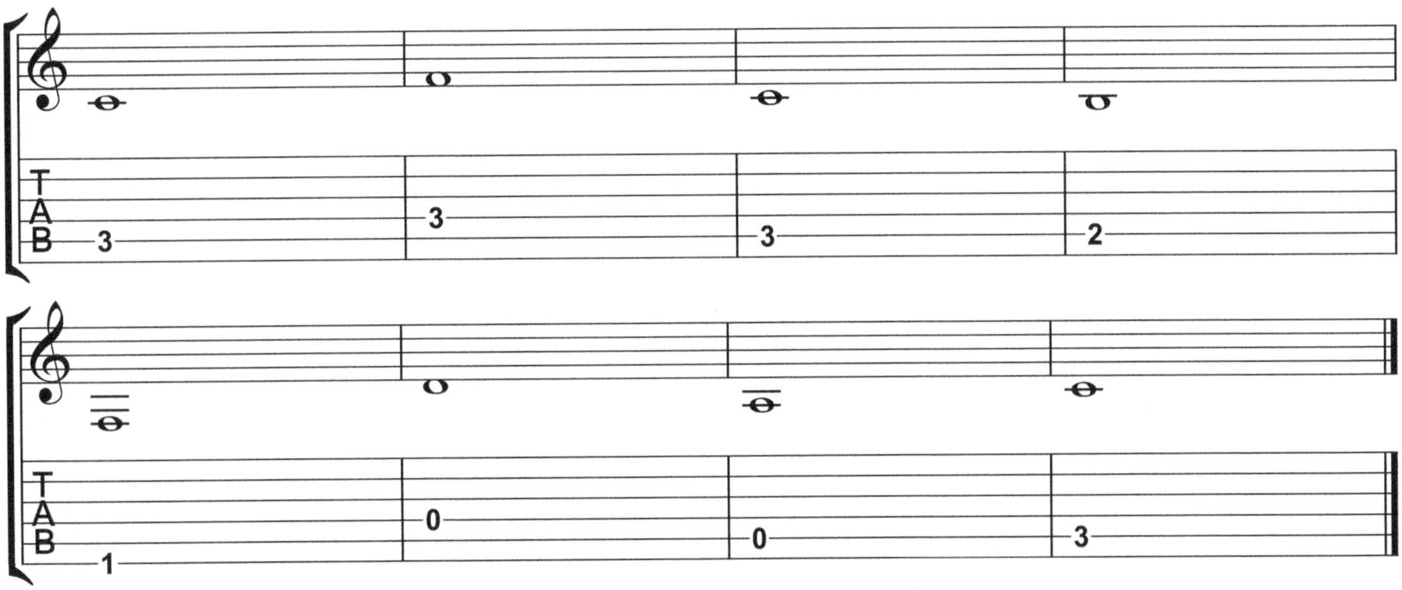

2. Add a middle note on the courses between the upper and bottom voices.

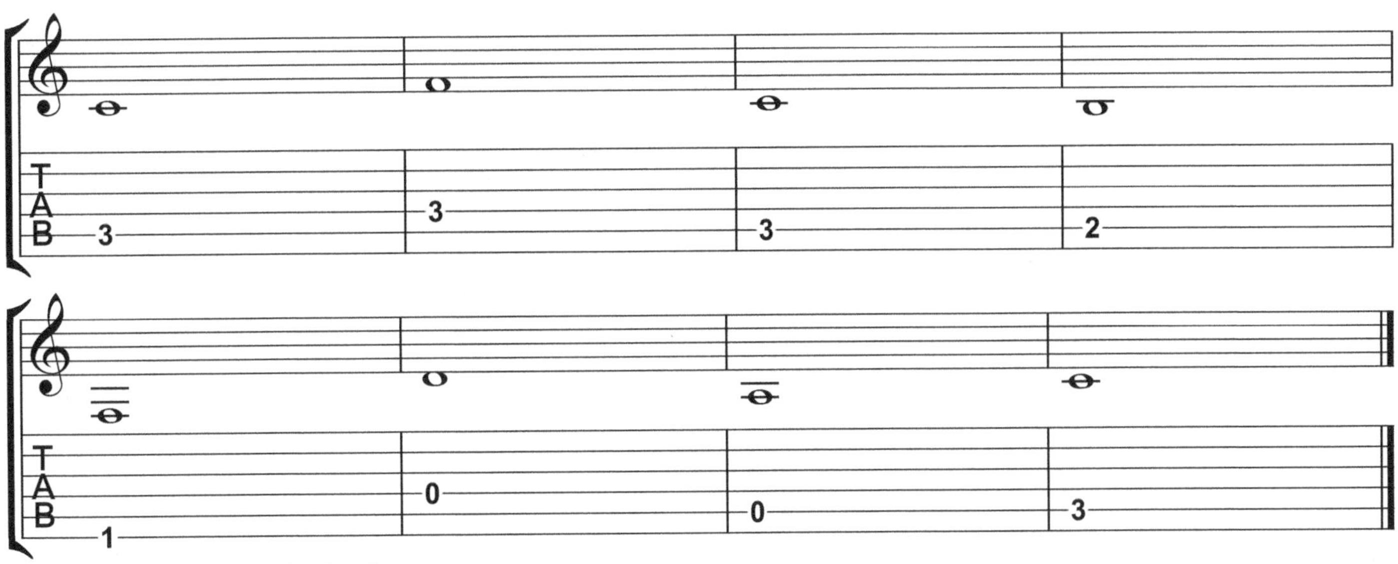

3. Improvise a melodic line on top.

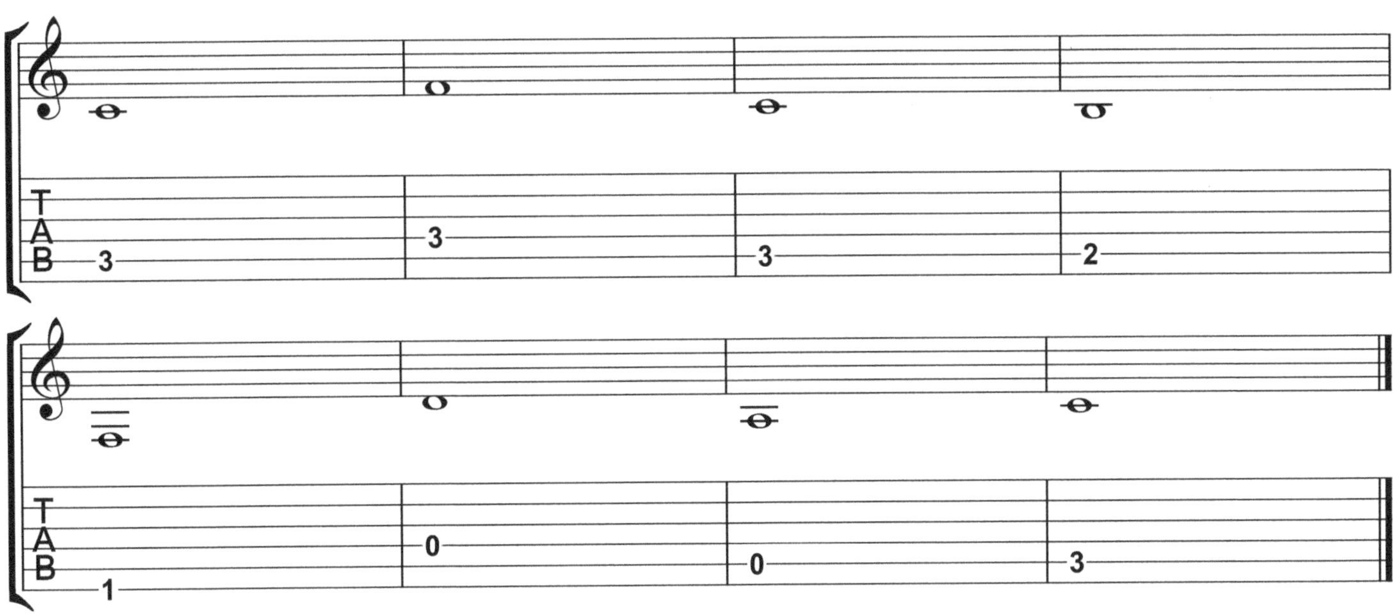

In chapter 4 we treated the root-root alteration. Let's practice this again on the bass progression.

1. Create dyads.

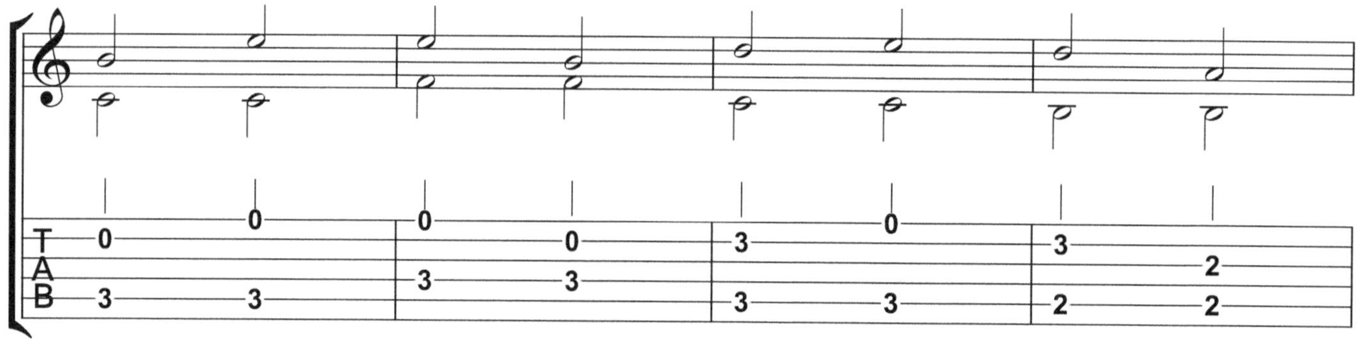

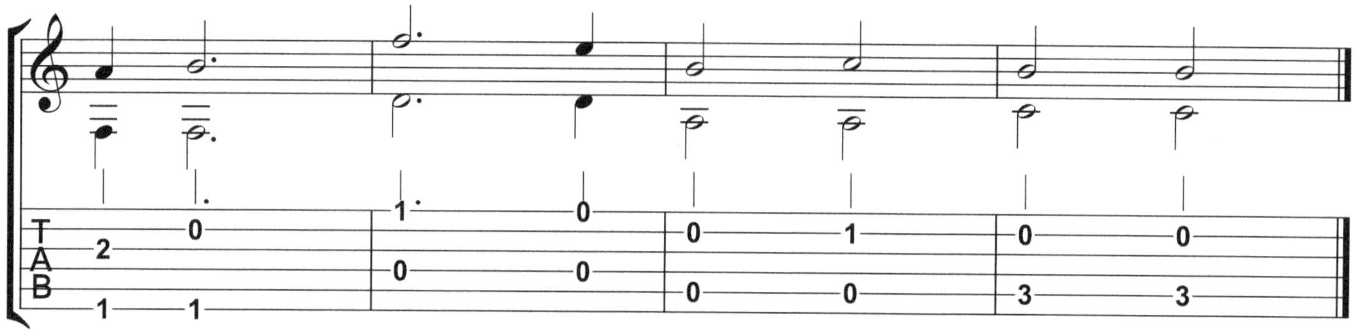

2. Add a note in the middle voice on the available courses from the C Major scale between the upper and bottom voices.

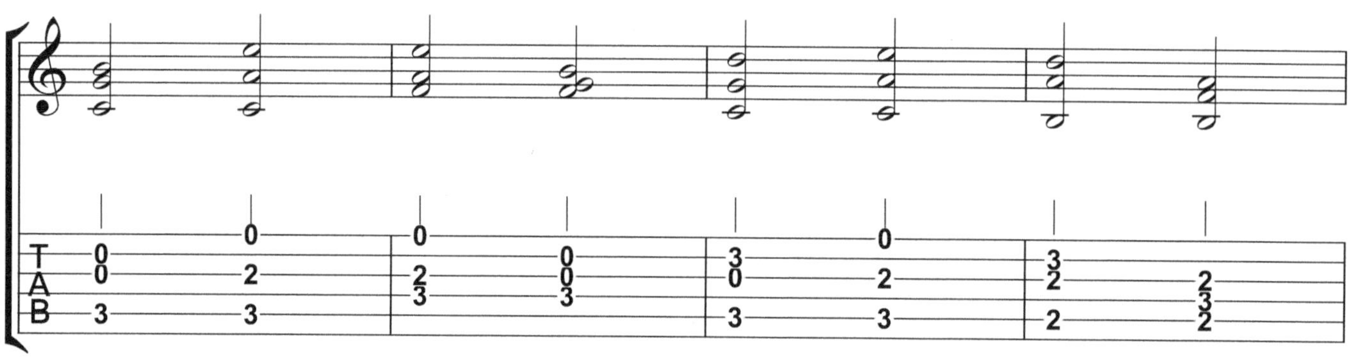

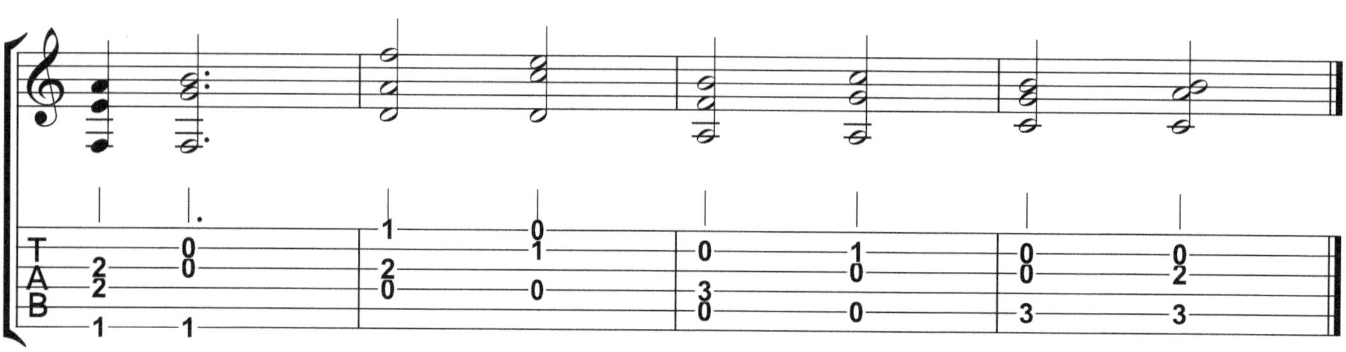

3. Improvise a melodic line on top.

Track 17

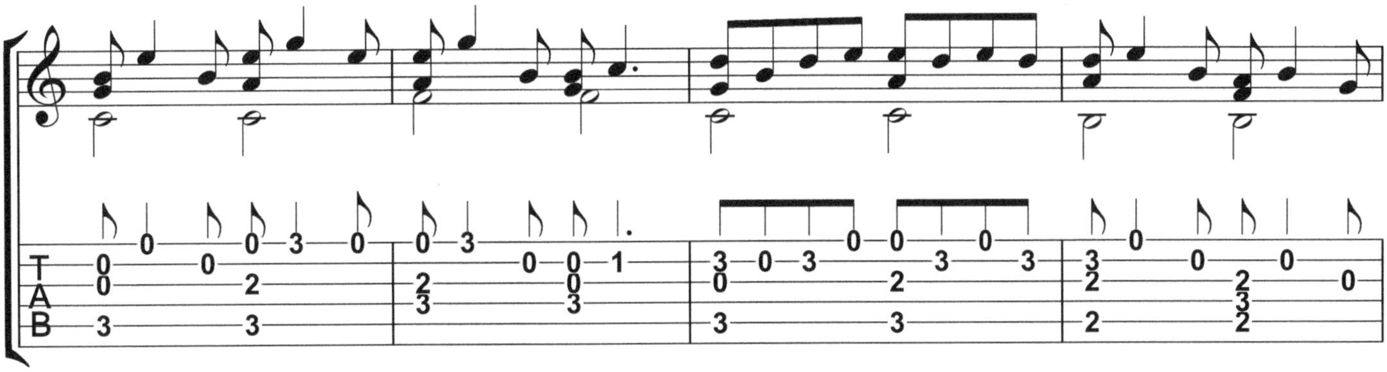

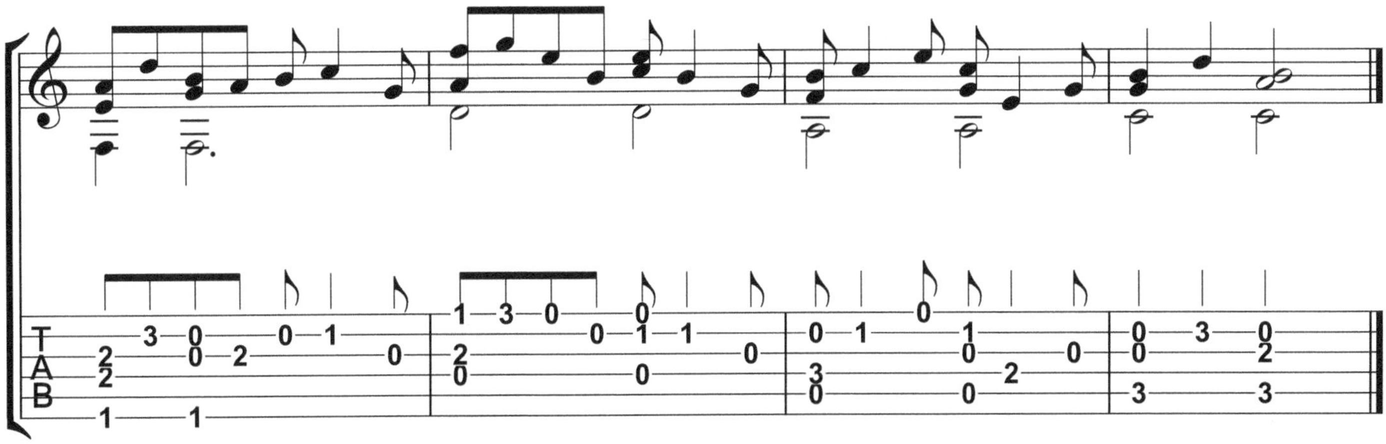

Your turn

1. Create dyads (root-root alteration).

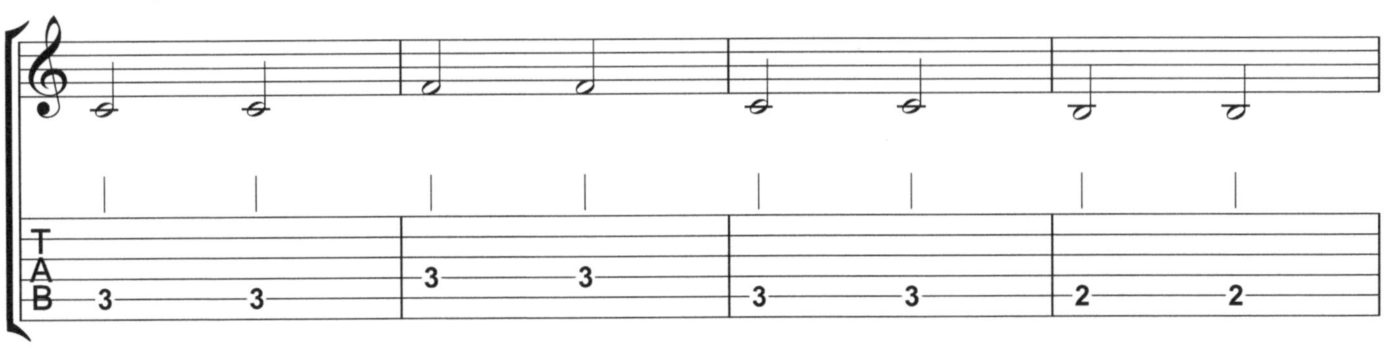

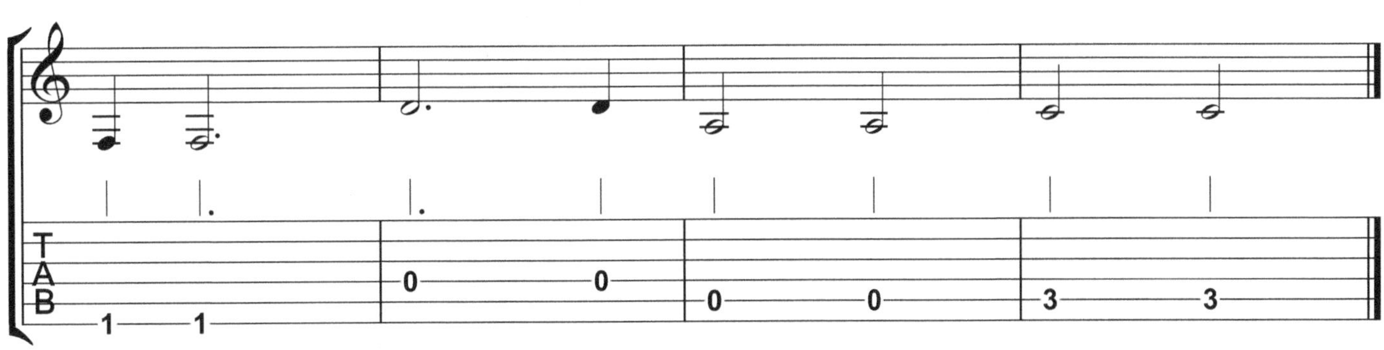

2. Add a middle note on the courses between the upper and bottom voices.

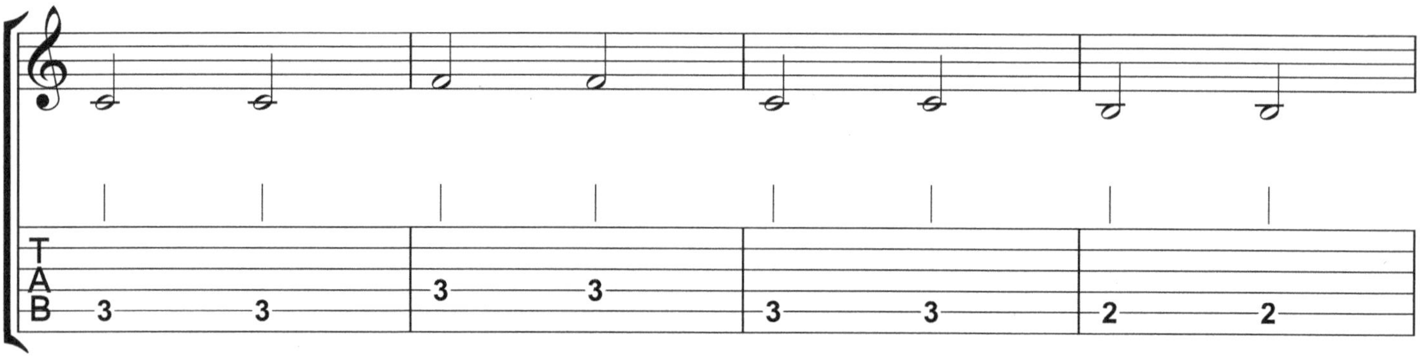

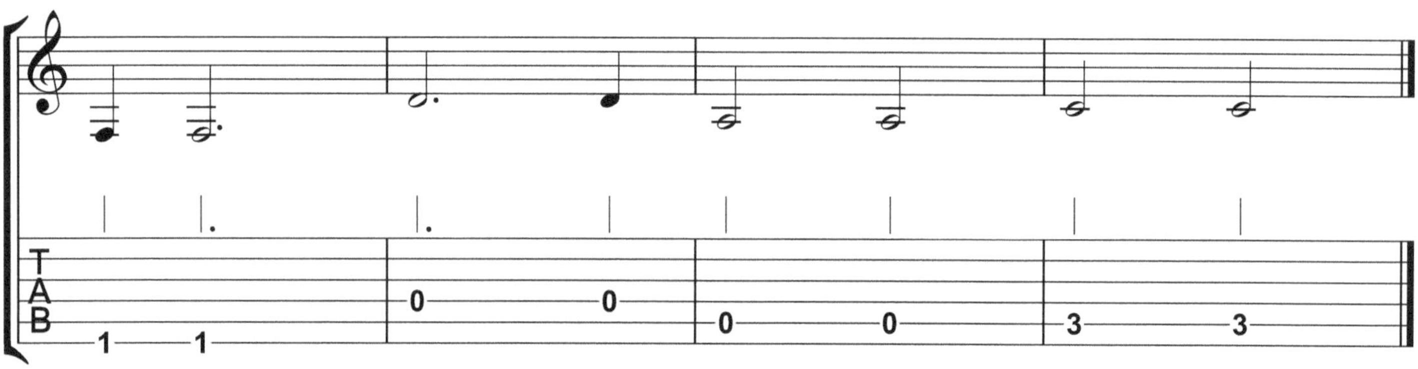

3. Improvise a melodic line on top.

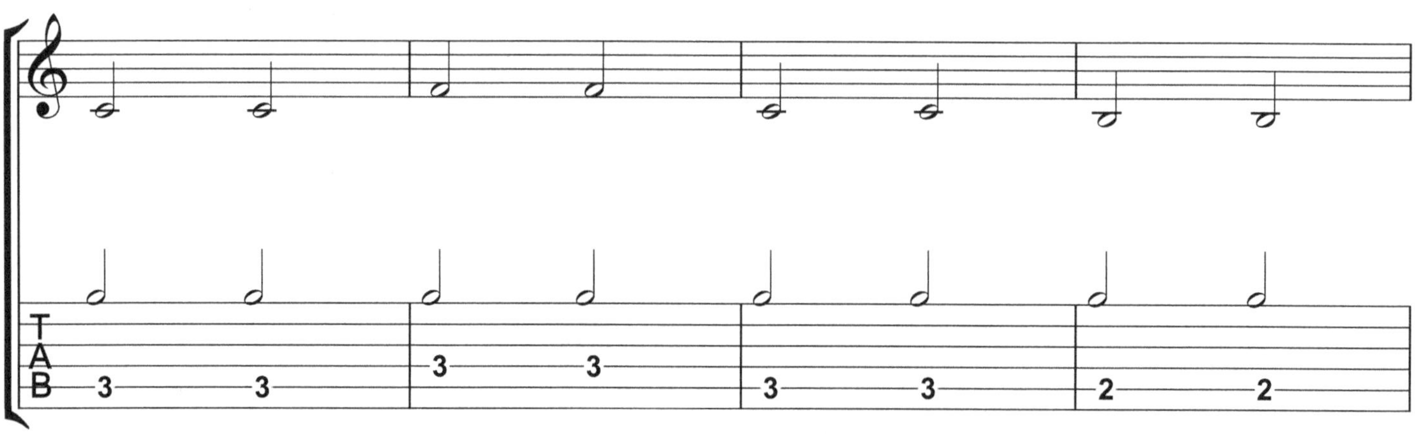

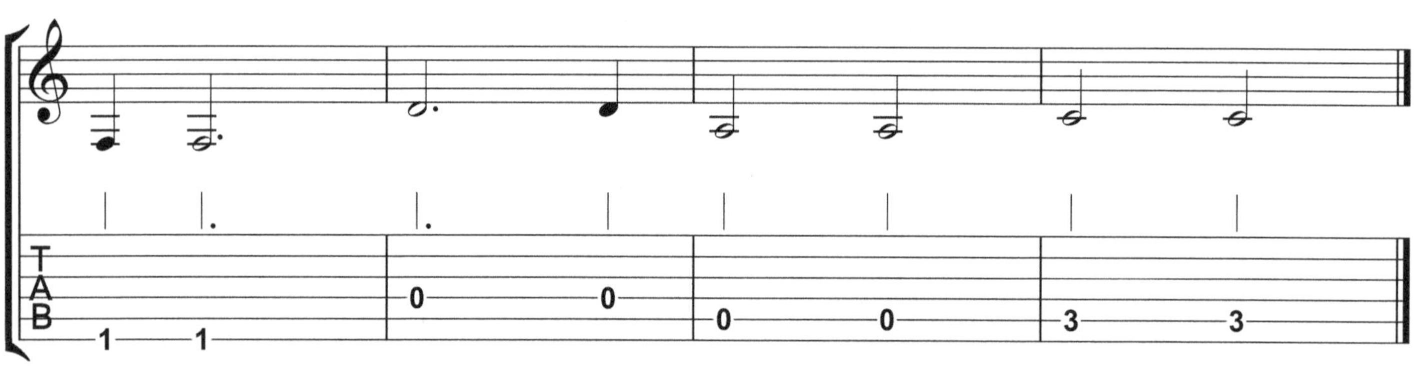

CHAPTER 6

More Movement in the Middle Voice

One bass per bar. The upper and bottom voices remain stationary.

Some examples:

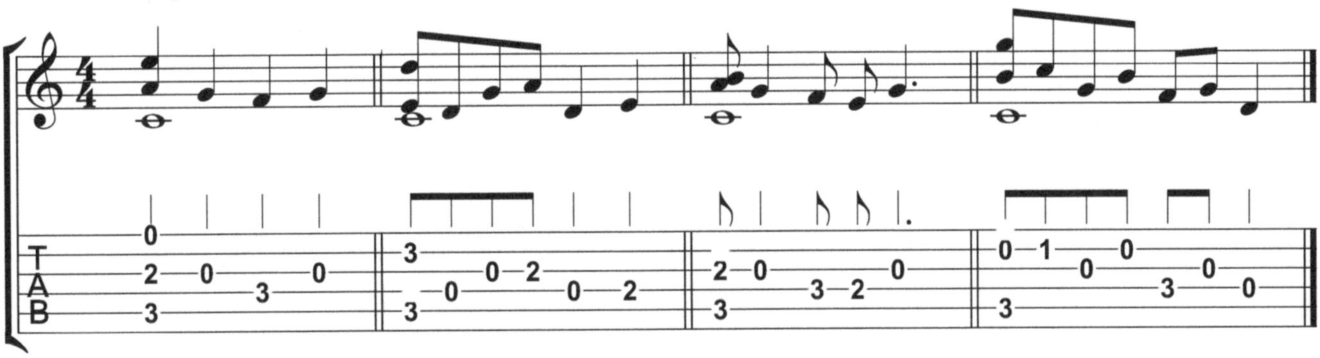

On a progression

Track 18

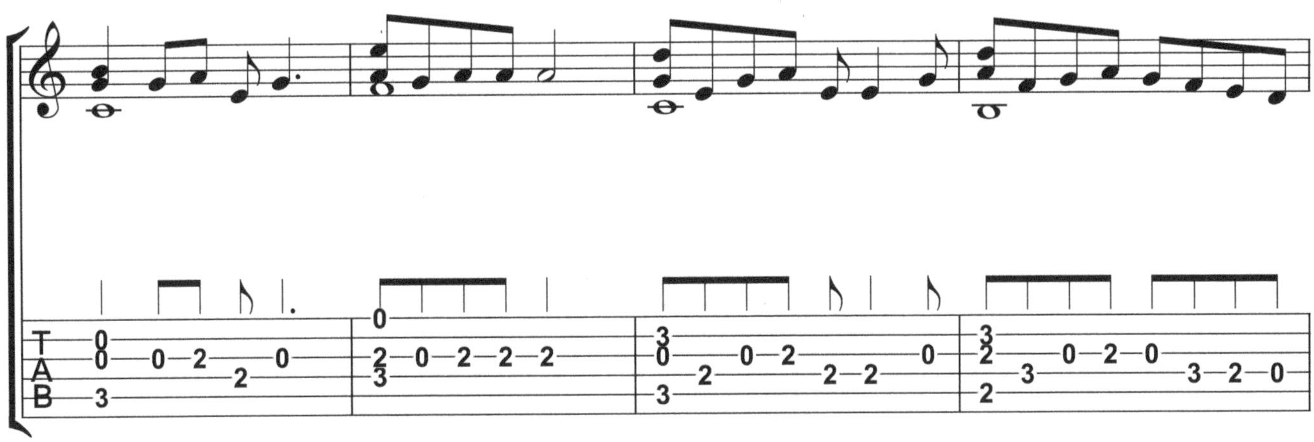

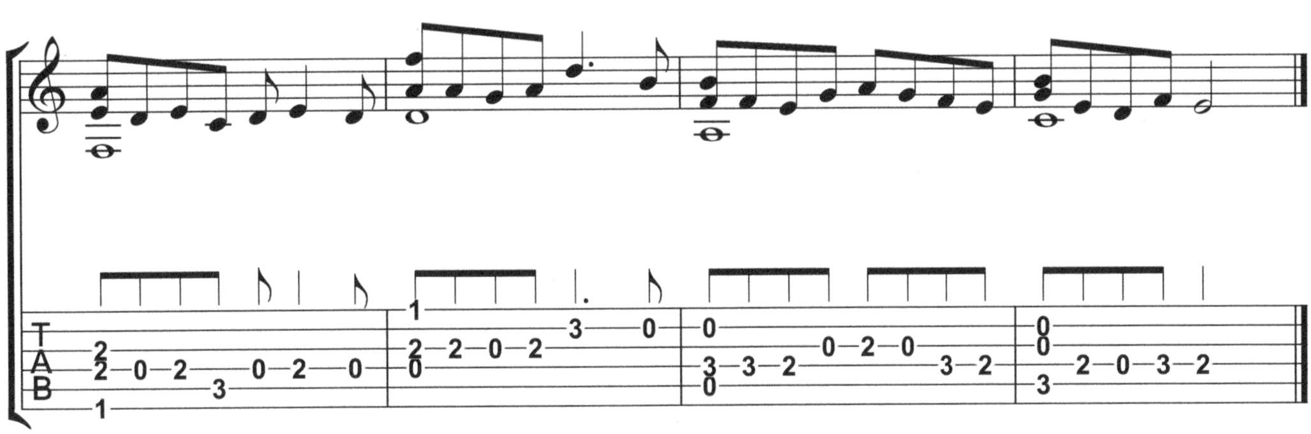

Your turn

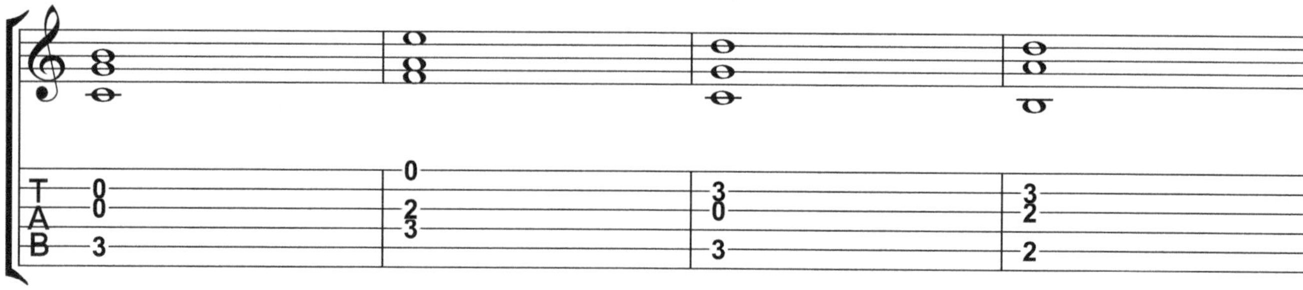

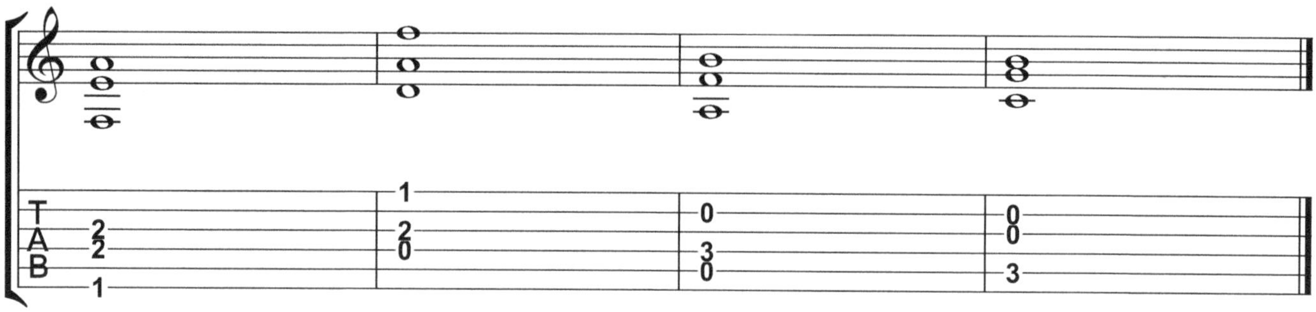

Two basses per bar

Some examples:

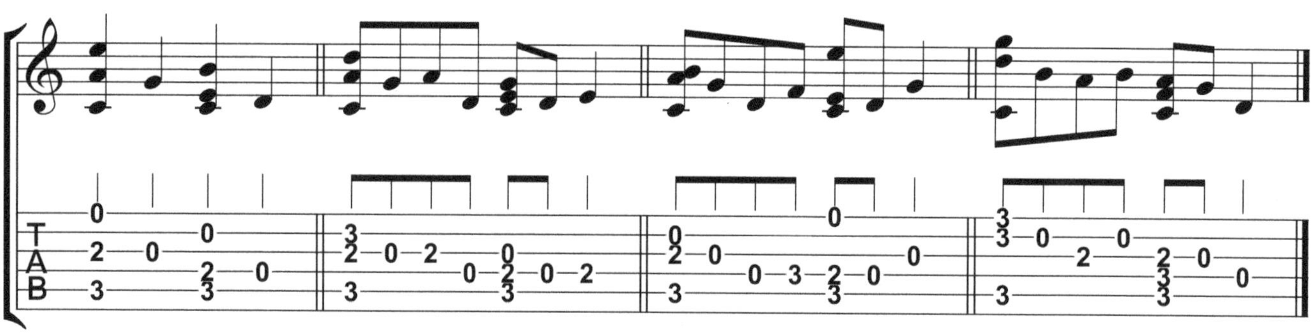

On a progression

Track 19

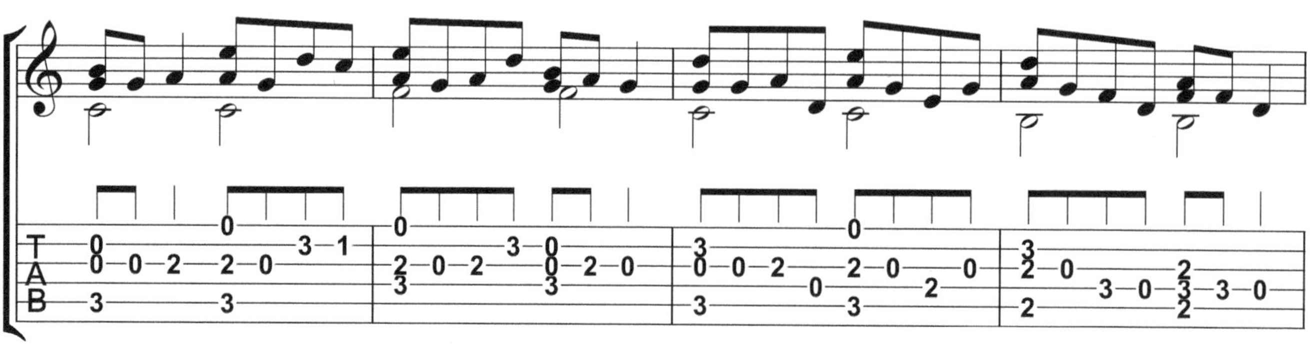

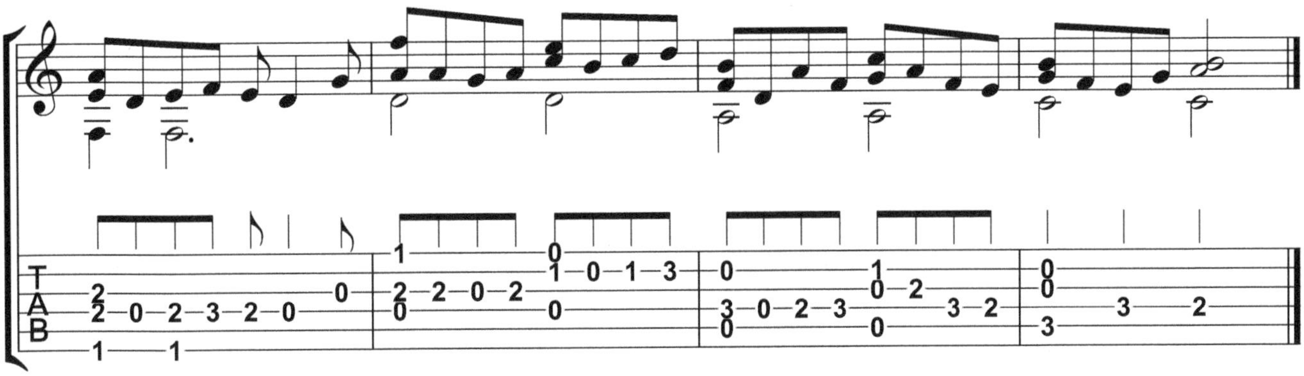

Your turn

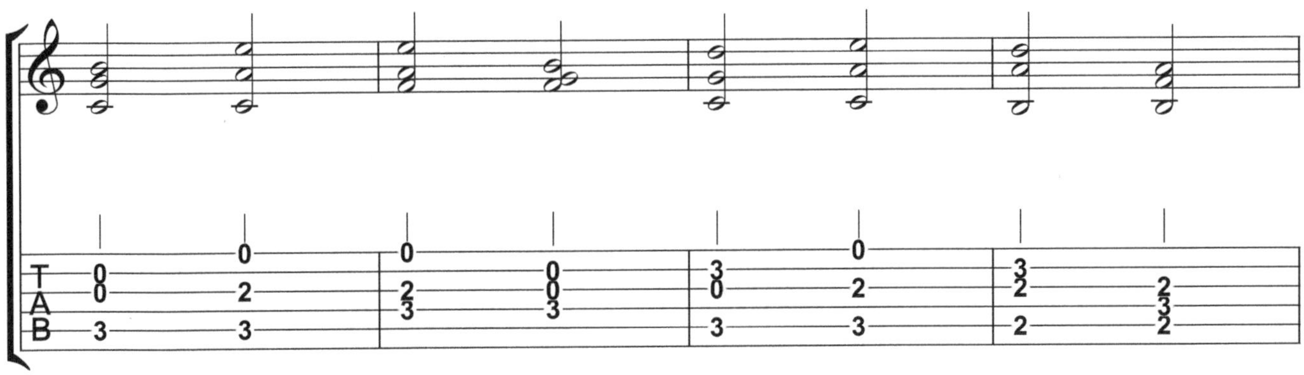

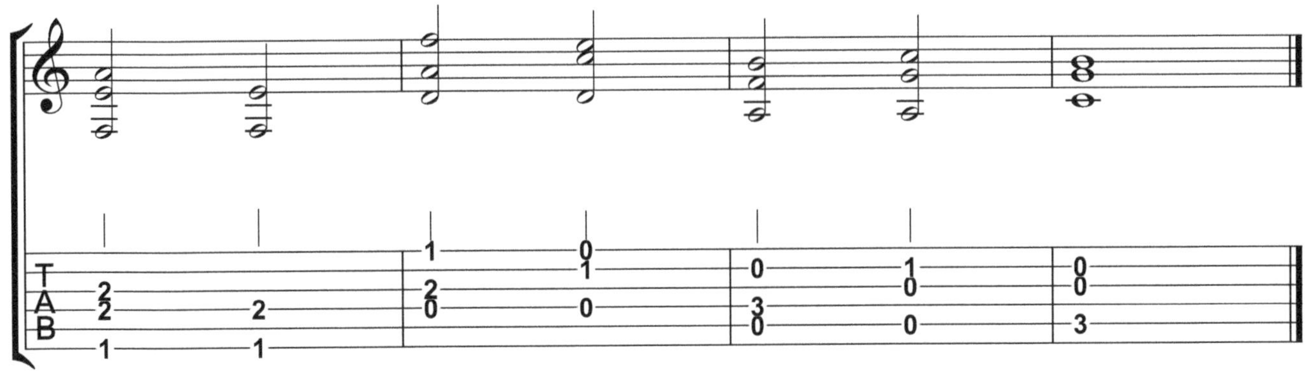

CHAPTER 7

Basic Chords

Thus far we have played quite a lot of 3-note chords. Most of these chords have a major or minor third in them. Thirds define whether the chord is a major or minor one. Chords are built by stacking intervals on top of each other, so make sure you know your intervals!!

If we look at the improvisation in the previous chapter, we could name these chords as:

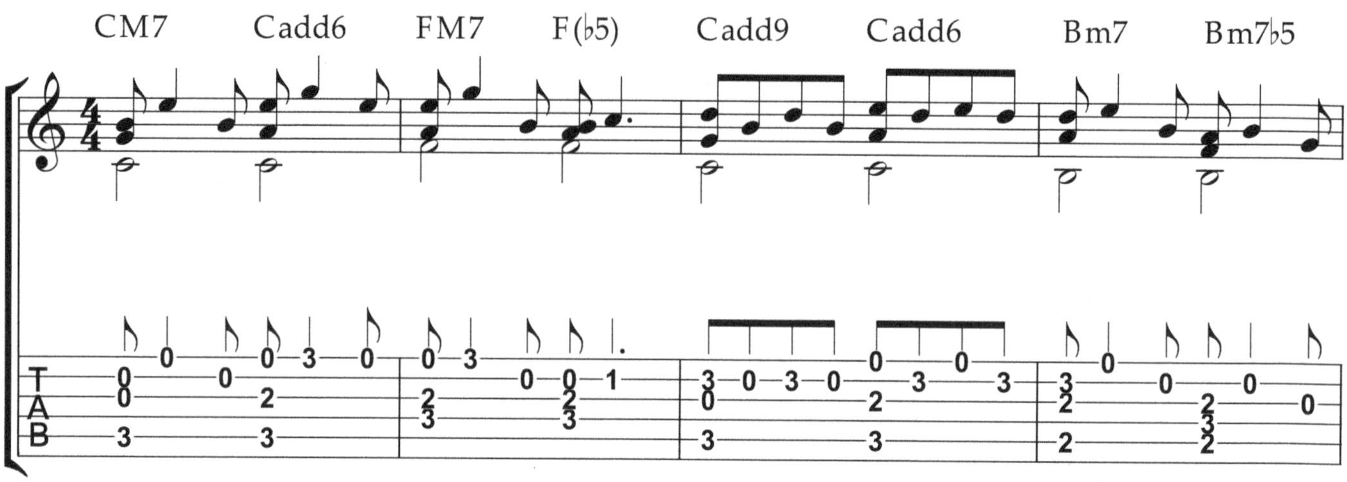

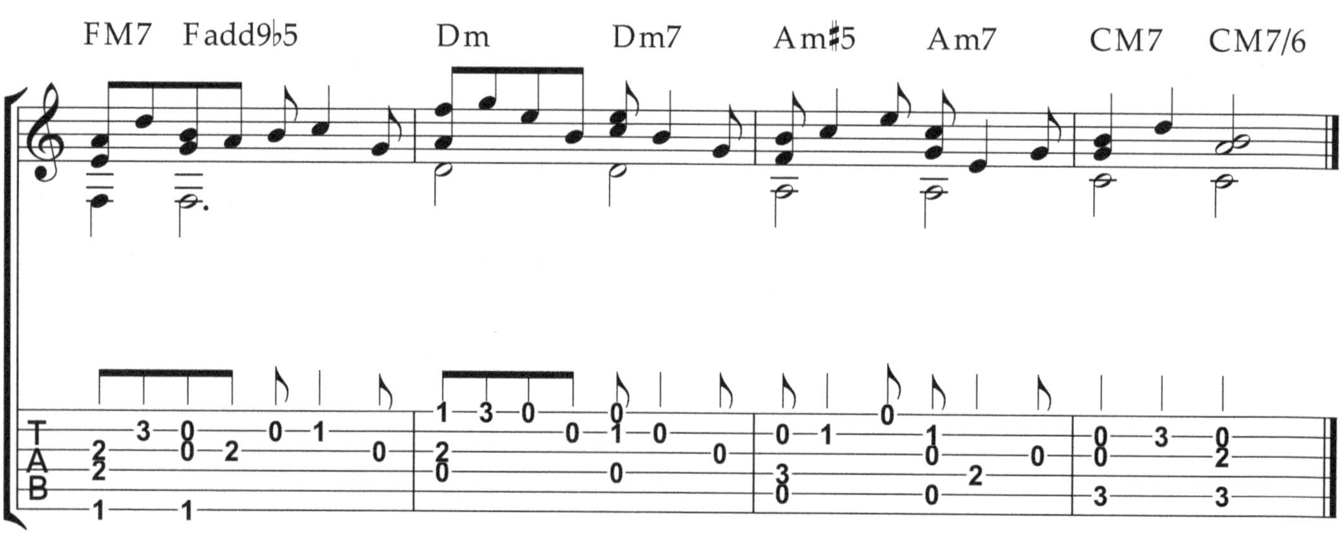

There are 3 basic chord families: The major, minor and dominant families.
The root, third and the seventh determine the family to which a chord belongs.

The C Major scale to the seventh:

Chord Name	Formula	Chord Tones
CM7	1,3,5,7	C E G B
Dm7	1,♭3,5,♭7	D F A C
Em7	1,♭3,5,♭7	E G B D
FM7	1,3,5,7	F A C E
G7	1,3,5,♭7	G B D F
Am7	1,♭3,5,♭7	A C E G
Bm7♭5	1,♭3,♭5,♭7	B D F A

All 3 chord families are represented here.

The major chord family (CM7, FM7)
The minor chord family (Dm7, Em7, Am7, Bm7♭5)
A m7♭5 is also referred to as a half diminished and fits into the minor chord family.
The dominant chord family (G7)
Additions to chords beyond the 7 are referred to as extensions.
1 2 3 4 5 6 7 8 9 10 11 12 13
C D E F G A B C D E F G A
Extensions are the 2 or 9 (D), the 4 or 11 (F), the 6 or 13 (A)
Chromatic tones are:
♭2/♭9 ♯2/♯9 ♯4/♭5 ♯5/♭13 ♭7
C♯/ D♯/ F♯ G♯ B♭

The Major Chord Family

We will refer to the major chords as **Major7ths (M7). You are however not limited to always playing chords with theM7th added. Feel free to eventually leave out the 7th or other notes such as the fifth, and replace them by any other scale notes that sound good to YOU.**
I will name the thus created chords '**Direct Substitutions**': chords of the same letter name that replace the original major, minor or dominant chord type.
Keep the third in the chord as it defines whether it is a major or minor chord.
It's good to play first the root-third so that you get familiar with their shapes.

CM7: 1,3,5,7

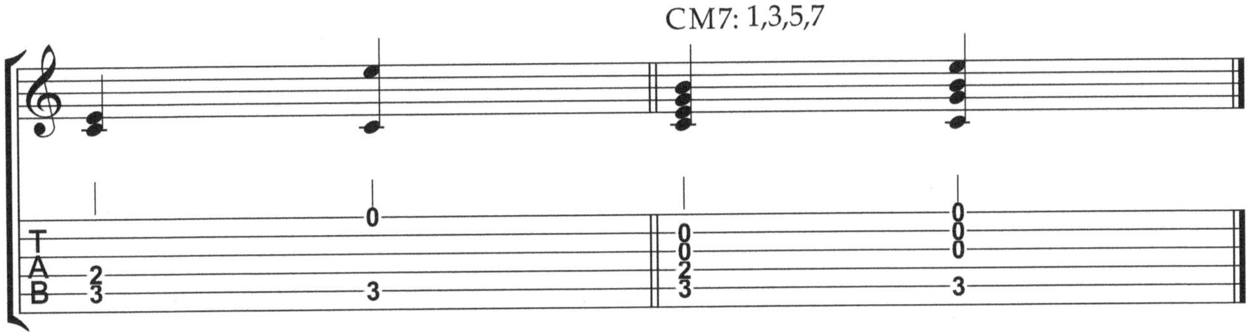

Some direct substitutions. Look for others. Name the intervals.

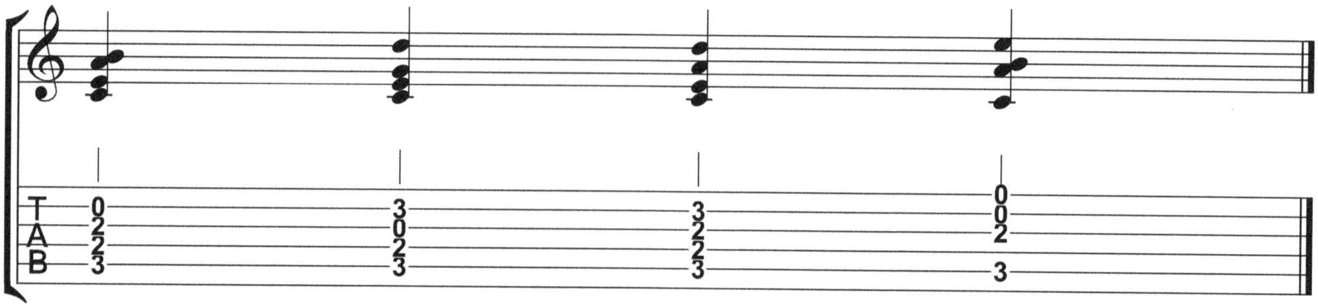

The F Major 7 chord (FM7)

In the C Major key, we play on FM7.

1 2 3 ♭5 5 6 7 1 9 3 ♯11 5 13 7 1

F G A B C D E F G A B C D E F

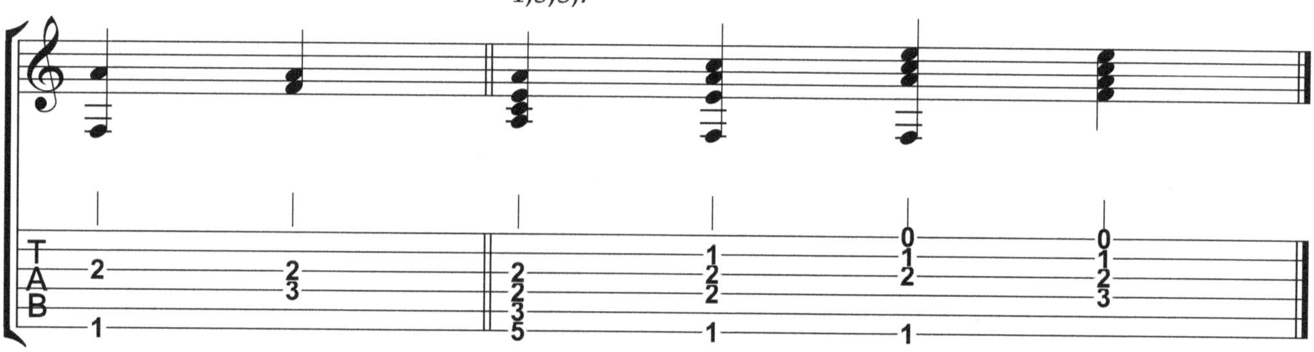

Some direct substitutions. Look for others.

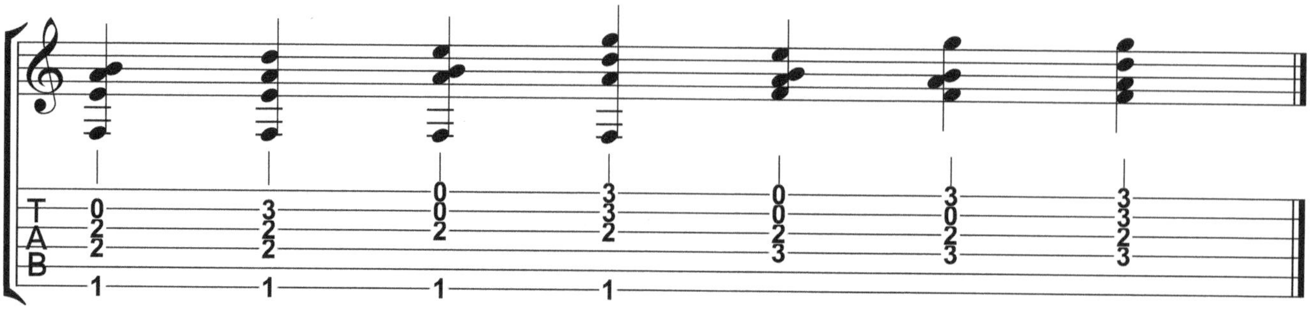

The Minor Chord Family

We will refer to the minor chords as Minor 7ths (m7).
Again, you are not limited to playing chords with only the m7th added.
Feel free to eventually leave out the 7th or other notes such as the fifth, and add extensions that sound good to YOU.
Keep the third in the chord, as it defines whether it is a major or minor chord.

The D minor 7 chord (Dm7)

In the key of C Major play:

1 2 ♭3 4 5 6 ♭7 1 9 ♭3 11 5 13 ♭7 1

D E F G A B C D E F G A B C D

1,♭3,5,♭7 Some direct substitutions.

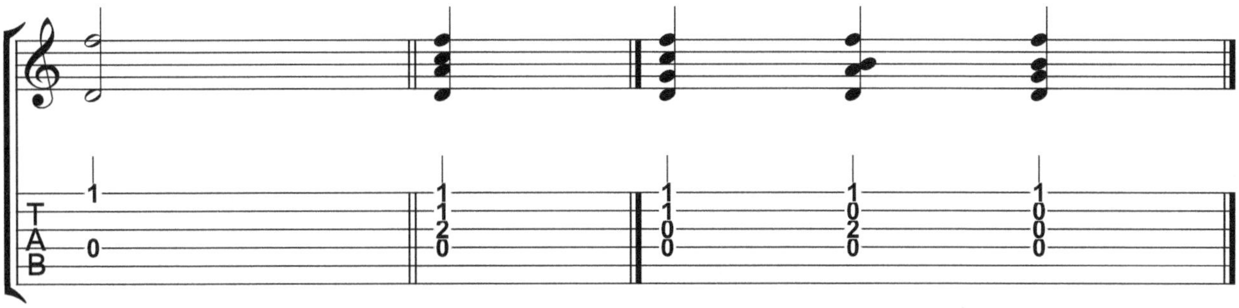

The E minor 7 chord (Em7)

In the key of C Major play:

1 ♭2 ♭3 4 5 ♯5 ♭7 1 ♭9 ♭3 4 5 ♭13

E F G A B C D E F G A B C

1,♭3,5,♭7

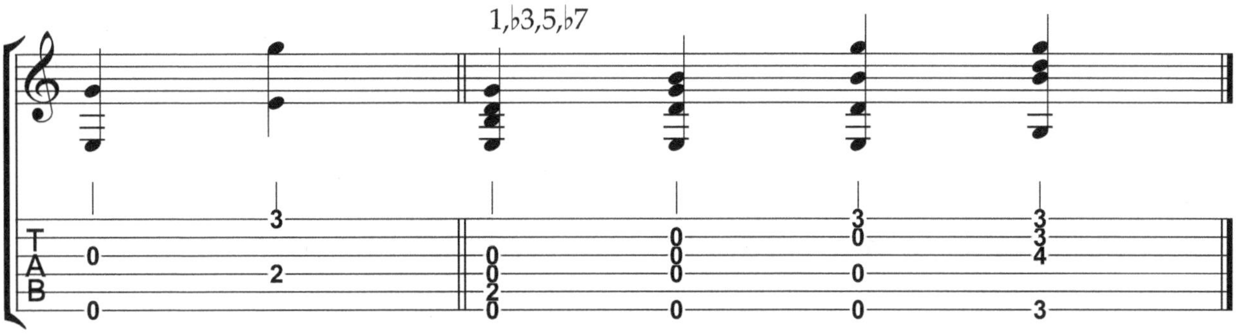

Some direct substitutions. Look for others.

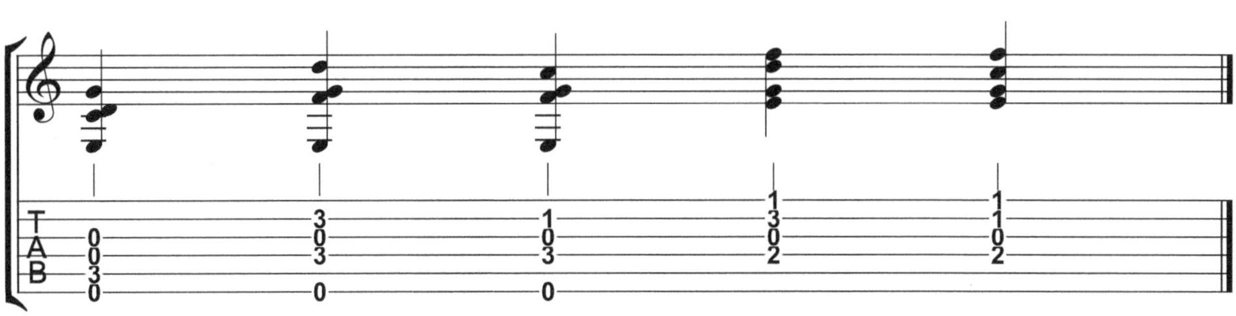

The A minor 7 chord (Am7)

In the key of C Major play:

1 2 ♭3 4 5 ♯5 ♭7 1 9 ♭3 11 5 ♭13 ♭7 1

A B C D E F G A B C D E F G A

1,♭3,5,♭7 Some direct substitutions. Look for others.

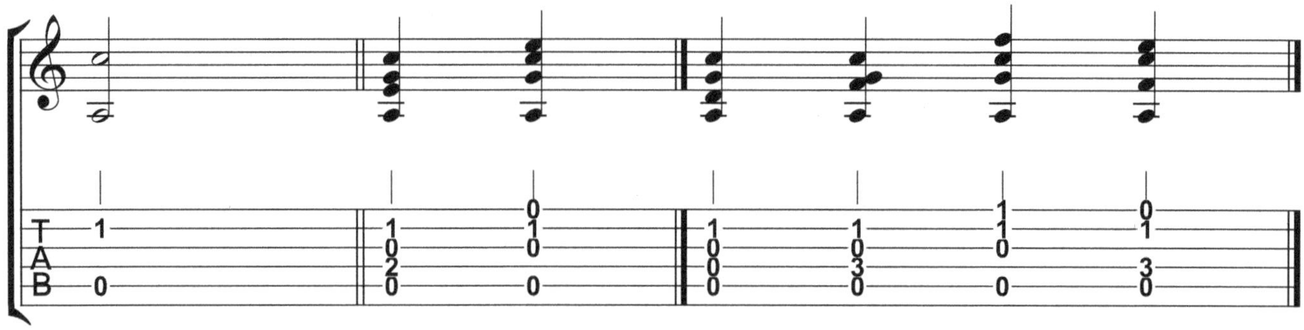

The B minor7 ♭5 or B half dminished chord chord (Bm7♭5)

The ♭3,♭5,♭7 are always present, so no other possiblities.

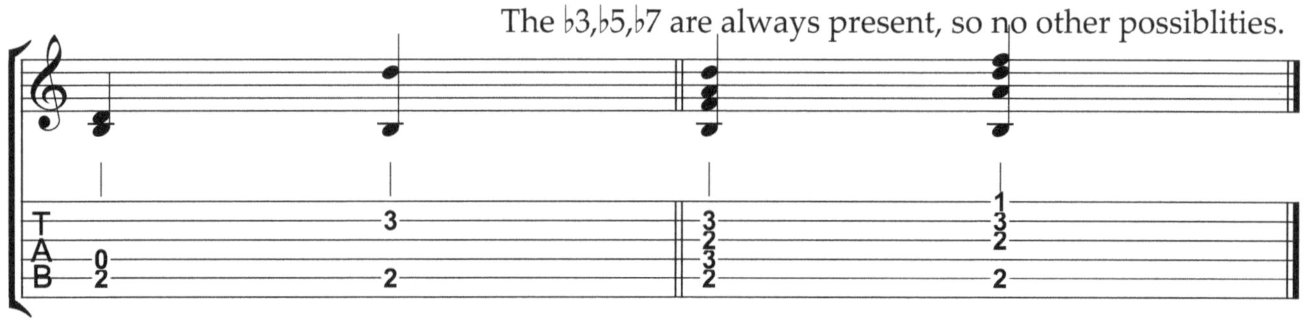

The Dominant Chord Family

The 7th is almost always present.

So keep the major third and the minor 7th (♭7) in the chord.

The G dom7 chord (G7)

In the key of C Major play:

1 2 3 4 5 6 ♭7 1 9 3 11 5 13 ♭7 1

G A B C D E F G A B C D E F G

1,3,5,♭7 Some direct substitutions. Look for others.

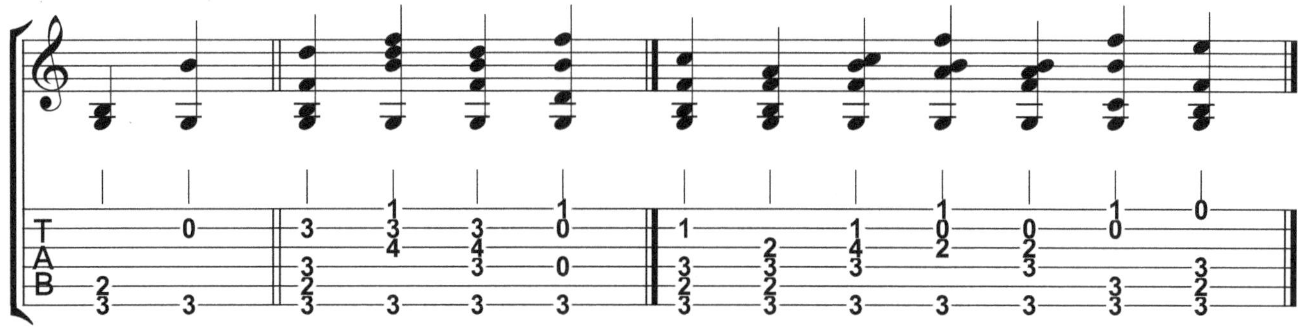

Play some of these chord possibilities on the following chord progression.

Track 20

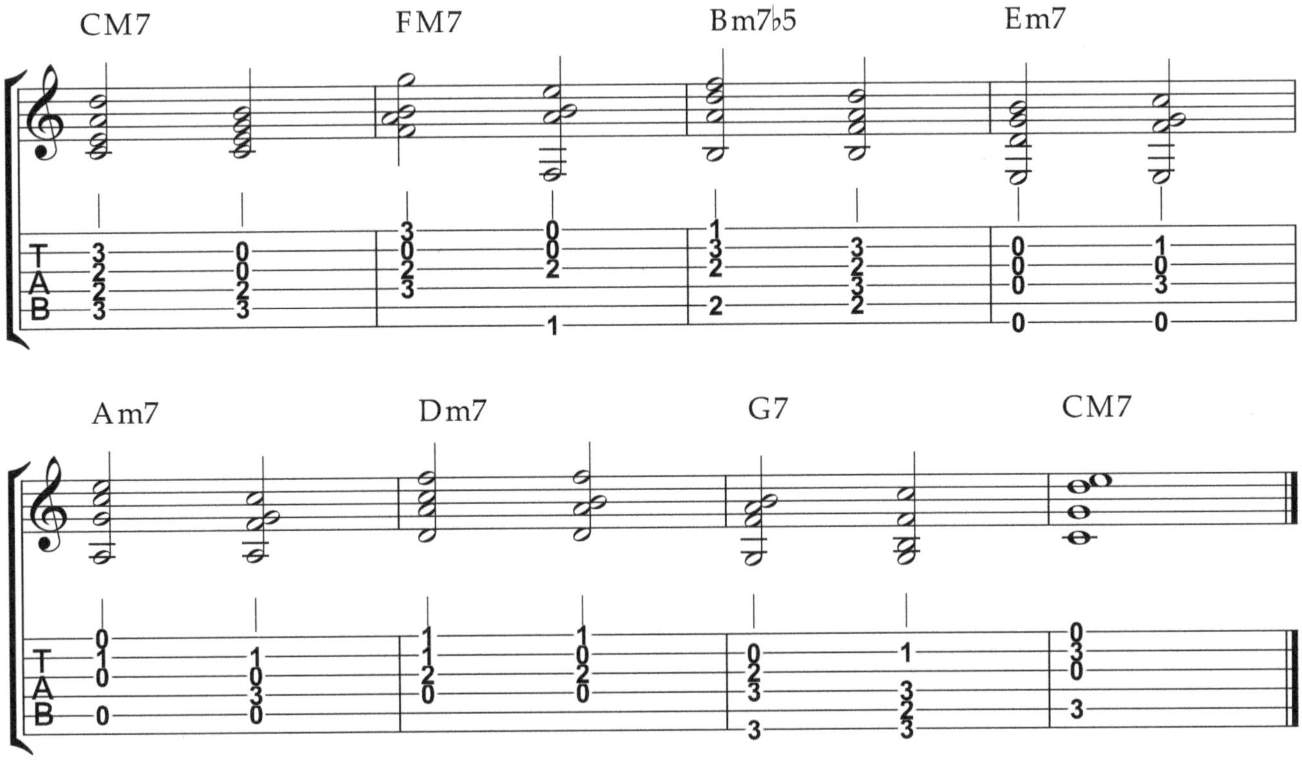

Your turn

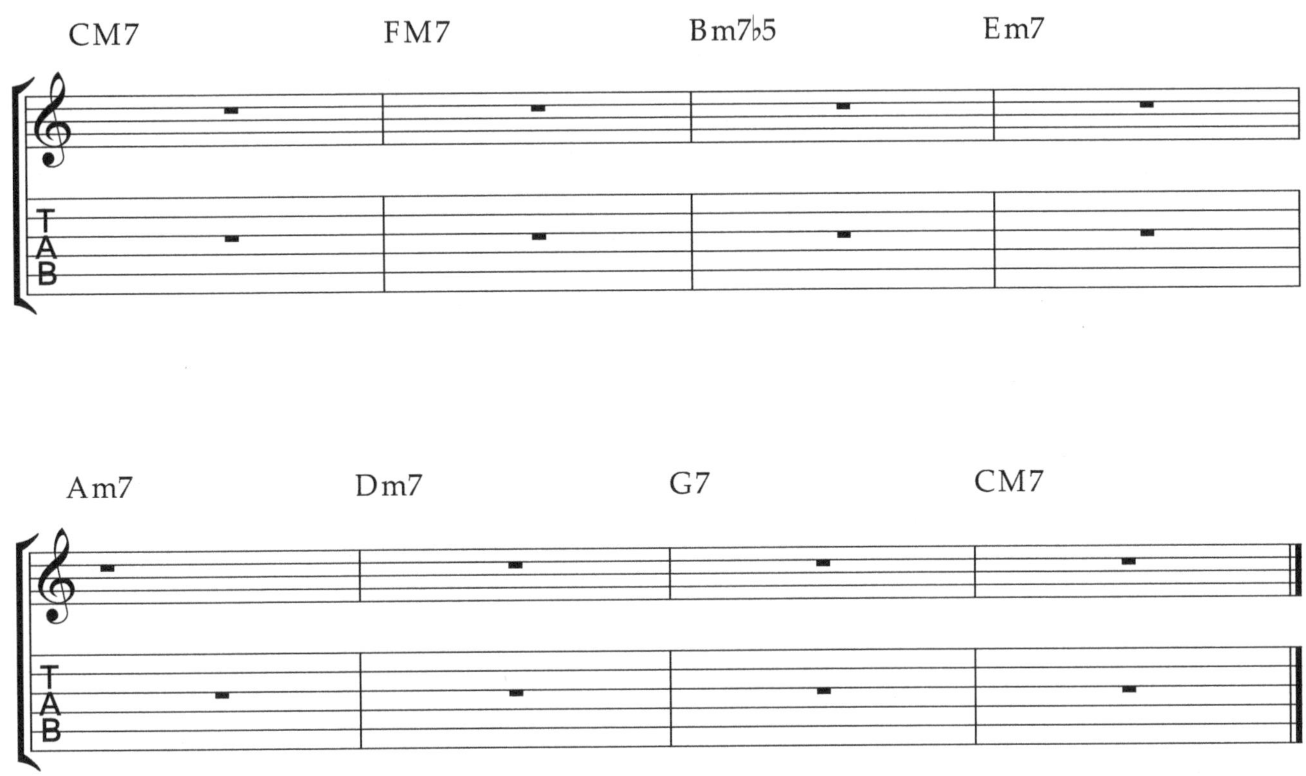

CHAPTER 8

Chord Arpeggiation

First, some new rhythms.

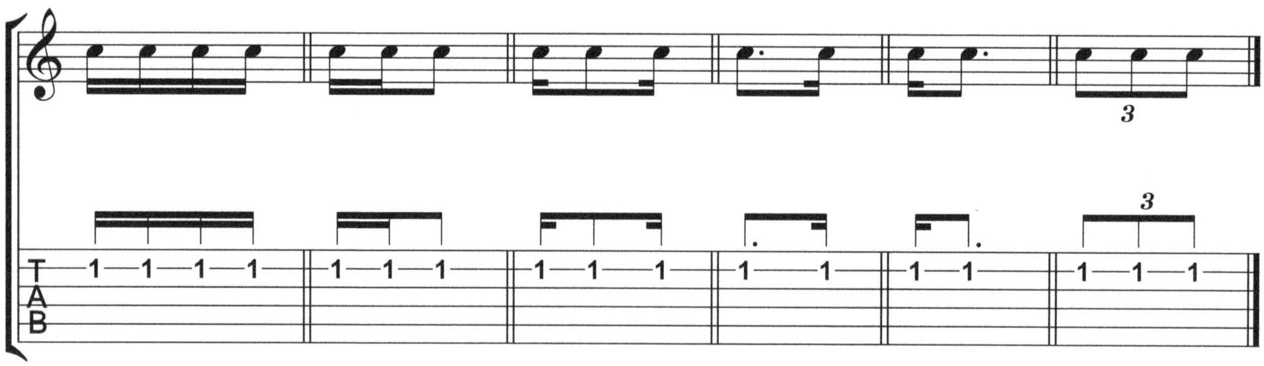

The chord shape notes are played one after the other, either ascending, descending, in various orders, with repetitions, or on different rhythmic patterns. Not all the chord shape notes should be used.

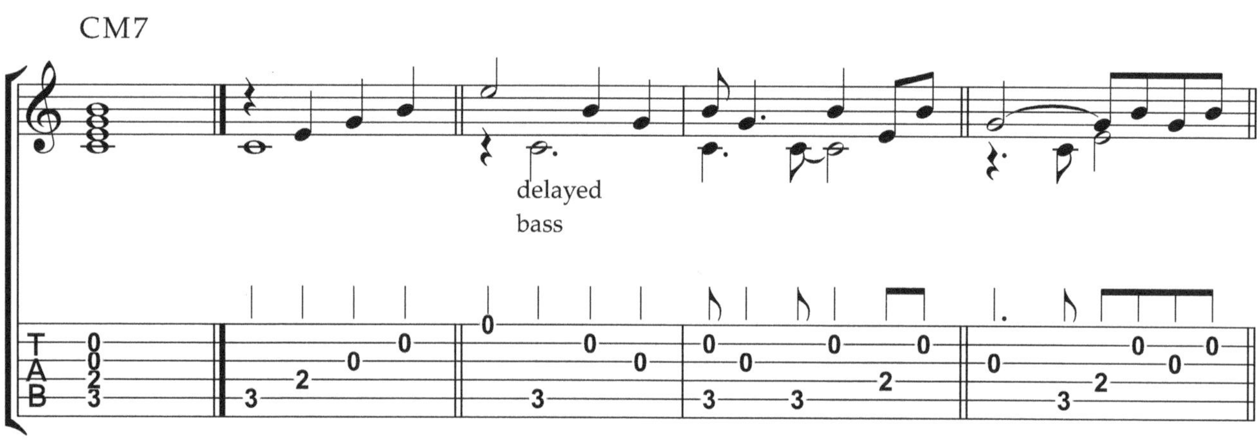

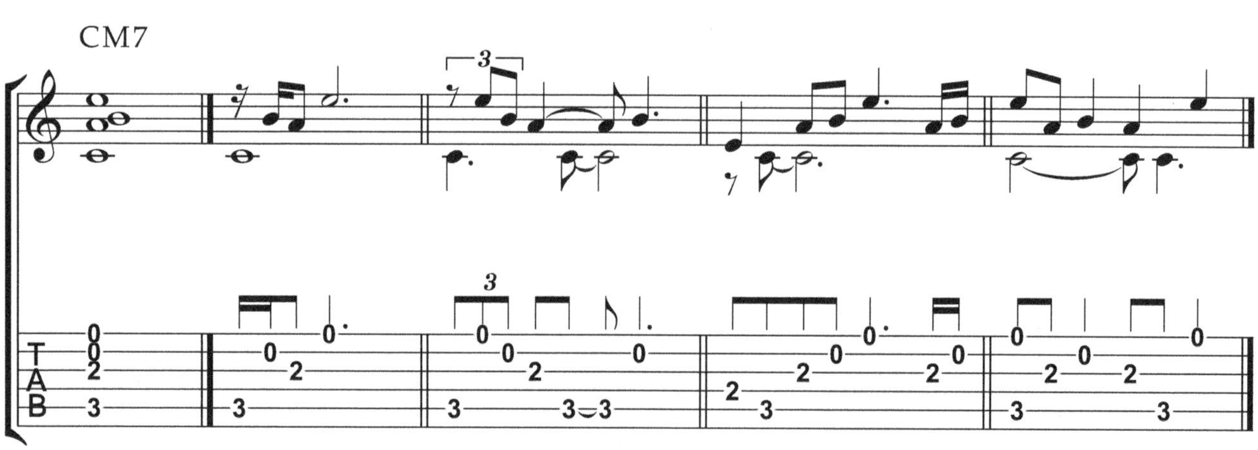

Your turn

Play some arpeggios on various rhythmic patterns on 2 different CM7 chords.

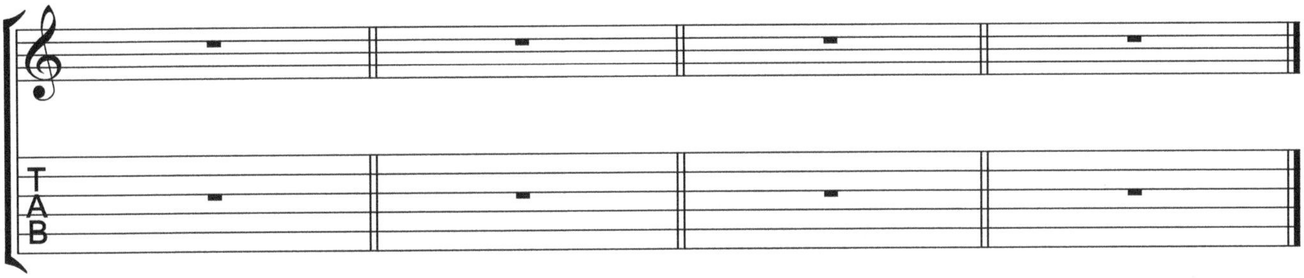

Arpeggiation and upper voice movement

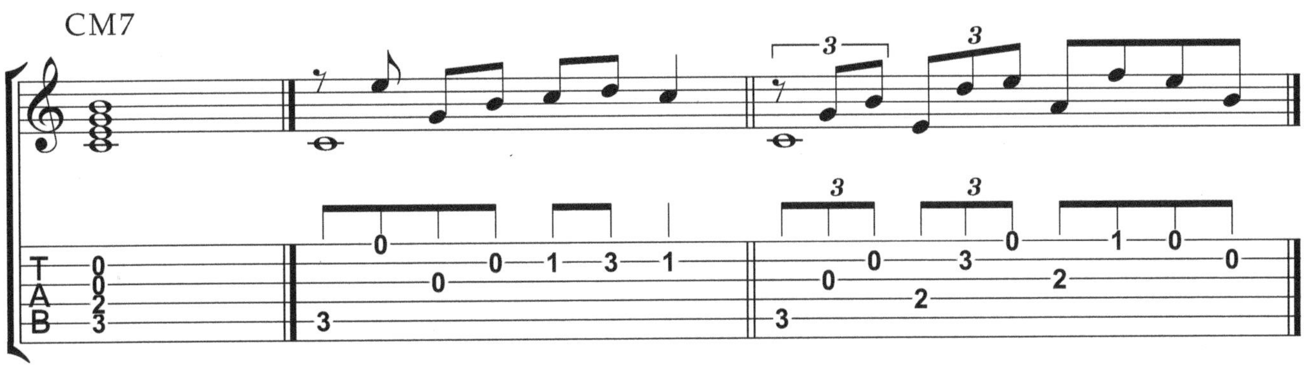

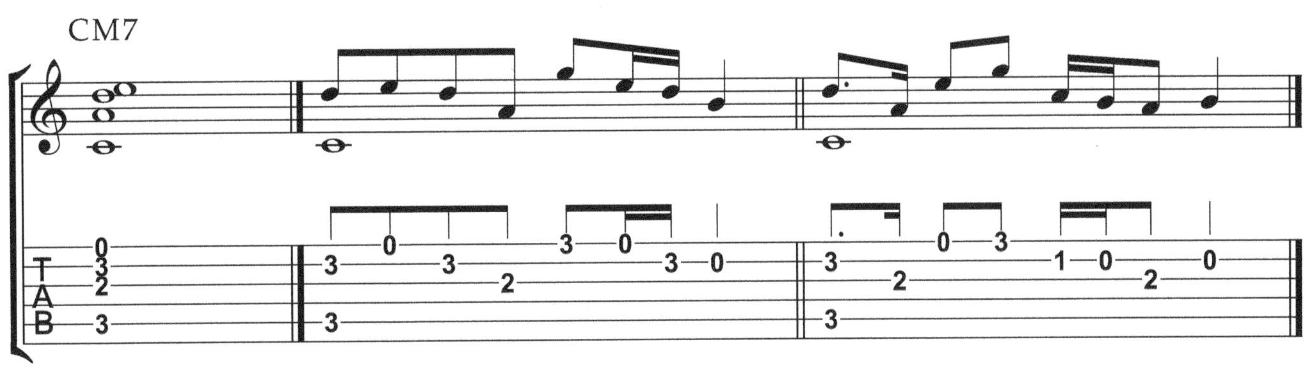

Your turn

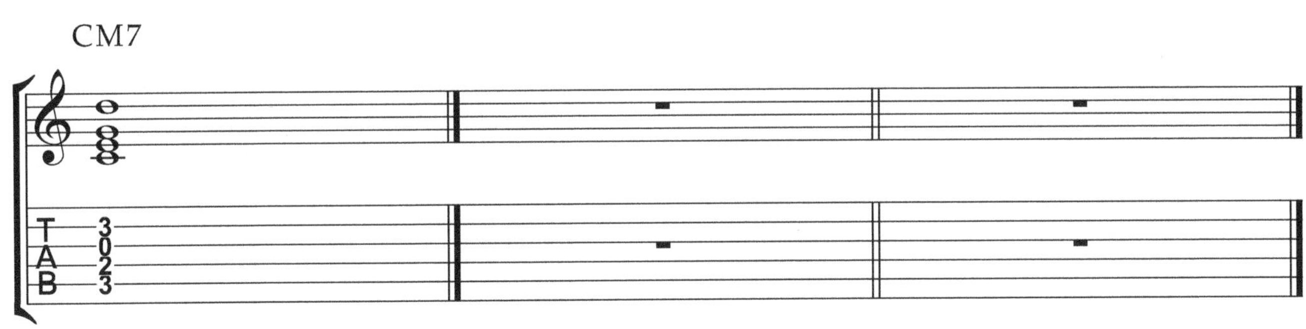

On a chord progression

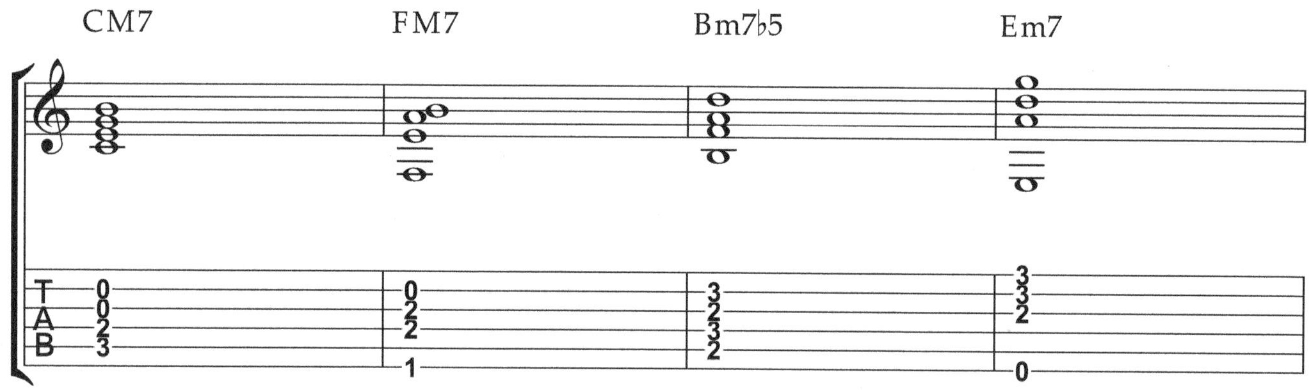

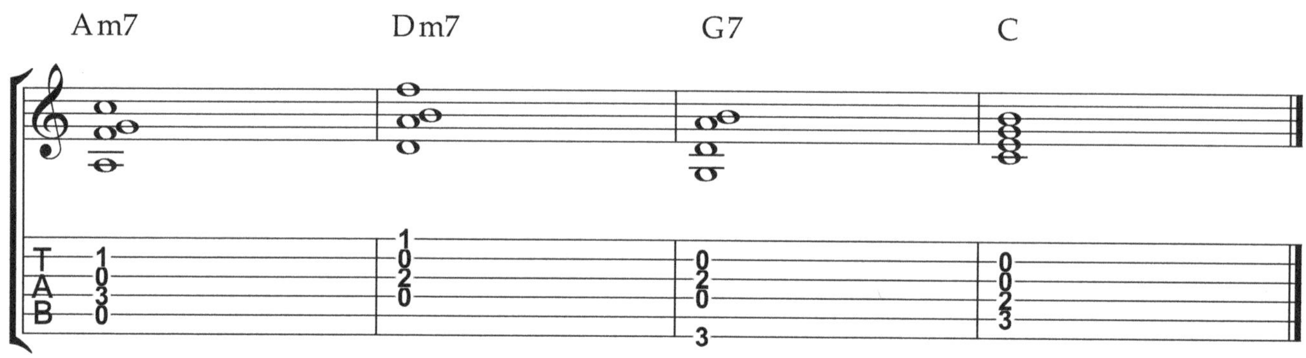

Track 21

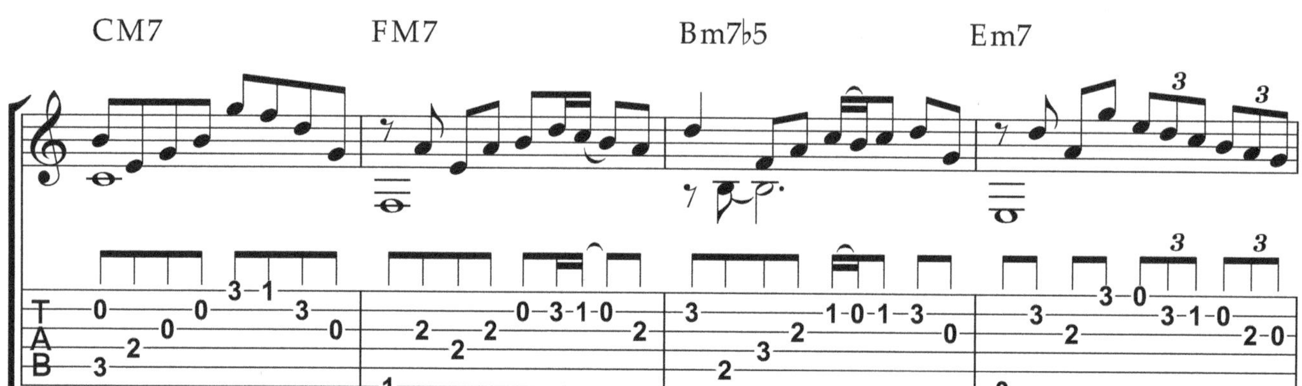

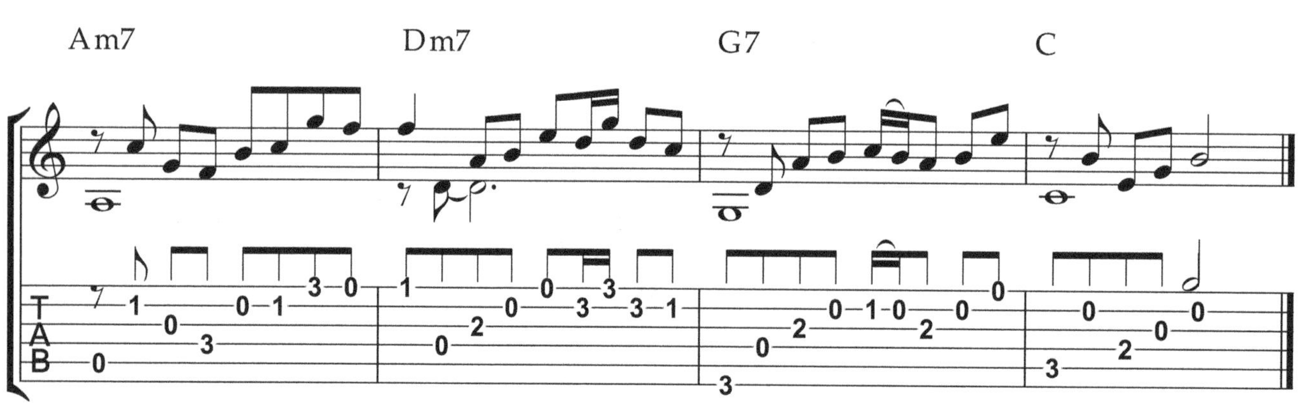

Your turn

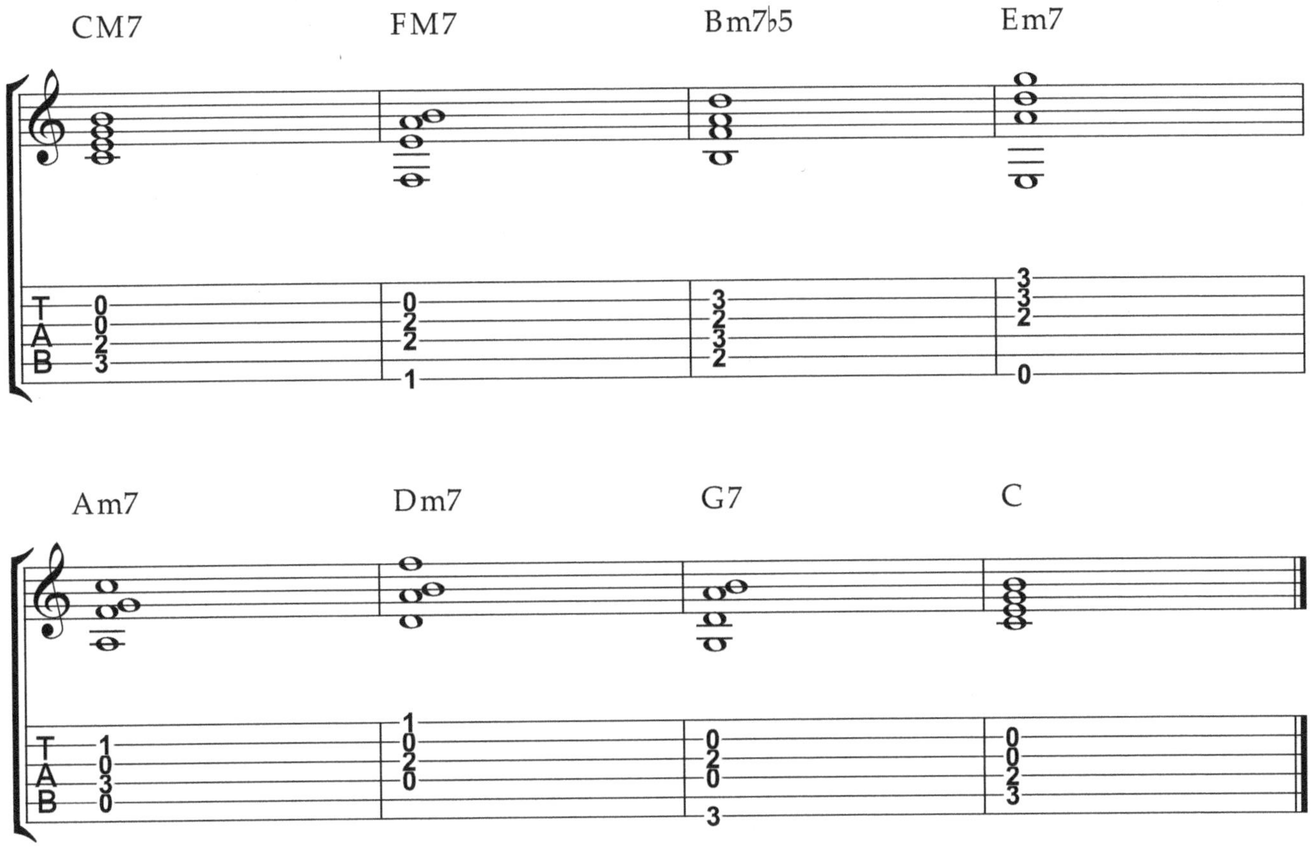

CHAPTER 9

Chord Parts and Upper Voice Movement

In this chapter, we will divide the chords into the 3 note and 2 note voicings (dyads).
Here are the possibilities for CM7.
Use them as a basis for upper voice movement.

CM7

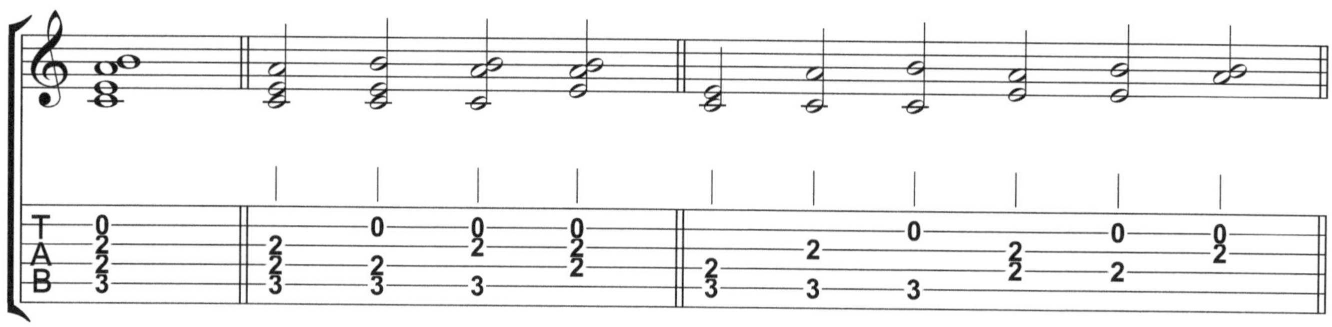

Some examples:

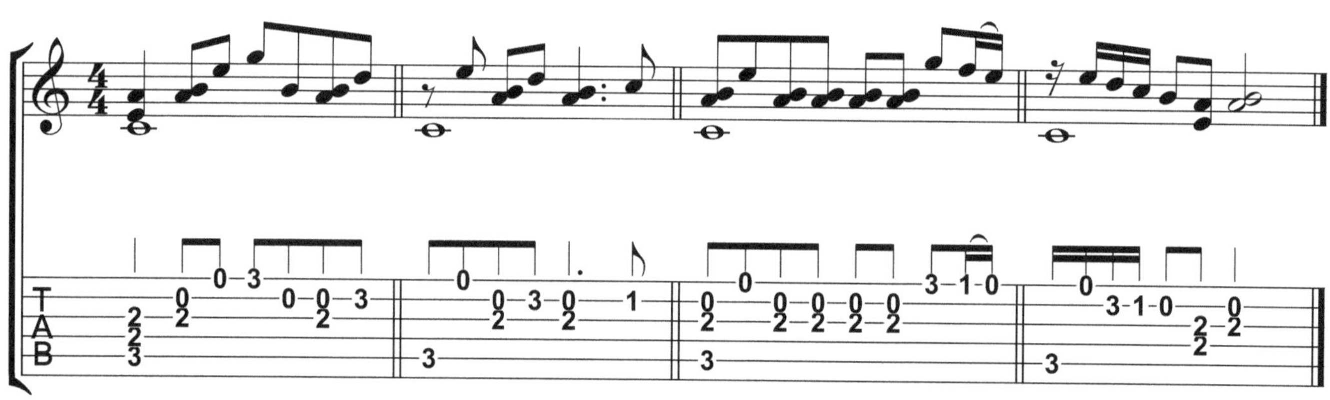

on G7

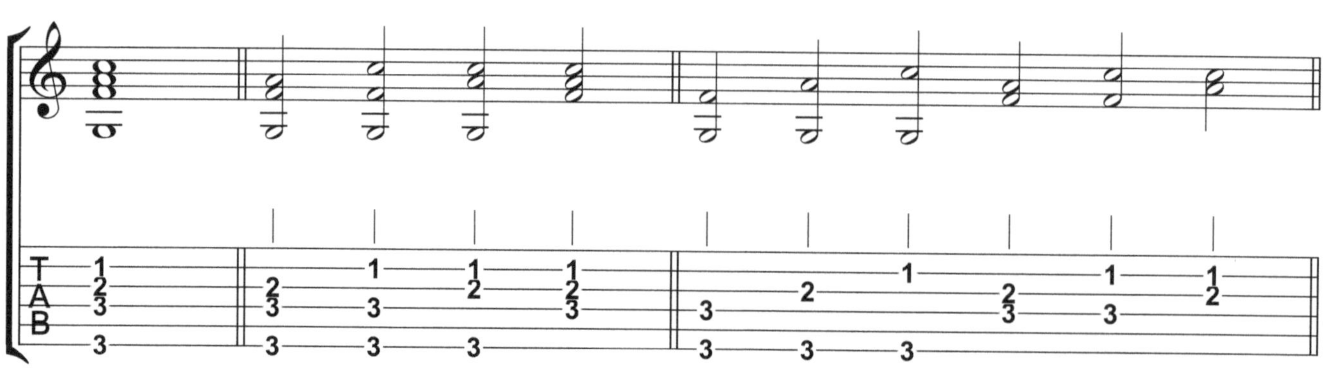

Some examples:

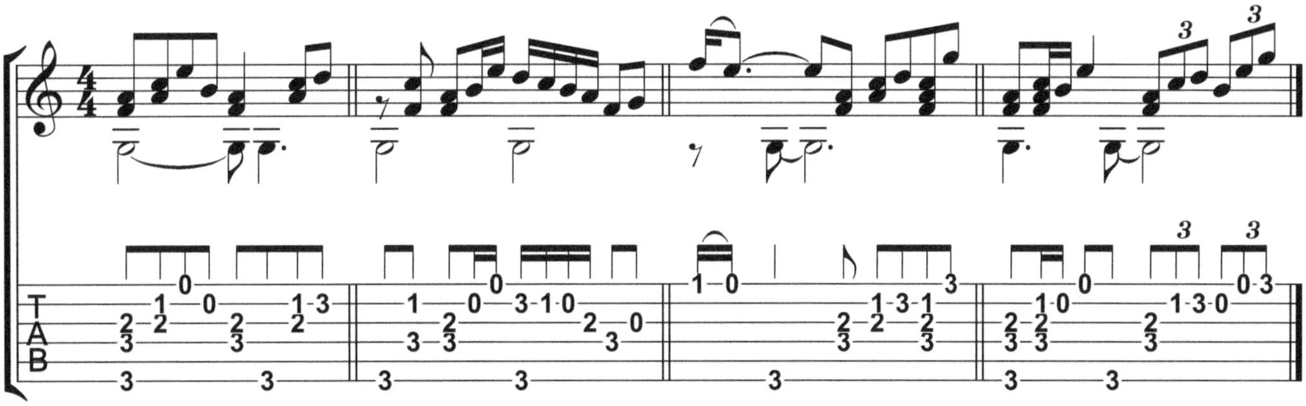

On a chord progression

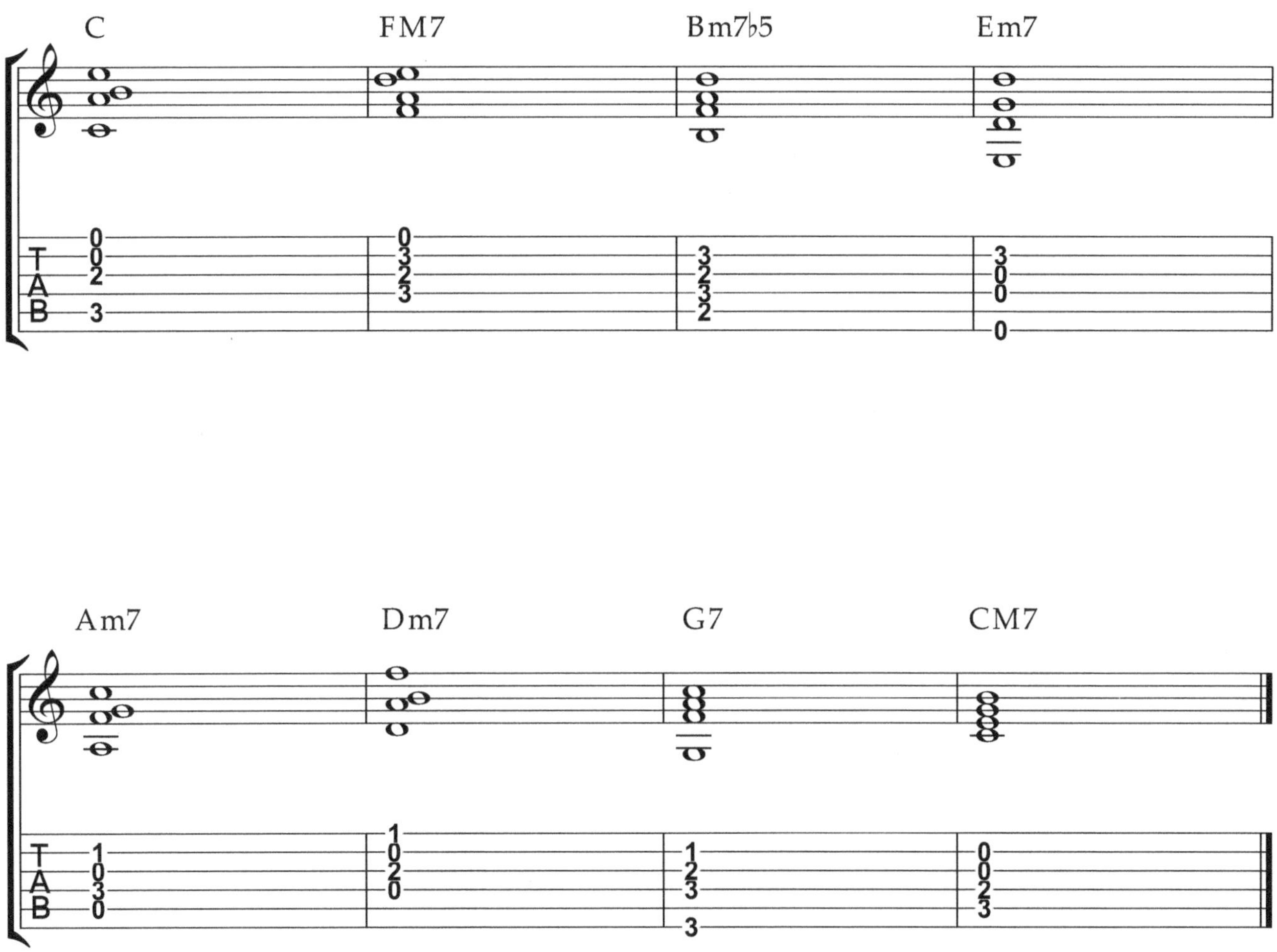

Example 1

Track 22

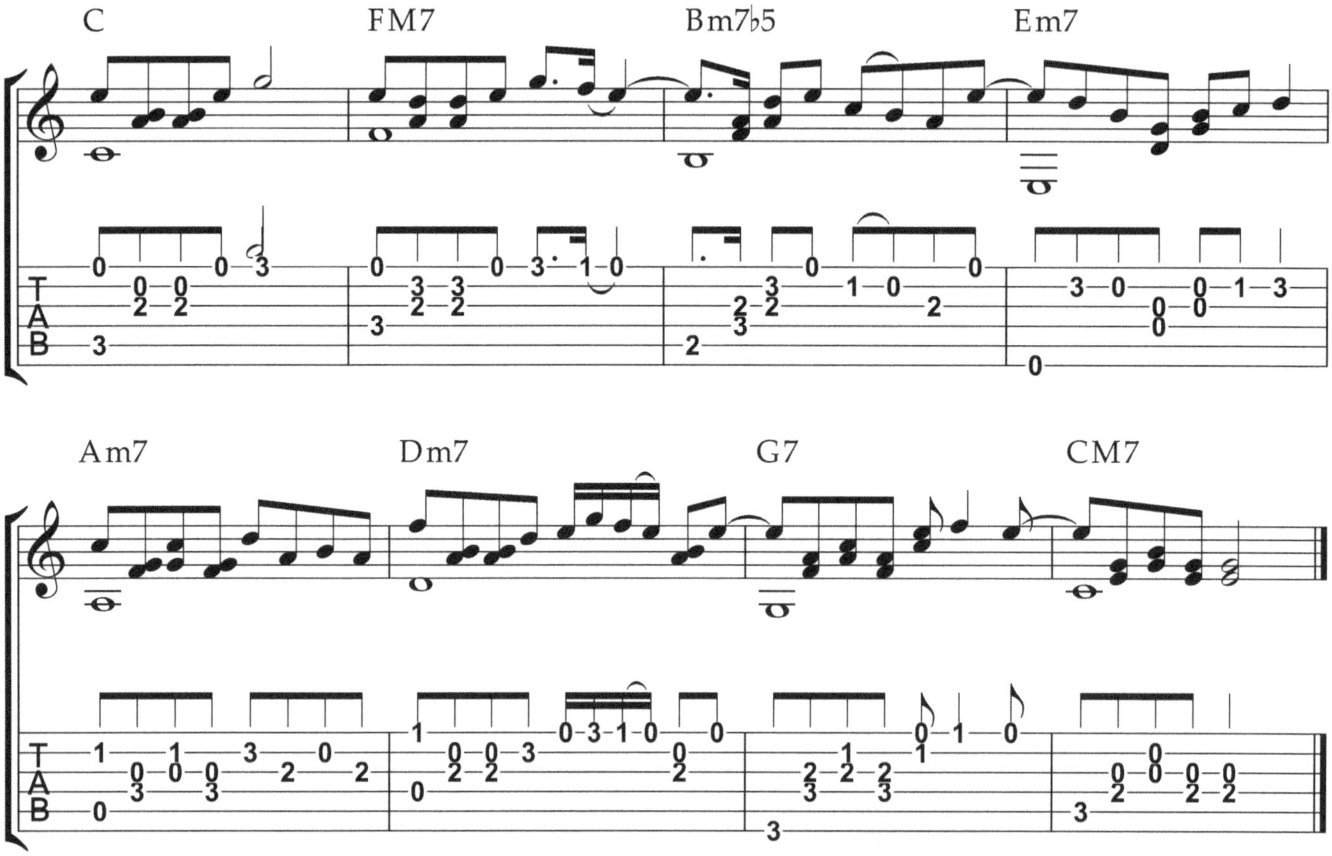

Example 2

Track 23

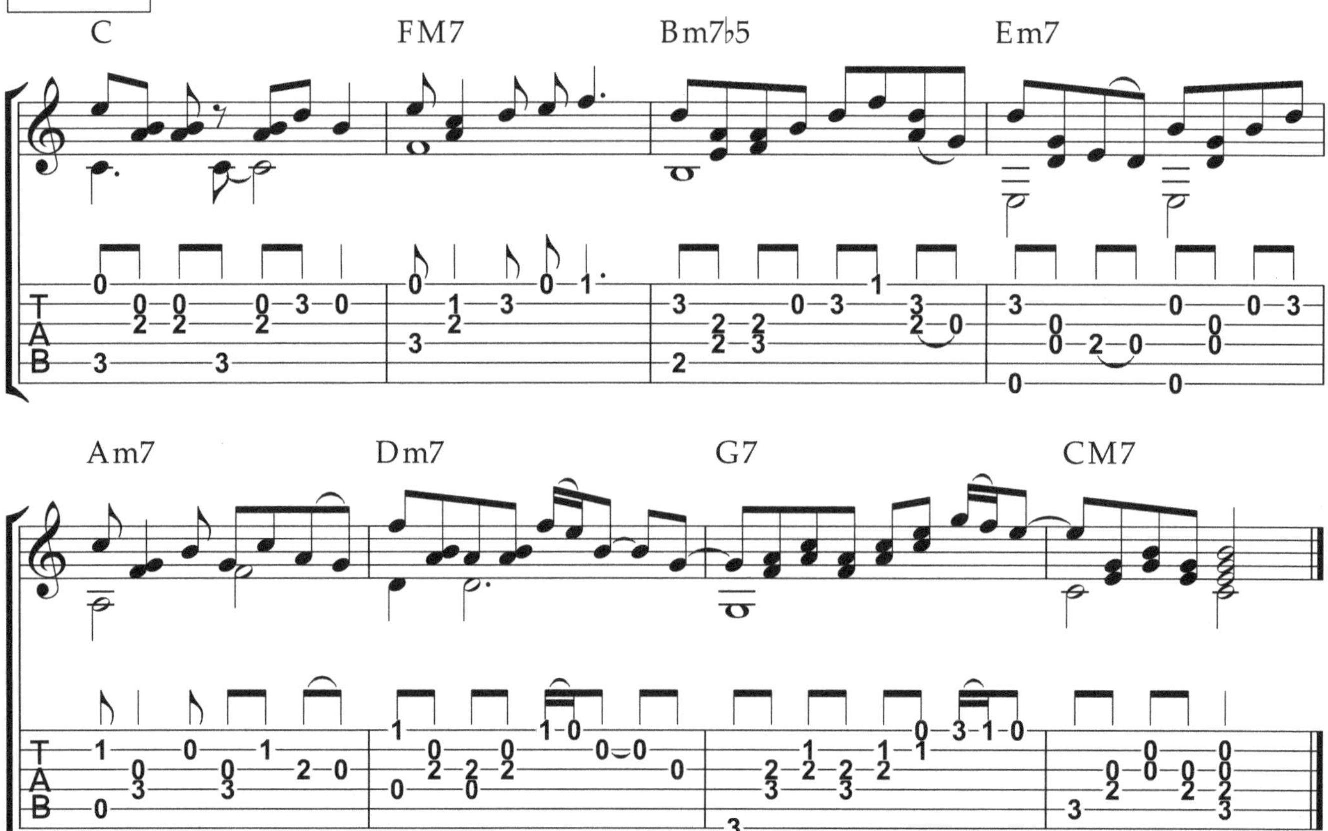

Your turn

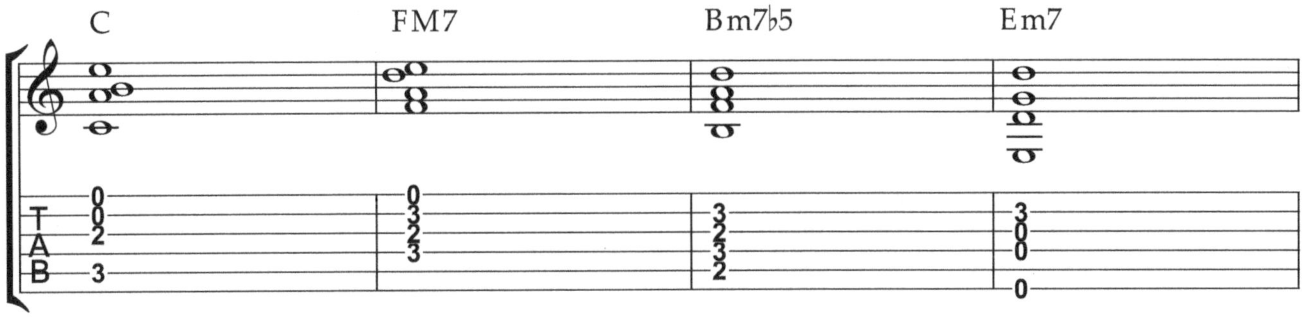

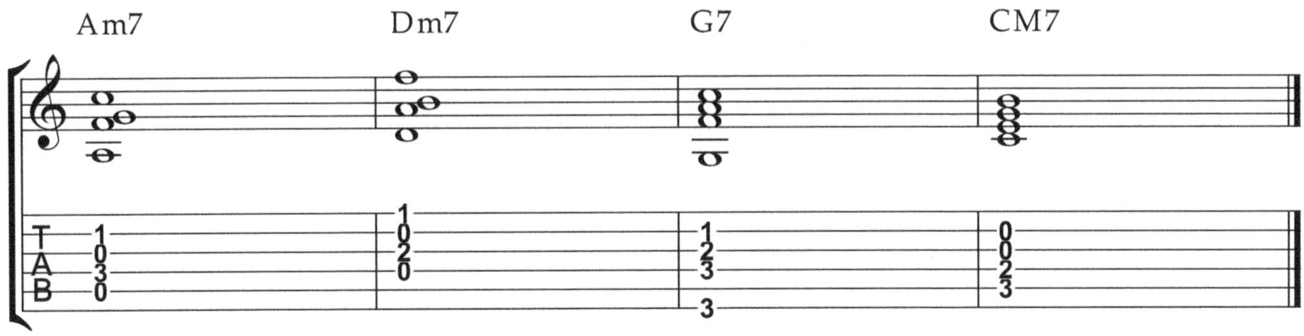

CHAPTER 10

Dyads Based on all the Scale Notes

Let's have a look at dyads consisting of scale notes only.

Dyads on:

a) the first and second string

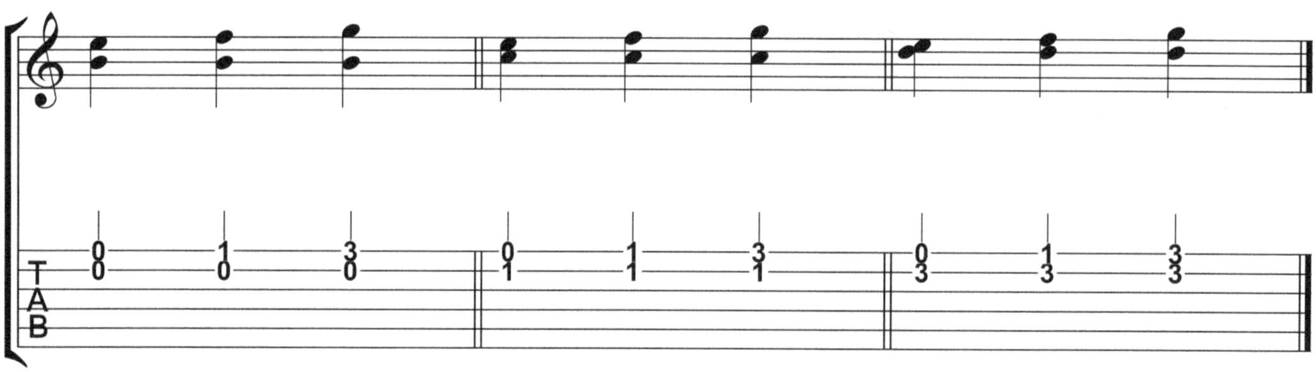

b) the second and third string

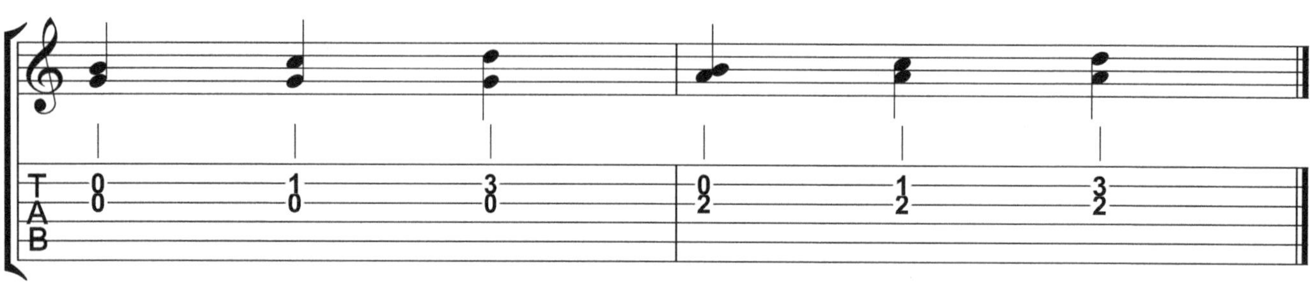

c) the third and fourth string

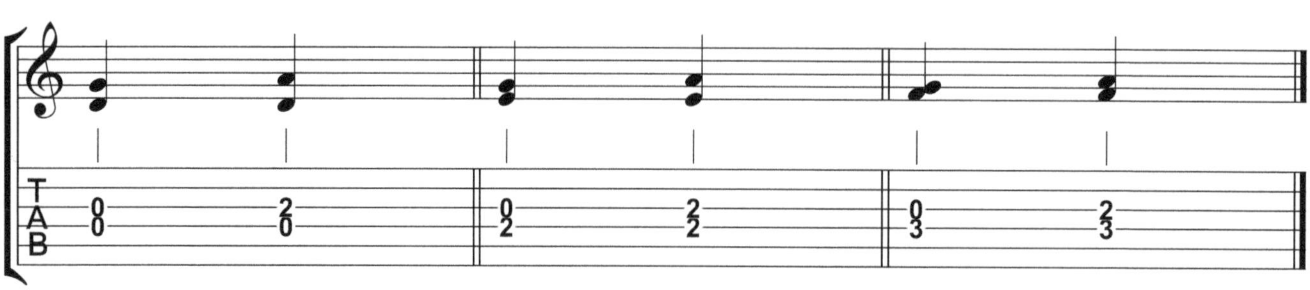

d) the first and third string

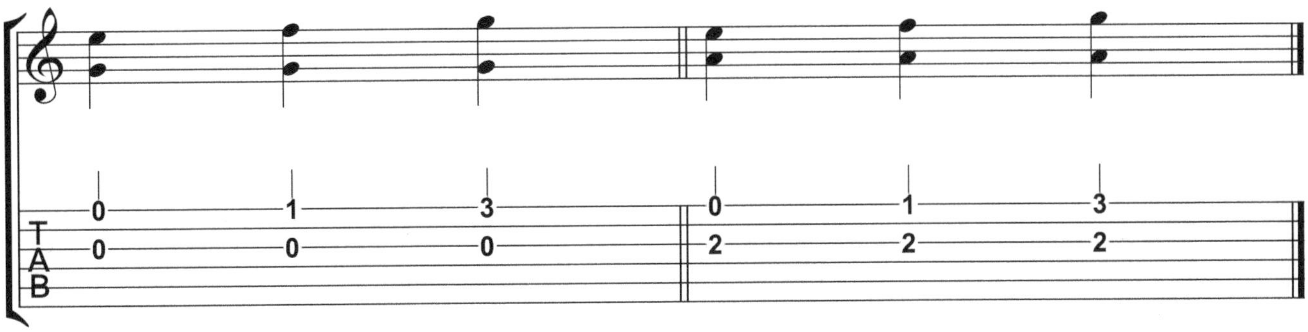

e) the second and fourth string

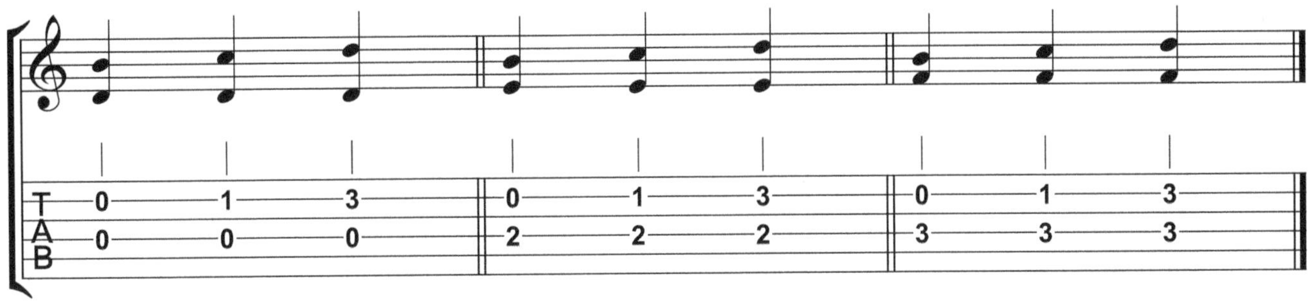

f) the first and fourth string

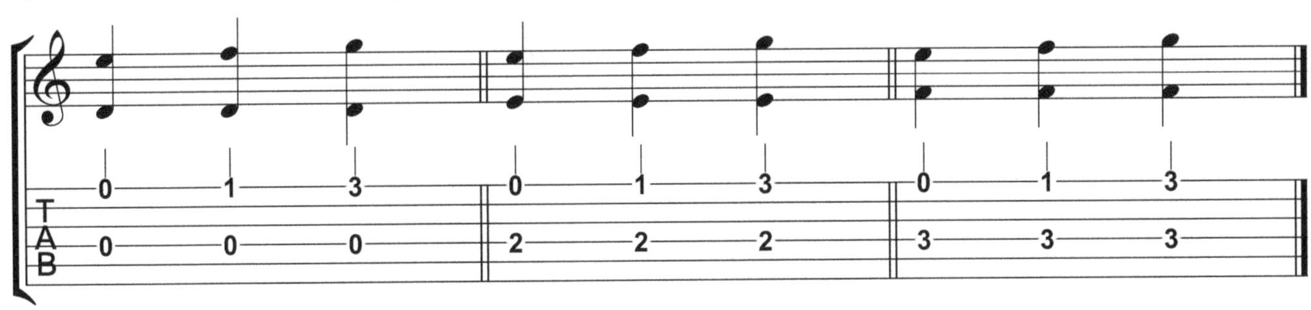

You can also create 3 note chords by using a dyad in combination with the root note.
Some examples:
Begin each bar with a full chord or a chord part for a clear harmonic outline.

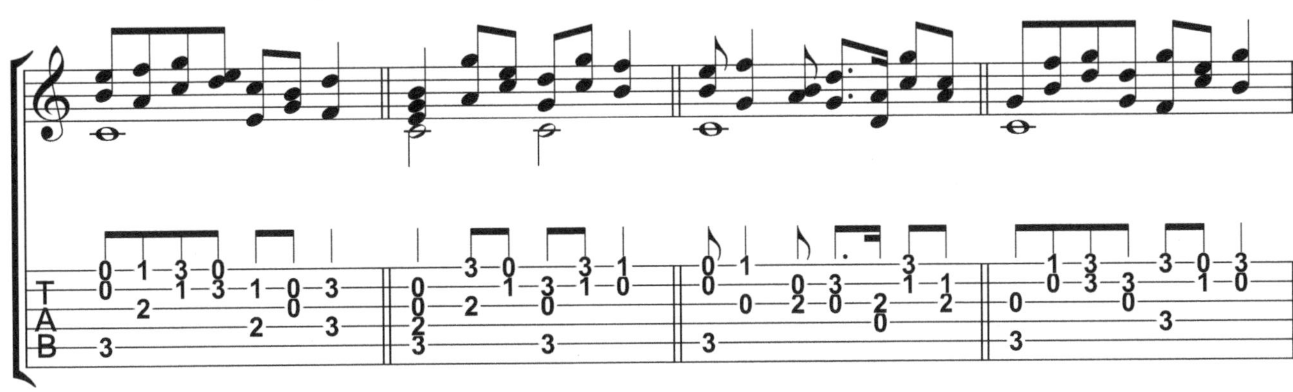

On a chord progression

Track 24

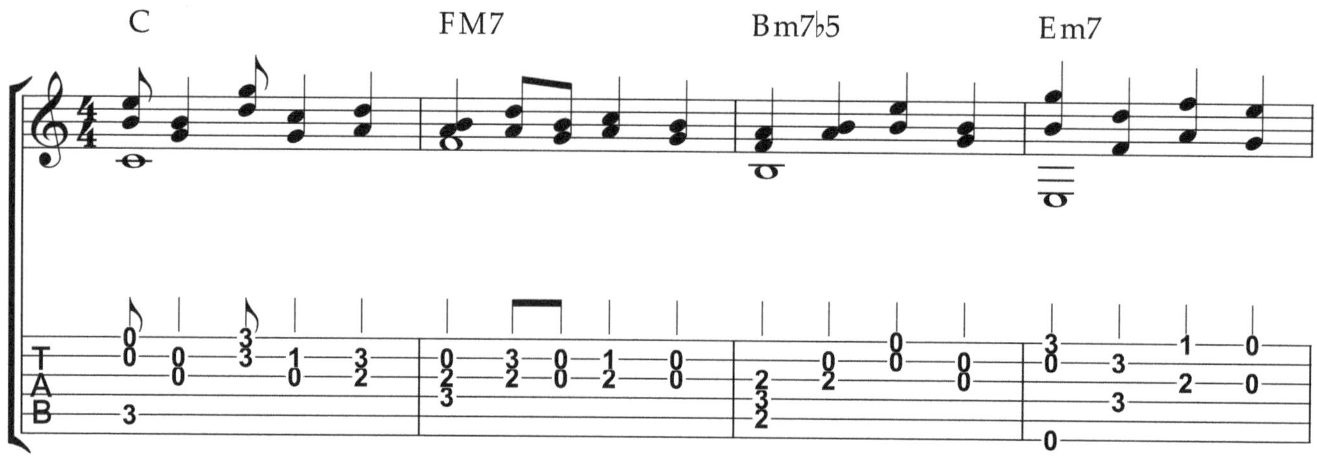

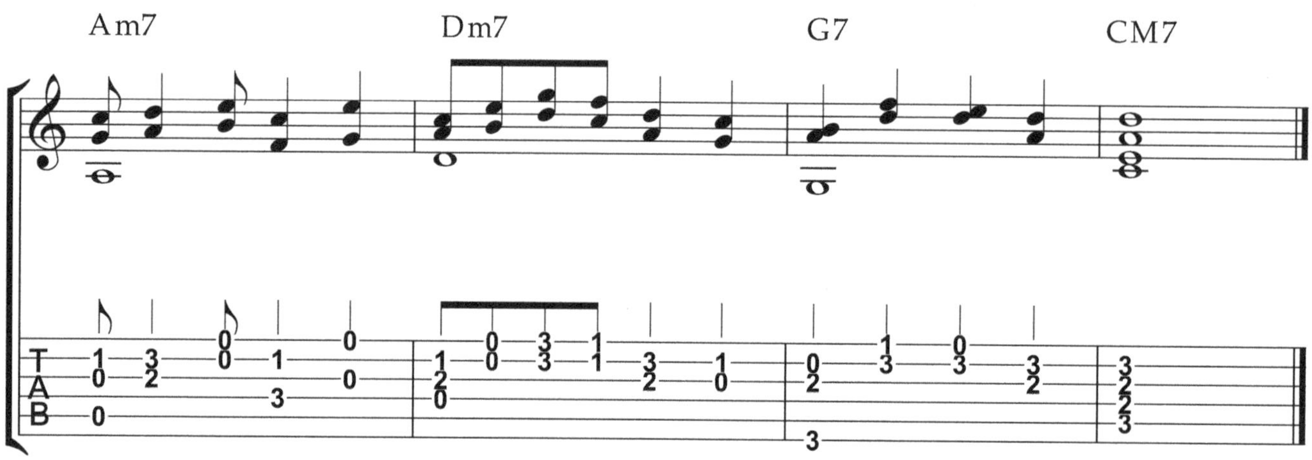

Your turn

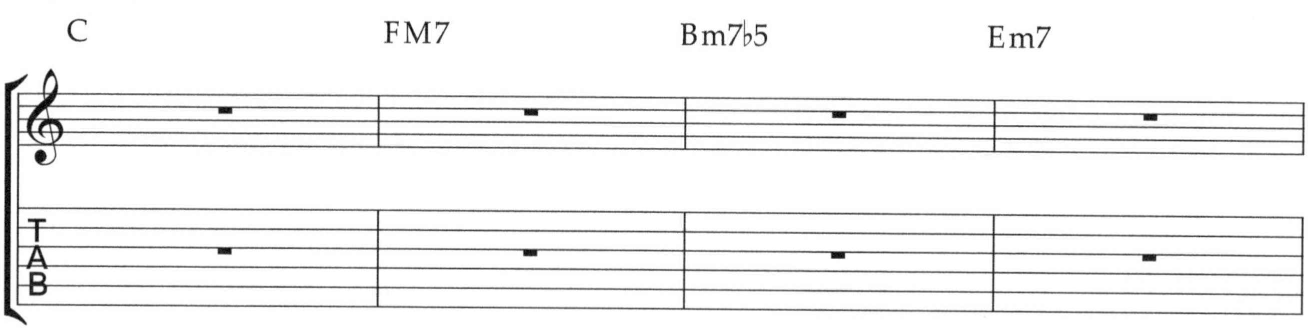

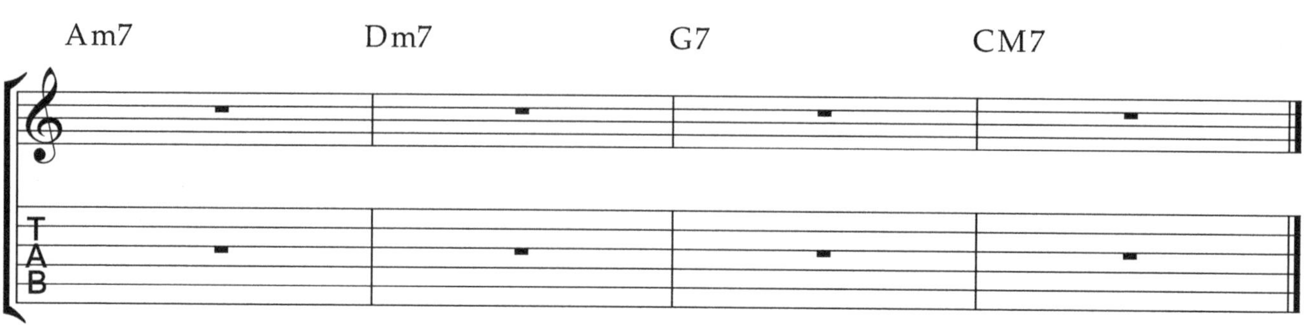

In combination with single note lines

Anticipation:
the root is played before its chord which is in the next bar

Track 25

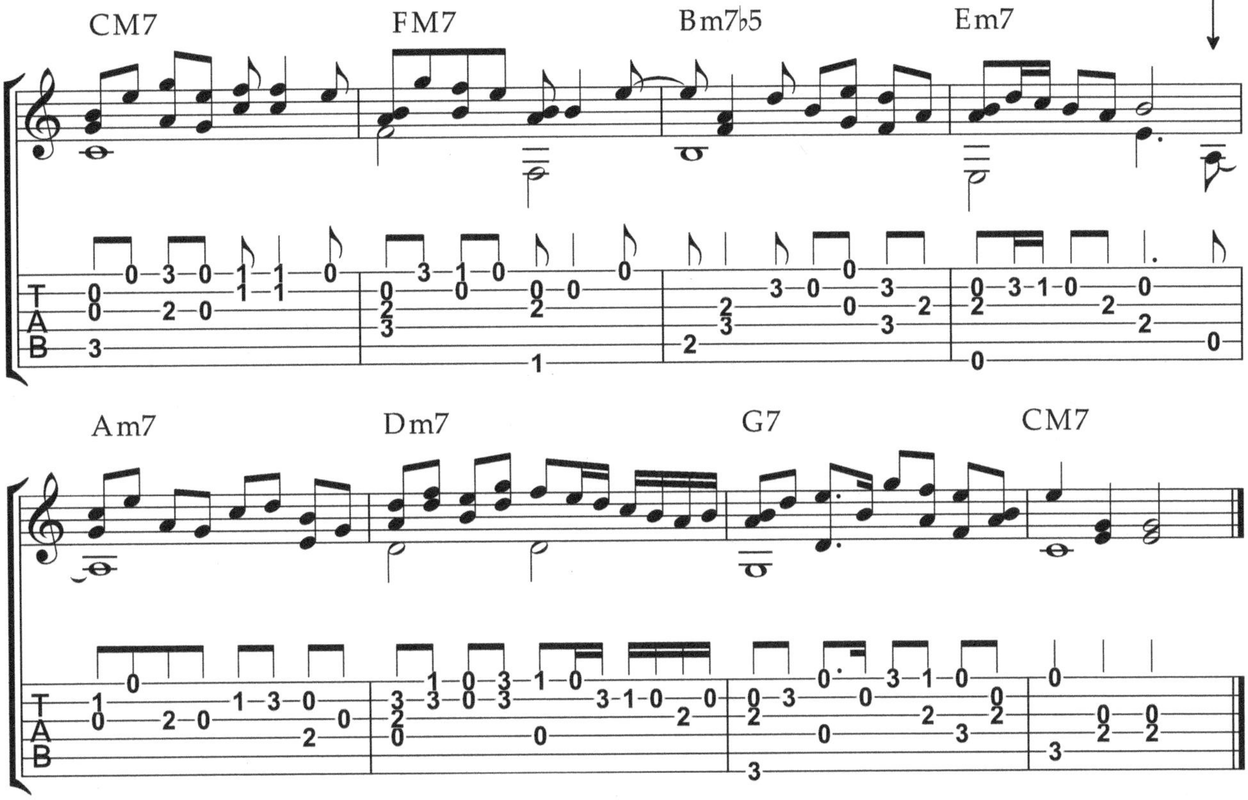

Your turn

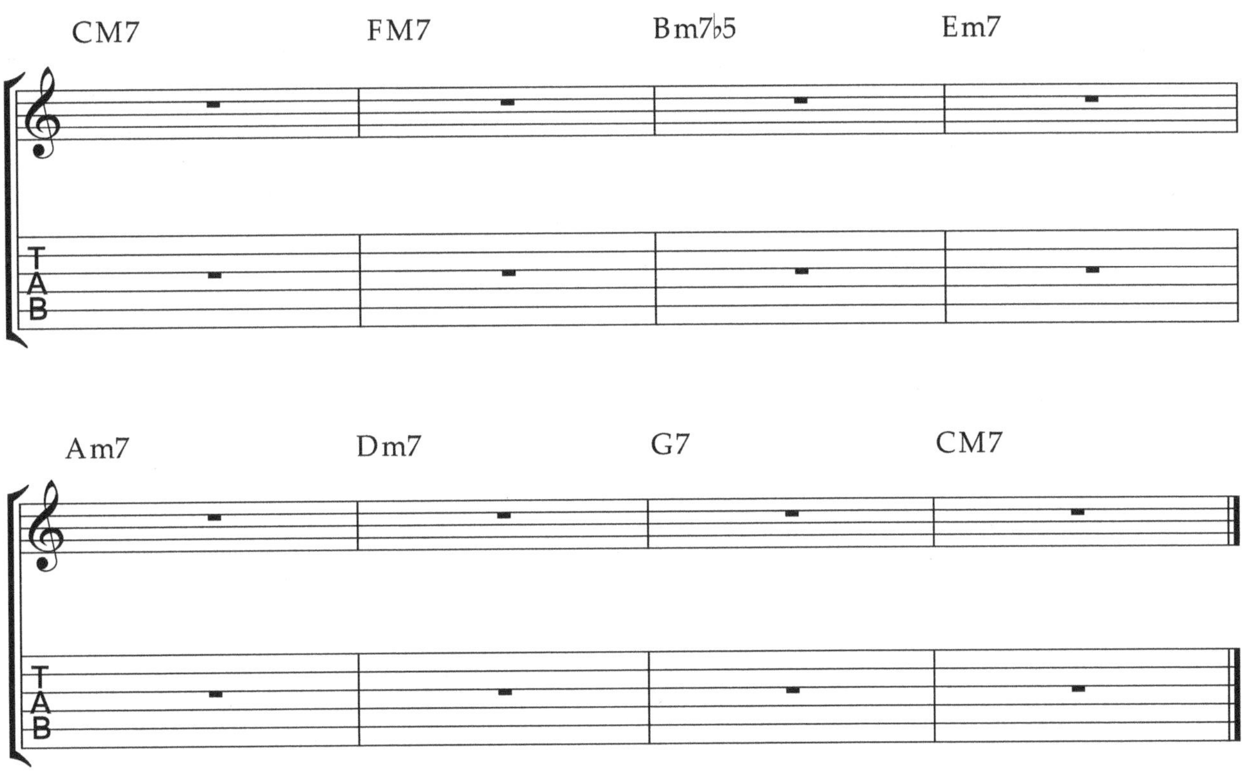

CHAPTER 11

All Approaches Thus Far

Use full chords, chord parts or any other notes from the scale: dyads, dyads + middle voice), middle voice movement, arpeggiation, chord parts. Play a melody preceded by a bass note, use the root-root alteration in the bottom voice,...

Track 26

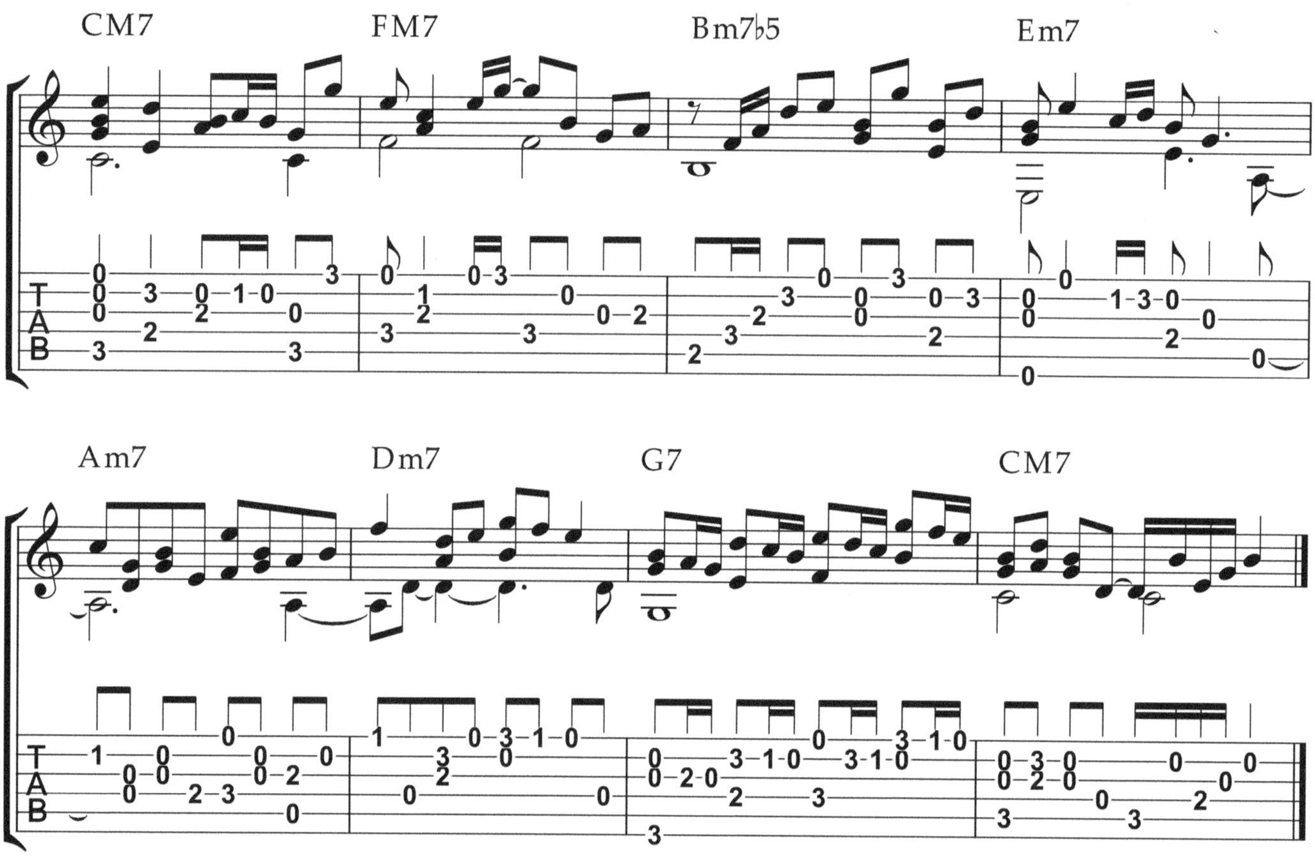

Your turn

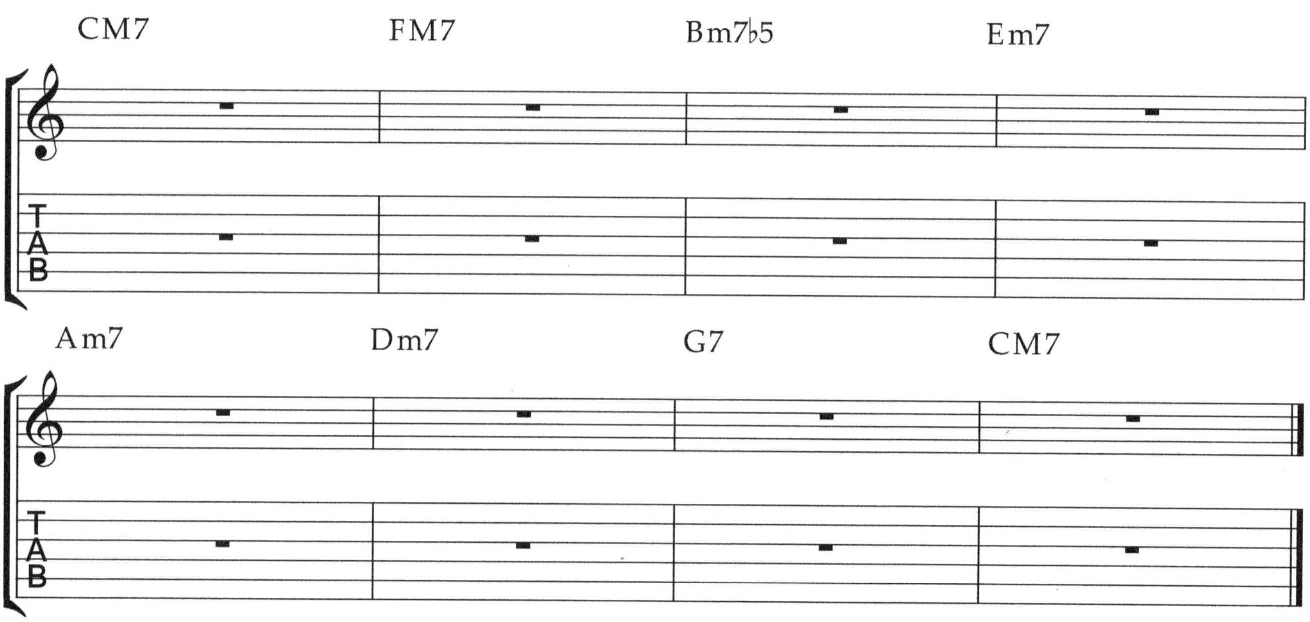

On a slightly different chord progression

C7	**F7**	**Bm7♭5**	**Em7**
Am7	**D7**	**B♭M7**	**CM7**

IMPORTANT! We will make things easy and more contemporary by just using the note of the C Major Scale (C D E F G A B C) of which one or more notes will be flattened or sharpened according to the chord tones.

For example:

F7 = F A C E♭ --) only E changes into E♭

The scale will be F G A B C D E♭ F. The B natural is a ♯4 or augmented 4th which creates an interesting modern sound.

As I like to mix fretted strings with open ones, I will also use an E natural in my soloing.

So the scale to be used could be F G A B C D E♭/E

A creative use of open strings can provide interesting harmonic and melodic possibilities as:

C7

C E G B♭

Direct substitutions

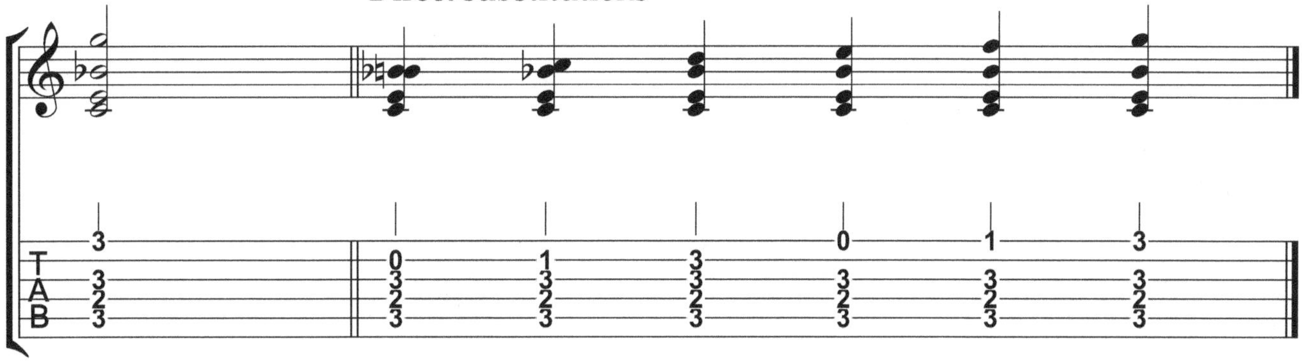

F7

F A C E♭

Here I left out the 5th

Some direct substitutions

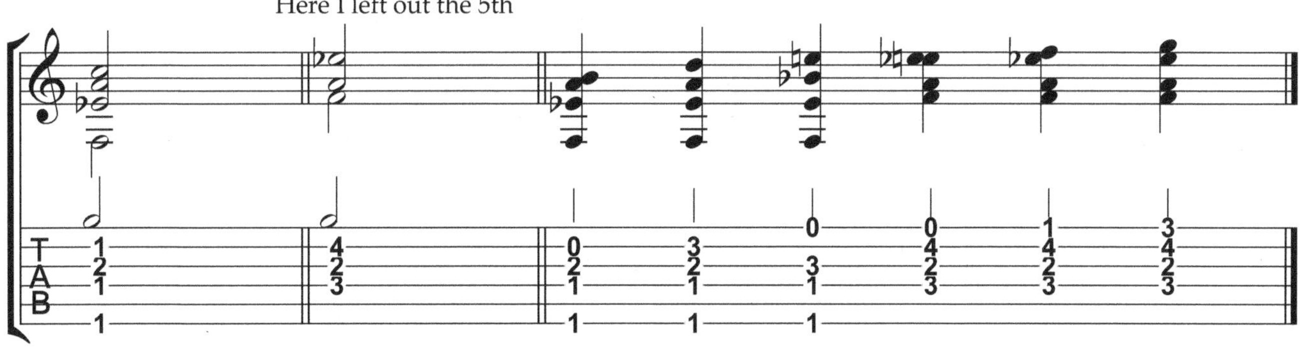

B♭M7

B♭ D F A

Some direct substitutions

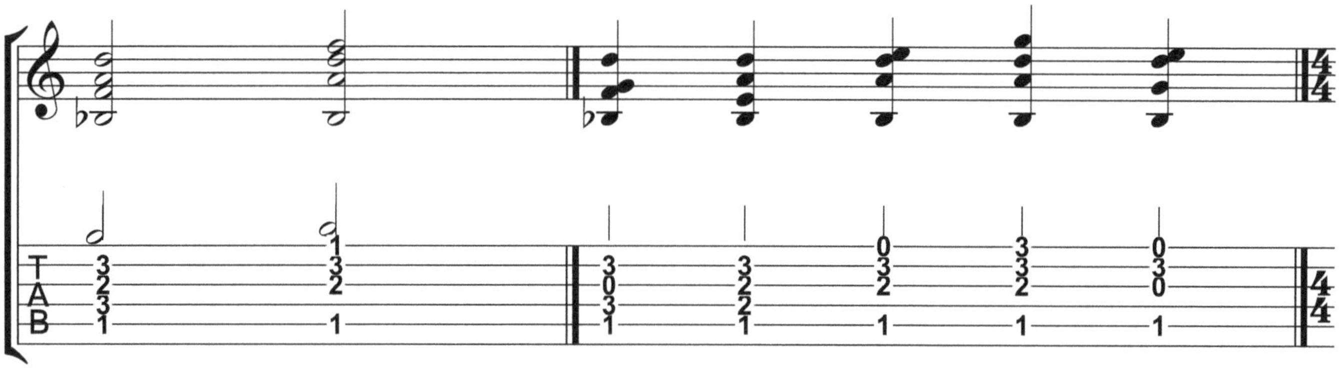

In the following examples, I will mix fretted and open strings and combine the C major scale note with the tones of a specific chord.

C7

C D E F G A B♭ C

F7

F G A B C D E♭ F

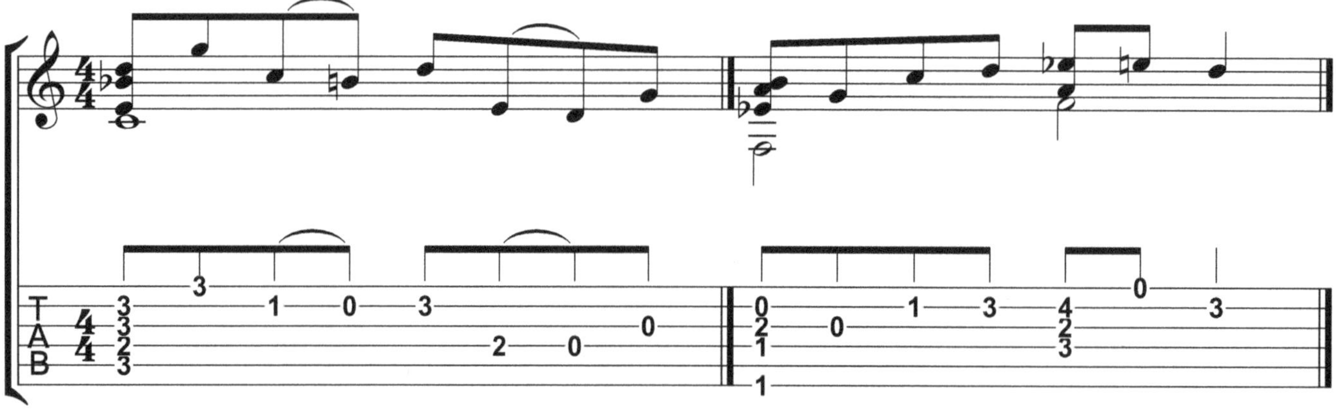

D7

D E F♯ G A B C

B♭M7

B♭ C D E F G A B♭

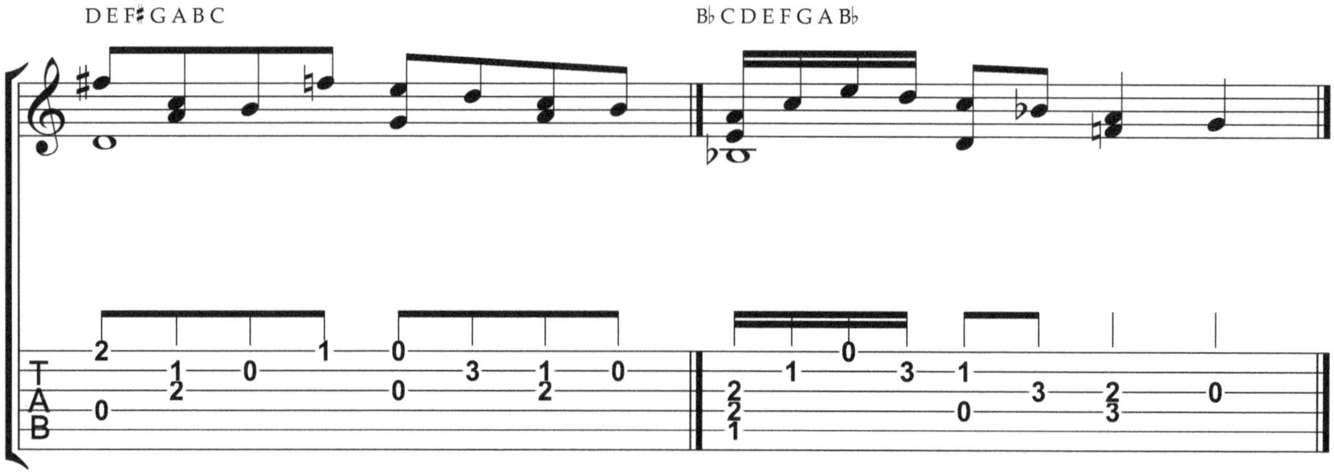

Example

Track 27

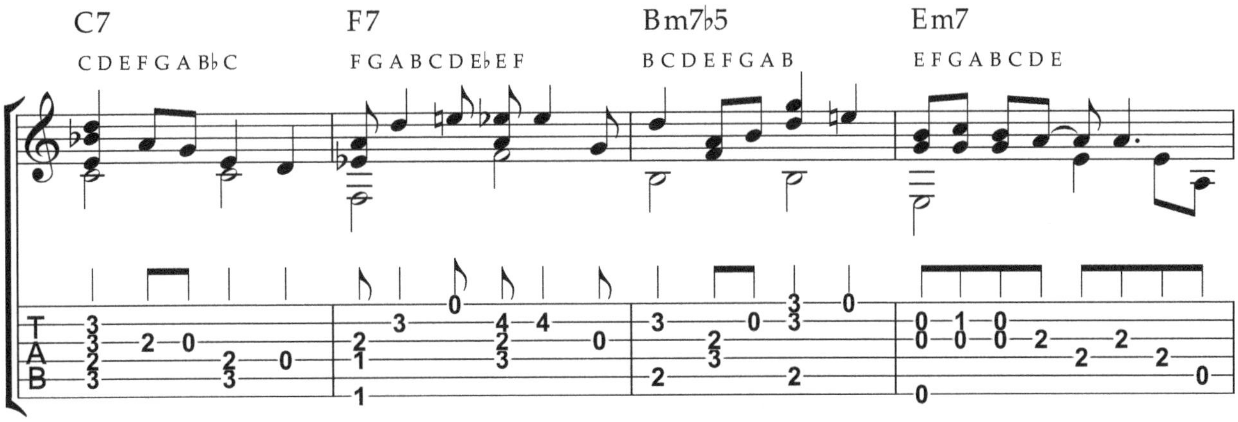

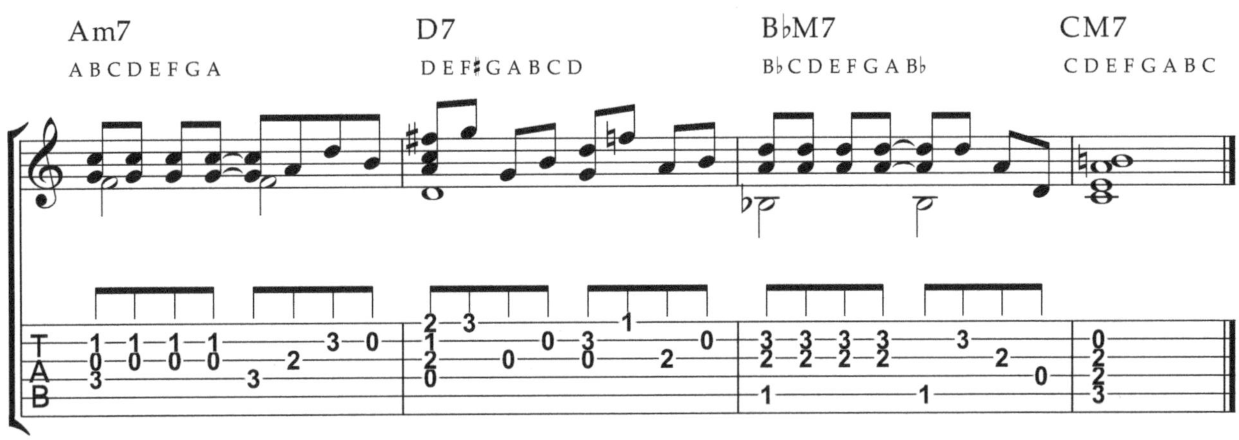

Your turn

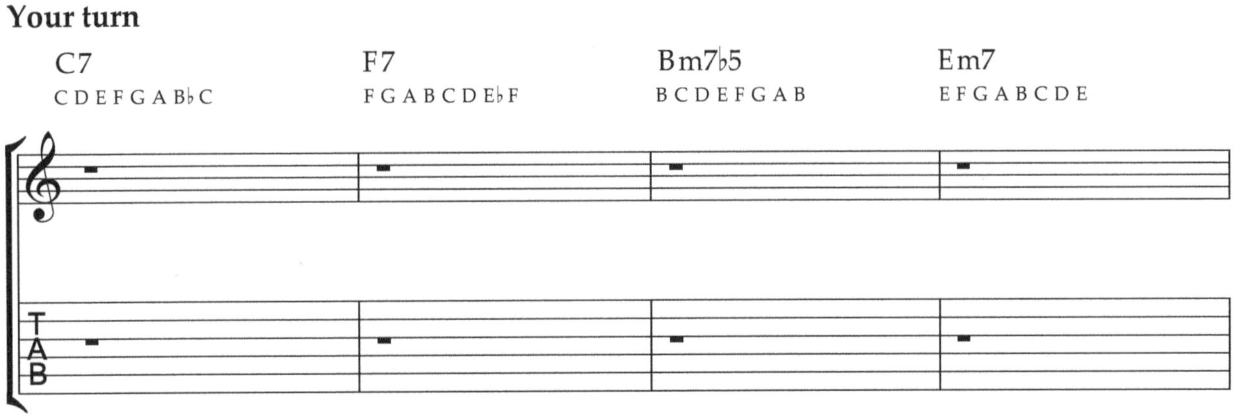

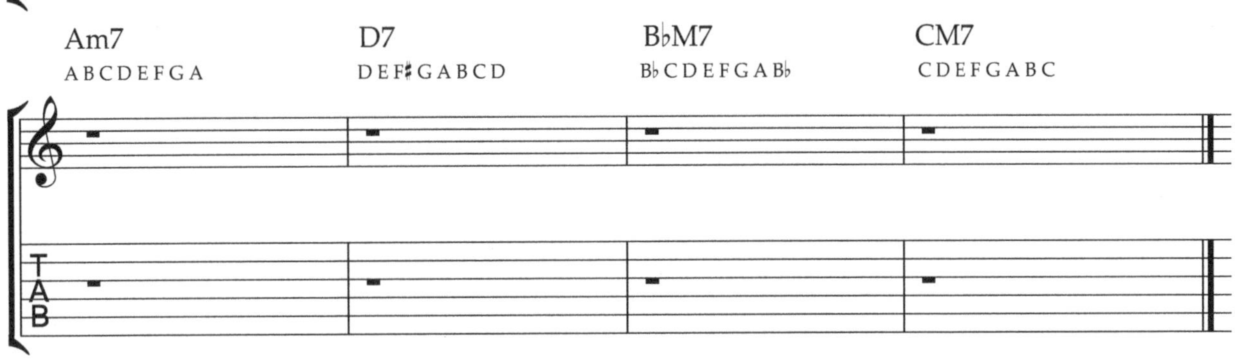

CHAPTER 12

Root-Third in the Bottom Voice

The third might be major or minor. These intervals must be completely internalized. From now on we will use them constantly.

But let's first explore the **A Minor scale: A B C D E F G A**
No accidentals!
Run through chapters 1 to 4 and play the exercises in the A minor scale.

The A minor scale in the first position:

Ascending

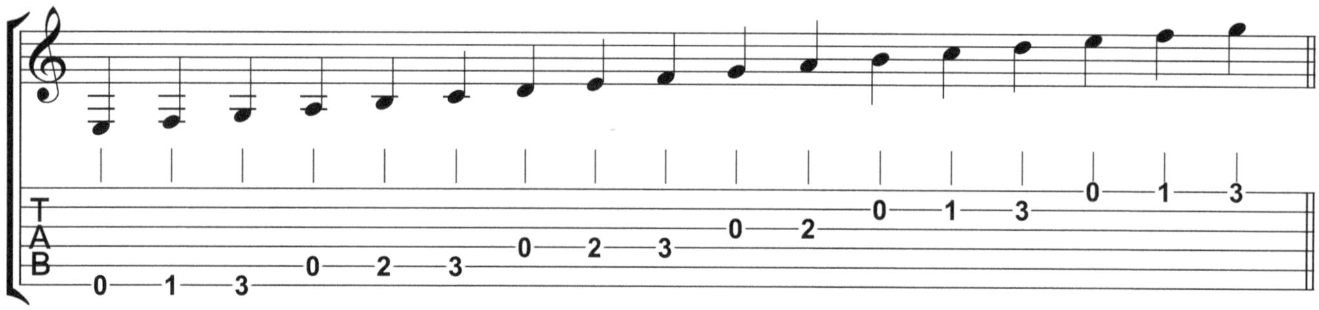

Descending

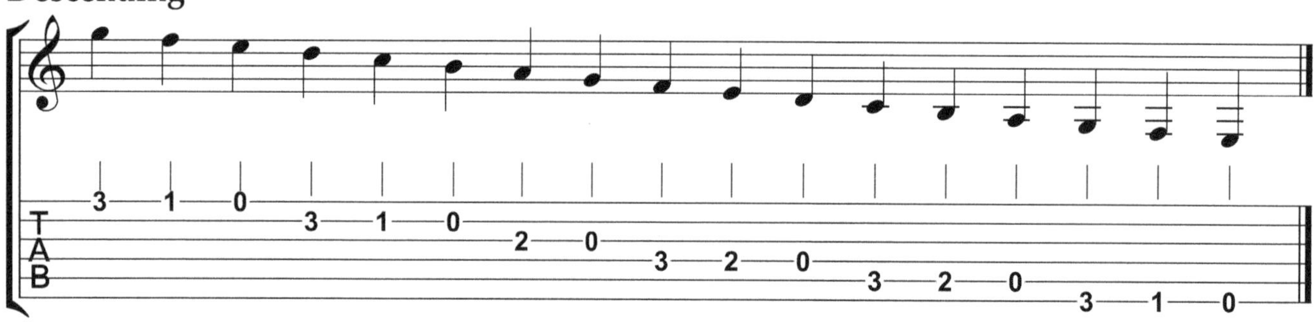

The thirds in the A minor scale are:
A-C; B-D; C-E; D-F; E-G; F-A; G-B Memorize these!!!
The A minor scale harmonized to the 7th:

Chord Name	Formula	Chord Tones
Am7	1,♭3,5,♭7	A C E G
Bm7♭5	1,♭3,♭5,♭7	B D F A
CM7	1,3,5,7	C E G B
Dm7	1,♭3,5,♭7	D F A C
Em7	1,♭3,5,♭7	E G B D
FM7	1,3,5,7	F A C E
G7	1,3,5,♭7	G B D F

The chords are the same as the ones of the C Major scale.

Root-Third

3 = Major third

♭3 = Minor third

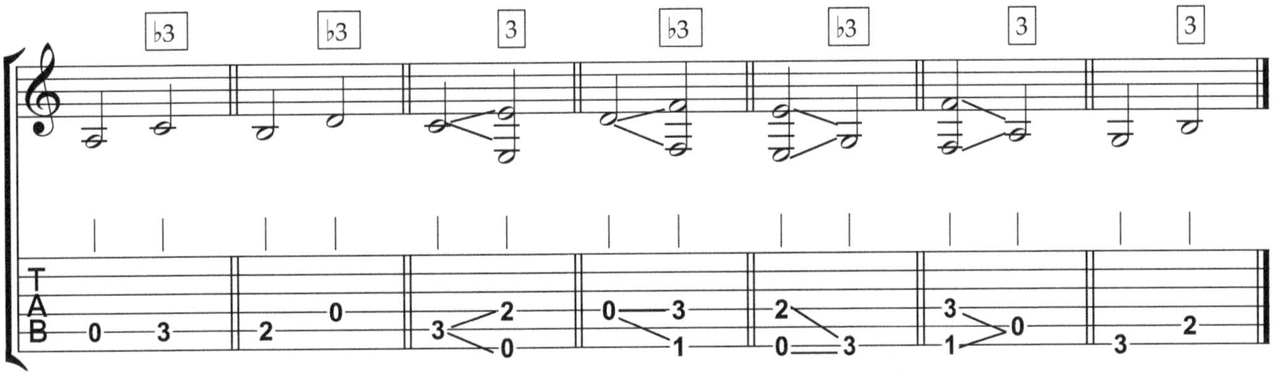

Some rhythmic possibilities:

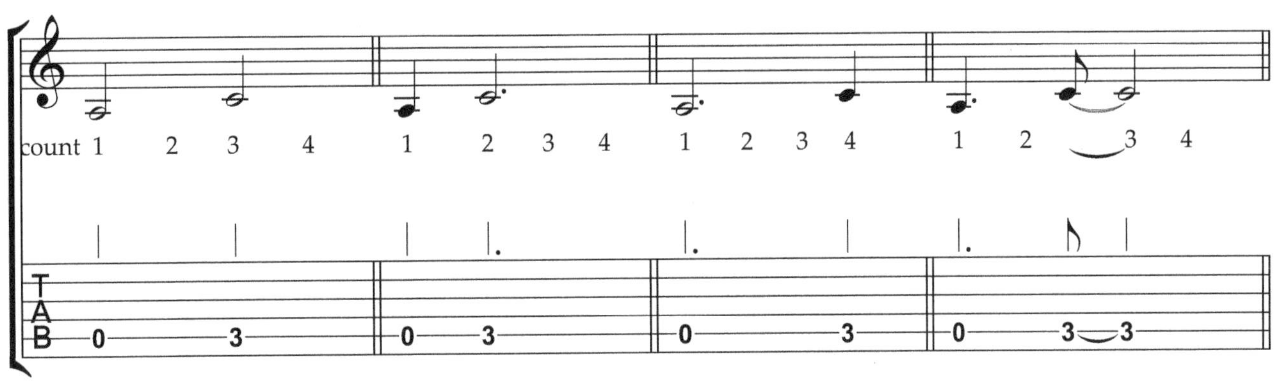

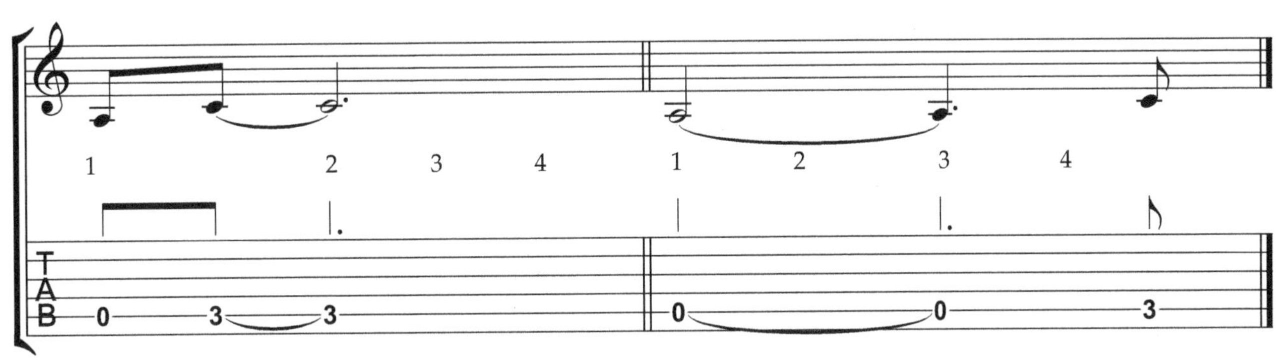

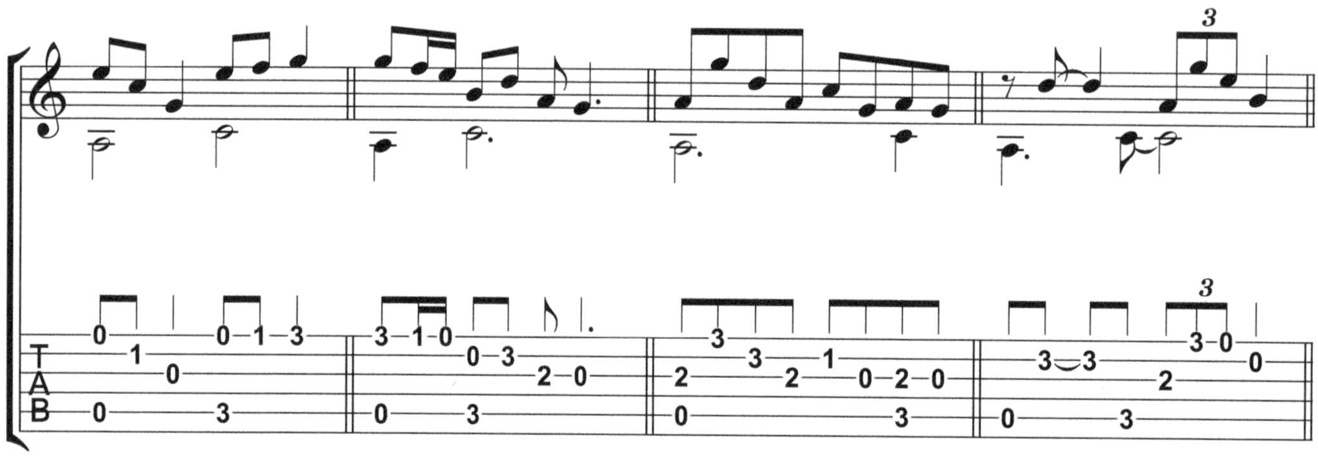

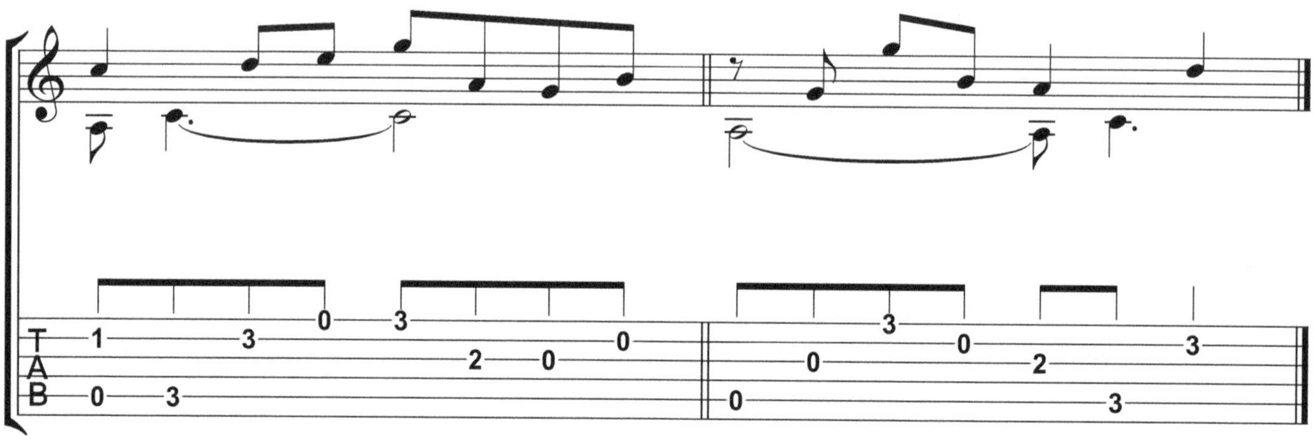

Your turn

Improvise on these Am7 bass lines.

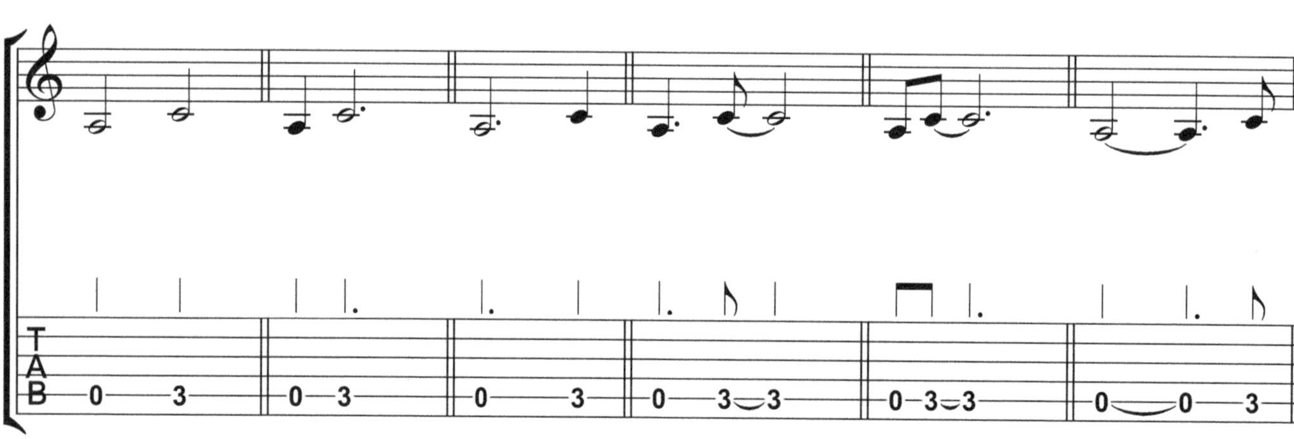

On a chord progression

Example 1

Track 28

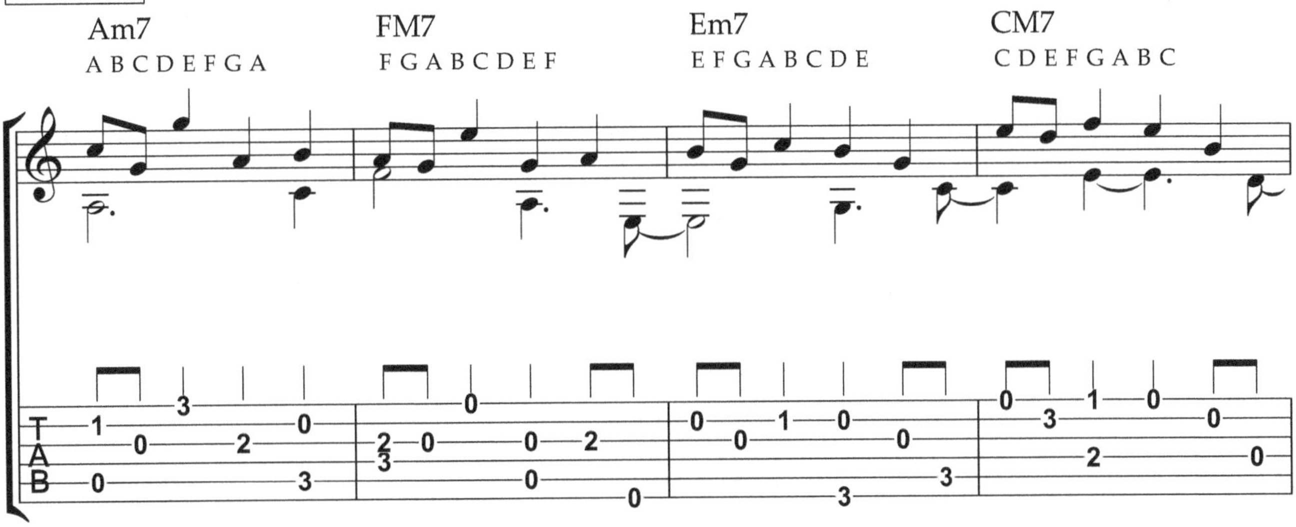

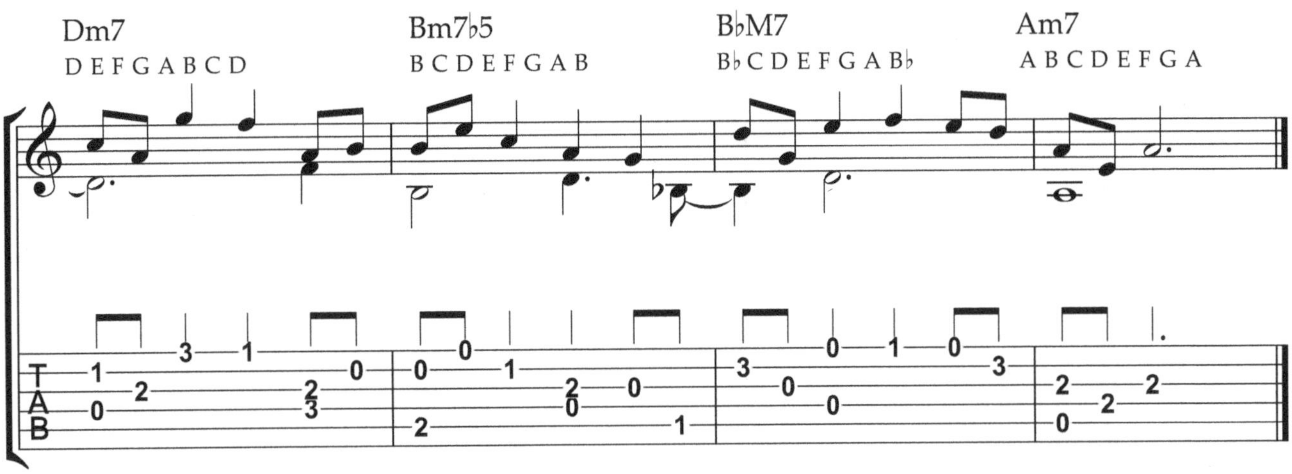

Example 2

Track 29

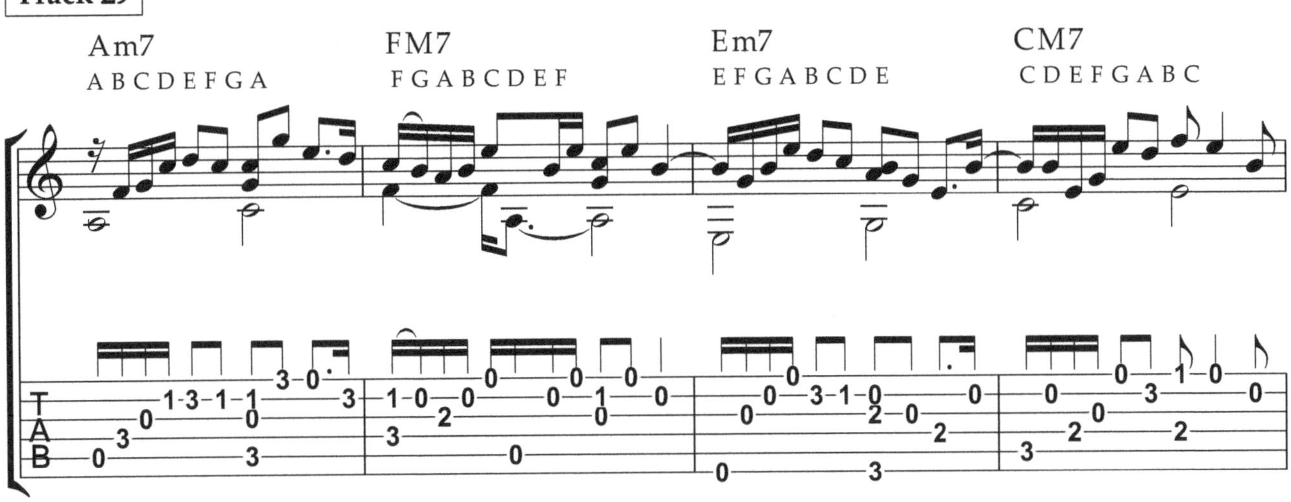

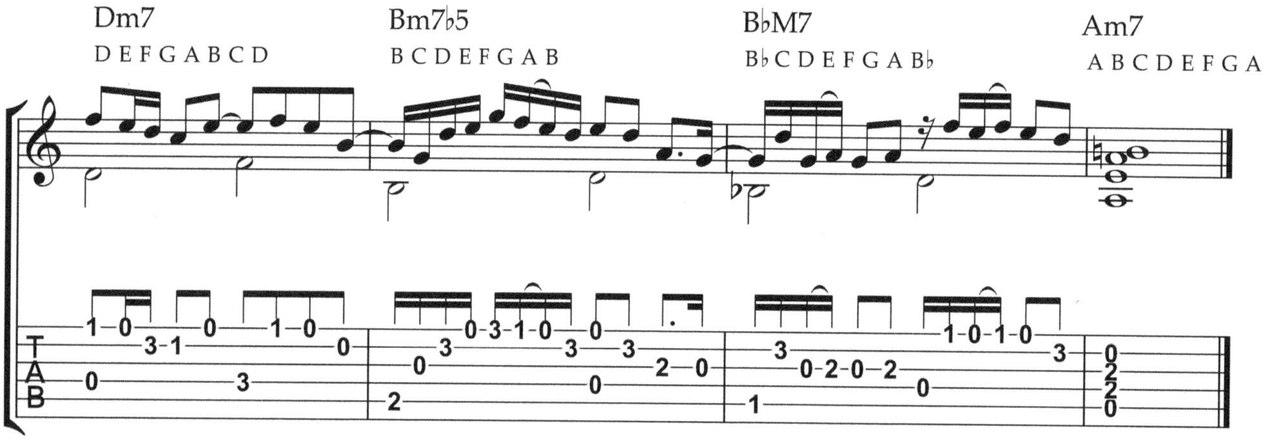
Dm7
D E F G A B C D
Bm7♭5
B C D E F G A B
B♭M7
B♭ C D E F G A B♭
Am7
A B C D E F G A

Your turn

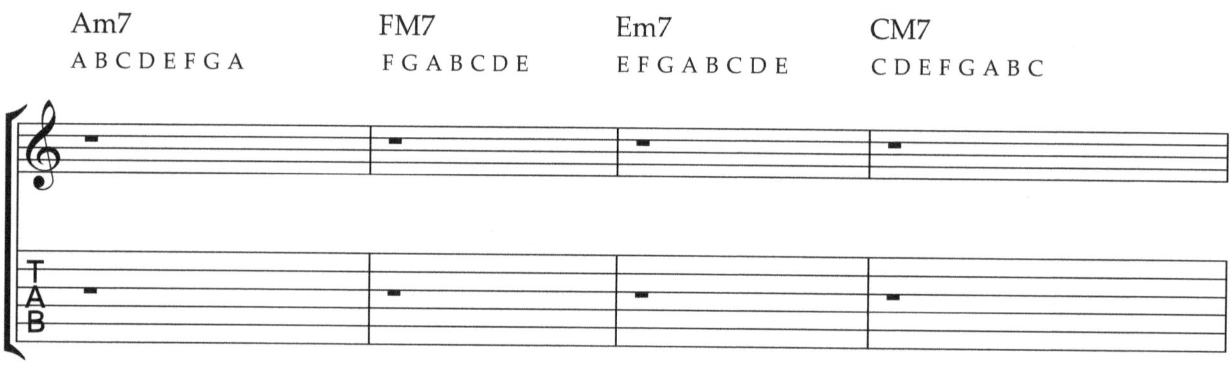
Am7
A B C D E F G A
FM7
F G A B C D E
Em7
E F G A B C D E
CM7
C D E F G A B C

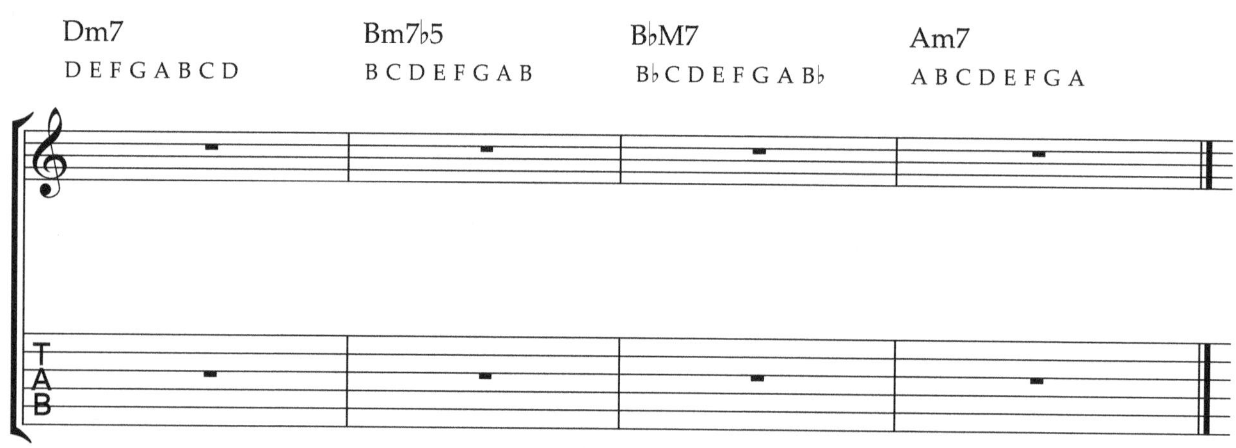
Dm7
D E F G A B C D
Bm7♭5
B C D E F G A B
B♭M7
B♭ C D E F G A B♭
Am7
A B C D E F G A

CHAPTER 13

Embellishing the Bass Line (Part 1)

Approach notes: Scale Tones/Chromatic Tones

We can add notes between the root-third or third-root.
Some notes are scalar and some are chromatic.
In the G Major Scale, scale tones are: G A B C D E F♯ G
Chromatic tones are: G♯ B♭ C♯ D♯ F
Let's first explore the G Major scale in the first position.
Only the F changes into F♯

Track 30

Ascending **Descending**

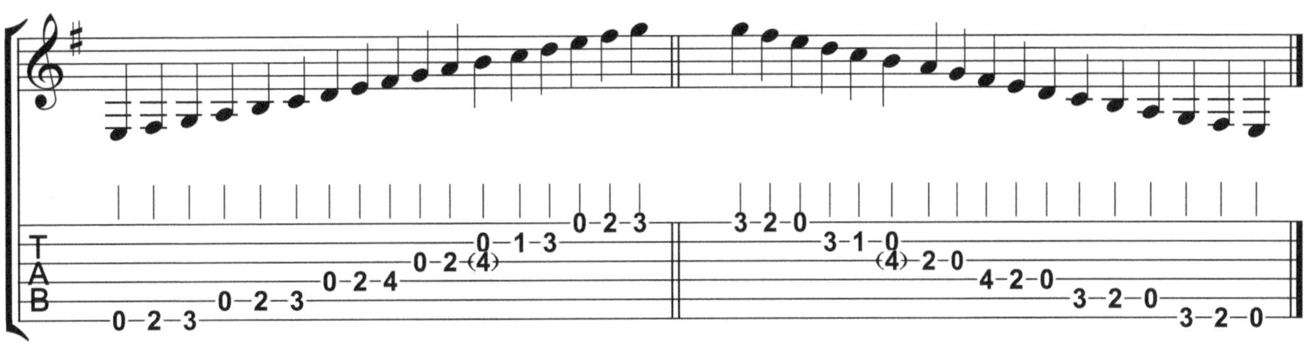

The G Major scale harmonized to the 7th

Chord Name	Formula	Chord Tones
GM7	1,3,5,7	G B D F♯
Am7	1,♭3,5,♭7	A C E G
Bm7	1,♭3,5,♭7	B D F♯ A
CM7	1,3,5,7	C E G B
D7	1,3,5,♭7	D F♯ A C
Em7	1,♭3,5,♭7	E G B D
F♯m7♭5	1,♭3,♭5,♭7	F♯ A C E

New chords

GM7

G B D F♯

Direct substitutions

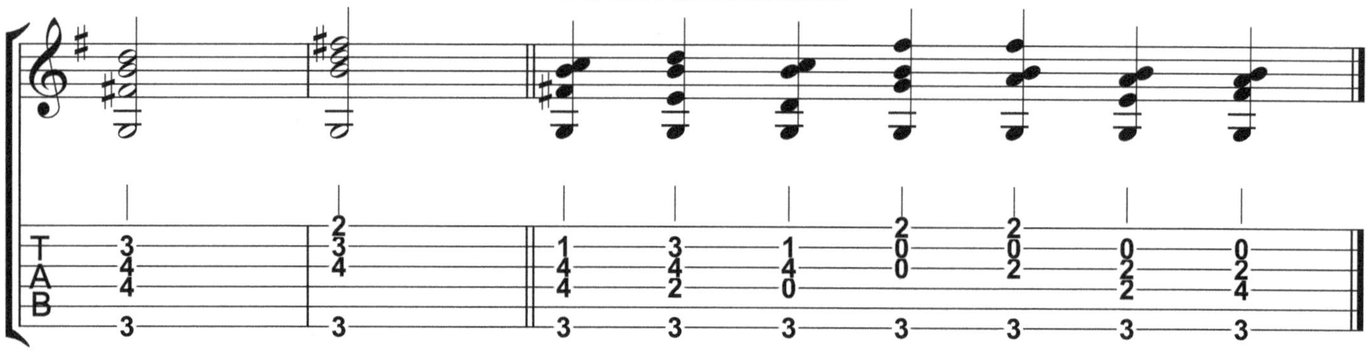

Bm7

B D F♯ A

Direct substitutions

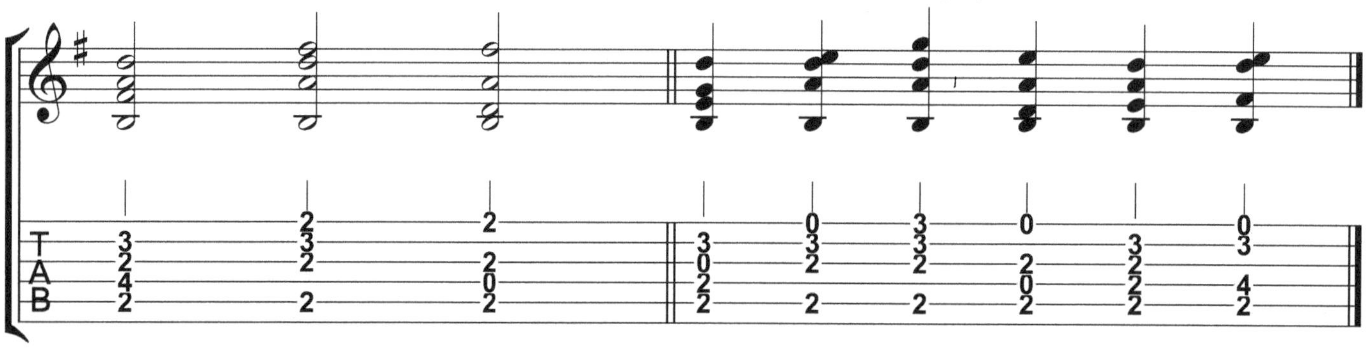

D7

D F♯ A C

Direct substitutions

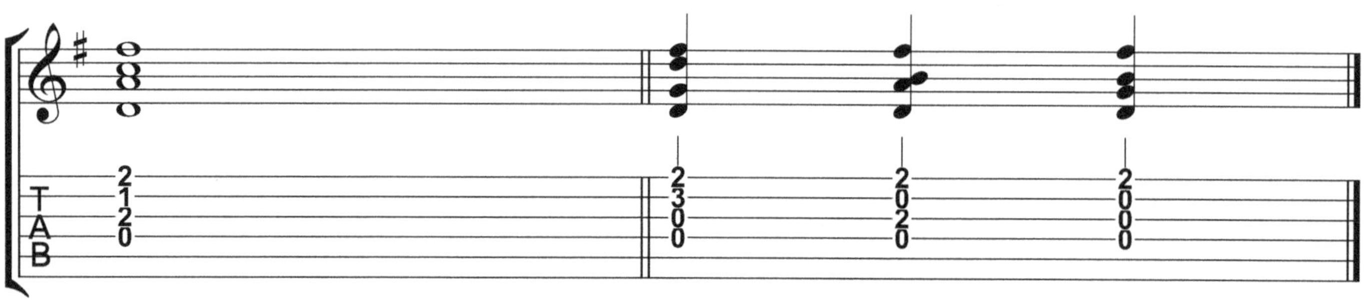

F♯m7♭5

F♯ A C E

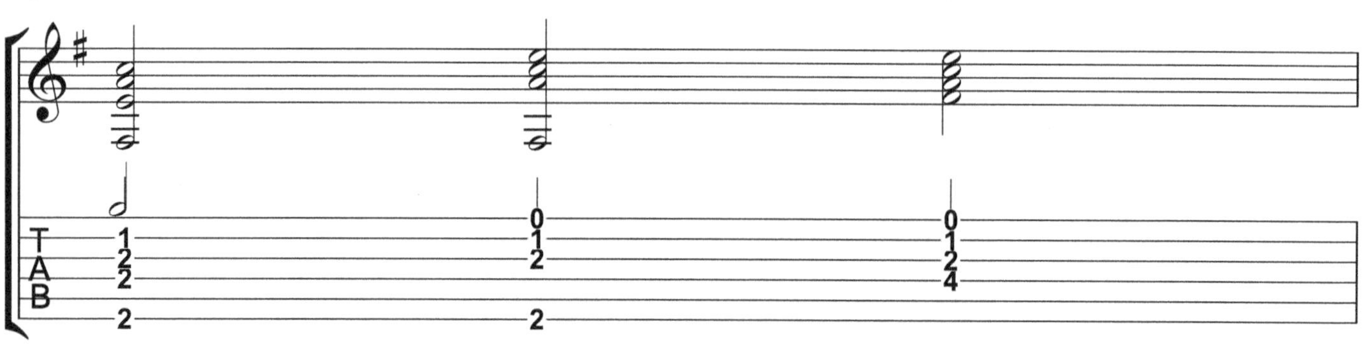

Root-Third

G-B; A-C; B-D; C-E; D-F♯; E-G; F♯-A Memorize these!!!

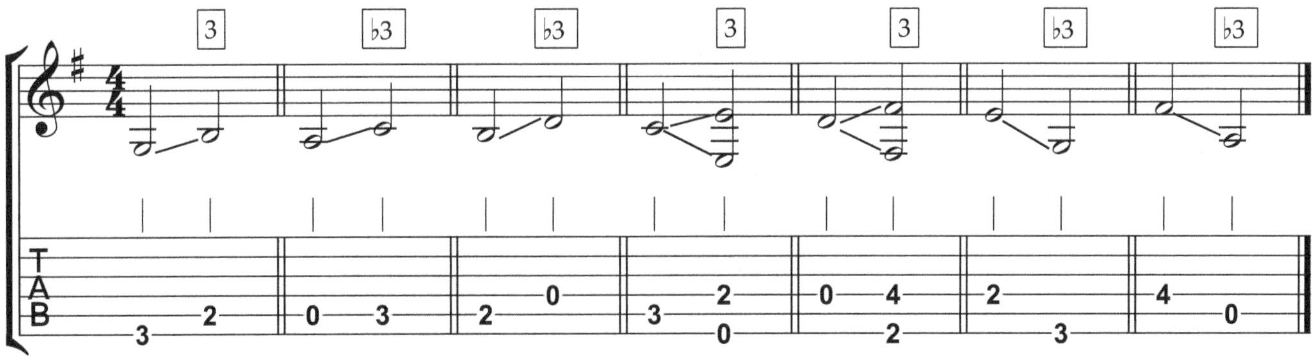

On a chord progression

Example 1

Track 31

GM7 G A B C D E F♯ G | Em7 E F♯ G A B C D E | CM7 C D E F♯ G A B C | Bm7 B C D E F♯ G A B

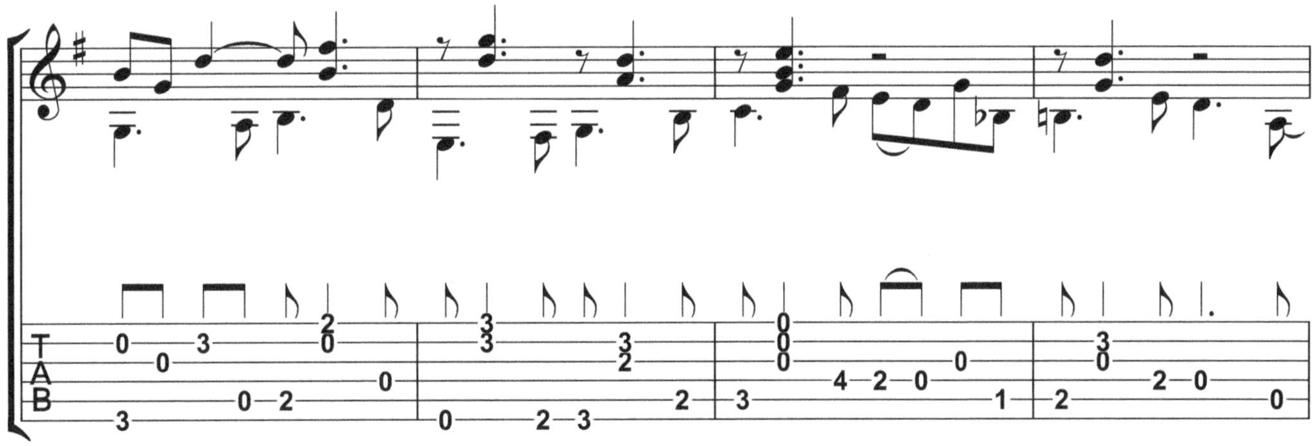

Am7 A B C D E F♯ G A | F♯m7♭5 F♯ G A B C D E F♯ | D7 D E F♯ G A B C | GM7 G A B C D E F♯ G

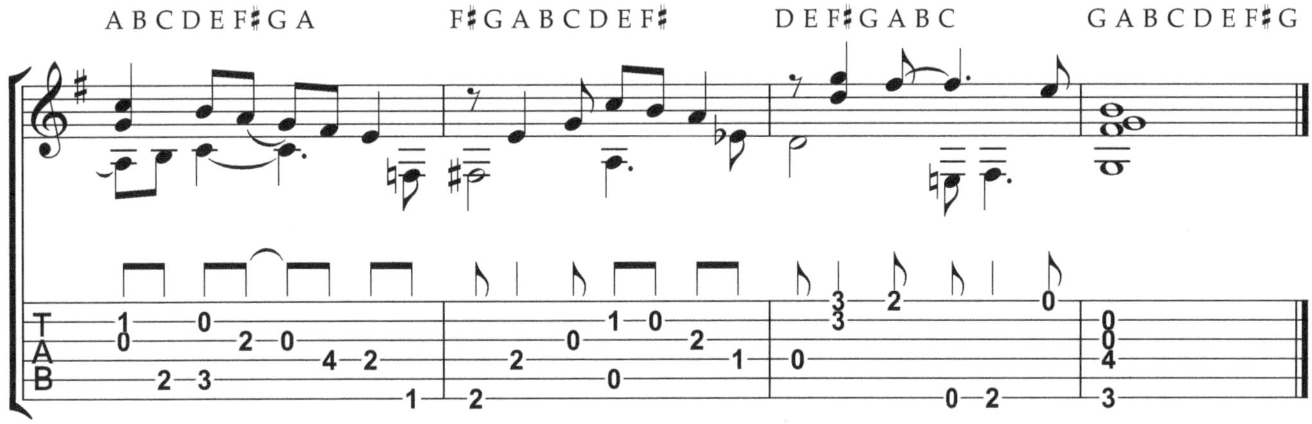

Example 2

Track 32

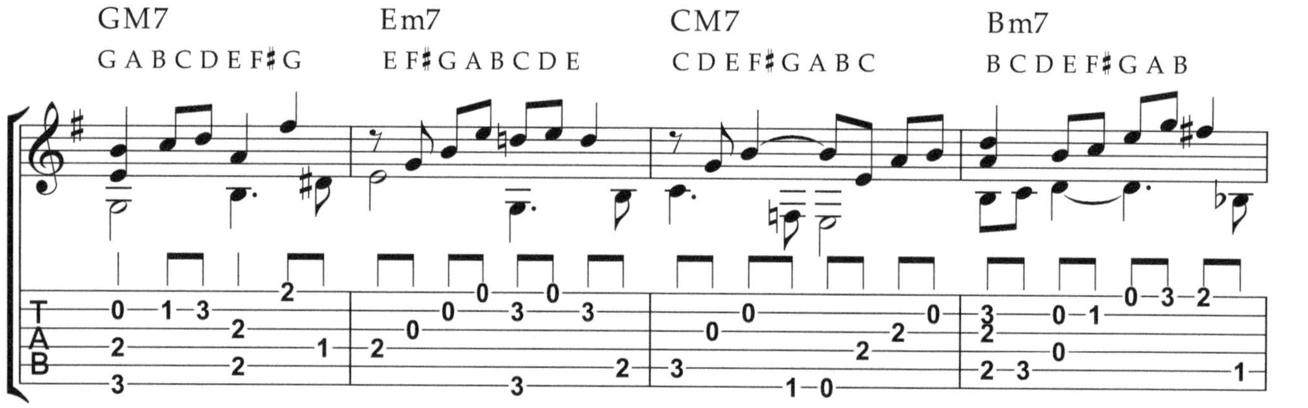

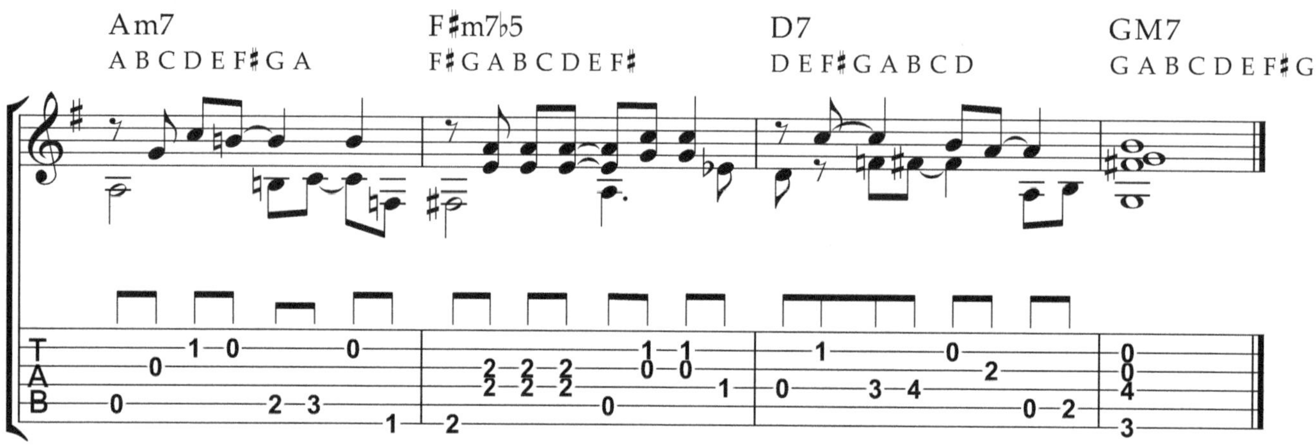

Your turn

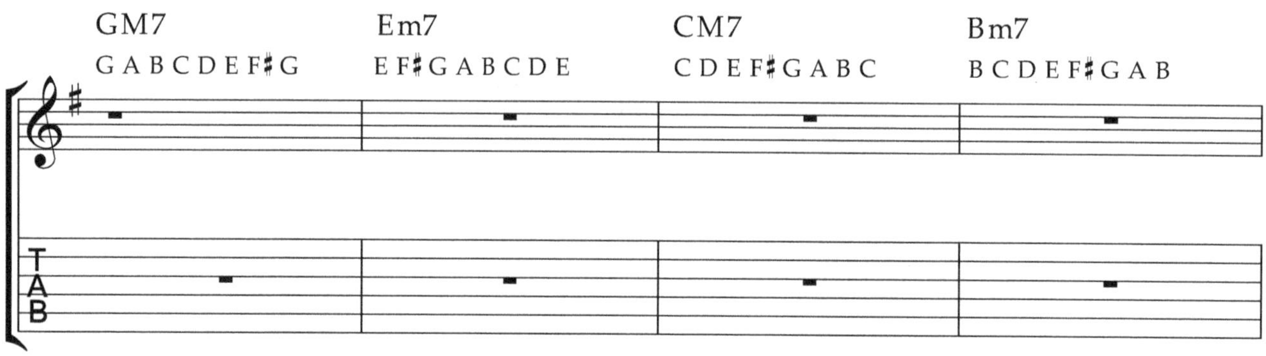

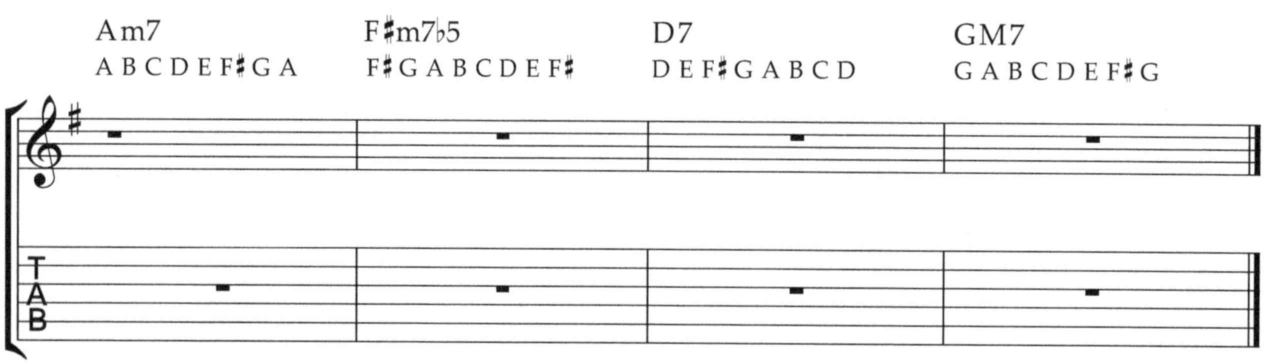

CHAPTER 14

Embellishing the Bass Line (Part 2)

A Freer Approach

Let's explore first the E Minor scale: E F♯ G A B C D E

F --) F♯ (same scale pattern as in chapter 13)

I like to use open strings whenever possible.

Ascending

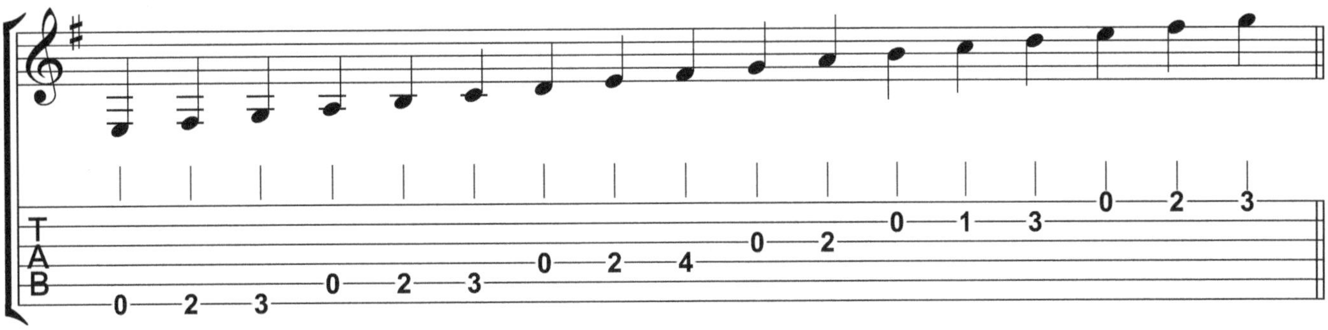

Descending

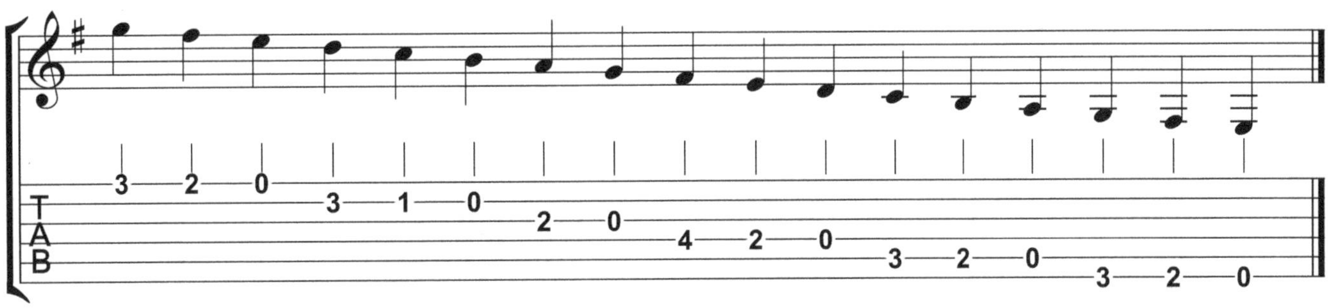

The E minor scale harmonized to the 7th
(the same chords as for the G Major scale)

Chord Name	**Formula**	**Chord Tone**
Em7	1,♭3,5,♭7	E G B D
F♯m7♭5	1,♭3,♭5,♭7	F♯ A C E
GM7	1,3,5,7	G B D F♯
Am7	1,♭3,5,♭7	A C E G
Bm7	1,♭3,5,♭7	B D F♯ A
CM7	1,3,5,7	C E G B
D7	1,3,5,♭7	D F♯ A C

Let's first practice bass lines on strings 6, 5, and 4.

String 6

Your turn

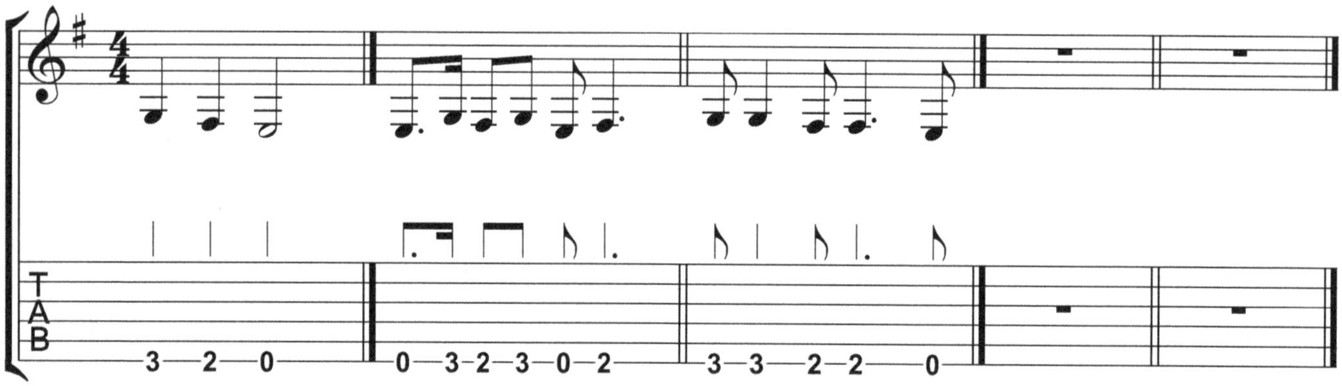

String 5

Your turn

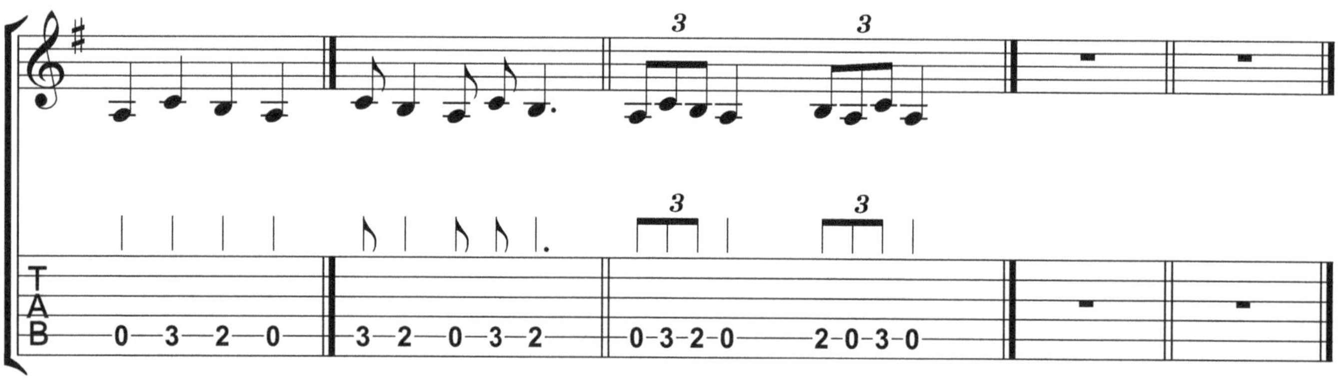

String 4

Your turn

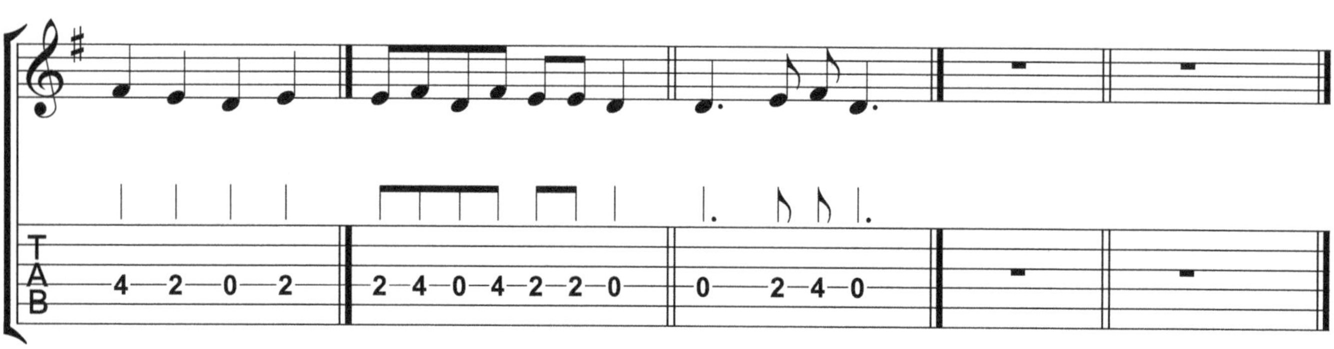

Strings 6 and 5

Your turn

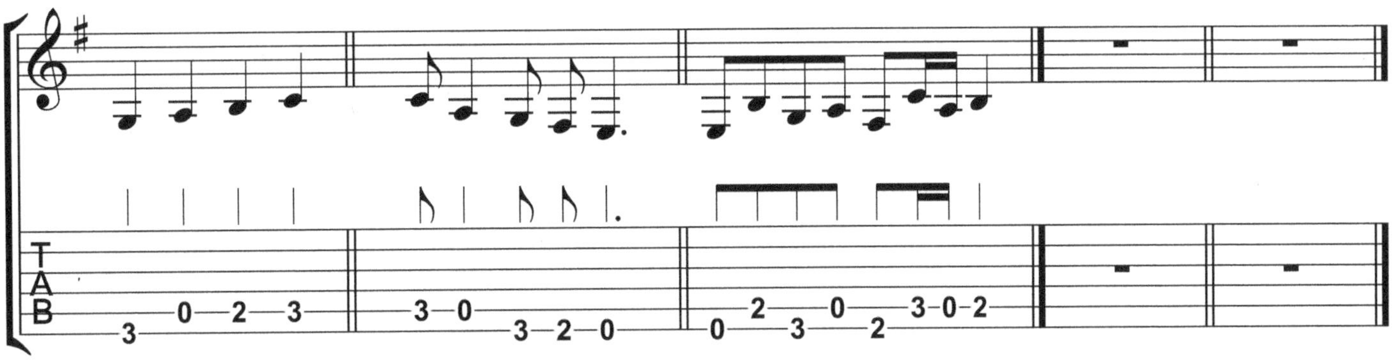

Strings 6 and 4

Your turn

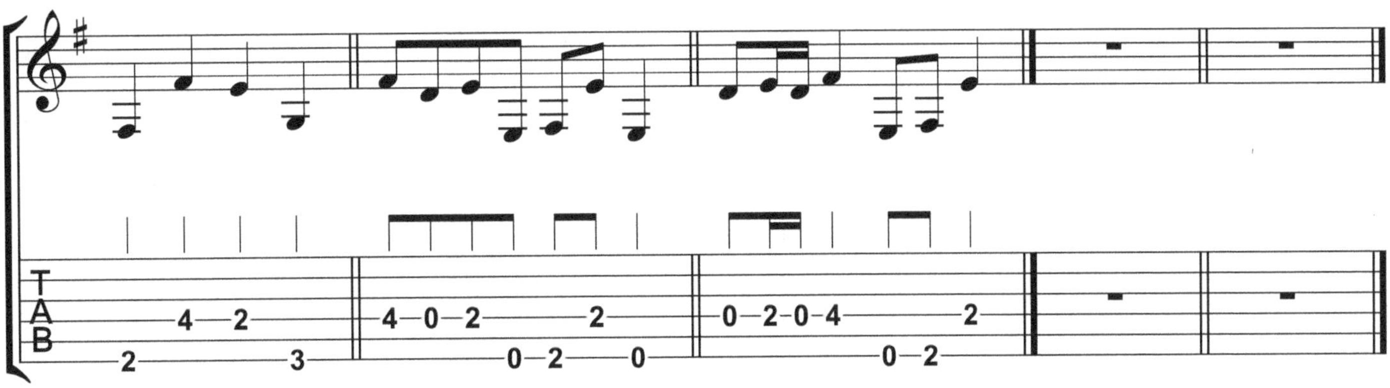

Strings 5 and 4

Your turn

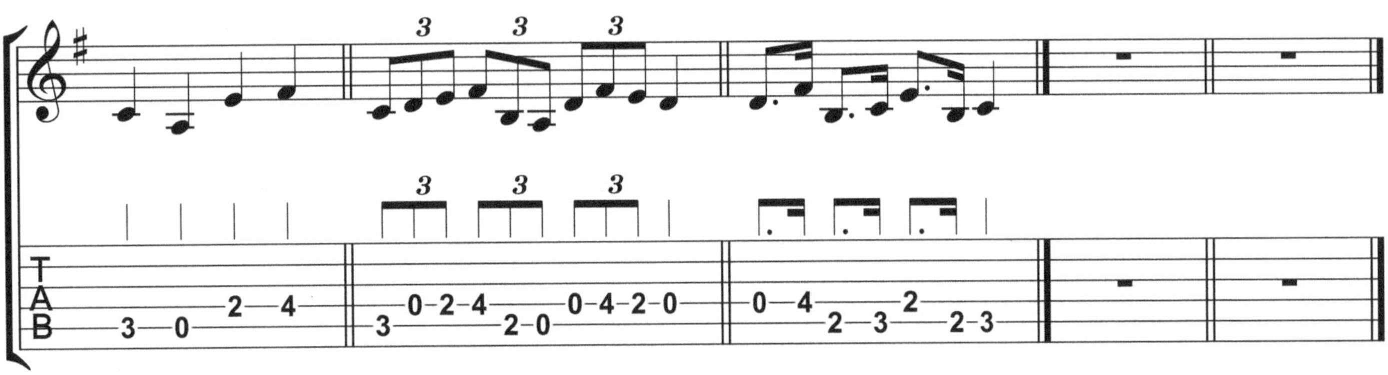

Strings 6, 5, 4

Your turn

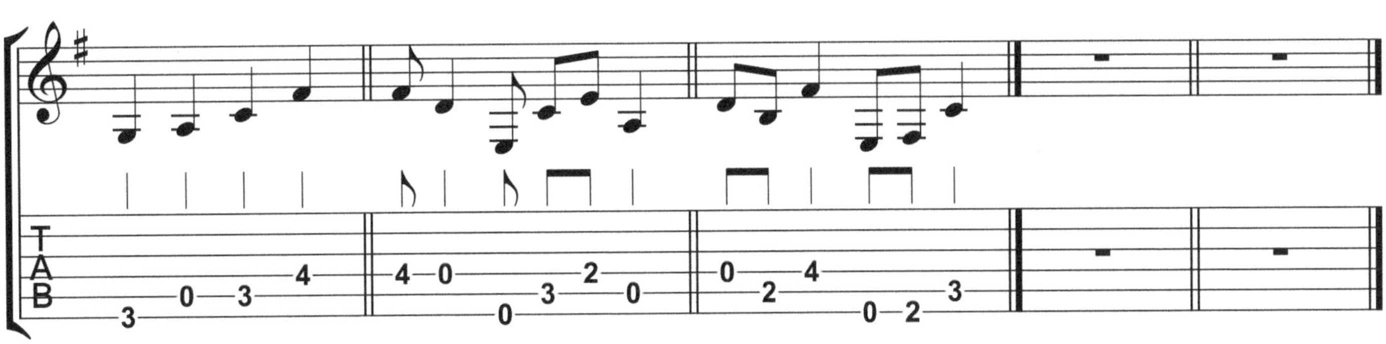

New chord

C♯m7

C♯ E G♯ B

Some direct substitutions

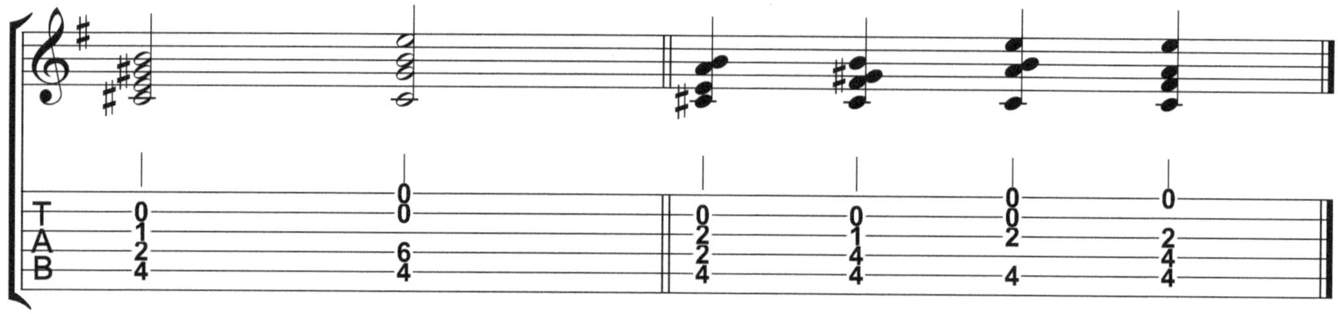

On a chord progression

Em7	Am7	D7	Bm7
C♯m7	F♯m7♭5	FM7	Em7

Example 1

Track 33

Em7 E F♯ G A B C D E — Am7 A B C D E F♯ G A — D7 D E F♯ G A B C D — Bm7 B C D E F♯ G A B

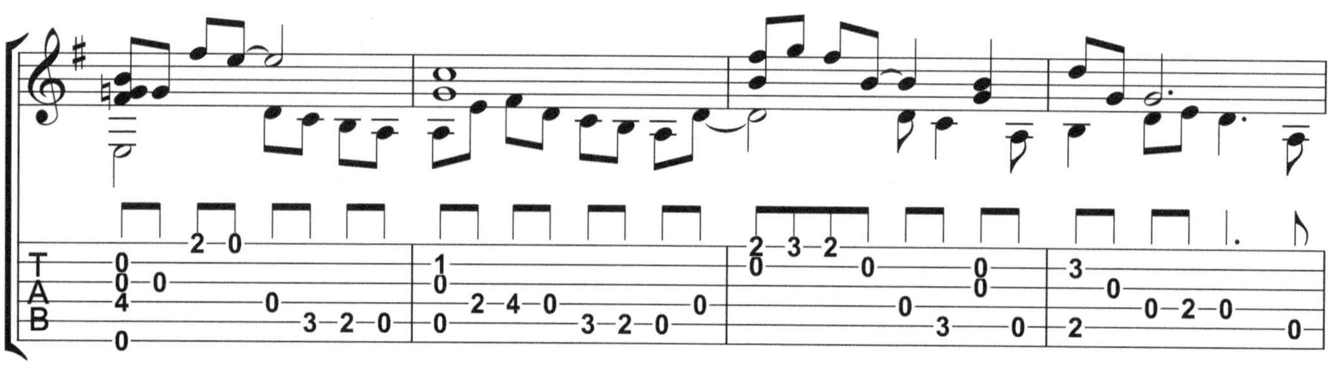

C♯m7 (C♯ E G♯ B) C♯ D E F♯ G♯ A B C♯ — F♯m7♭5 F♯ G A B C D E F♯ — FM7 F G A B C D E F — Em7 E F♯ G A B C D E

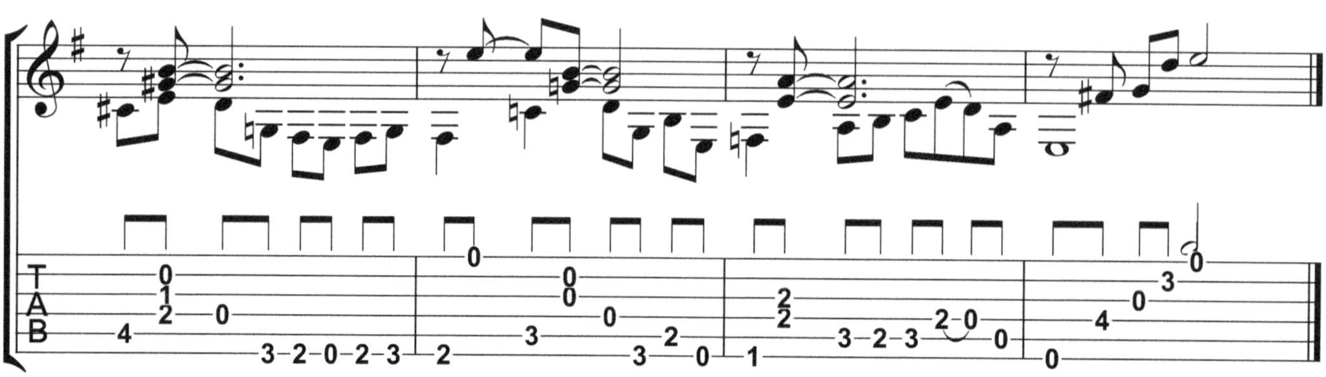

Example 2

Track 34

Em7 — E F♯ G A B C D E | Am7 — A B C D E F♯ G A | D7 — D E F♯ G A B C D | Bm7 — B C D E F♯ G A B

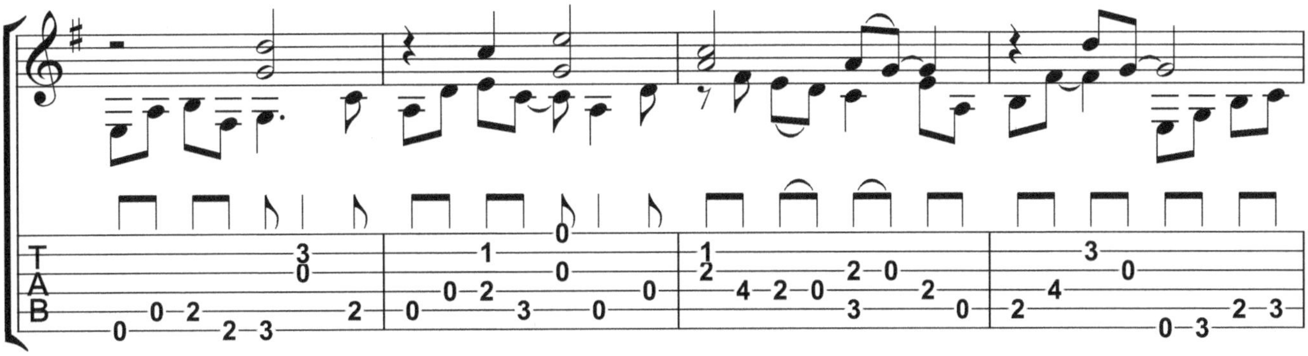

C♯m7 (C♯ E G♯ B) — C♯ D E F♯ G♯ A B C♯ | F♯m7♭5 — F♯ G A B C D E F♯ | FM7 — F G A B C D E F | Em7 — E F♯ G A B C D E

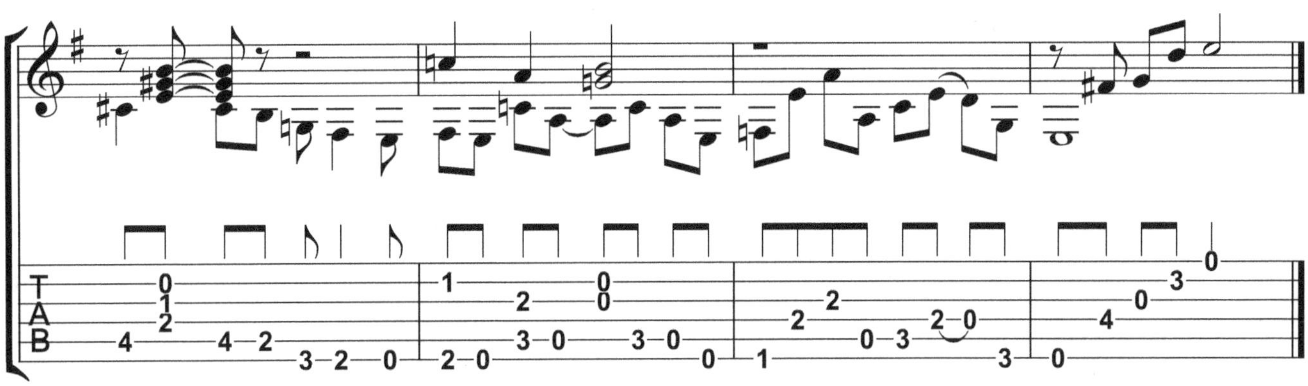

Your turn

Em7 — E F♯ G A B C D E | Am7 — A B C D E F♯ G A | D7 — D E F♯ G A B C D | Bm7 — B C D E F♯ G A B

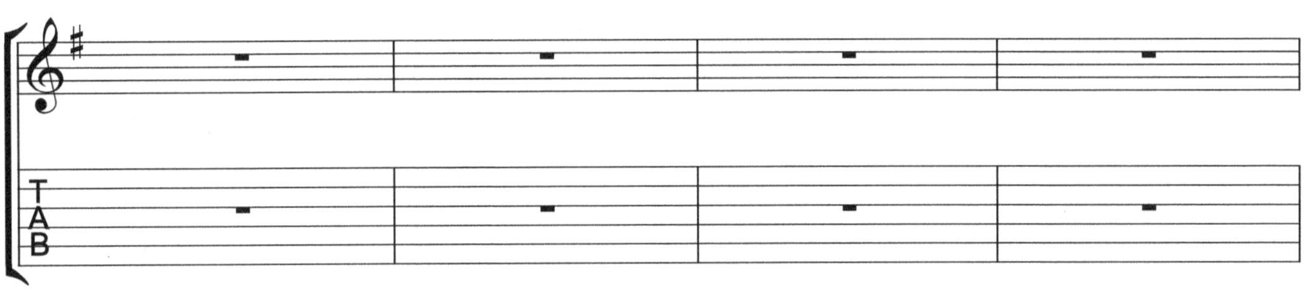

C♯m7 (C♯ E G♯ B) — C♯ D E F♯ G♯ A B C♯ | F♯m7♭5 — F♯ G A B C D E F♯ | FM7 — F G A B C D E F | Em7 — E F♯ G A B C D E

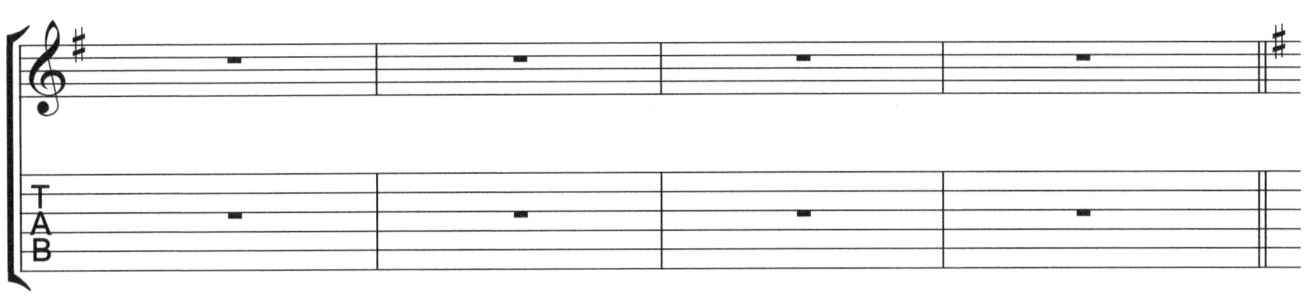

CHAPTER 15

Adding Chromatic Tones in the Melody

A **chromatic** note is any note that is not in the scale you are playing.
In the E minor scale (E F♯ G A B C D E) the chromatic notes are F, G♯, B♭, C♯ and D♯
Chromatic notes are usually (but not always) added on weak beats.
Chromaticism, used tastefully and occasionally, may add great color and emotion to your melodic lines.

Some examples of adding chromaticism to a melody line:

Em7

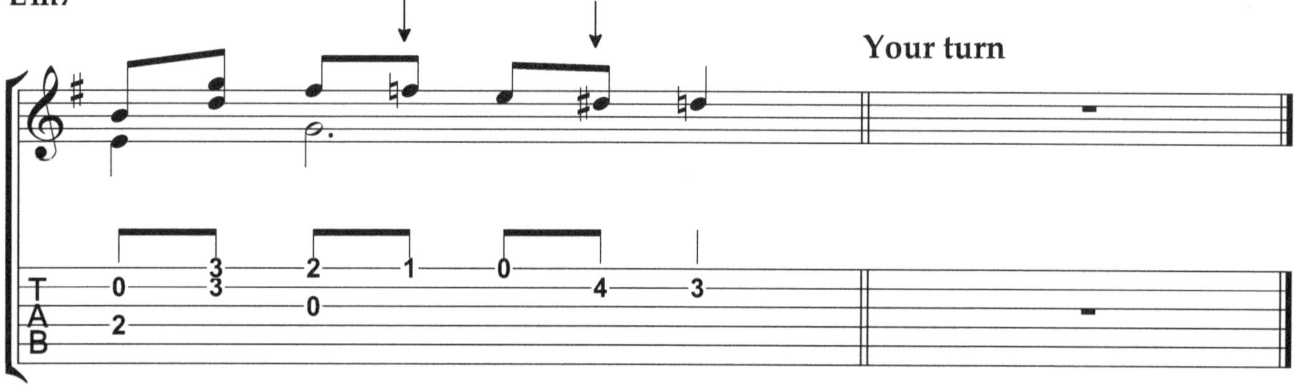

F♯m7♭5

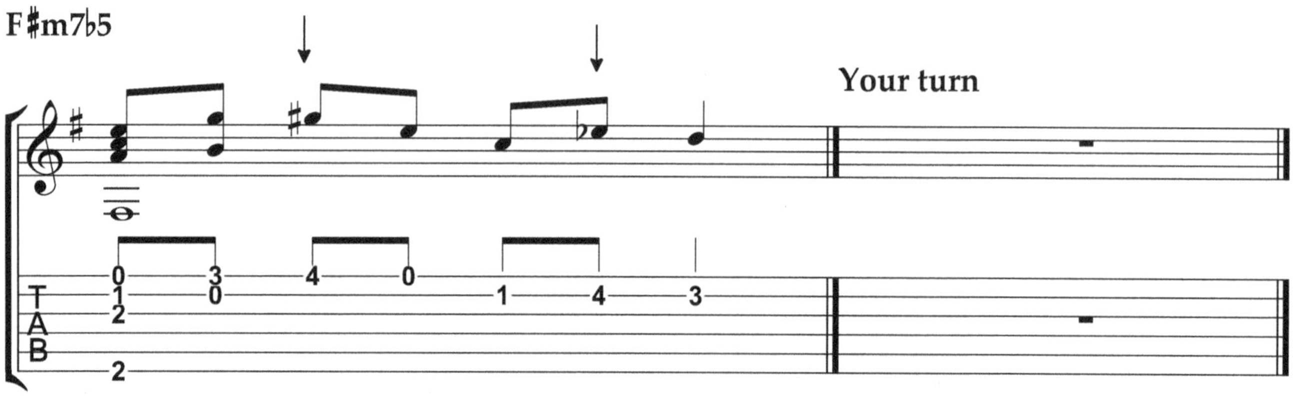

GM7

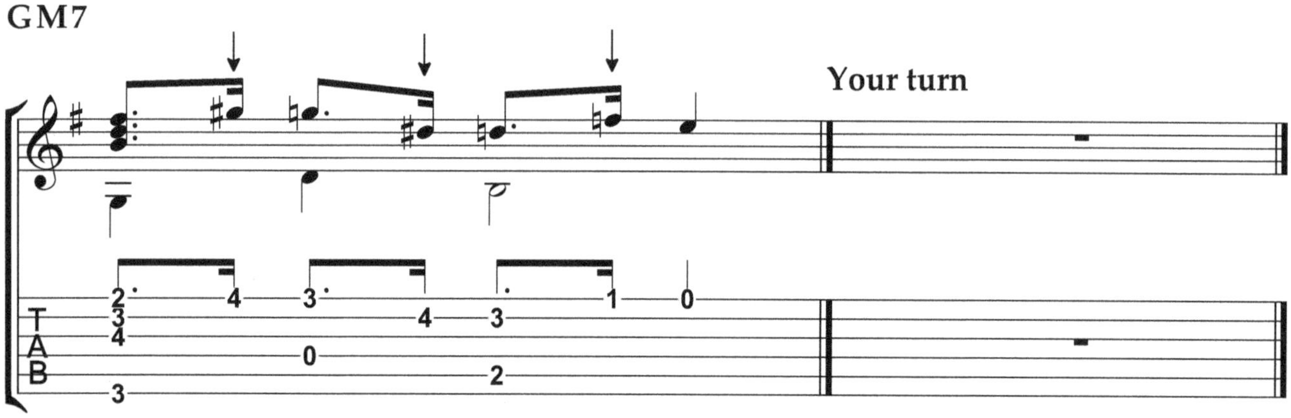

Am7

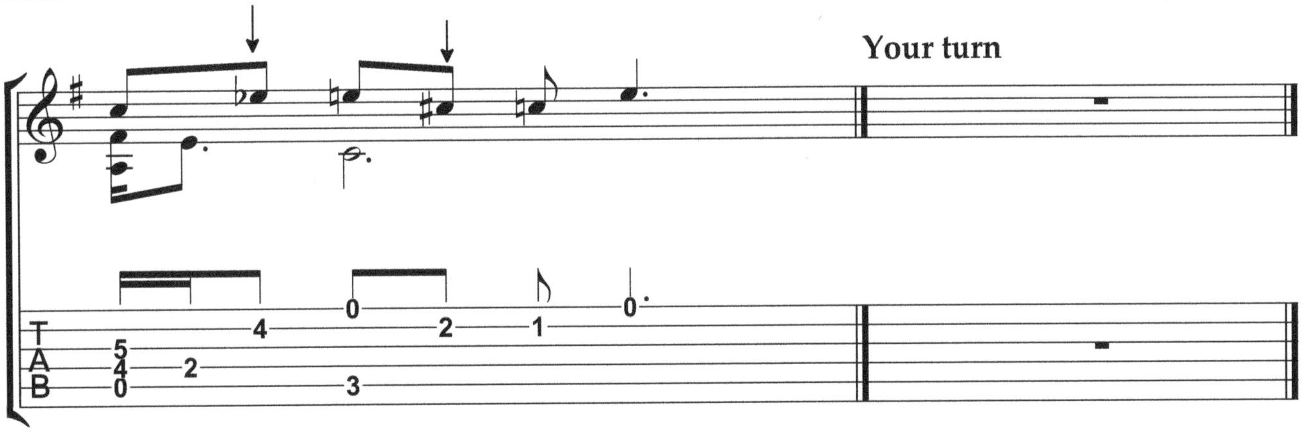

Bm7

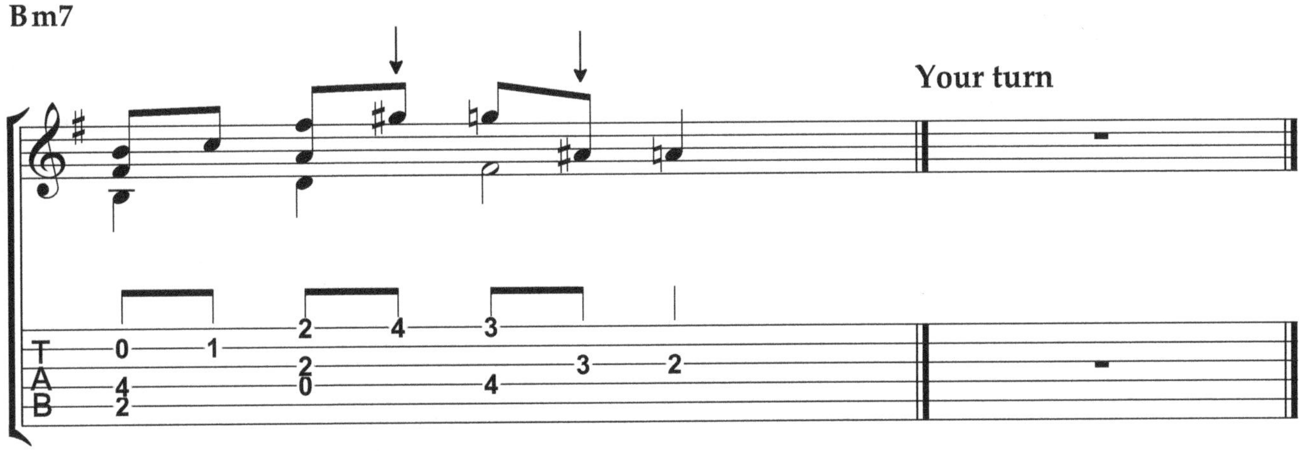

CM7

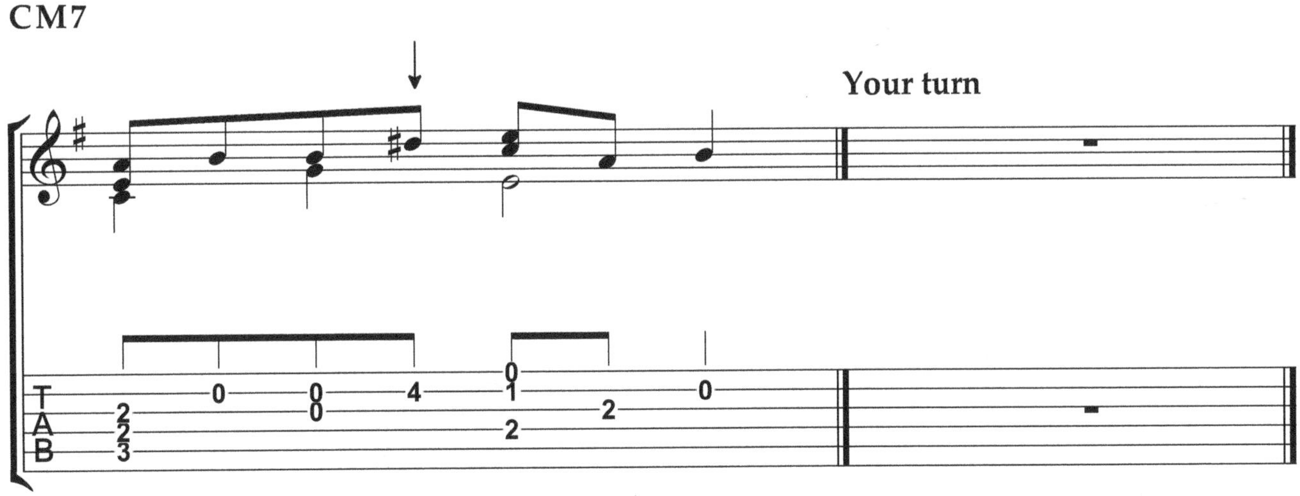

Track 35

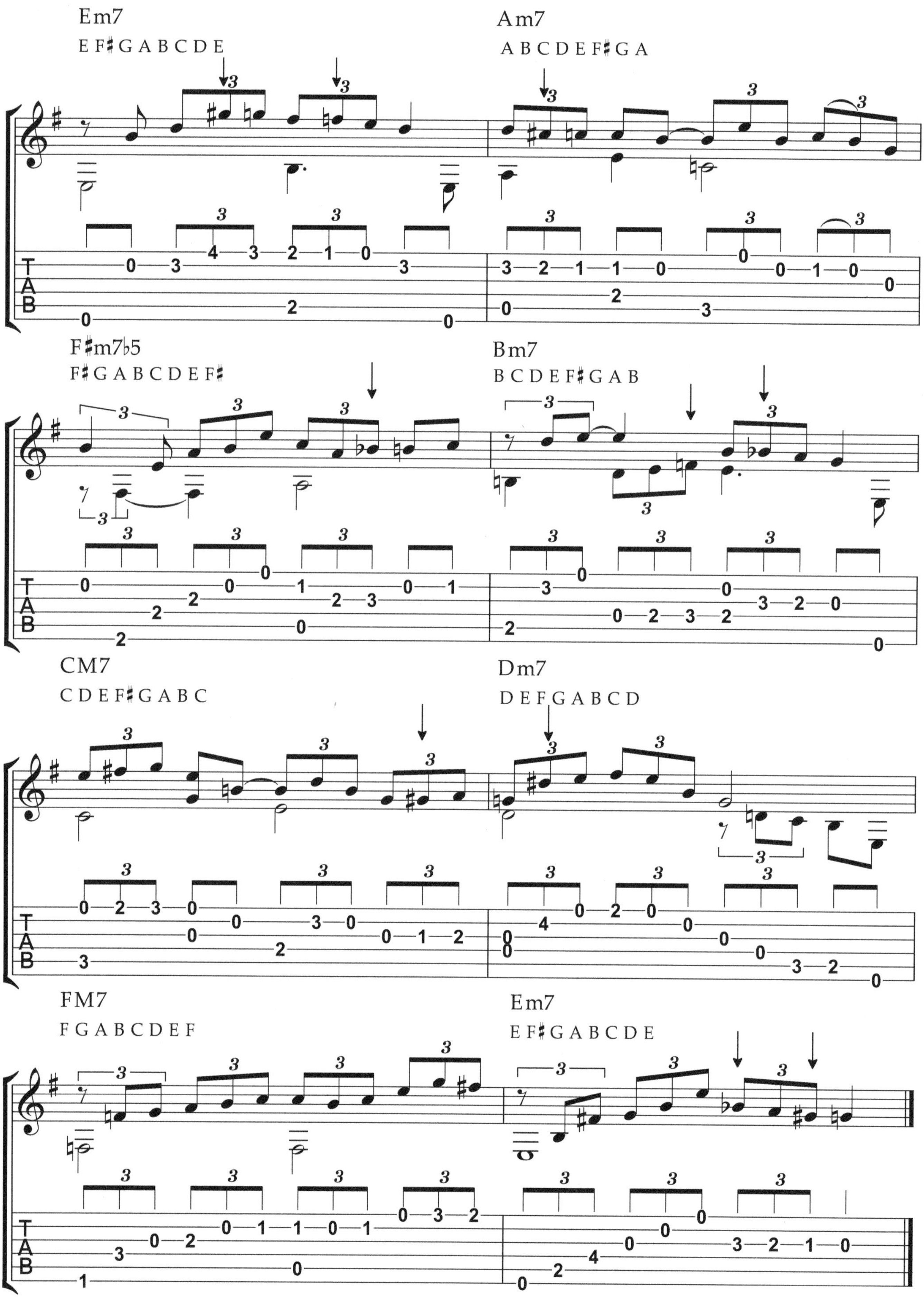
Em7
E F♯ G A B C D E
Am7
A B C D E F♯ G A
F♯m7♭5
F♯ G A B C D E F♯
Bm7
B C D E F♯ G A B
CM7
C D E F♯ G A B C
Dm7
D E F G A B C D
FM7
F G A B C D E F
Em7
E F♯ G A B C D E

Your turn

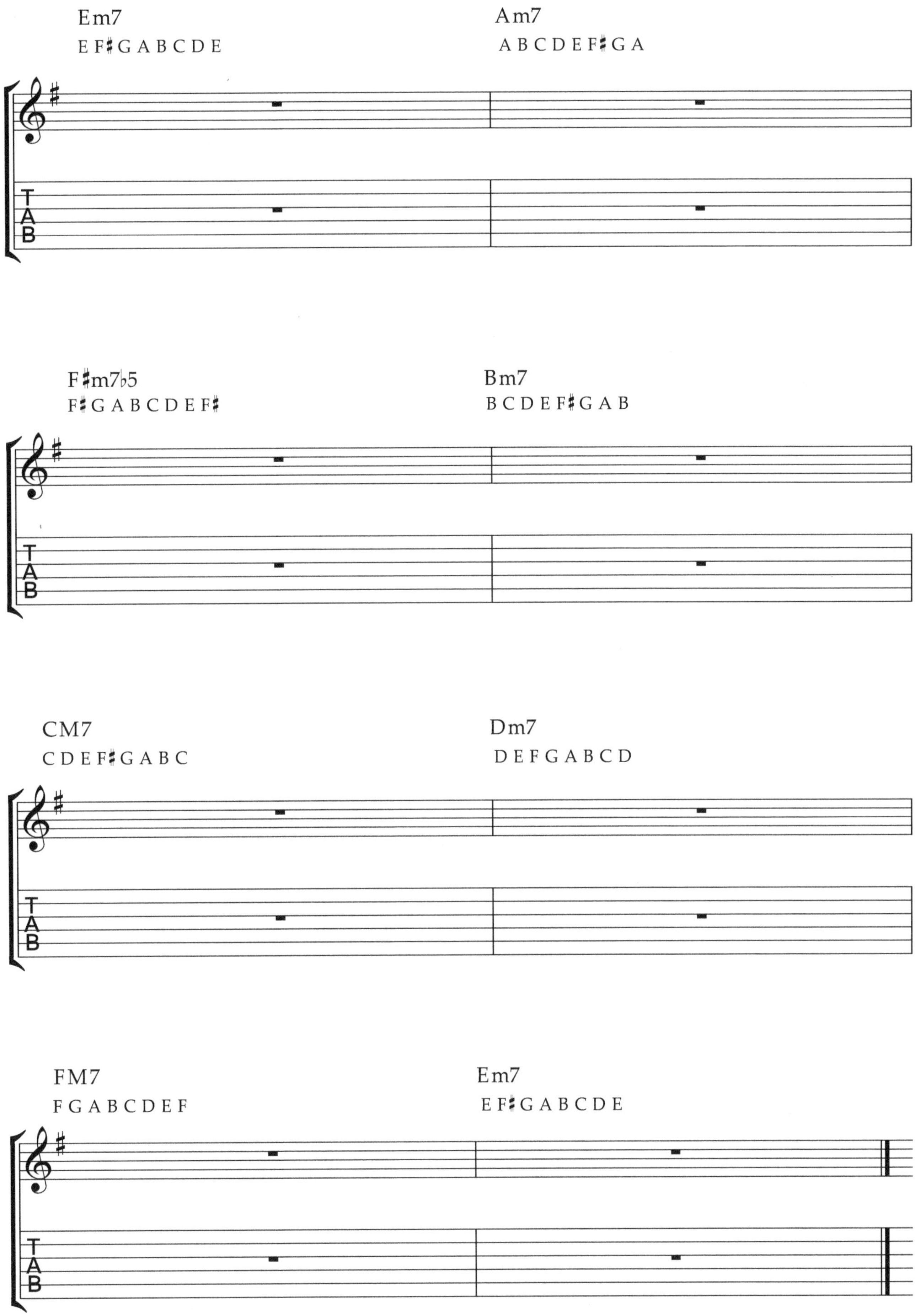
Em7
E F♯ G A B C D E
Am7
A B C D E F♯ G A
F♯m7♭5
F♯ G A B C D E F♯
Bm7
B C D E F♯ G A B
CM7
C D E F♯ G A B C
Dm7
D E F G A B C D
FM7
F G A B C D E F
Em7
E F♯ G A B C D E

CHAPTER 16

Modern Sounds (Part 1): ♭5 and ♯5 in the Middle Voice

For a more contemporary sound, I like to spice the middle voice with a ♭**5** or a ♯**5.**
They are considered as mild dissonances.
They are very easy to locate: just lower or raise the 5th with a half step (one fret).
To make things as straightforward as possible, it is best to focus on the idea of raising or lowering the fifth by a semitone and then describing that note in the simplest and most intuitive way.
Strictly speaking, we are flattening or sharpening the fifth and this sometimes results in unfamiliar ways of writing notes. For example, flattening the note C becomes C♭, but it is much easier to read this as the note B. Flattening the note F is F♭ but it is much easier to think of the note E and sharpening the note F is F♯♯, but it is simpler just to think of the note G.

The following examples use the easiest ways of describing the notes from raising or lowering them, not the strict names as dictated by theory.

In the key of C Major

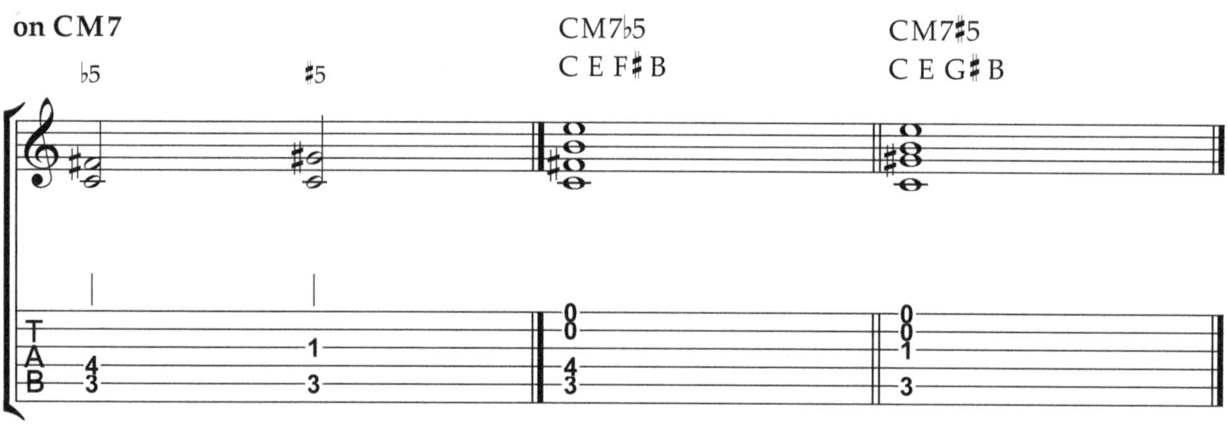

Play C D E F G A B C in the upper and bottom voice, add F♯ or G♯ into the middle voice.

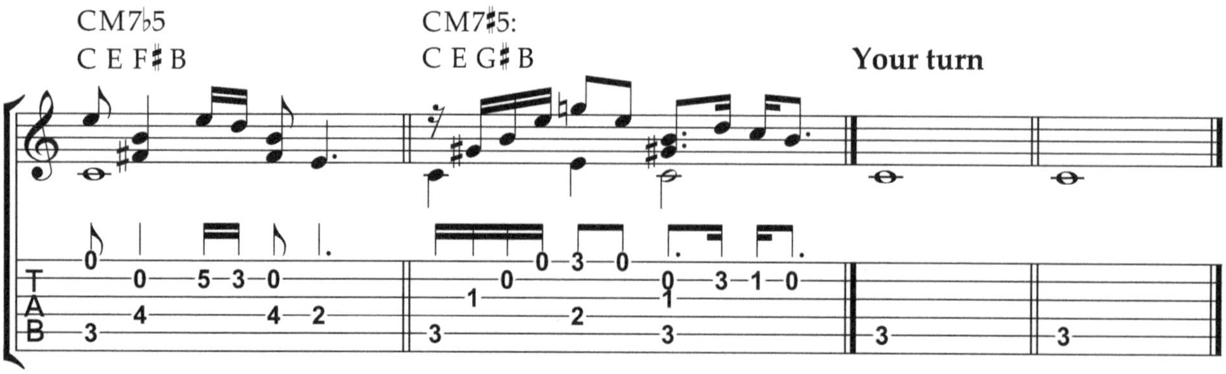

on Dm7

♭5 ♯5

Dm7♭5: D F A♭ C

Dm7♯5: D F B♭ C

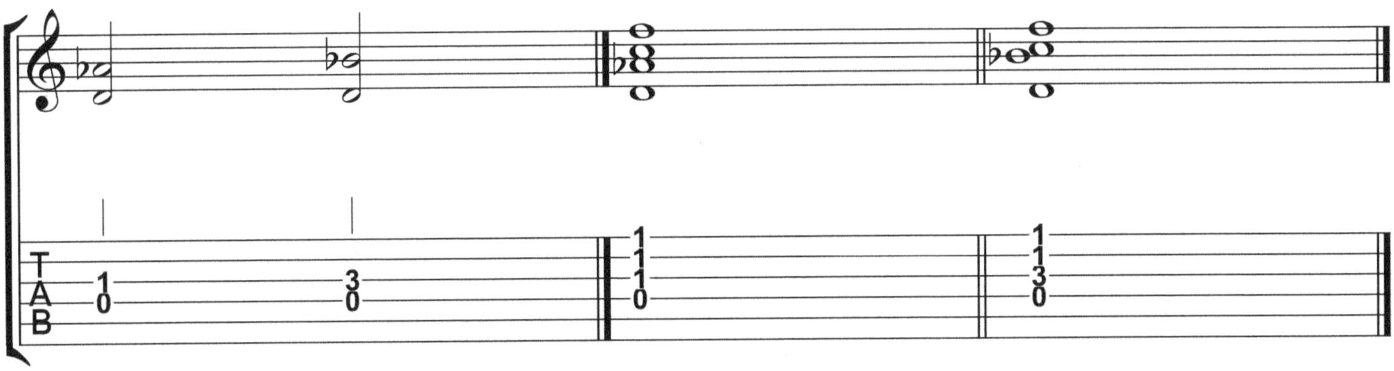

Play D E F G A B C in the upper and bottom voice.
Add A♭ and/or B♭ into the middle voice.

Your turn

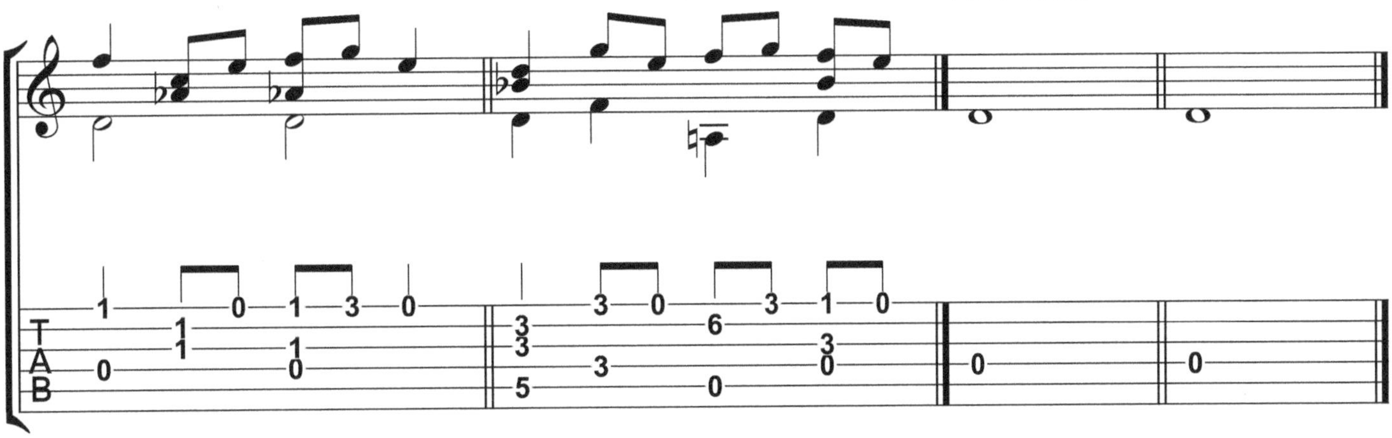

on Em7

♭5 ♯5

Em7♭5: E G B♭ D

Em7♯5: E G C D

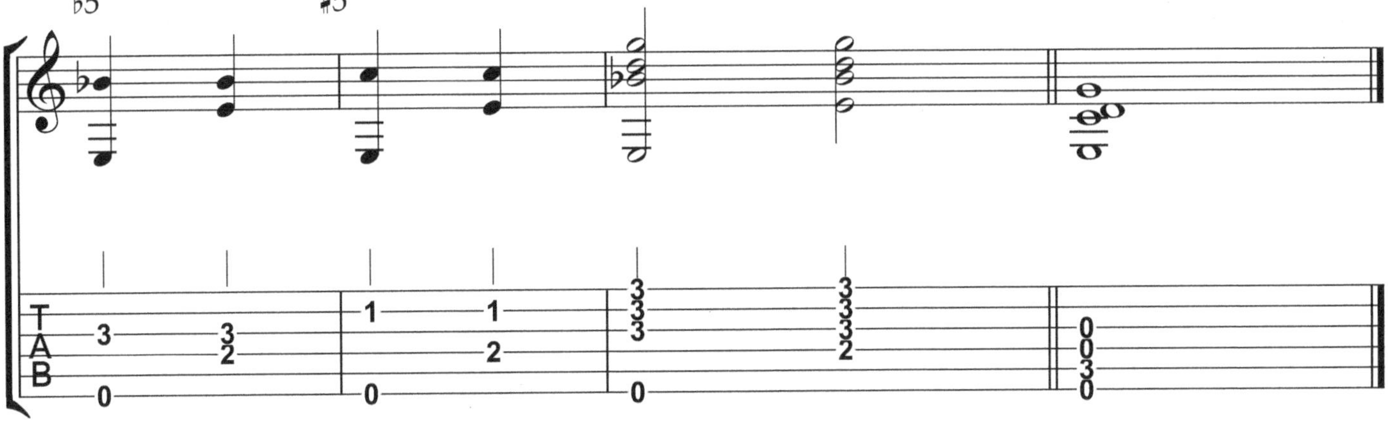

Play E F G A B C D E in the upper and bottom voice.
Add B♭ and/or C into the middle voice.

Your turn

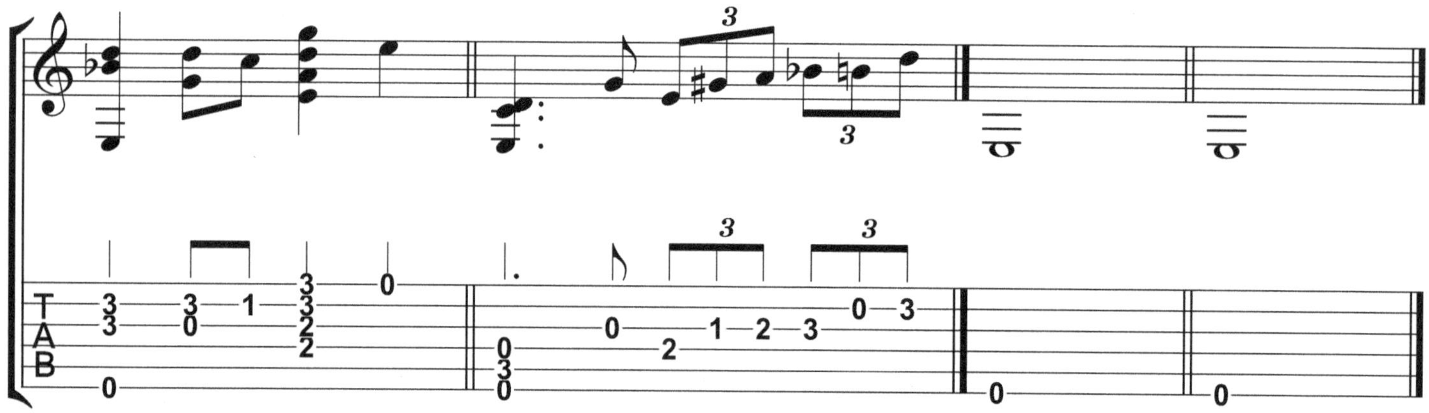

on FM7

♭5 ♯5

FM7♭5:
F A B E

FM7♯5:
F A C♯ E

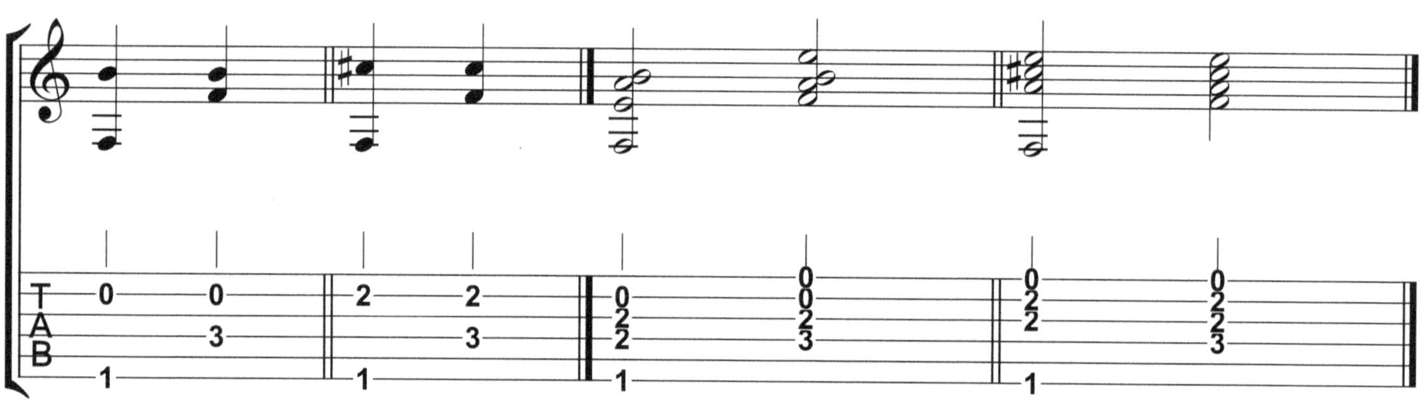

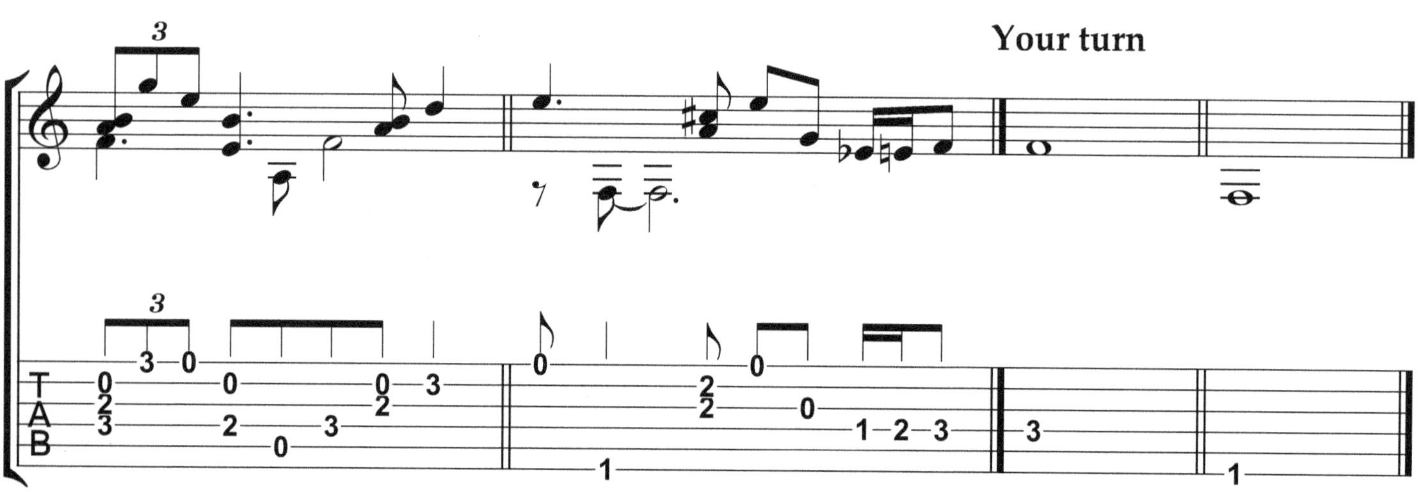

on G7

♭5 ♯5 G7♭5: G B D♭ F G7♯5: G B D♯ F

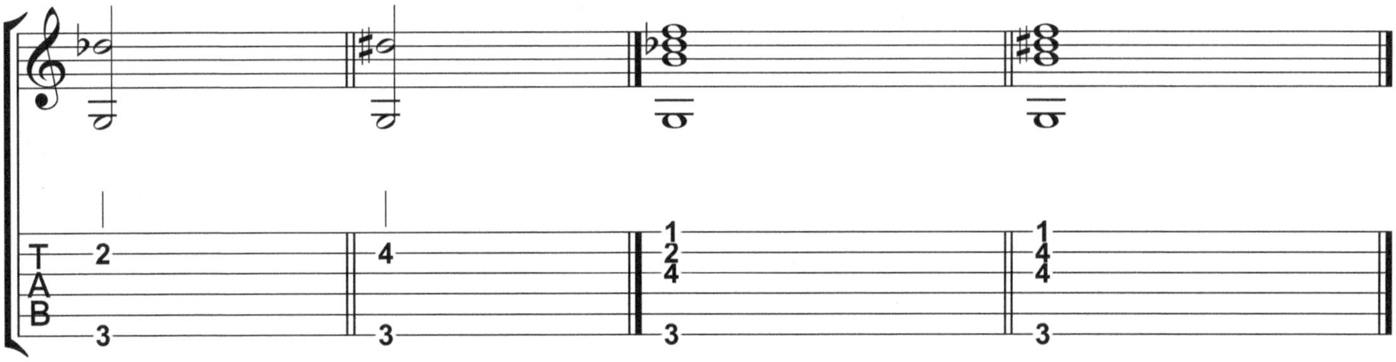

Play G A B C D E F G in the upper and bottom voice.
Add D♭ and/or D♯ into the middle voice.

Your turn

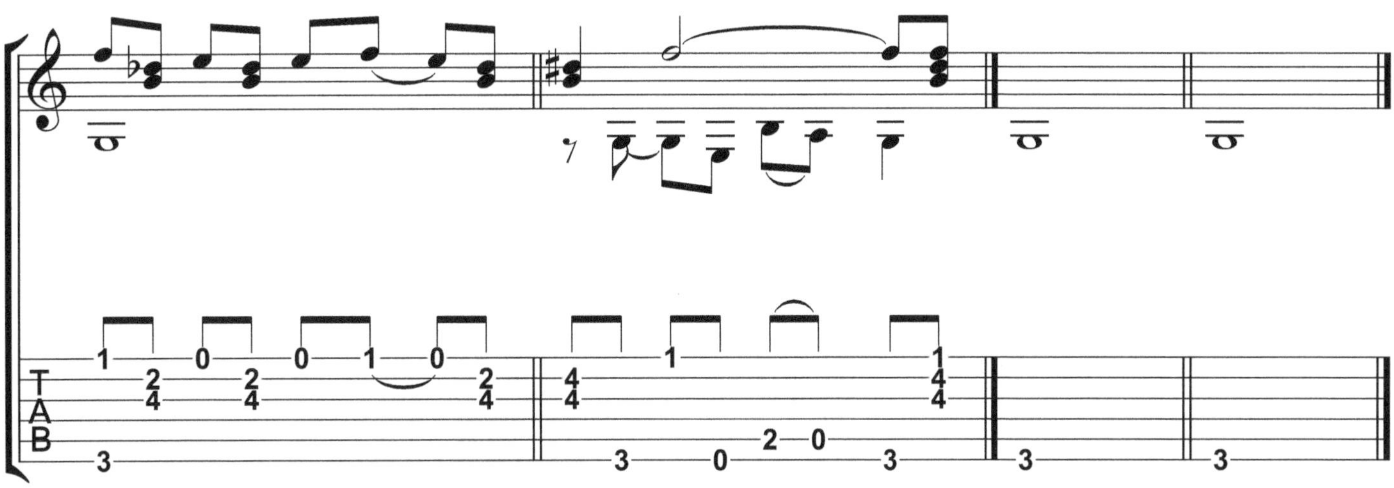

on Am7

♭5 ♯5 Am7♭5: A C E♭ G Am7♯5: A C F G

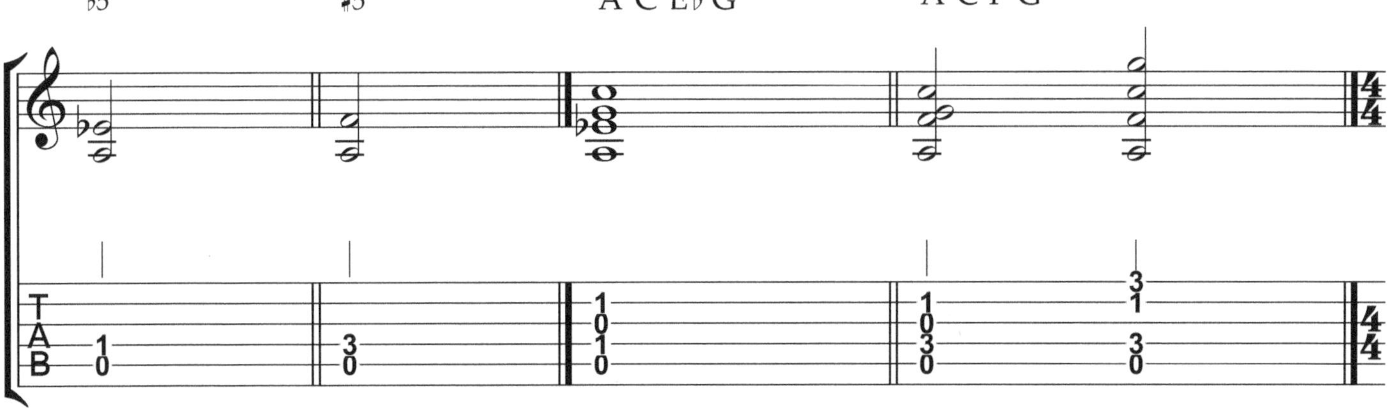

Play A B C D E F G A in the upper and bottom voice.
Add E♭ and/or F into the middle voice.

Your turn

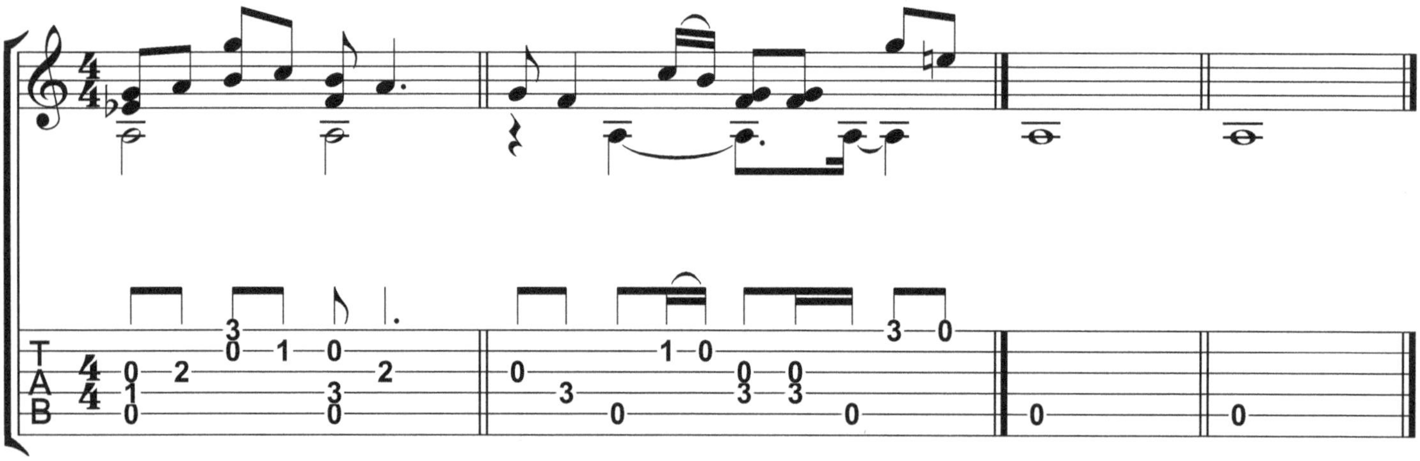

on Bm7♭5

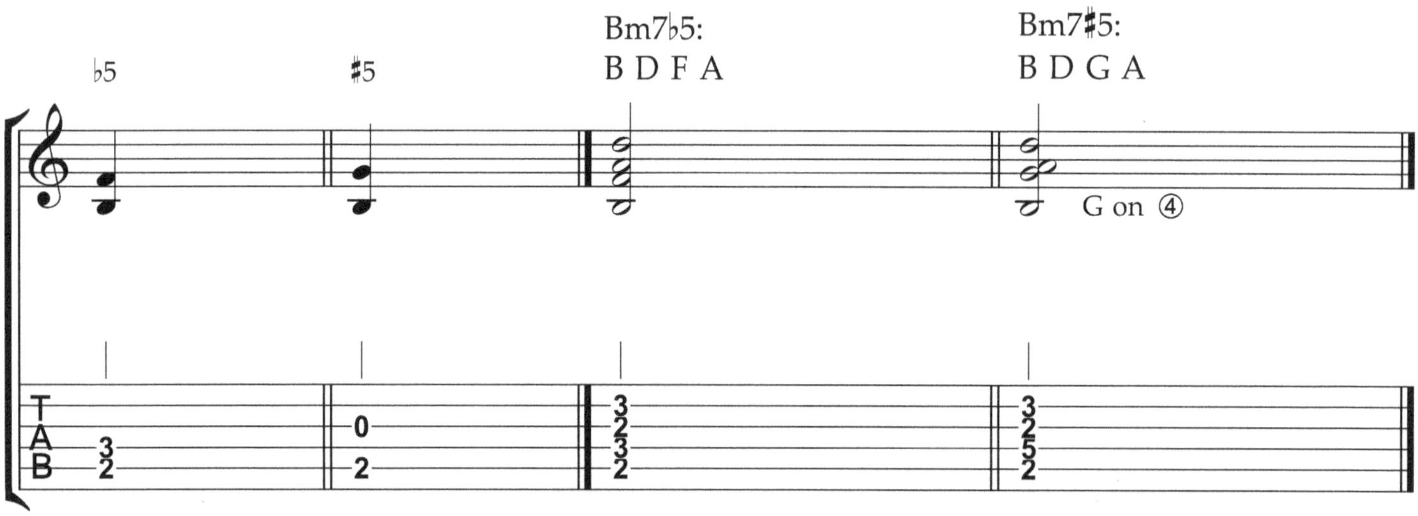

Here the ♭5 is already part of the chord.
Play B C D E F G A B in the upper and bottom voice.
Add F and/or G into the middle voice.

Your turn

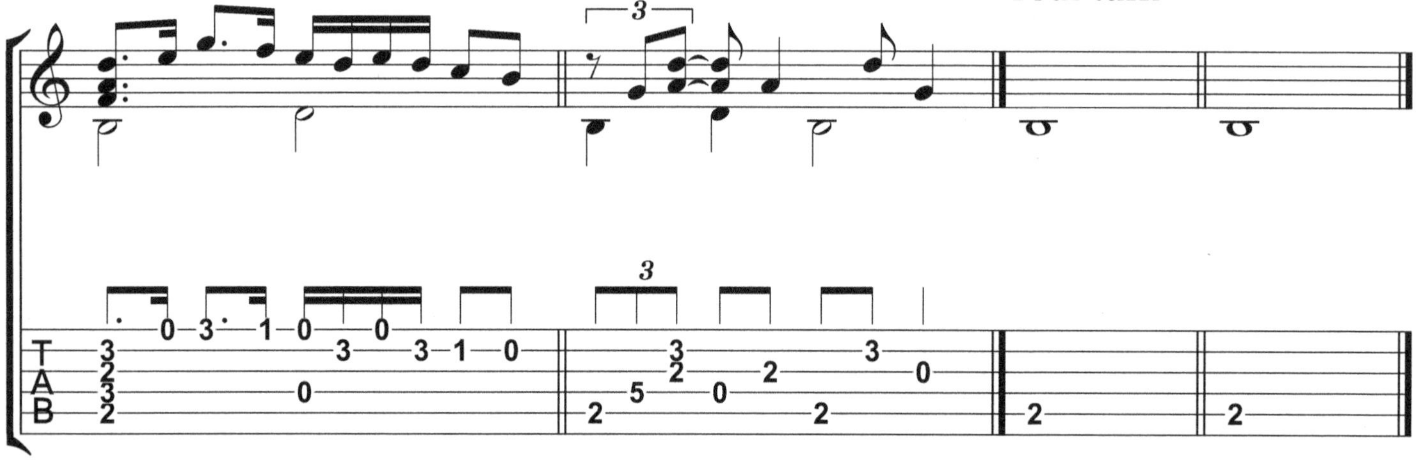

On a chord progression

Track 36

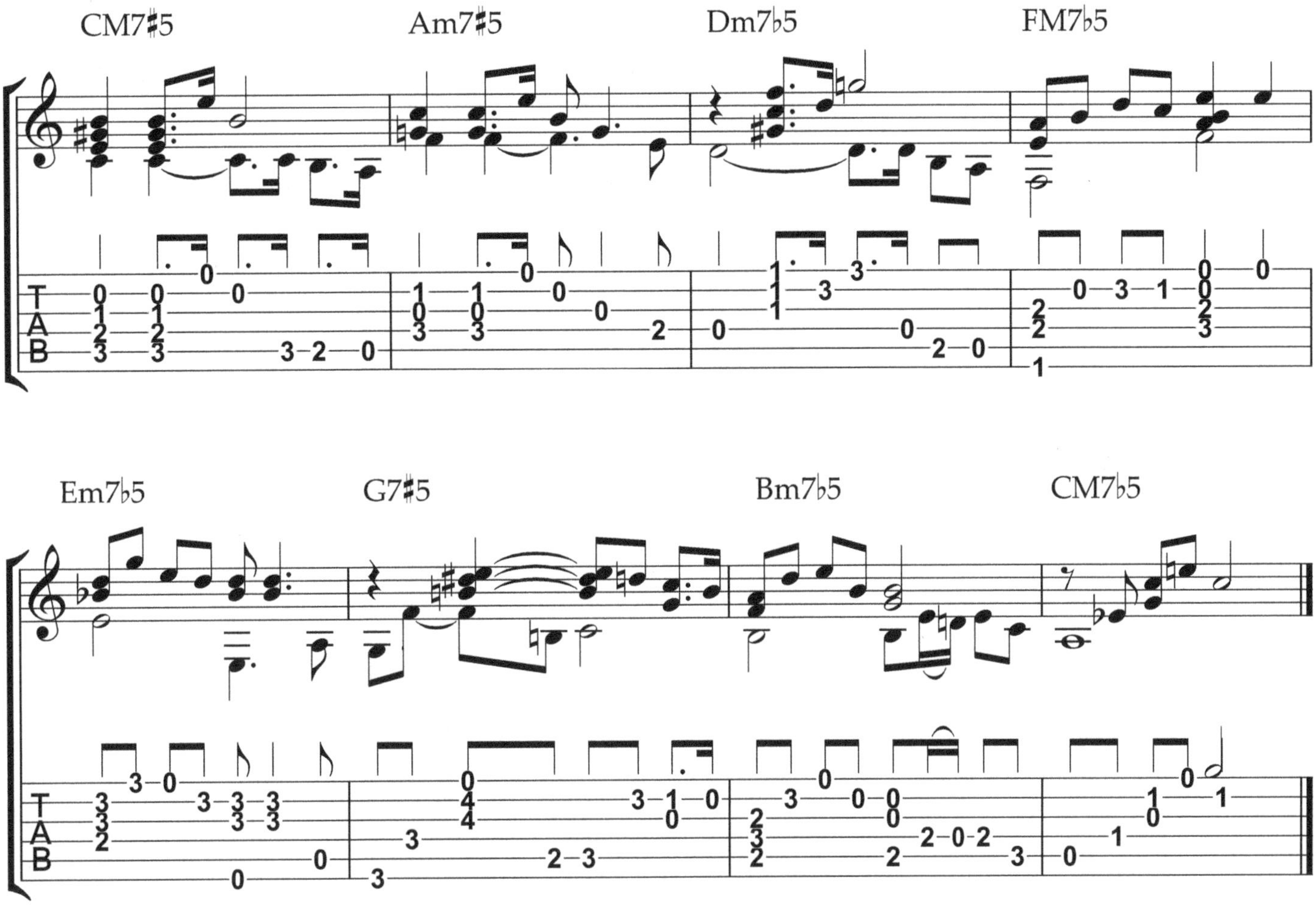

Your turn

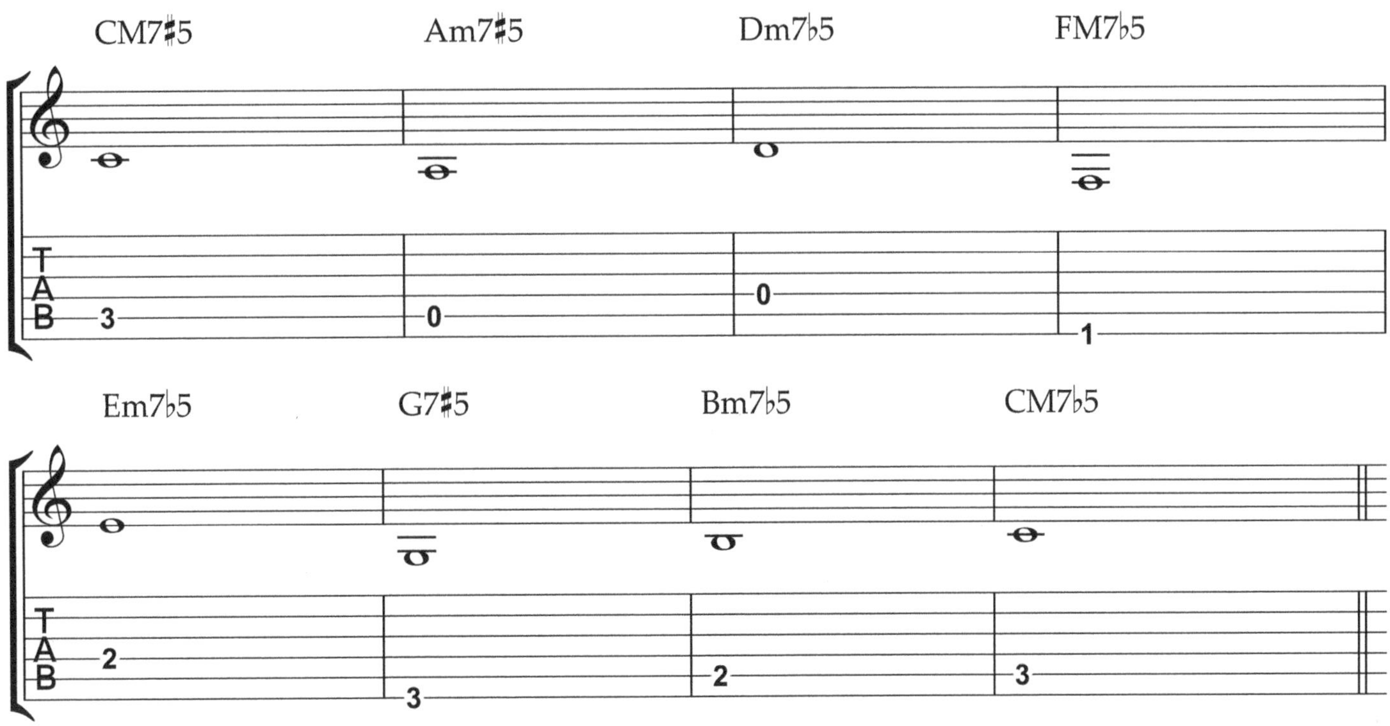

CHAPTER 17

Modern Sounds (Part 2): Adding an M7 to Minor Chords in the Middle Voice

By adding a M7 to a minor chord, you create an mM7 chord
Just raise the ♭7th with a half step. For example, C E♭ B♭ becomes C E♭ B

Let's experiment on some Minor Major chords in the C Major Scale (as explained in Chapter 16.)
First is a chord example, then the dyad followed by some examples.

CmM7
C E♭ G B

Some direct substitutions

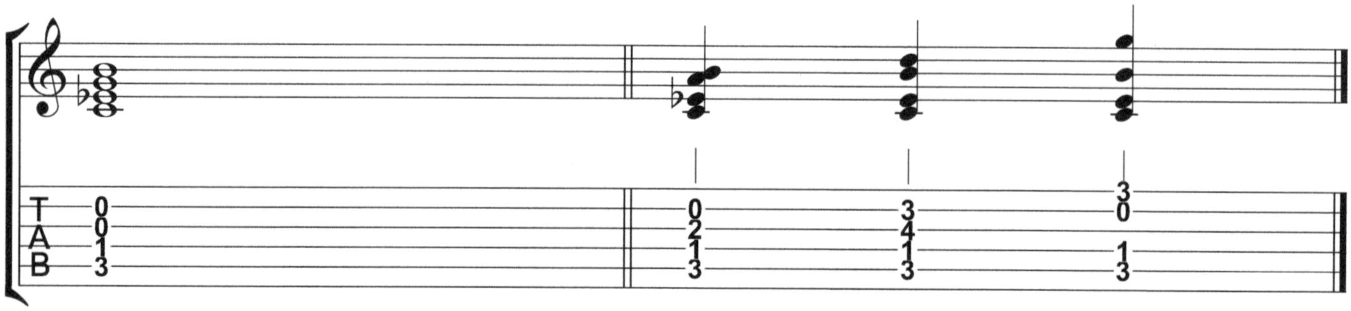

DmM7
D F A C♯

A direct substitution

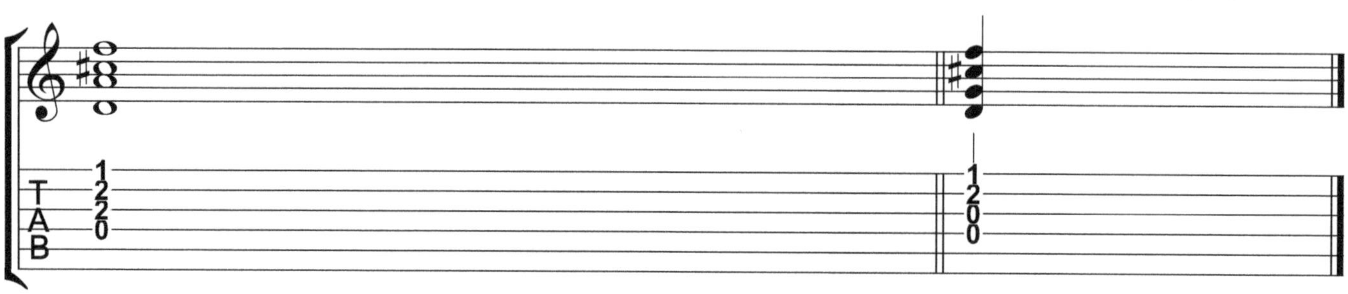

EmM7
E G B D♯

Some direct substitutions

Some direct substitutions

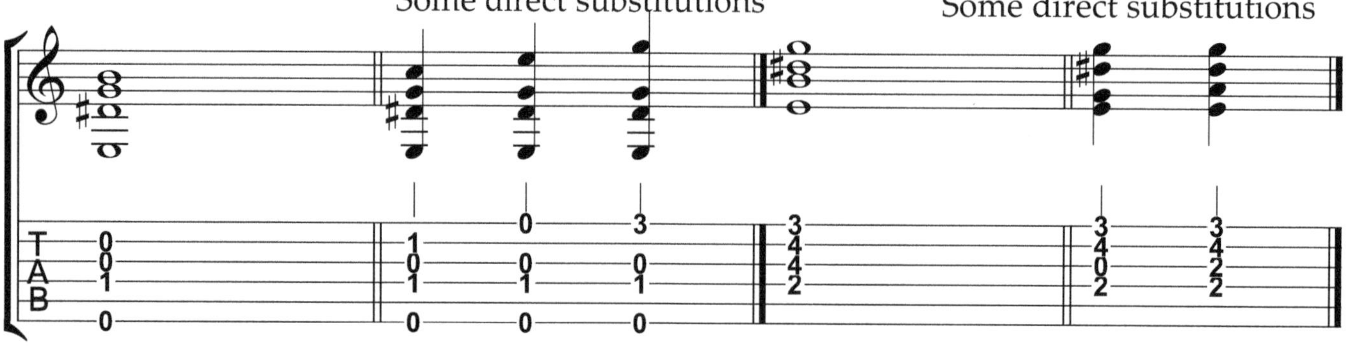

FmM7

F A♭ C E

Some direct substitutions

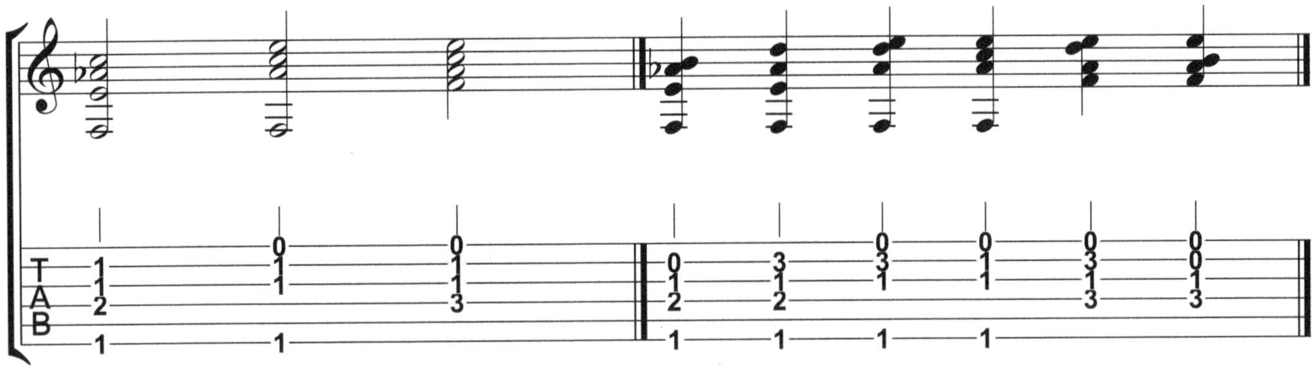

GmM7

G B♭ D F♯

Some direct substitutions

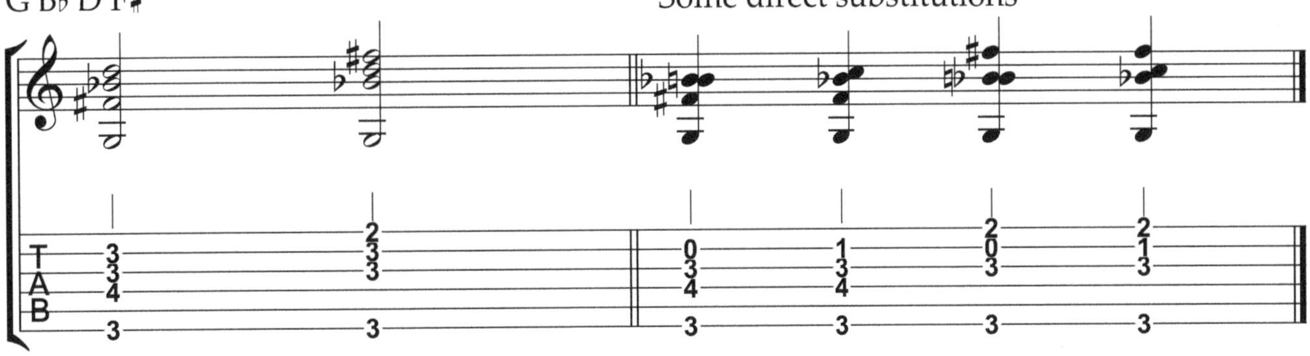

AmM7

A C E G♯

Some direct substitutions

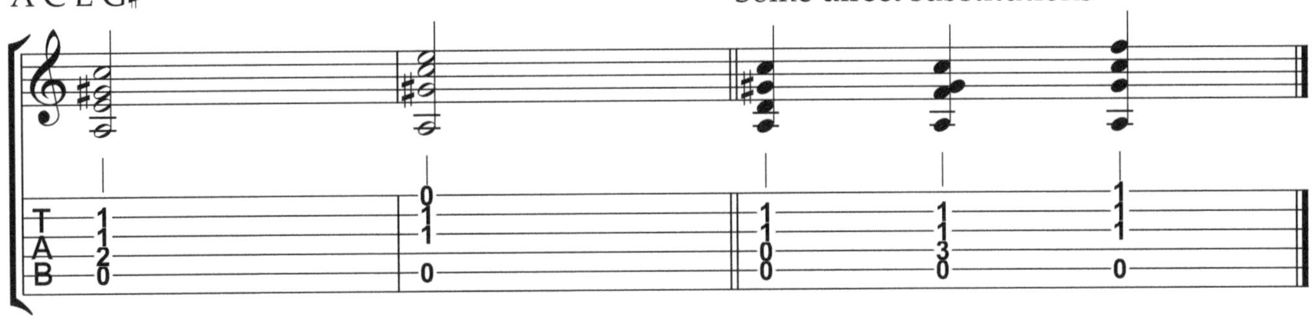

BmM7

B D F♯ A♯

Some direct substitutions

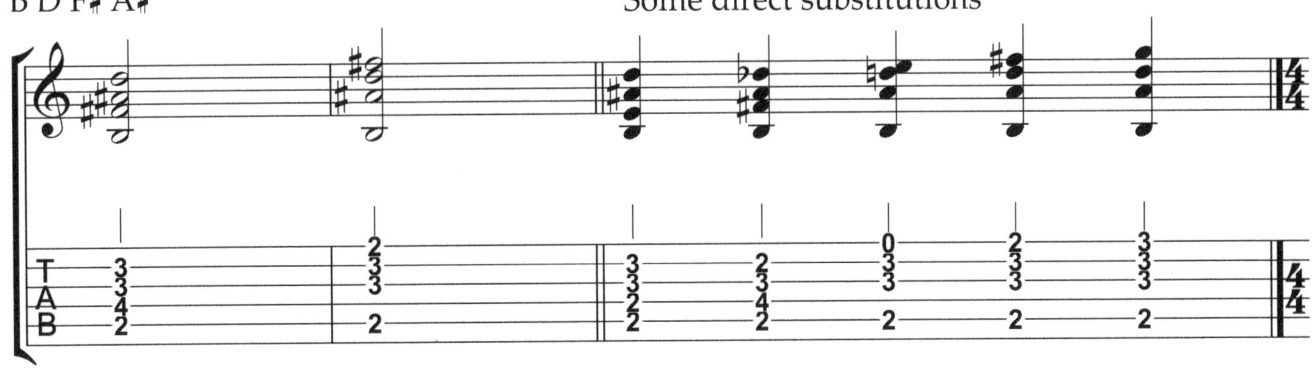

On a chord progression in C Major

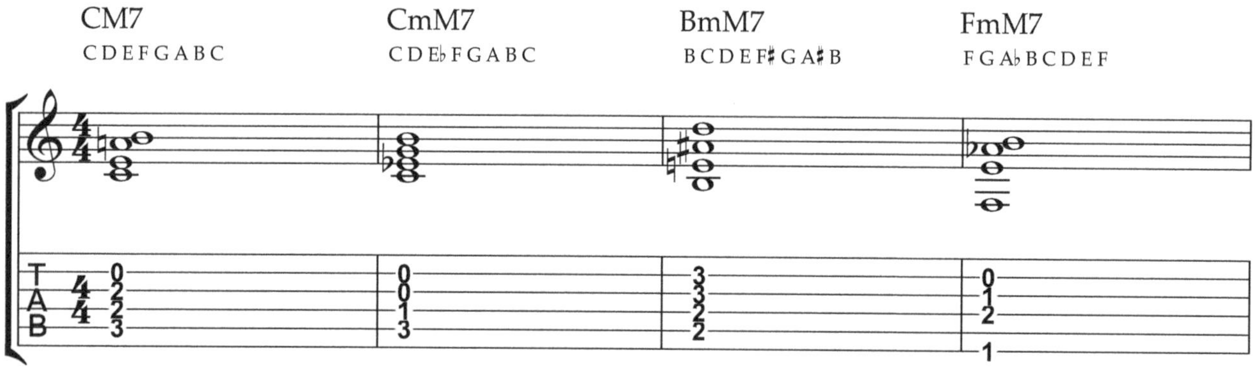

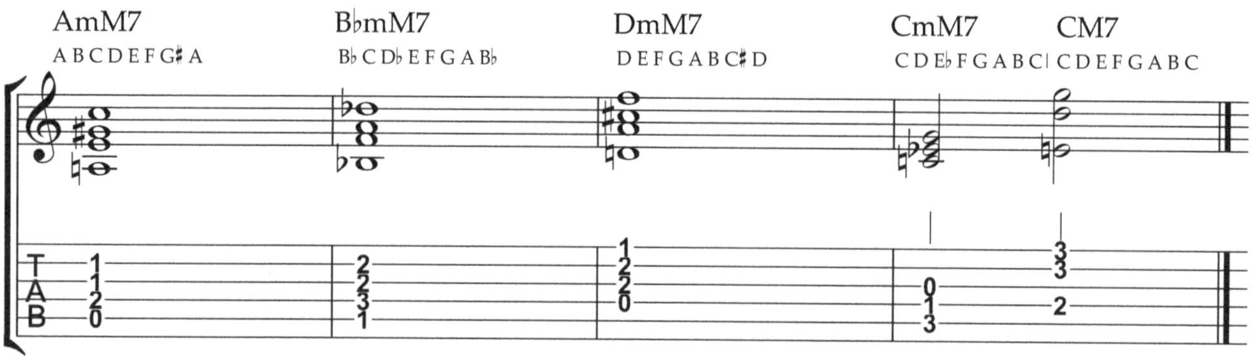

Example

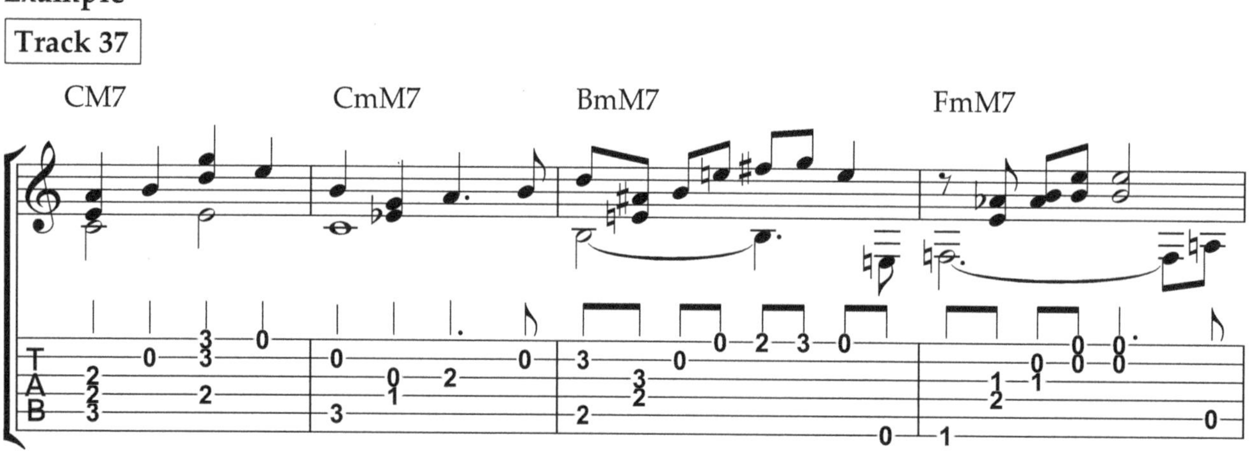

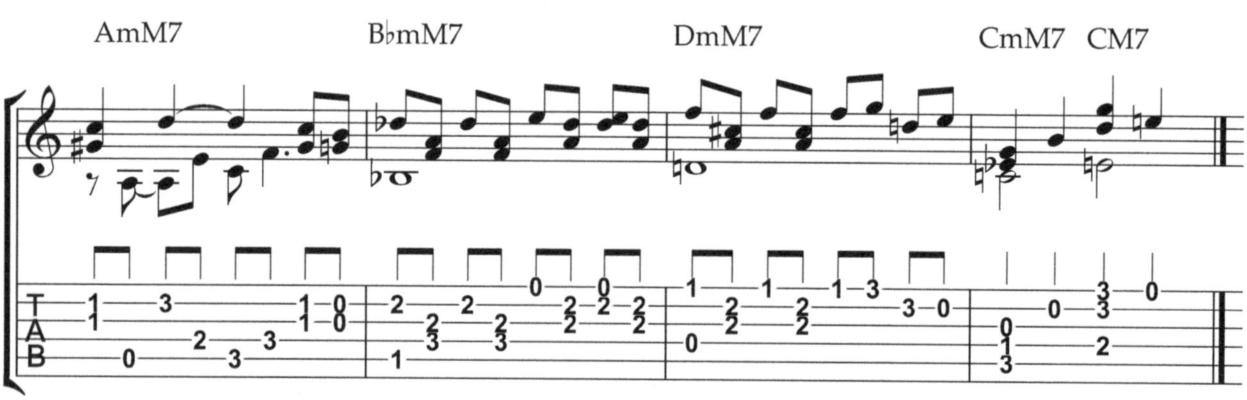

Your turn

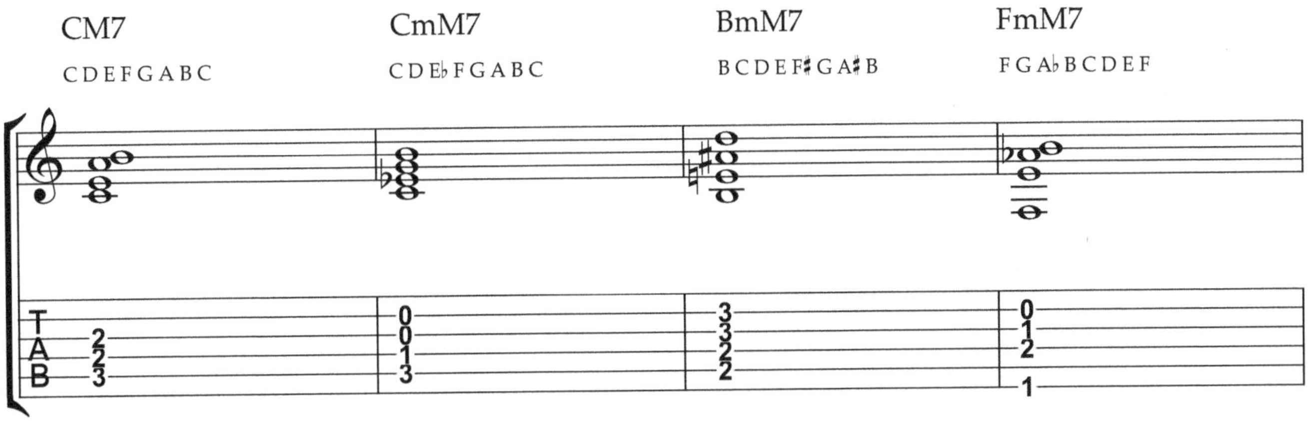

CM7
C D E F G A B C
CmM7
C D E♭ F G A B C
BmM7
B C D E F♯ G A♯ B
FmM7
F G A♭ B C D E F

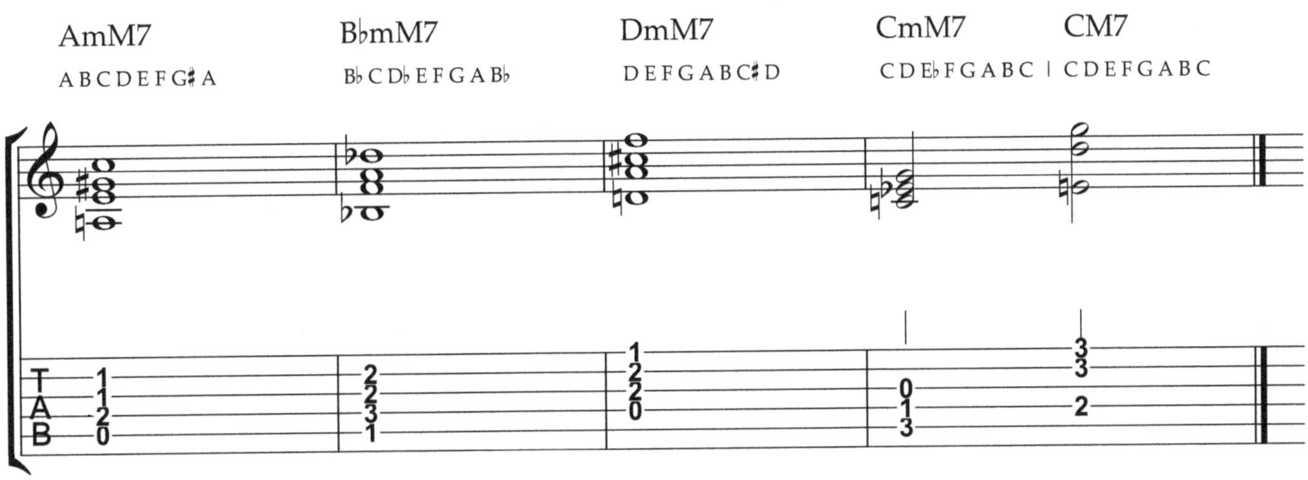

AmM7
A B C D E F G♯ A
B♭mM7
B♭ C D♭ E F G A B♭
DmM7
D E F G A B C♯ D
CmM7
C D E♭ F G A B C
CM7
C D E F G A B C

CHAPTER 18

Modern Sounds (Part 3): Adding Major and Minor Seconds in the Middle Voice

Major and minor seconds can be added to create intriguing contemporary sounds.
Possibilities in the first position

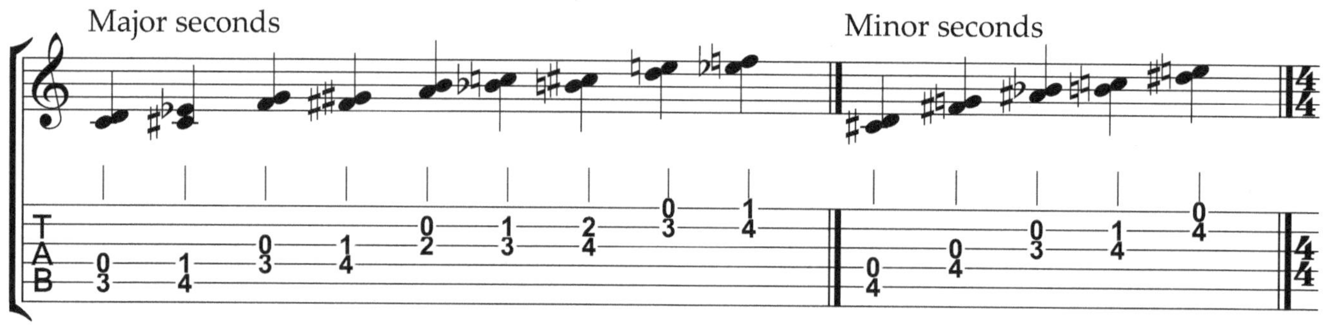

CM7

Your turn

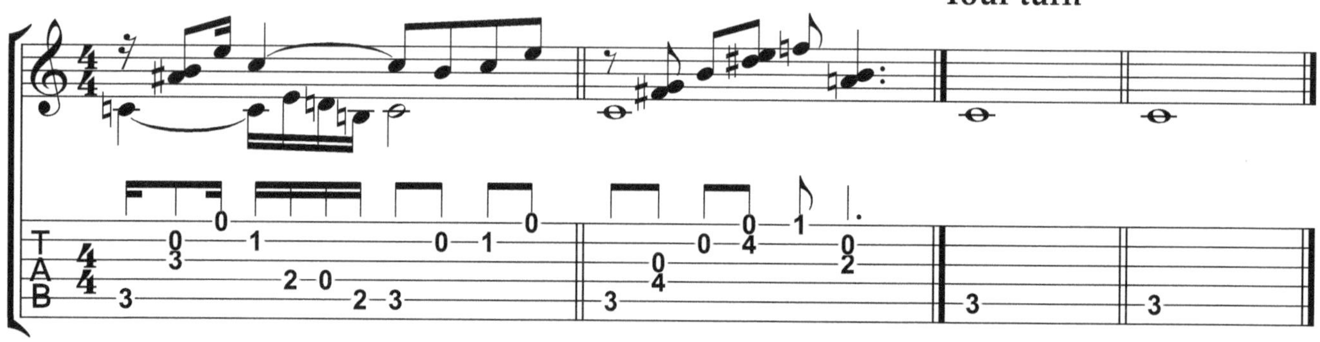

Dm7

Your turn

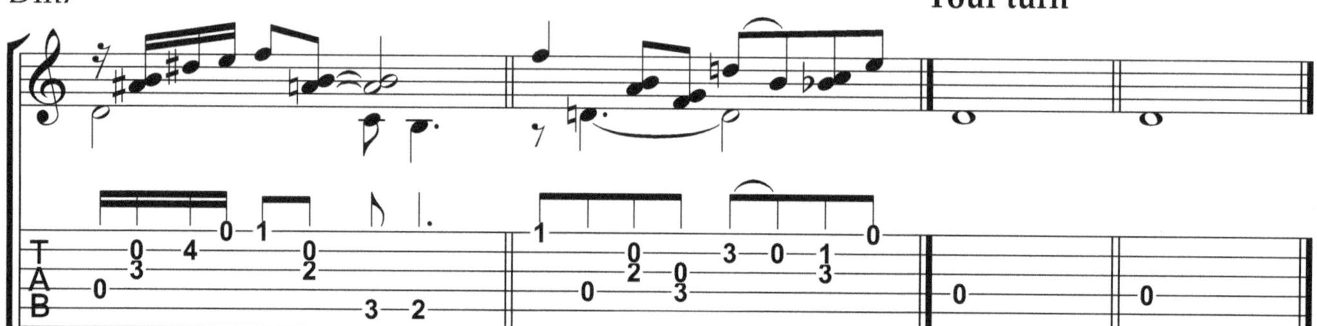

Em7

Your turn

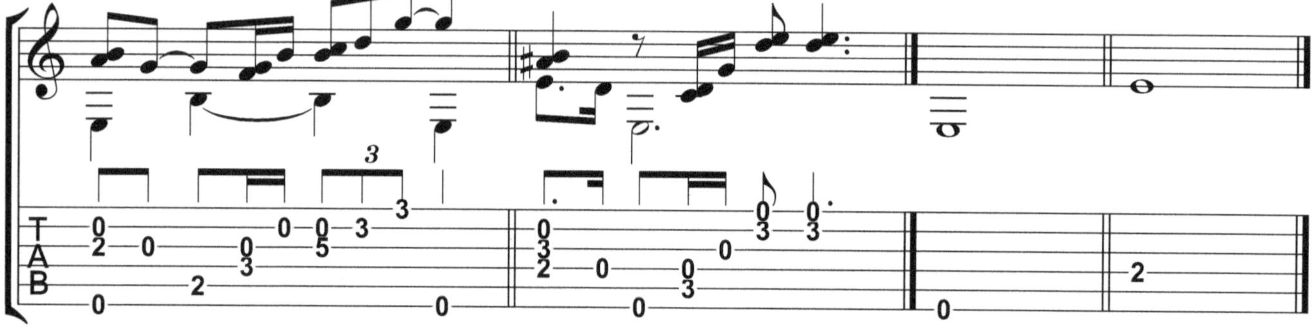

FM7

Your turn

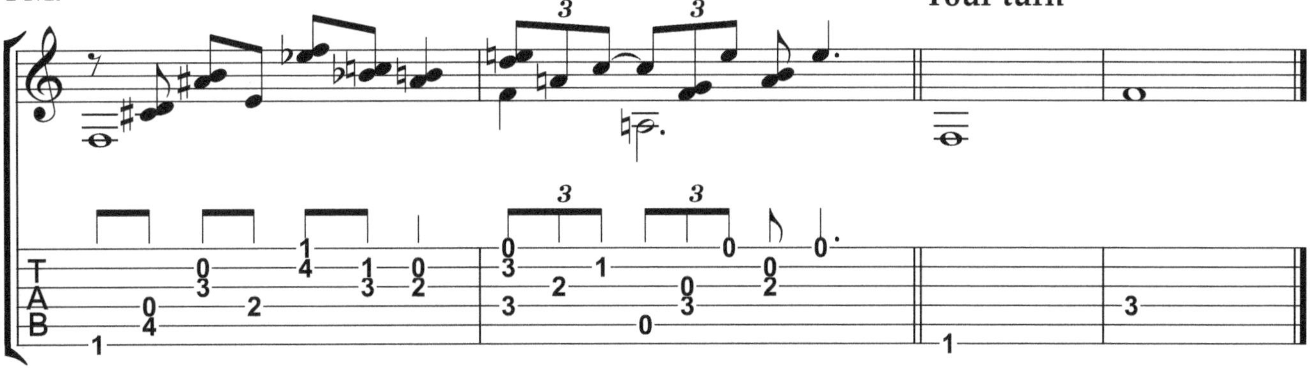

G7

Your turn

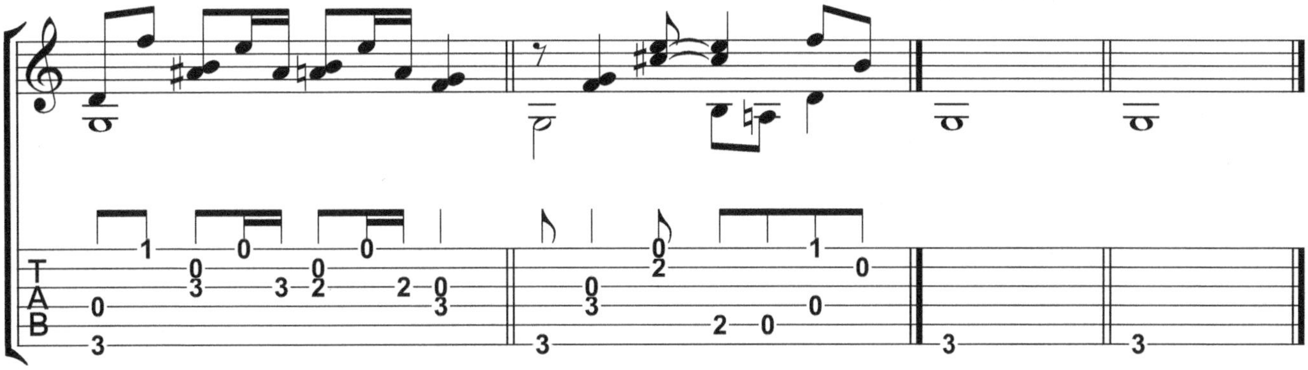

Am7

Your turn

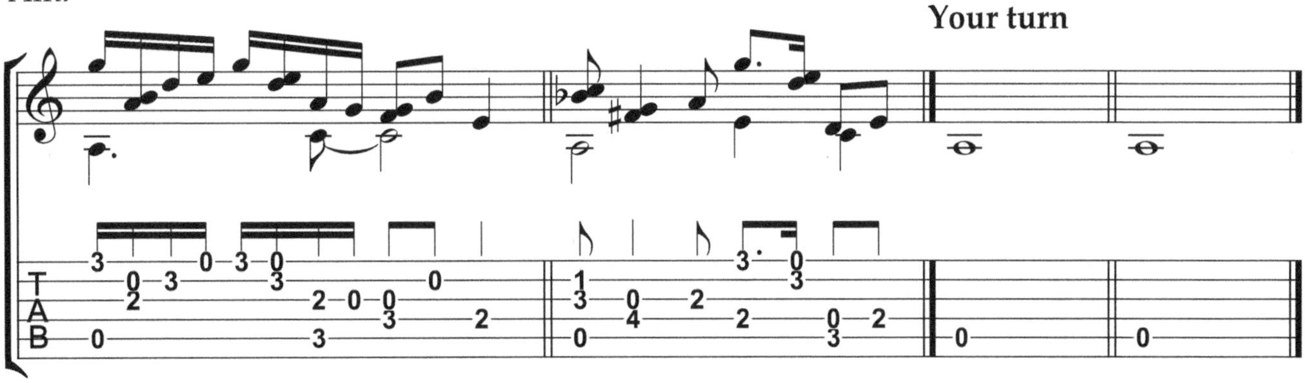

Bm7♭5

Your turn

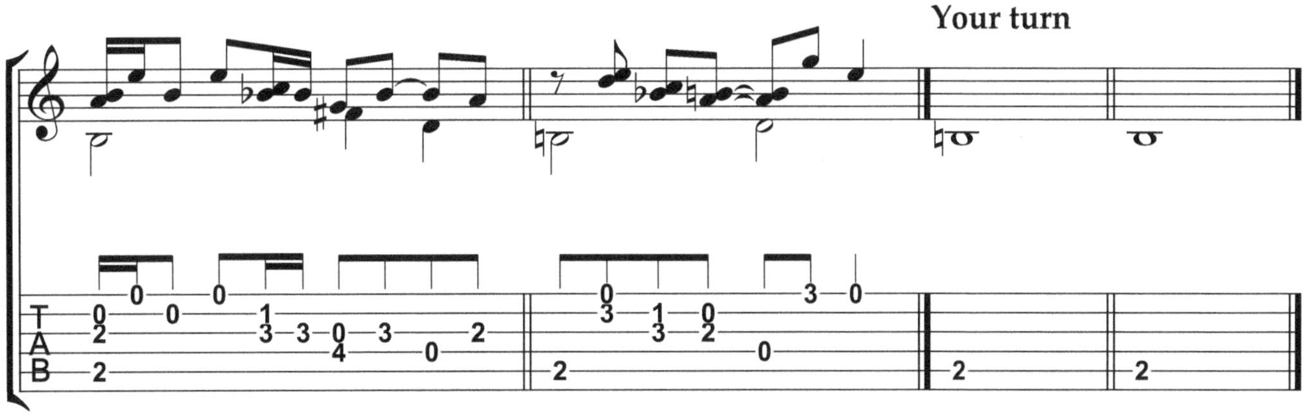

On a chord progression in 3/4!!

Track 38

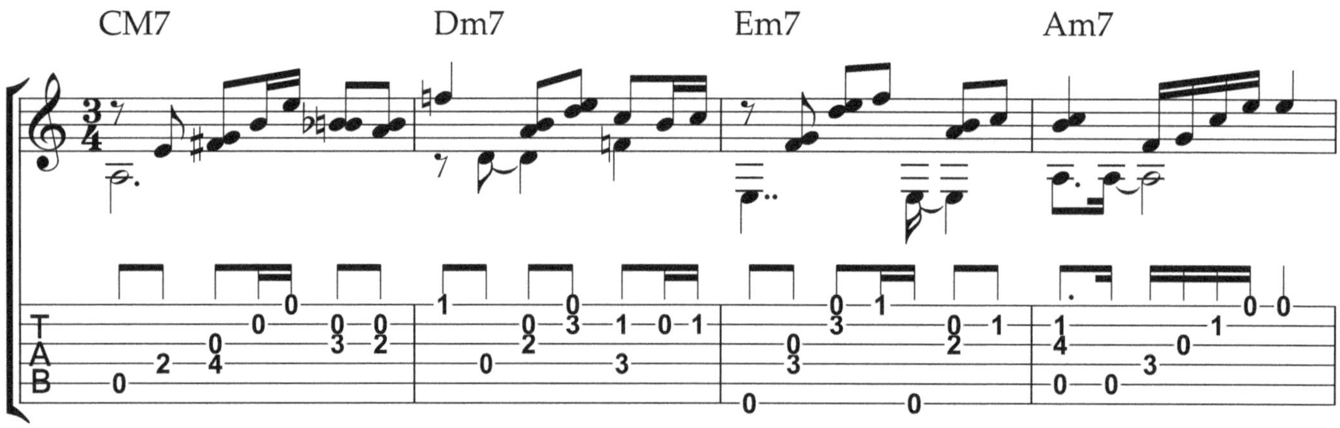

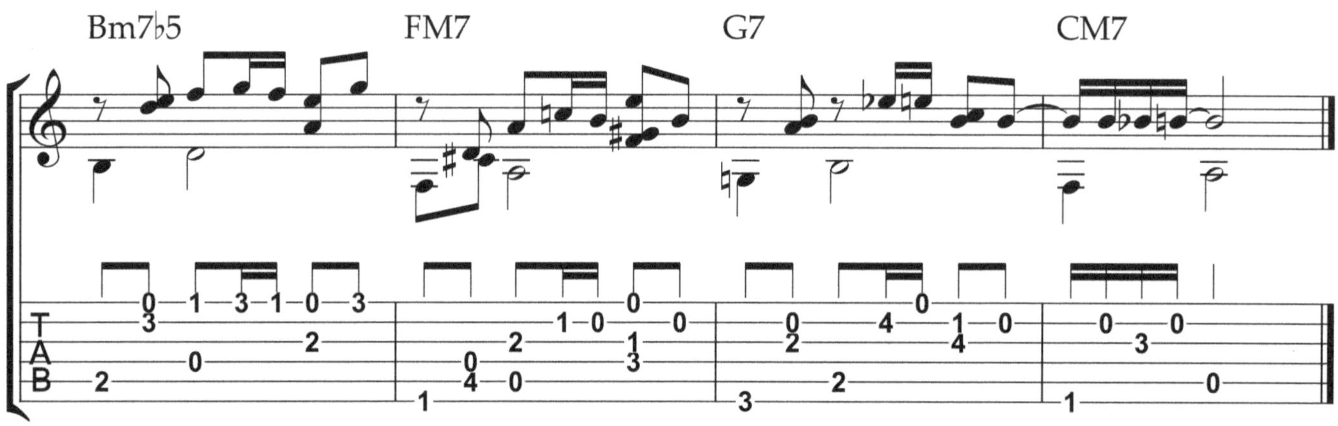

Your turn

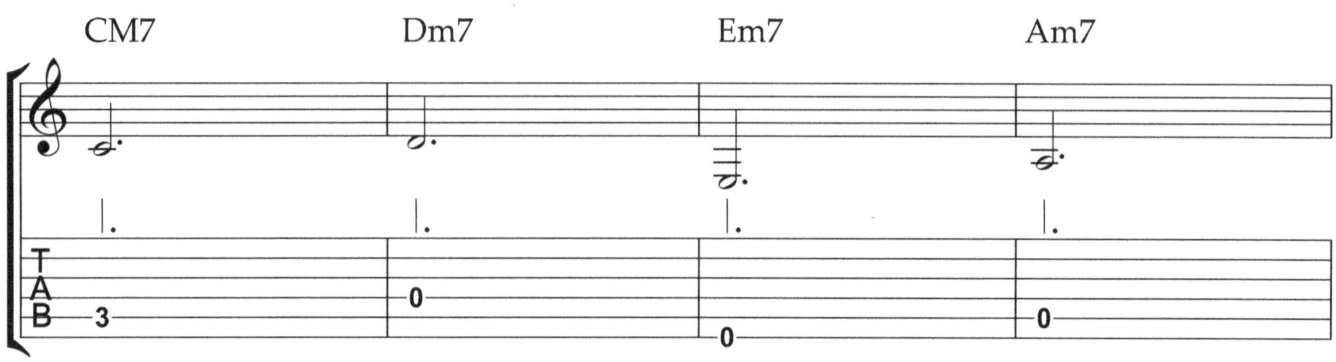

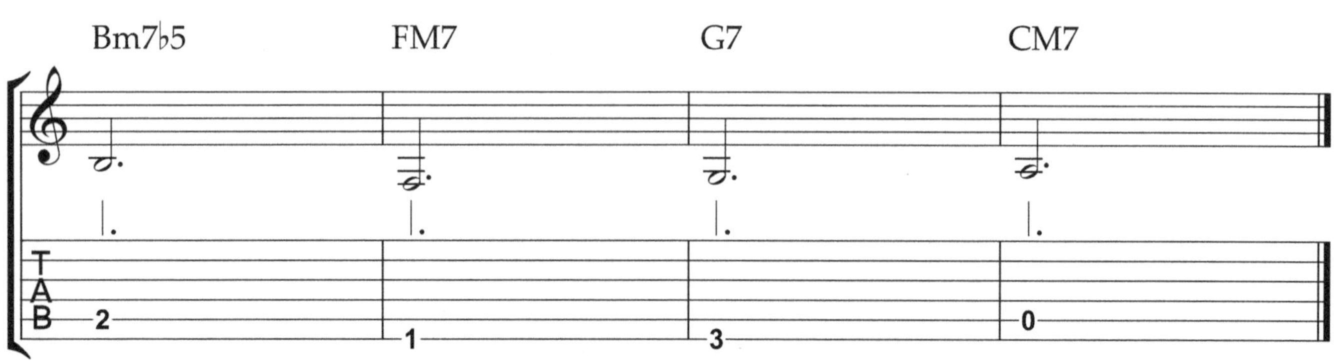

CHAPTER 19

Modern Sounds (Part 4): Sus2 and Sus4 Chords

In a sus2 chord the major or major 3rd is replaced by a 2nd.
In sus4 chords, the major or minor 3rd is replaced with a 4th.
The lack of a minor or major third creates an open, refreshing sound.

Sus2 = 1, 2, 5 or just 1, 2
Sus4 = 1, 4, 5 or just 1, 4

Some examples:

For C

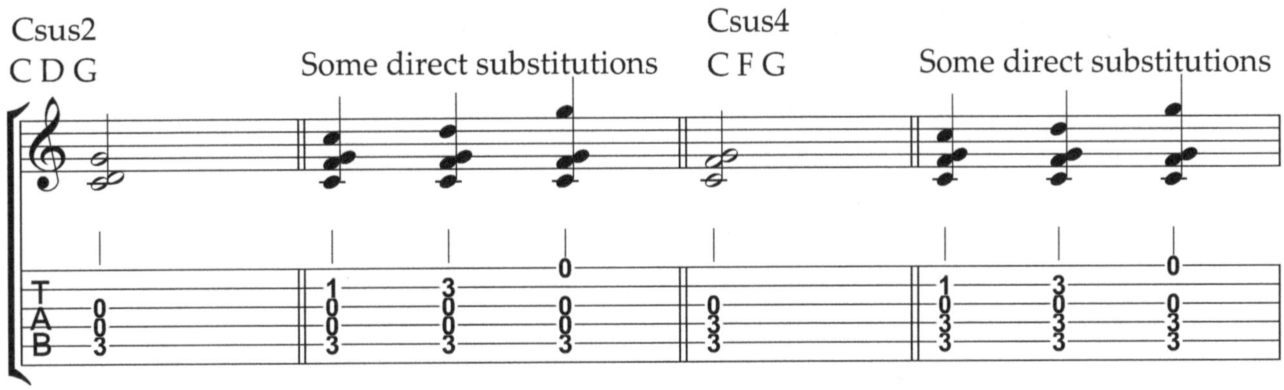

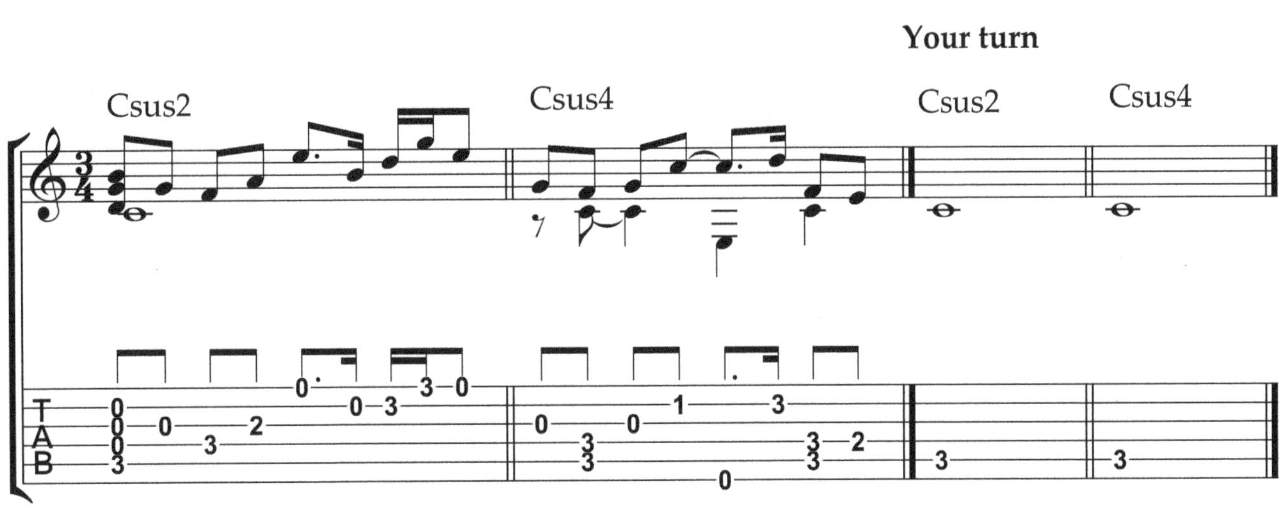

for Dm

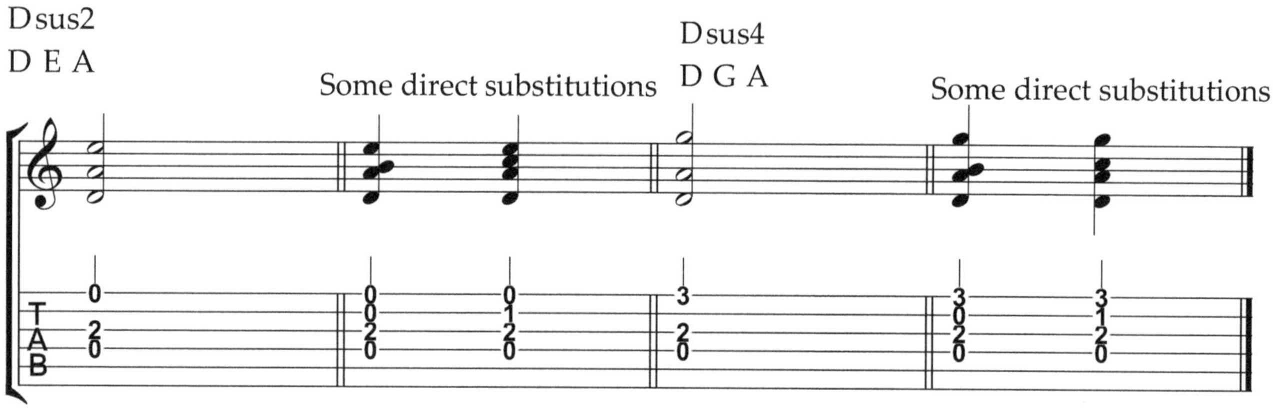
Dsus2
D E A
Some direct substitutions
Dsus4
D G A
Some direct substitutions

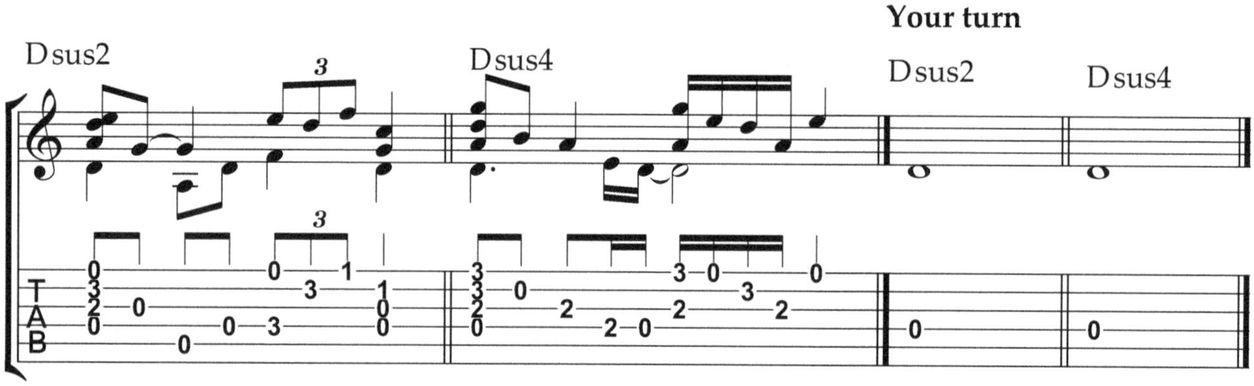
Dsus2
Dsus4
Your turn
Dsus2
Dsus4

for Em

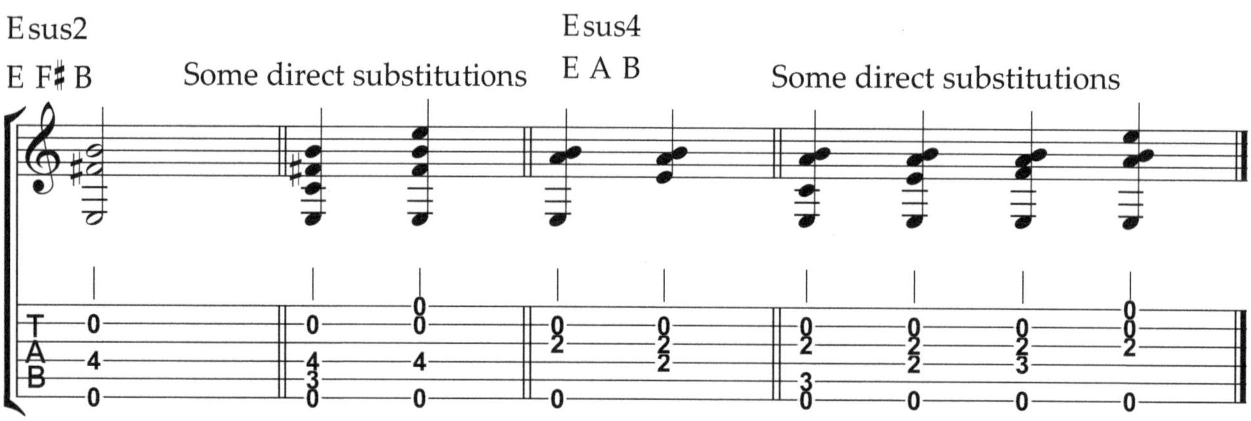
Esus2
E F♯ B
Some direct substitutions
Esus4
E A B
Some direct substitutions

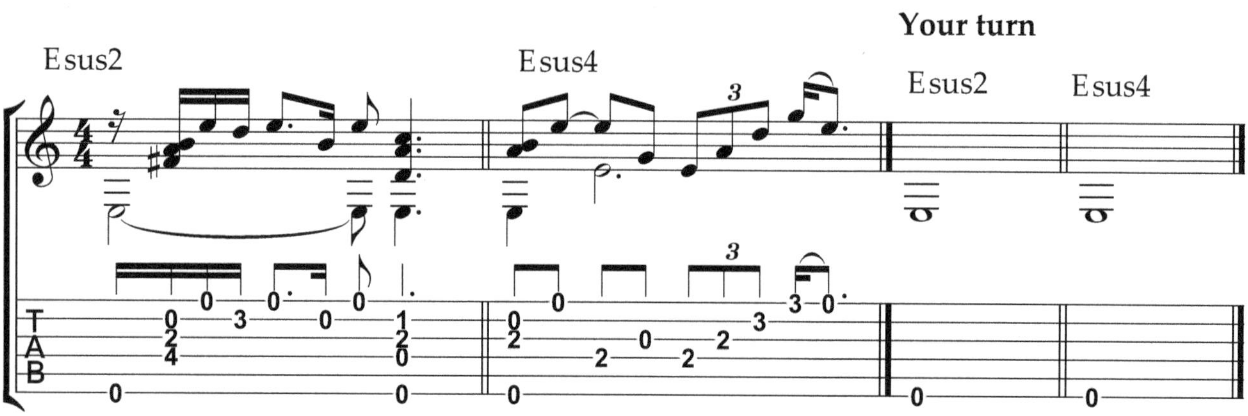
Esus2
Esus4
Your turn
Esus2
Esus4

for F

Fsus2
F G C

Some direct substitutions

Fsus4
F B♭ C

Some direct substitutions

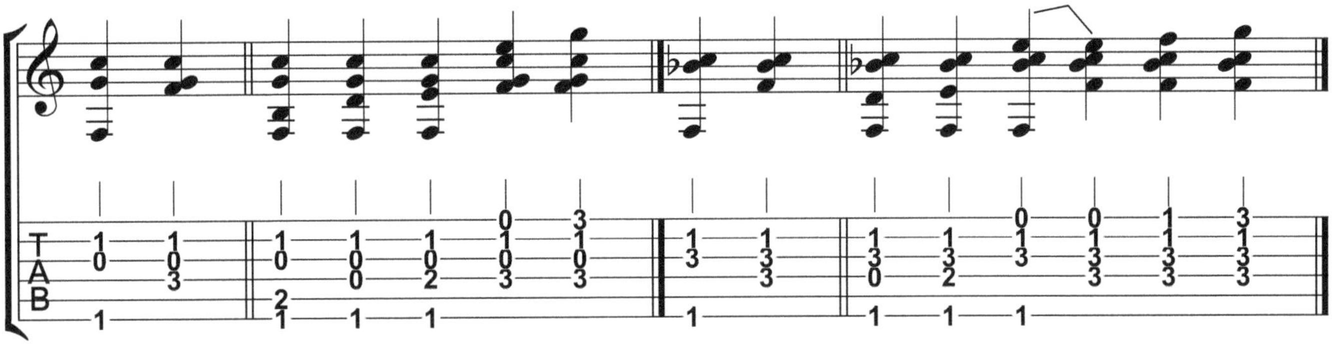

Fsus2 Fsus4

Your turn

Fsus2 Fsus4

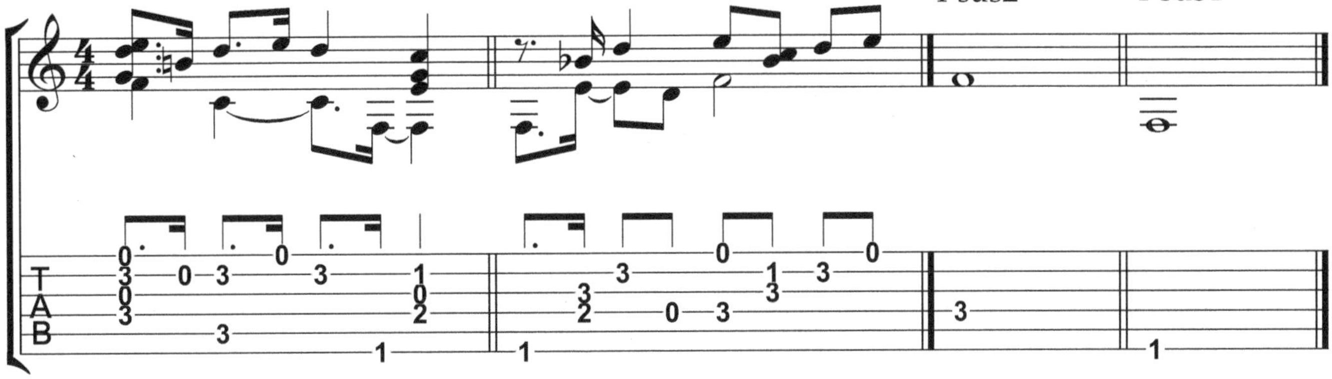

for G

Gsus2
G A D

Some direct substitutions

Gsus4
G C D

Some direct substitutions

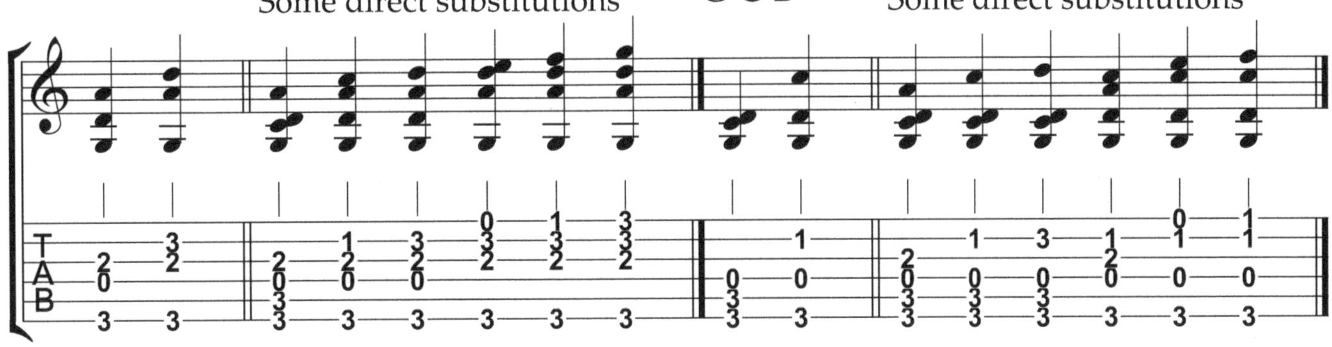

Gsus2 Gsus4

Your turn

Gsus2 Gsus4

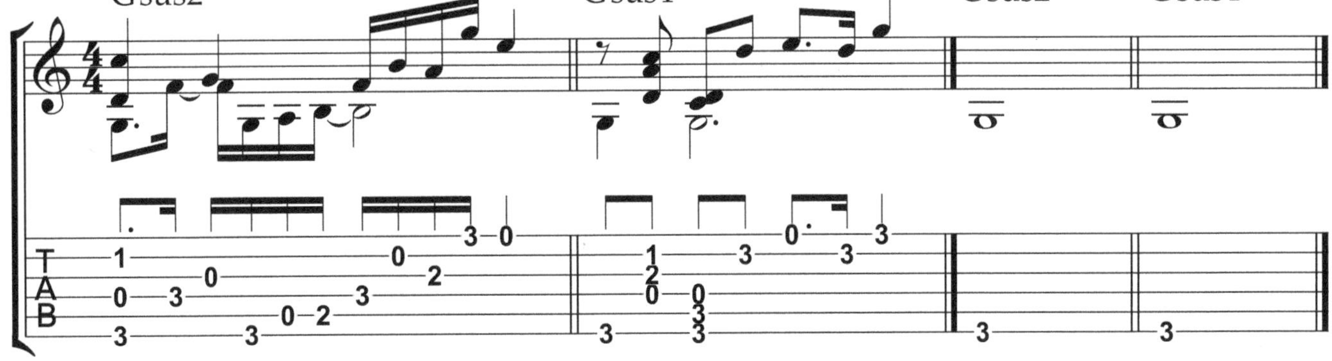

for Am

Asus2
A B E

Some direct substitutions

Asus4
A D E

Some direct substitutions

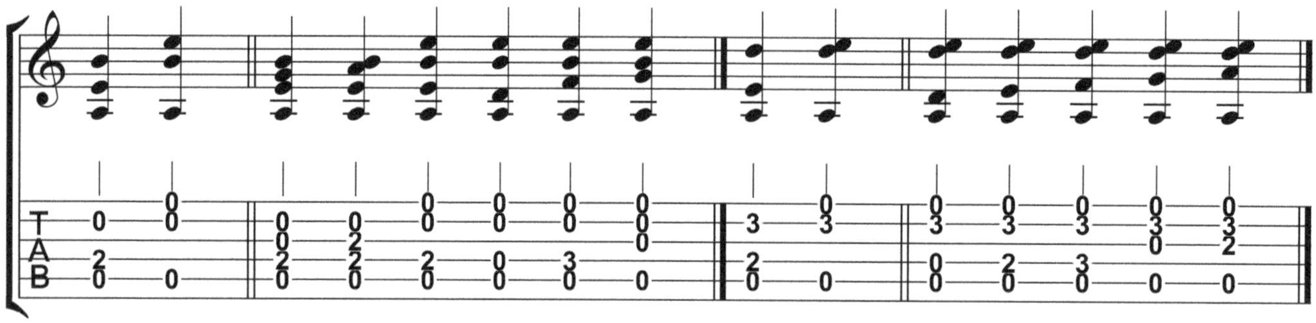

Asus2 Asus4

Your turn

Asus2 Asus4

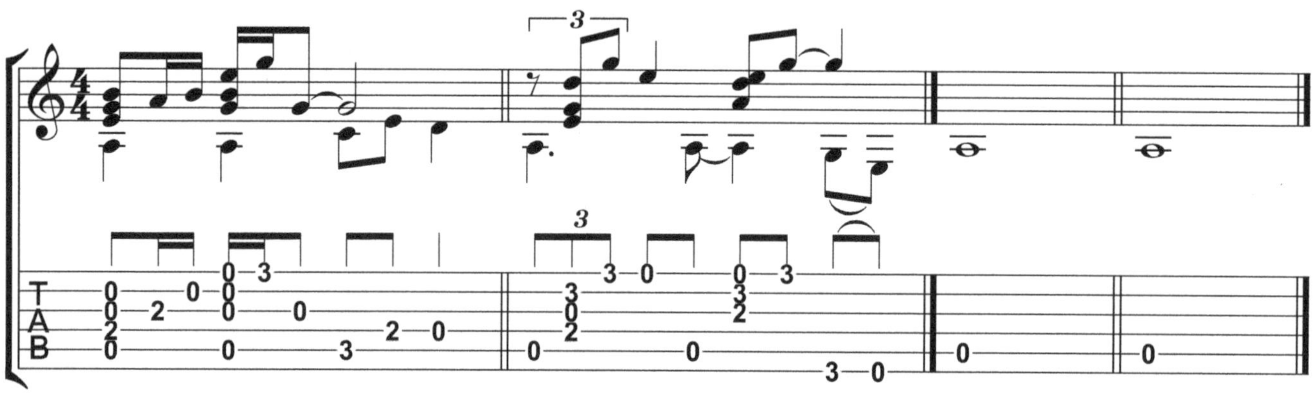

for Bm

Bsus2
B C♯ F♯

Some direct substitutions

Bsus4
B E F♯

Some direct substitutions

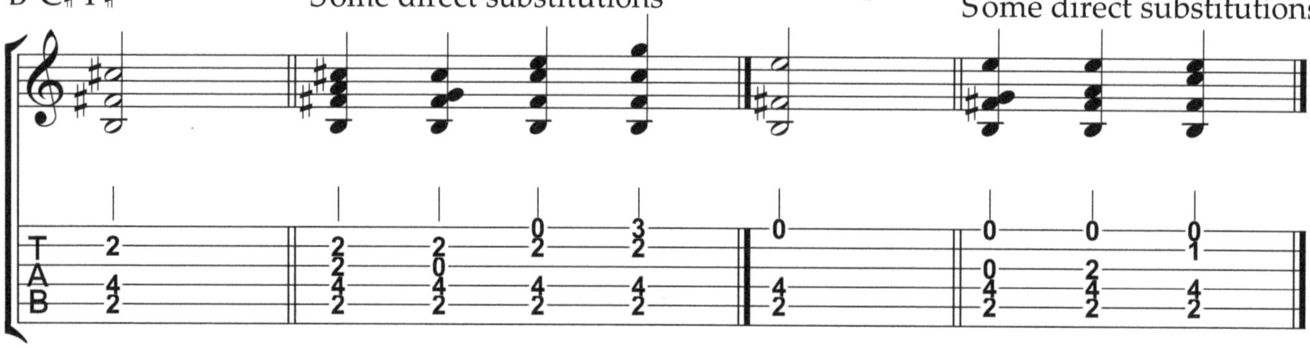

Bsus2 Bsus4

Your turn

Bsus2 Bsus4

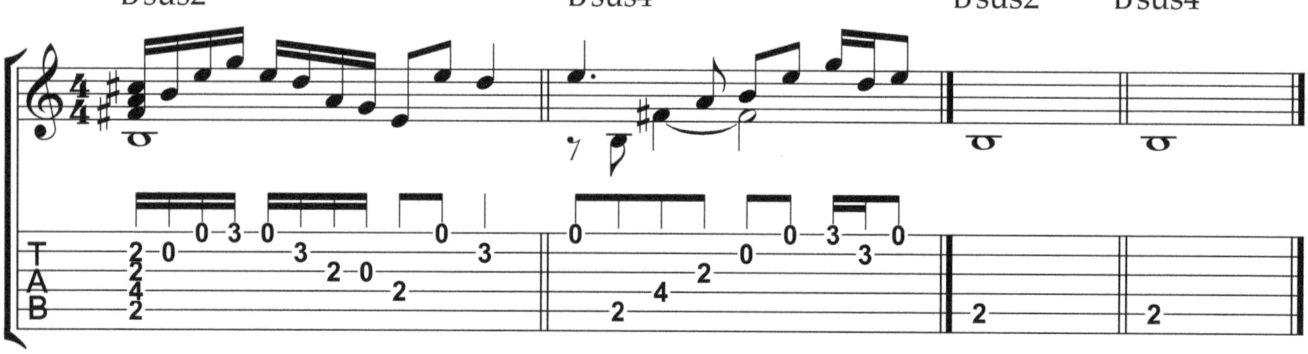

On a chord progression in 2/4

Track 39

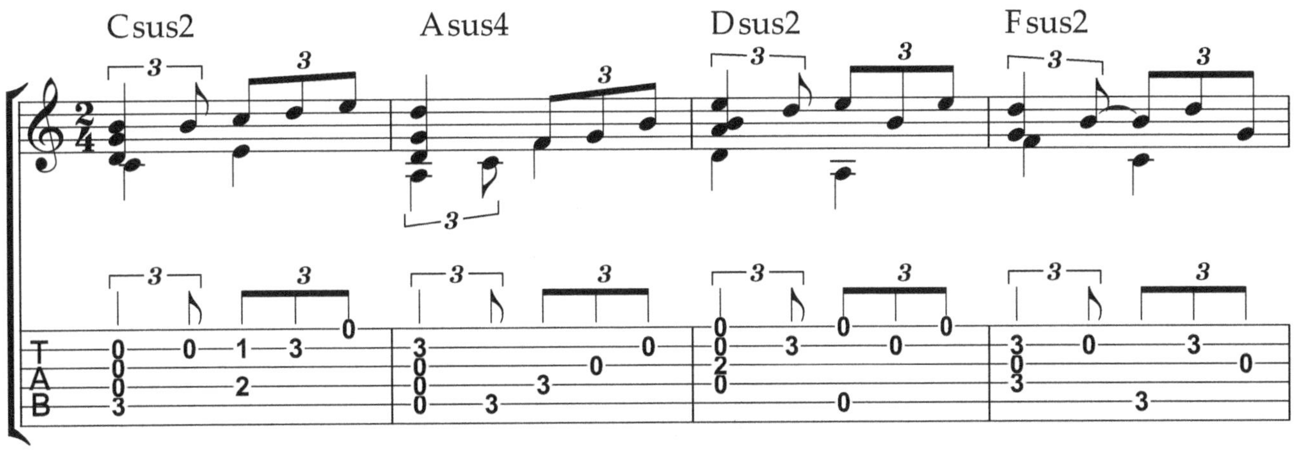

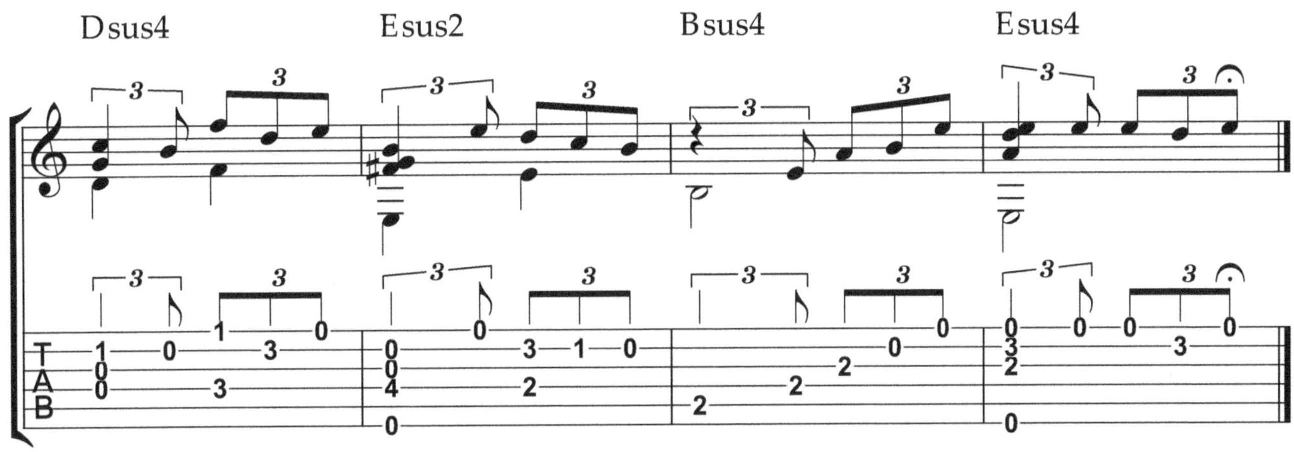

Your Turn

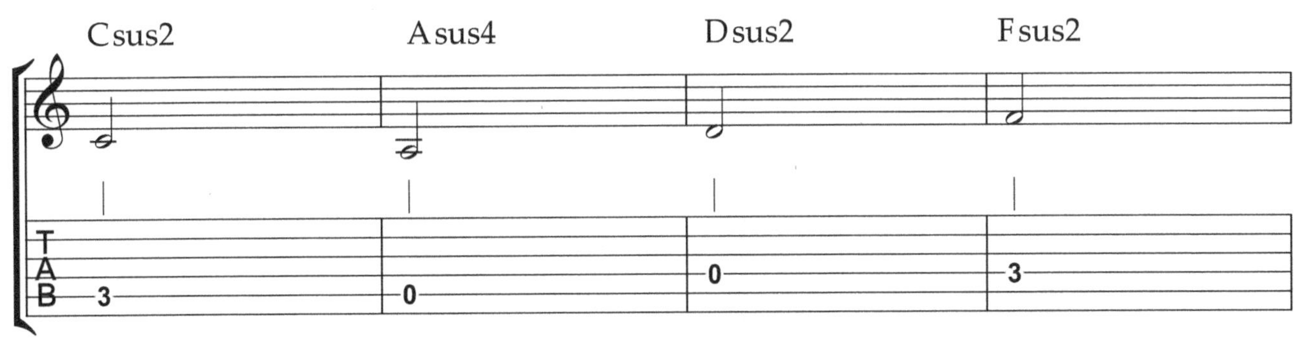

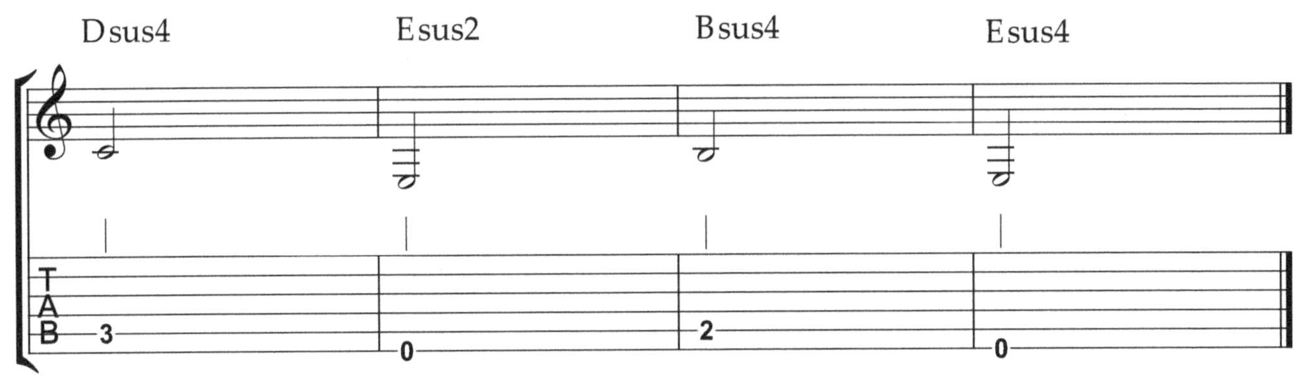

CHAPTER 20

The C Major Scale in Higher Positions on the Fretboard

Before we improvise let's explore the C Major scale in different positions on the fingerboard. Play the note fretted or mix fretted notes and open strings.

Second Position

Track 40

Ascending Descending

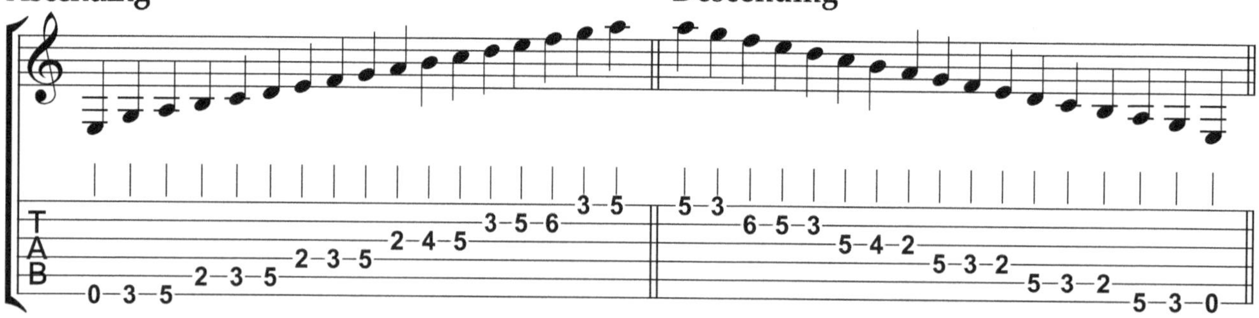

Track 41

Ascending Descending

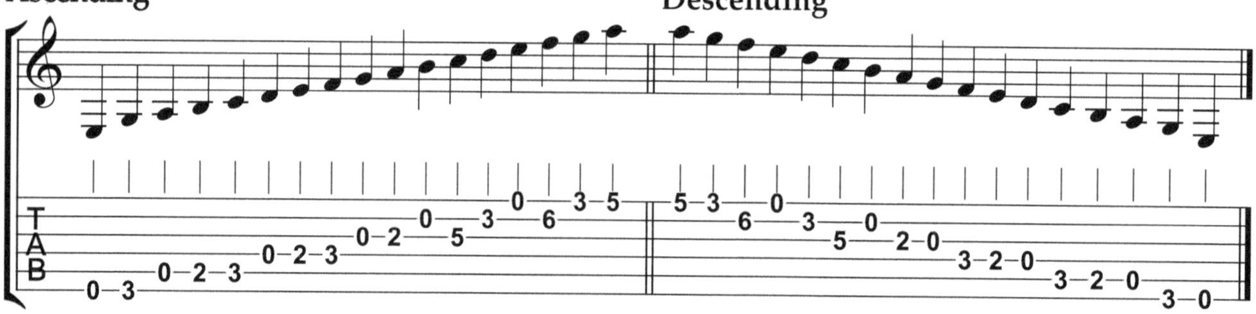

Fifth Position

Track 42

Ascending Descending

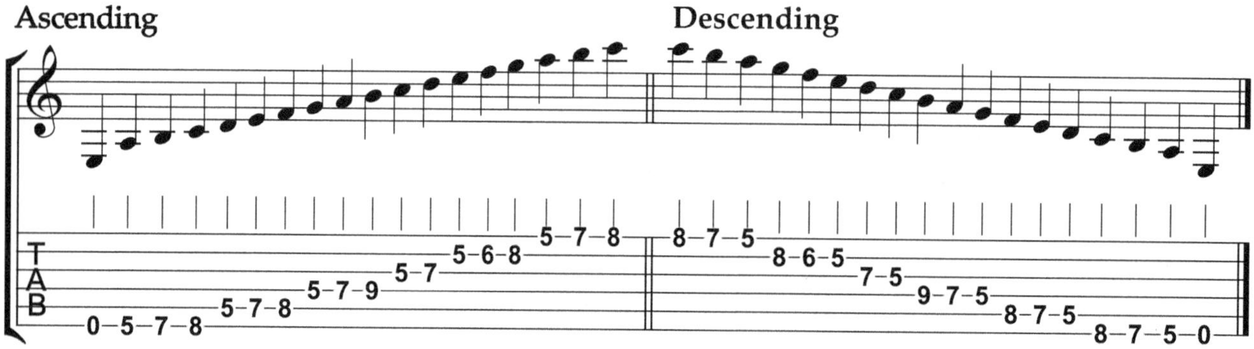

Fifth Position

Track 43

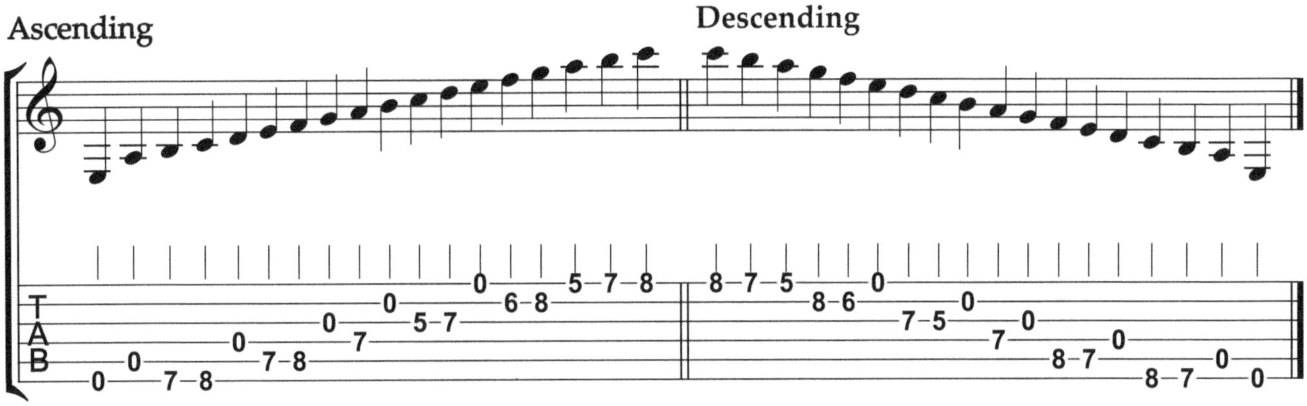

Seventh Position

Track 44

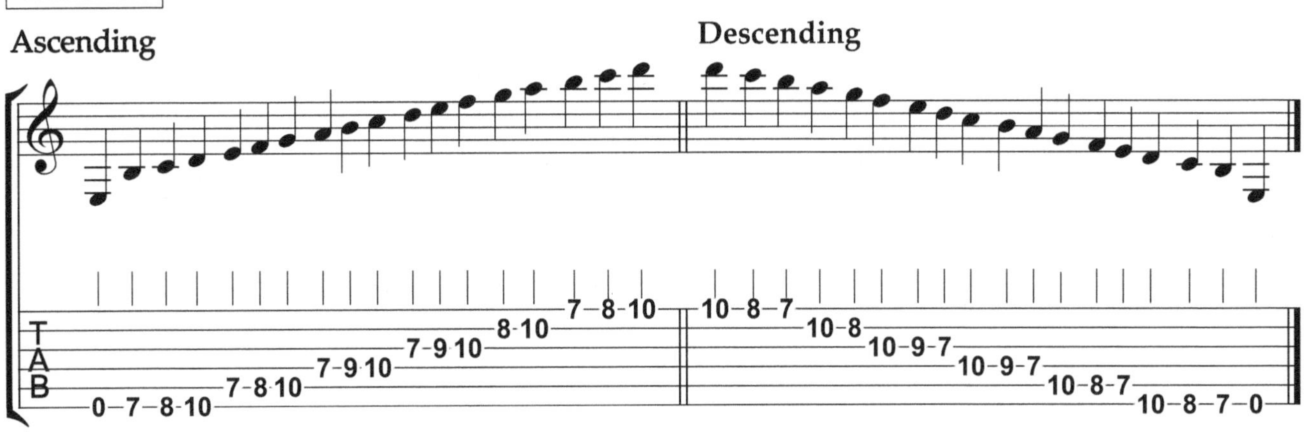

Track 45

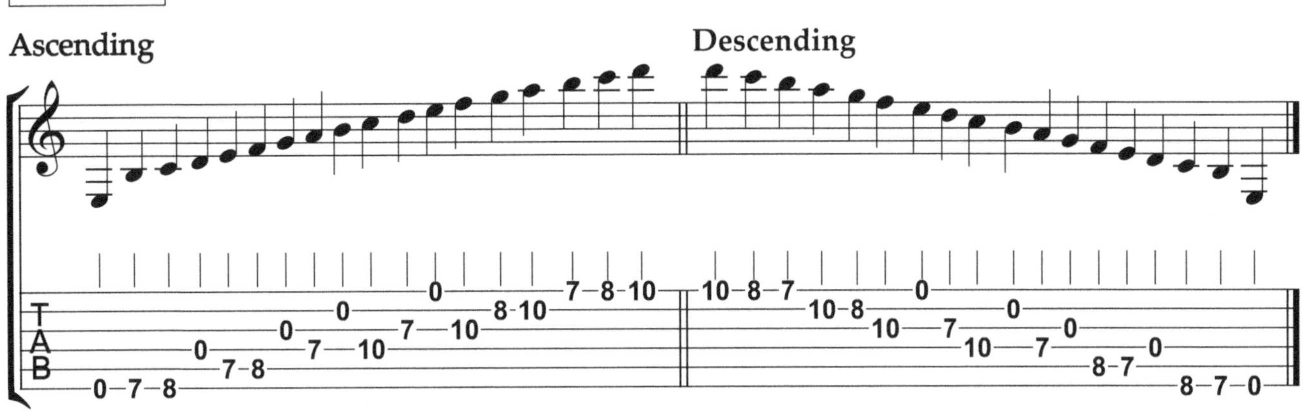

Ninth Position

Track 46

Ascending   Descending

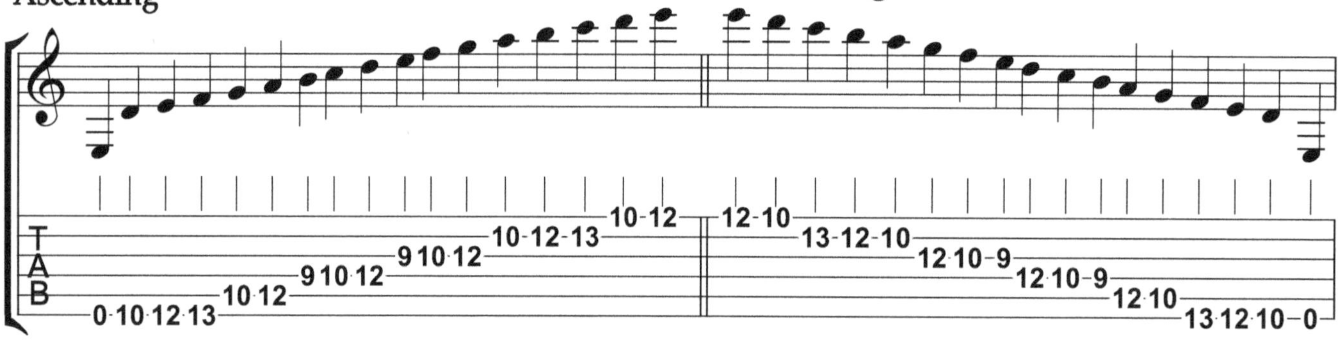

Track 47

Ascending   Descending

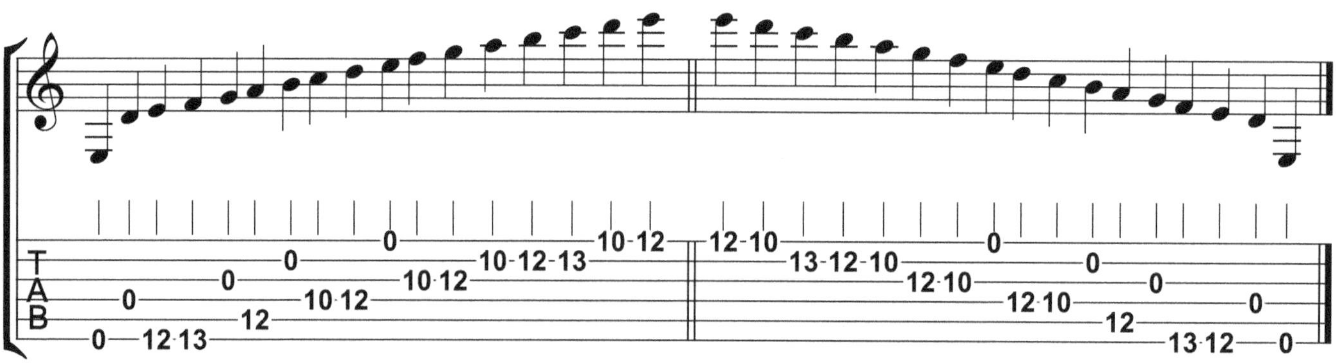

Now improvise melodies proceeded or combined with the root note.
Locate the root first. If possible, play the root as an open string too.
Some examples in the **second position**

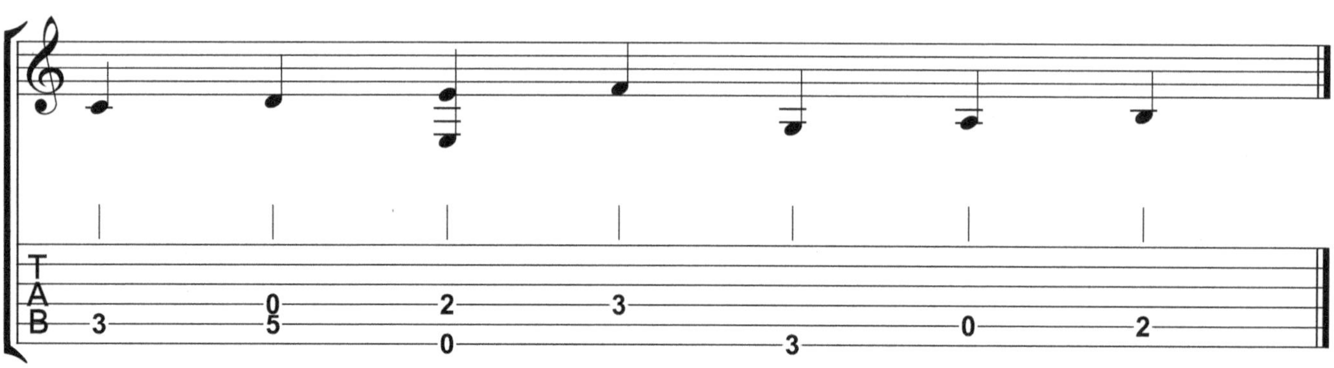

Example

Track 48

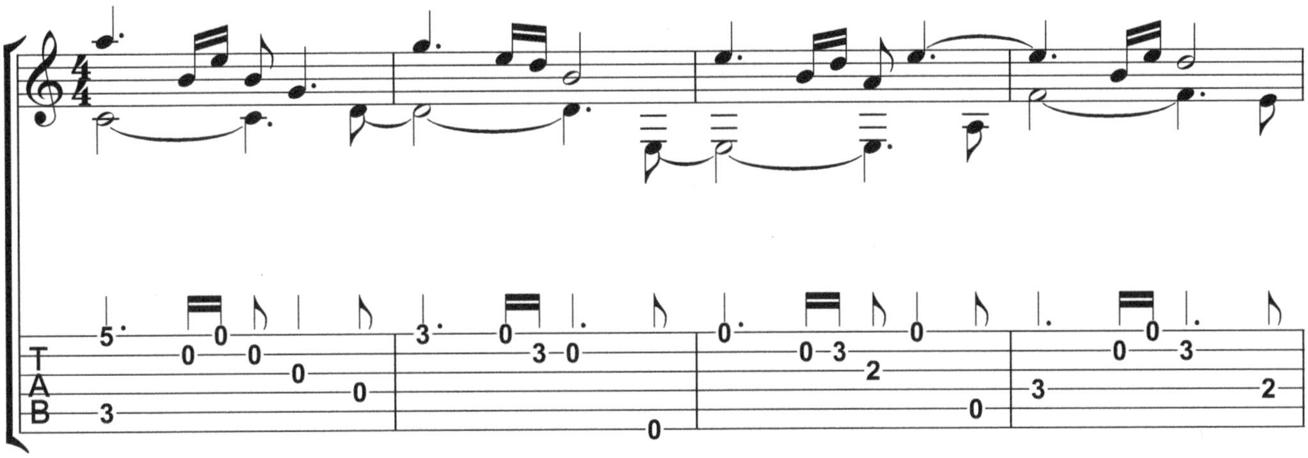

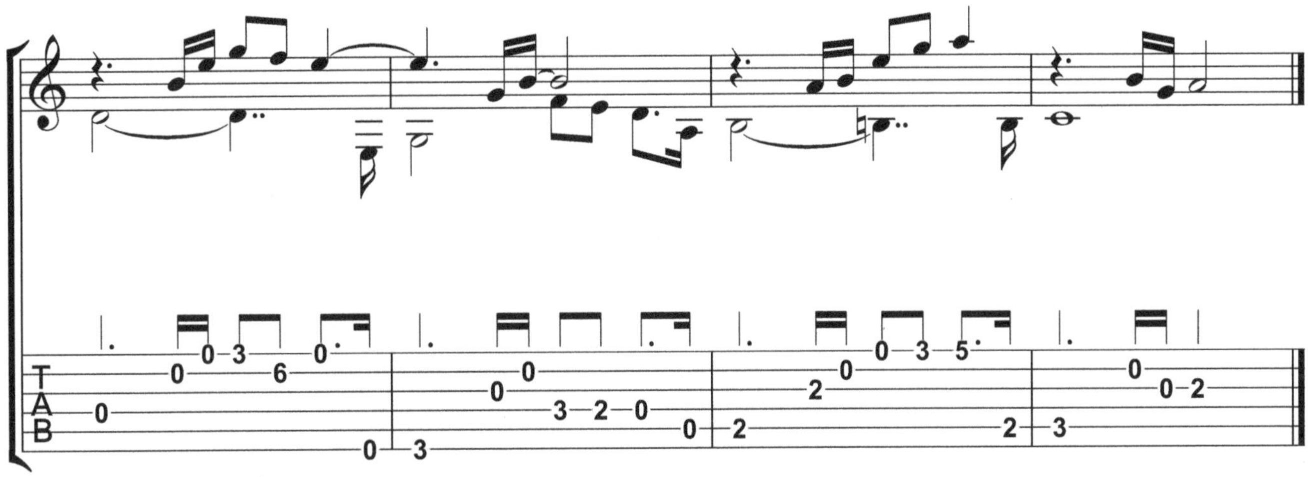

Your turn

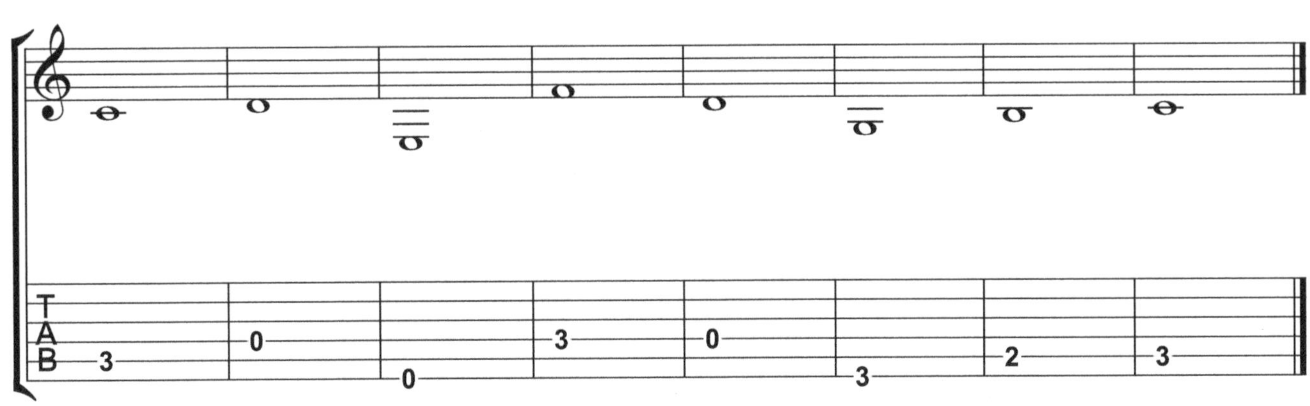

Some examples in the **fifth postion**

Locate the root first. If possible, play the root as an open string too.

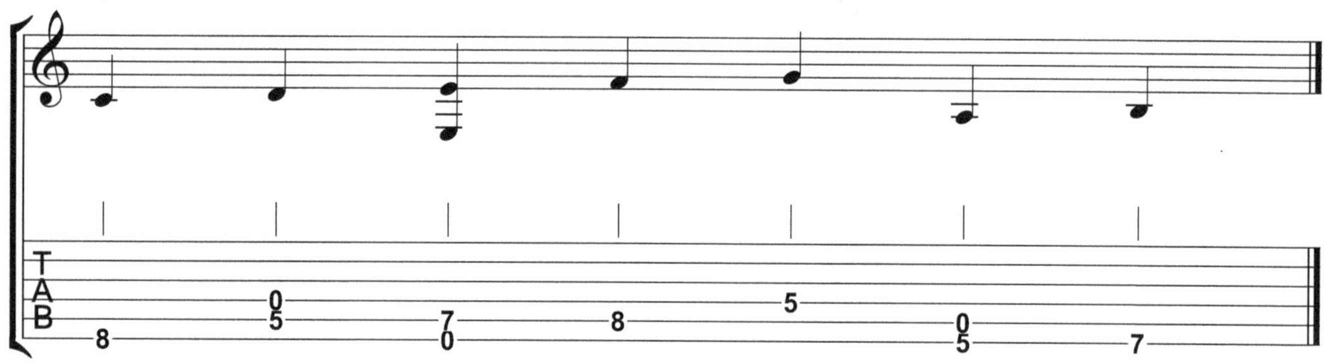

Track 49

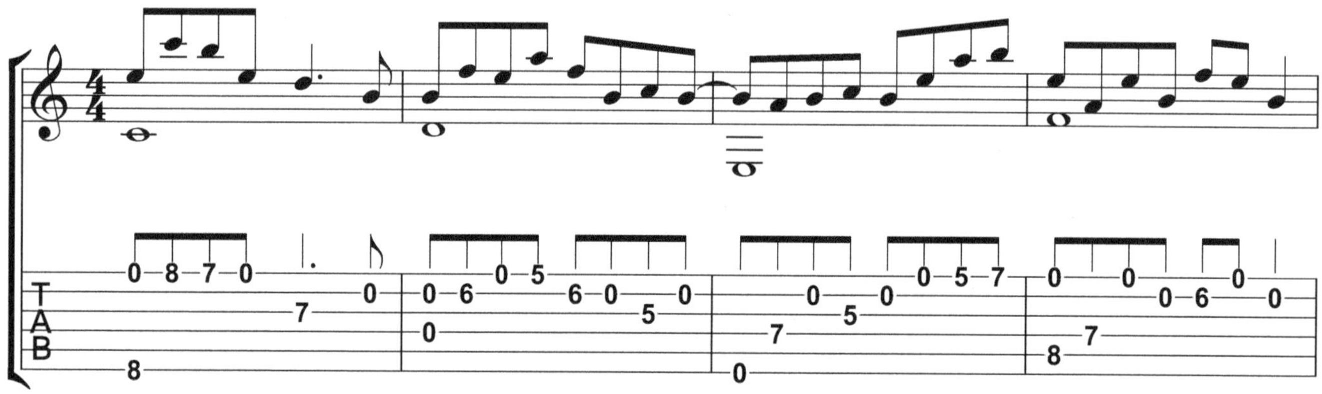

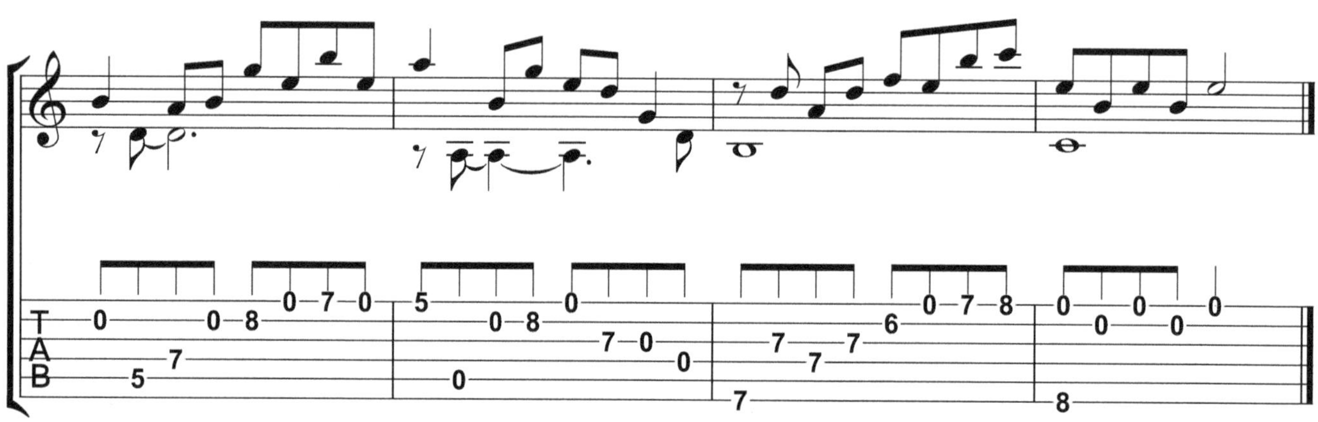

Your turn

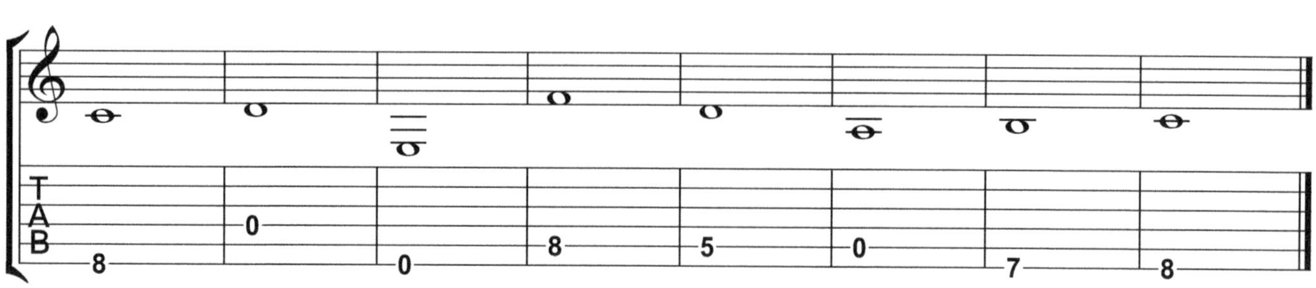

Some examples in the **seventh postion**

Locate the root first. If possible, play the root as an open string too.

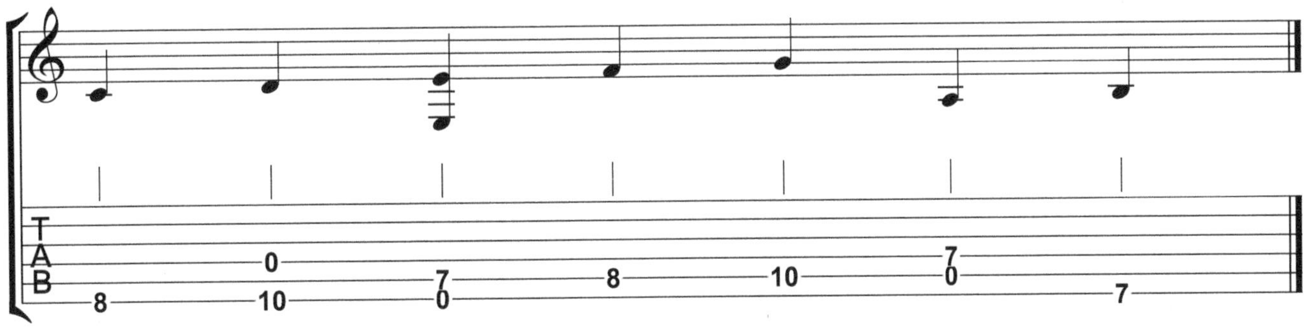

Track 50

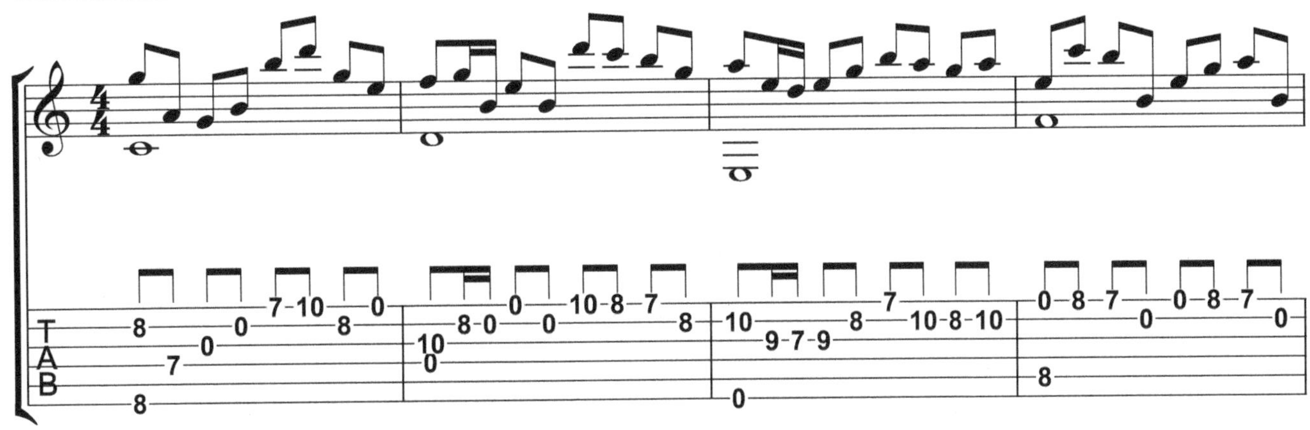

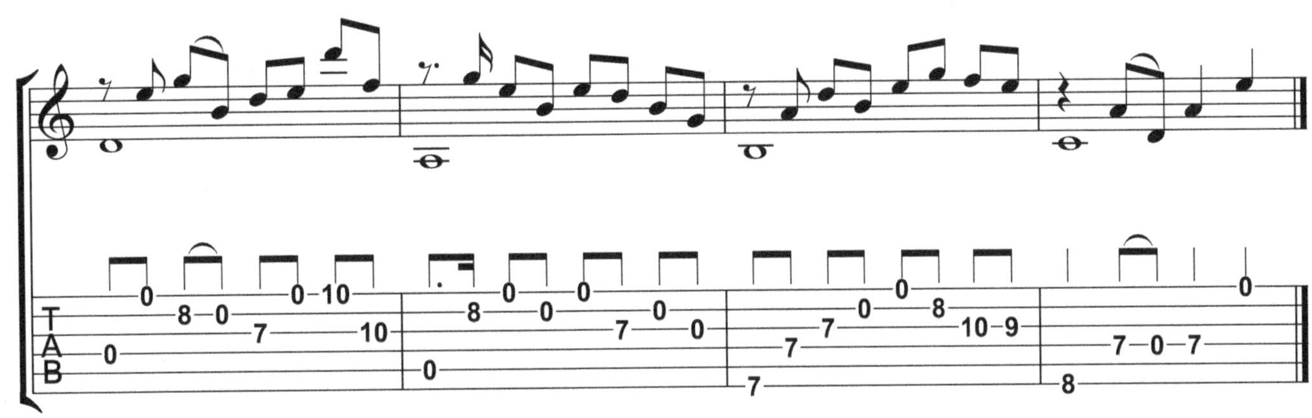

Your turn

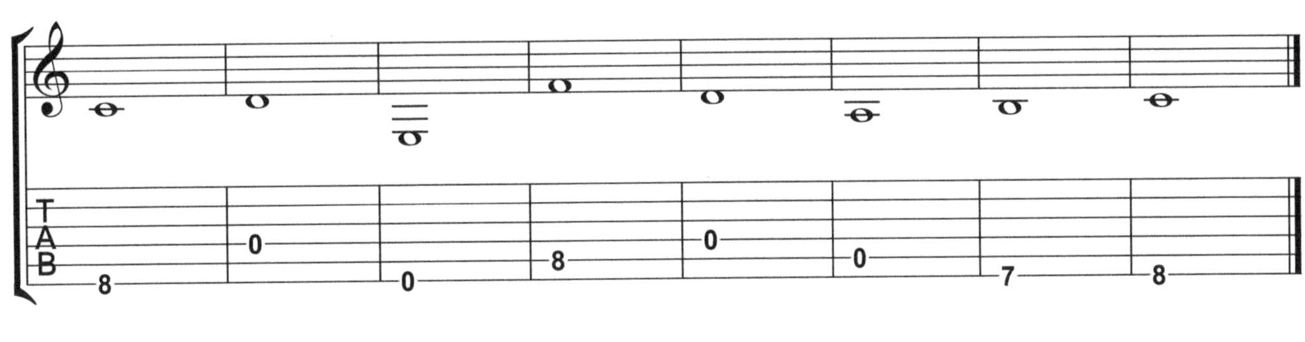

Some examples in the **ninth postion**
Locate the root first. If possible, play the root as an open string too.

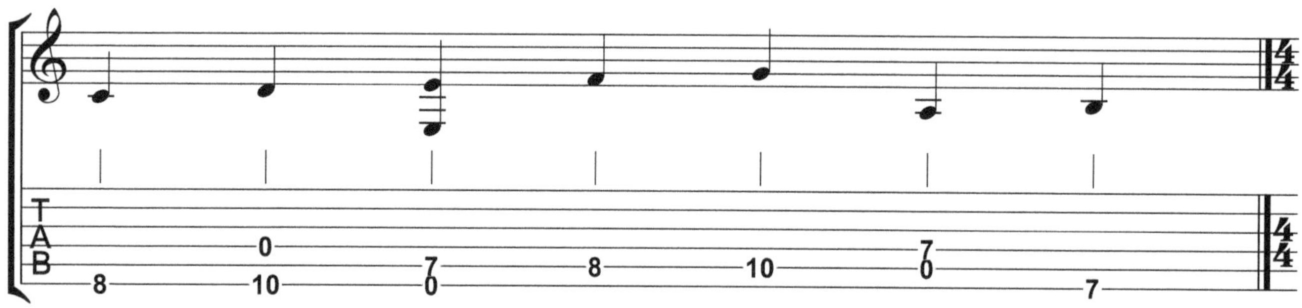

Track 51

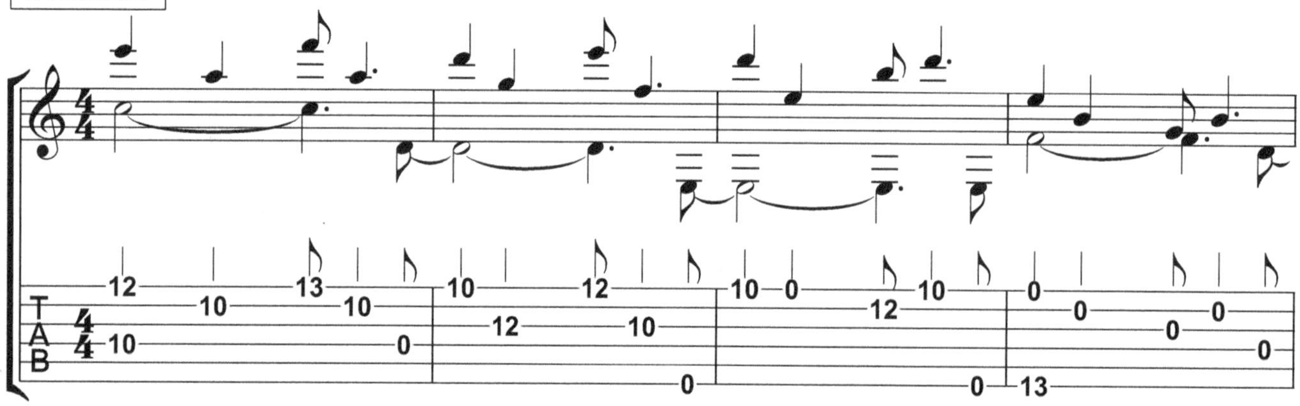

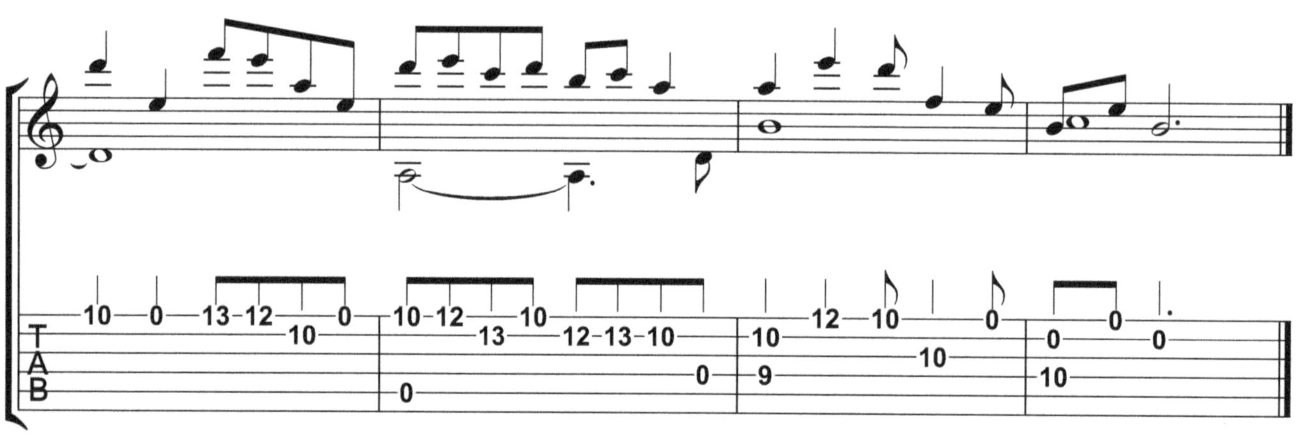

Your turn

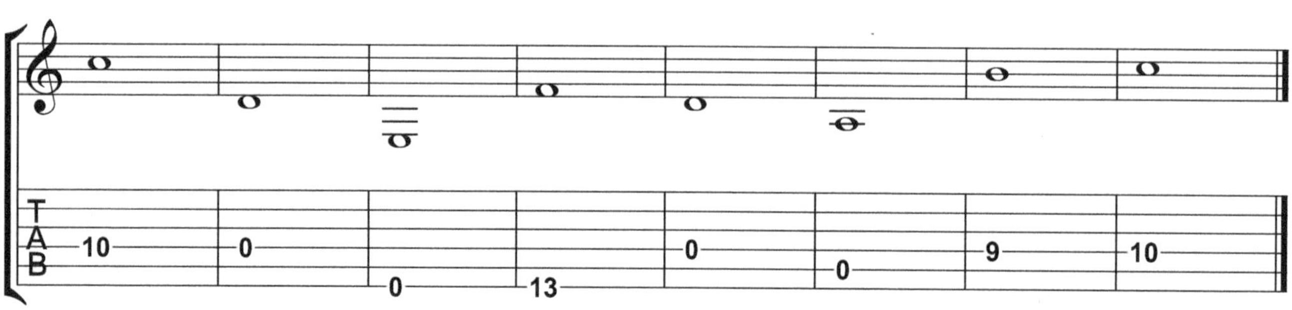

CHAPTER 21

Root-Third in Higher Positions

When improvising on chord progressions first look for the root-third, as the third is defining whether the chord is a major or minor one.
I like to use 4 locations.

Major 3rd Minor 3rd

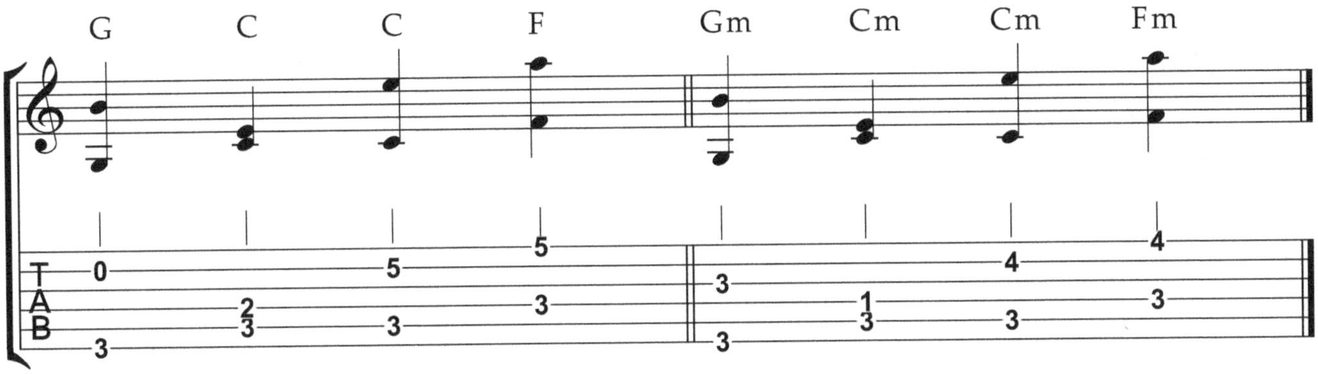

Play these two shapes all over the neck and name them.

Major 3rd Minor 3rd

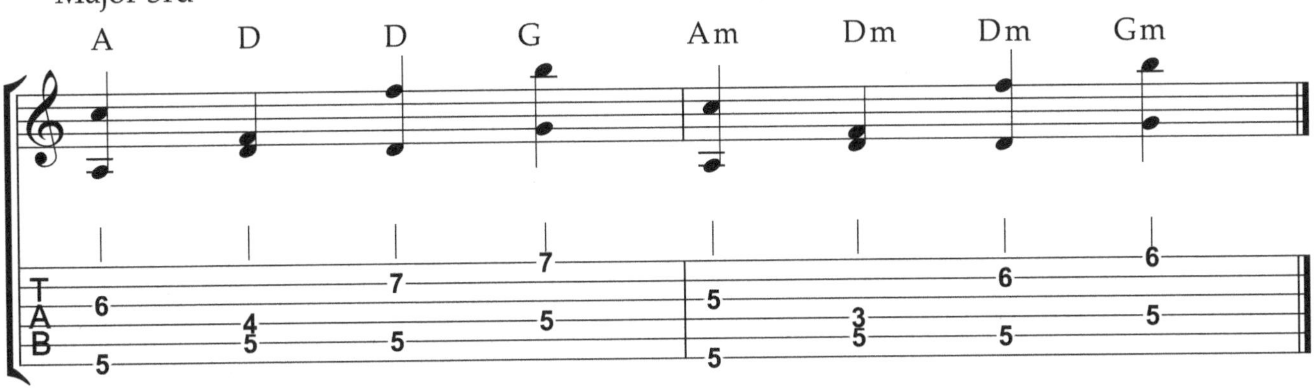

Root on the 6th string

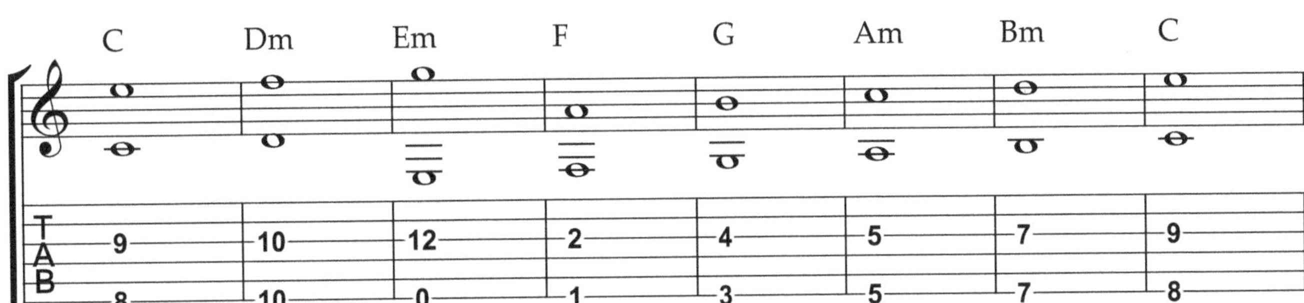

Root on the 5th string

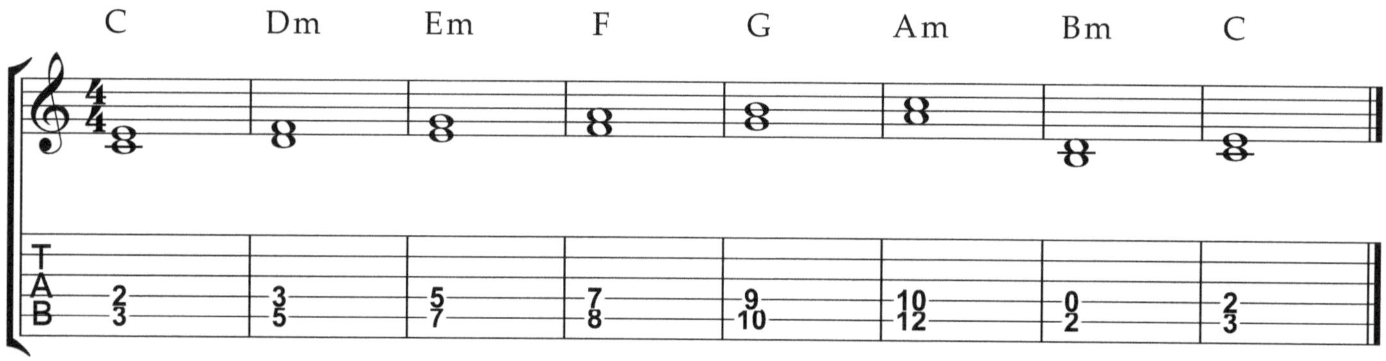

Root on the 5th string

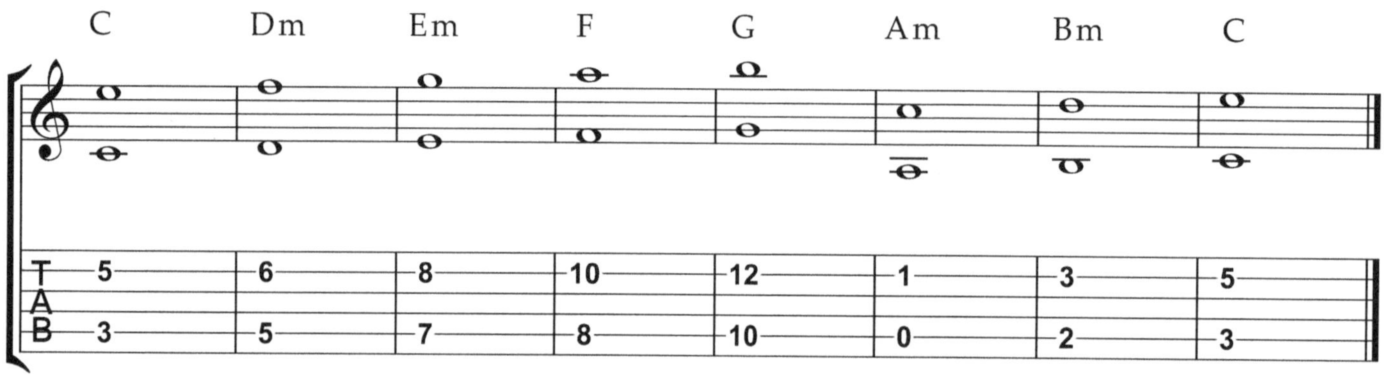

Root on the 4th string

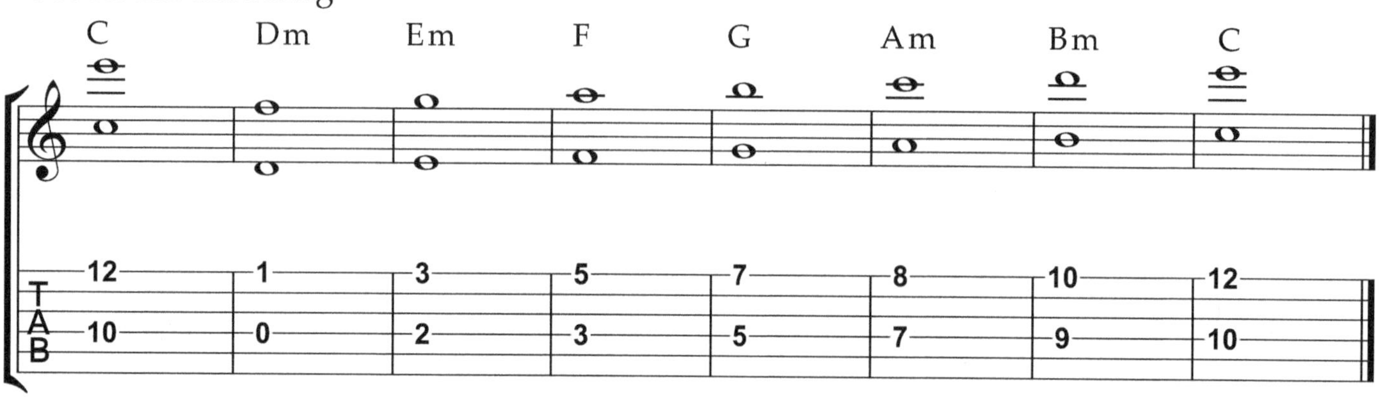

Root on 6th, 5th and 4th strings in any order

Track 52

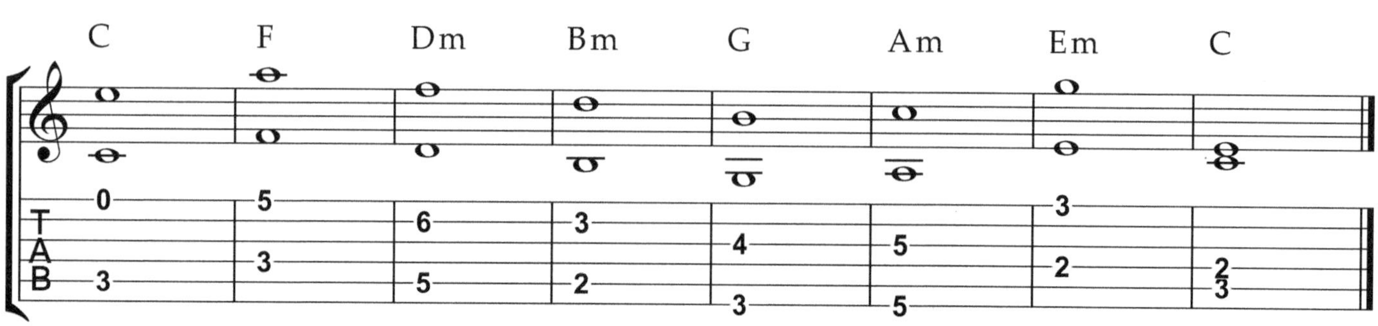

Track 53

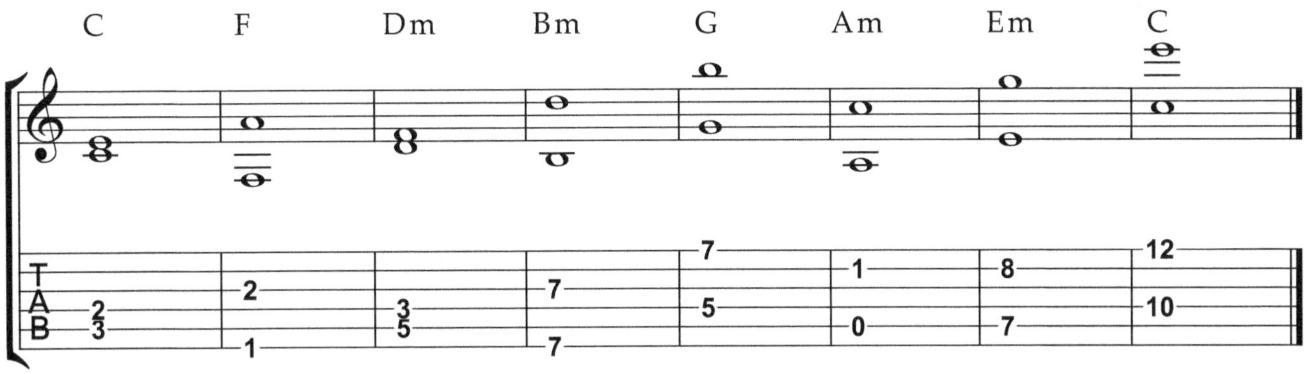

Your turn

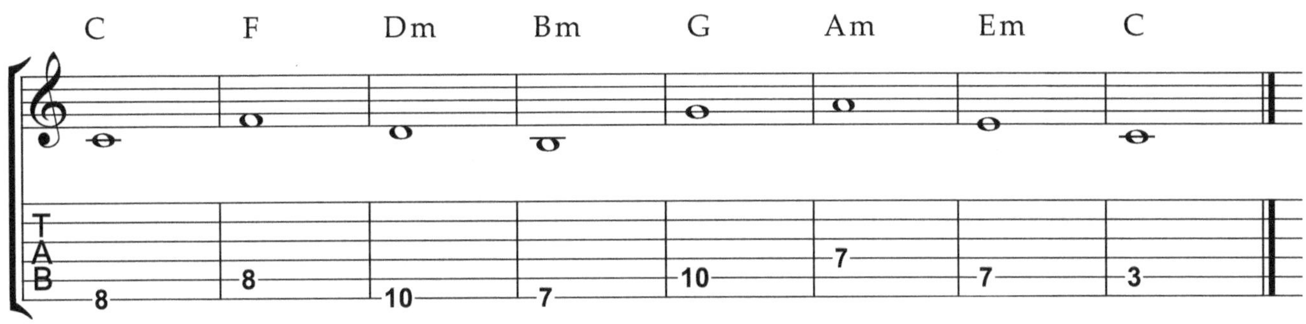

CHAPTER 22

Root-Third: Two-Part Playing

Add notes in the upper and/or bottom voice. The notes may be scalar (belonging to the scale of G Major: G A B C D E F♯ G) and some may be chromatic (G♯, B♭ C♯,D♯)

On a chord progression

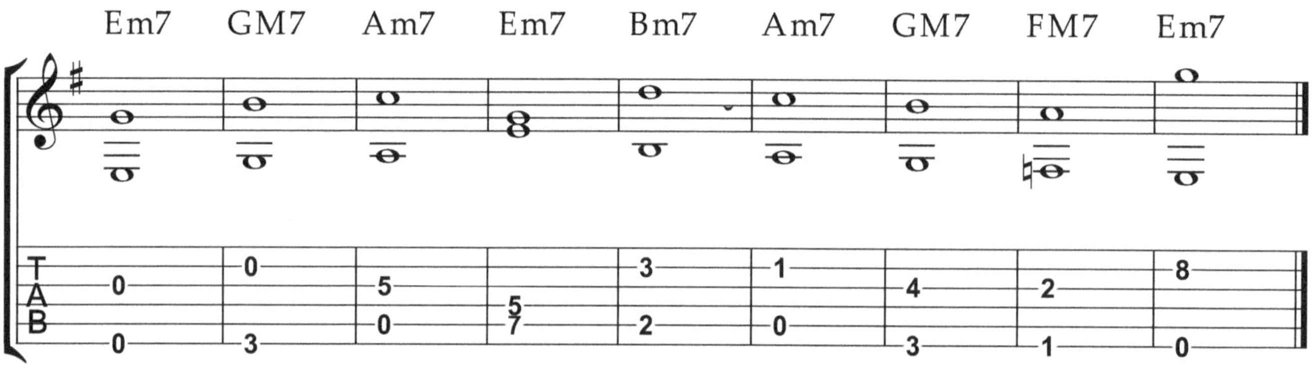

Example 1

Track 54

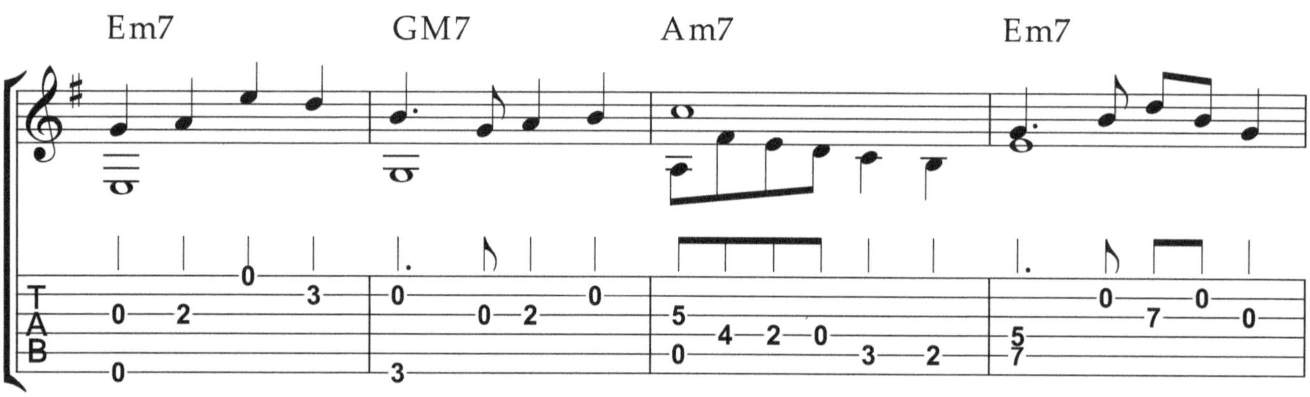

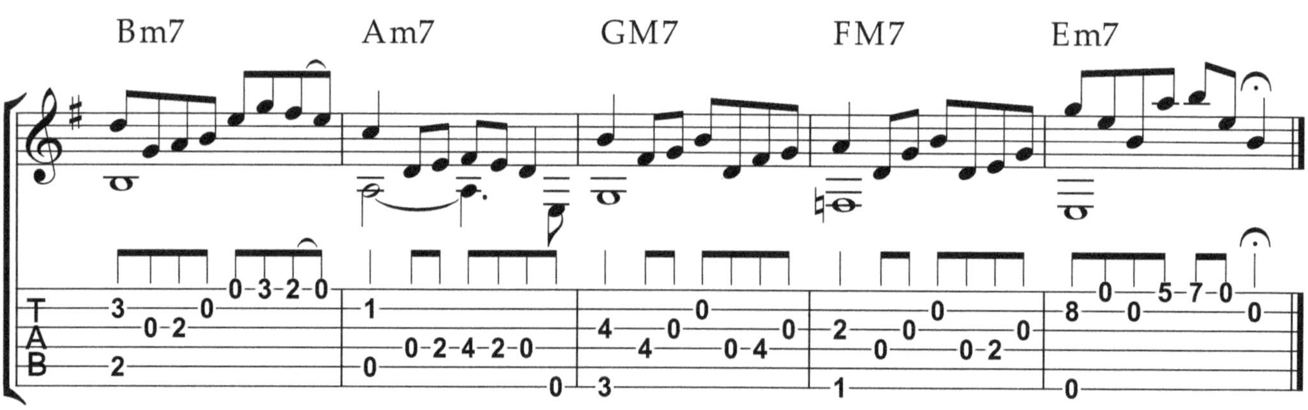

Example 2 in 3/4

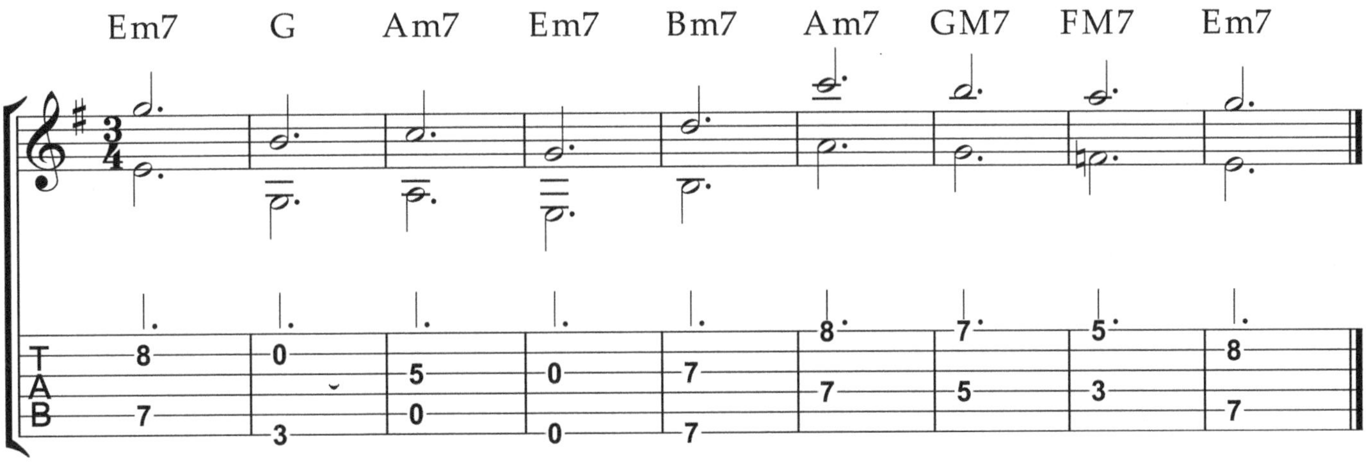

Track 55

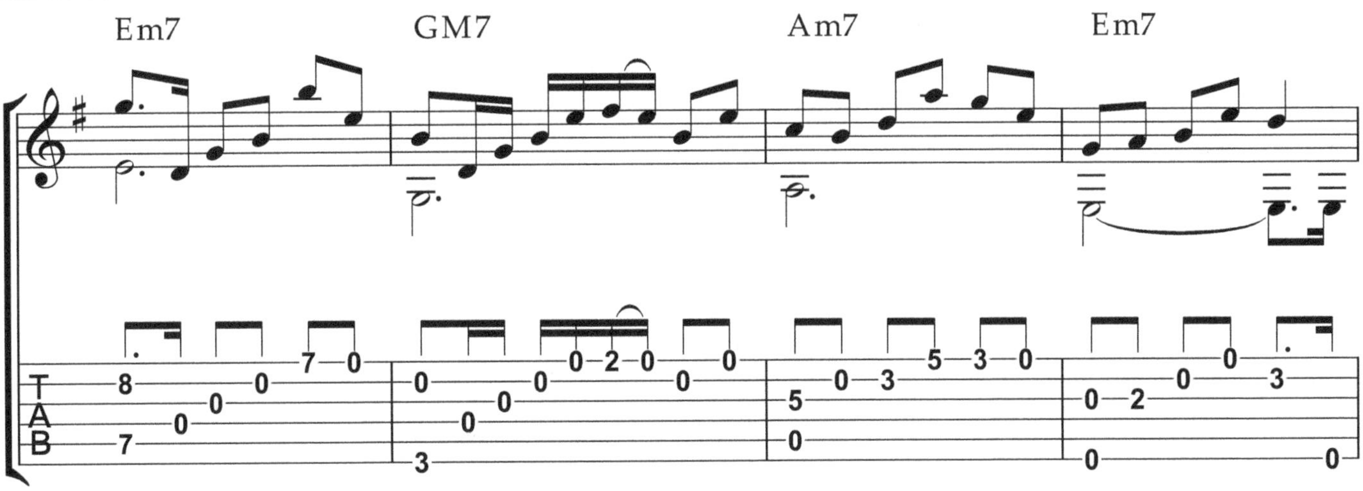

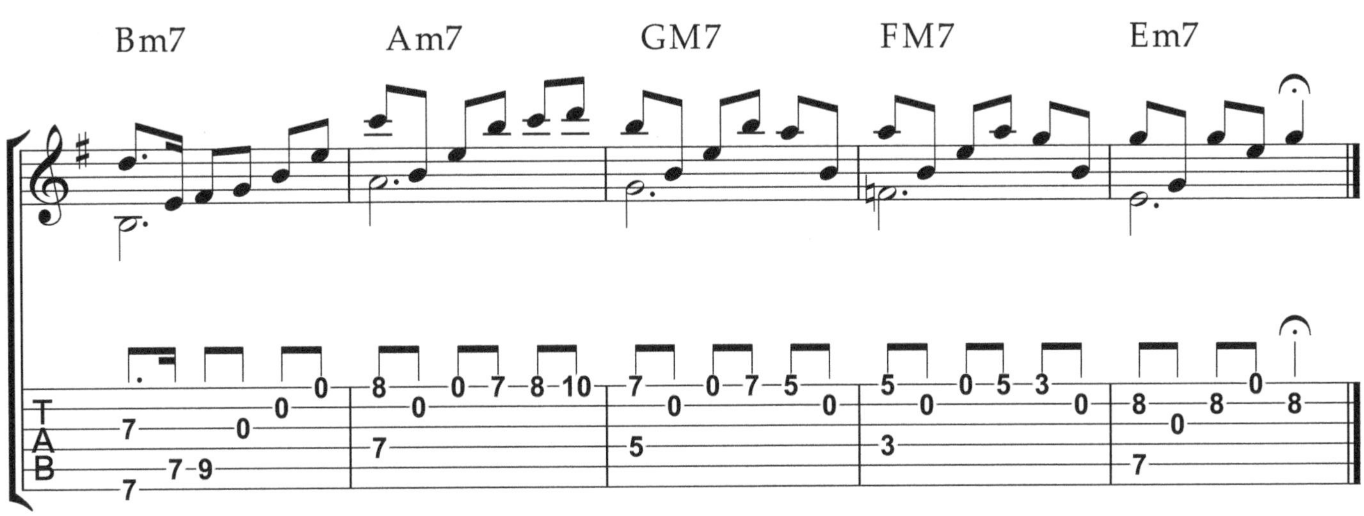

Your turn

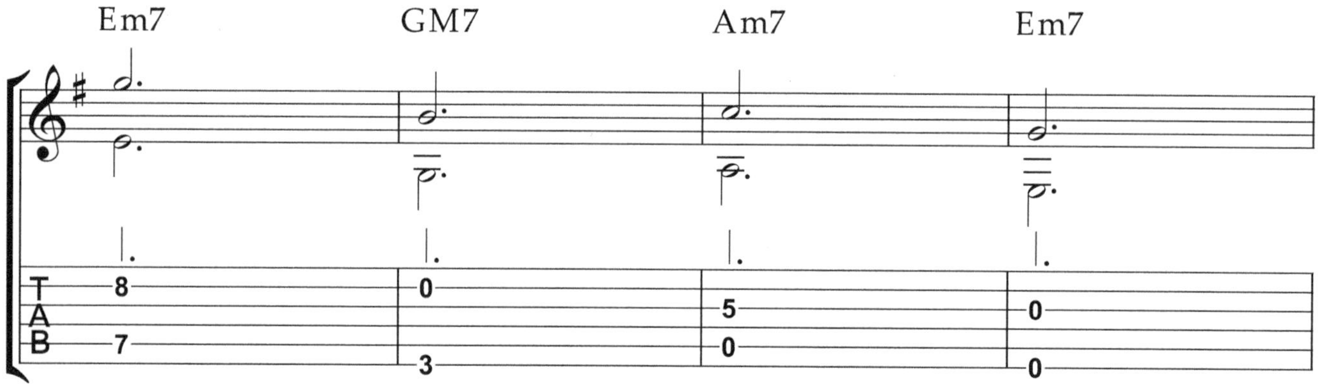

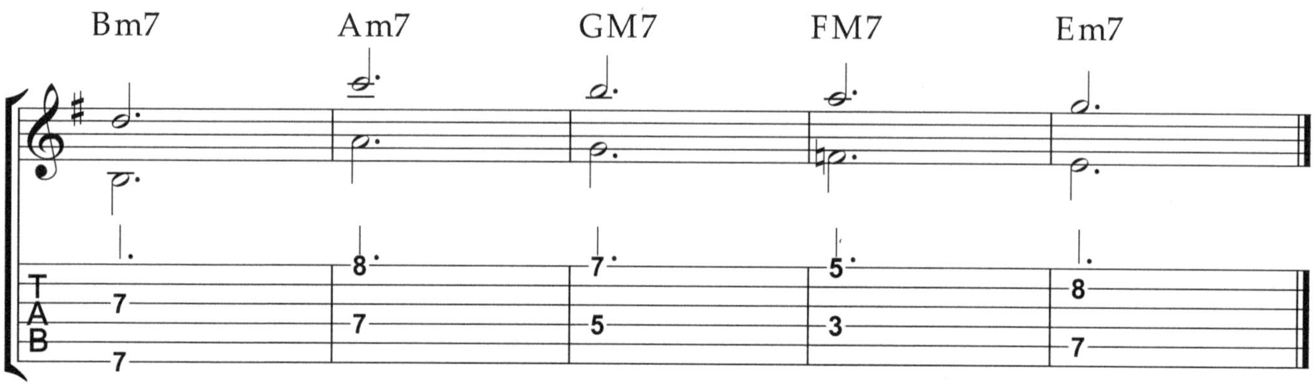

CHAPTER 23

Shell Voicings

A **Shell Voicing** combines the root-third-seventh.
Memorize these shapes and move them across the fingerboard.

Major 7ths — Minor 7ths

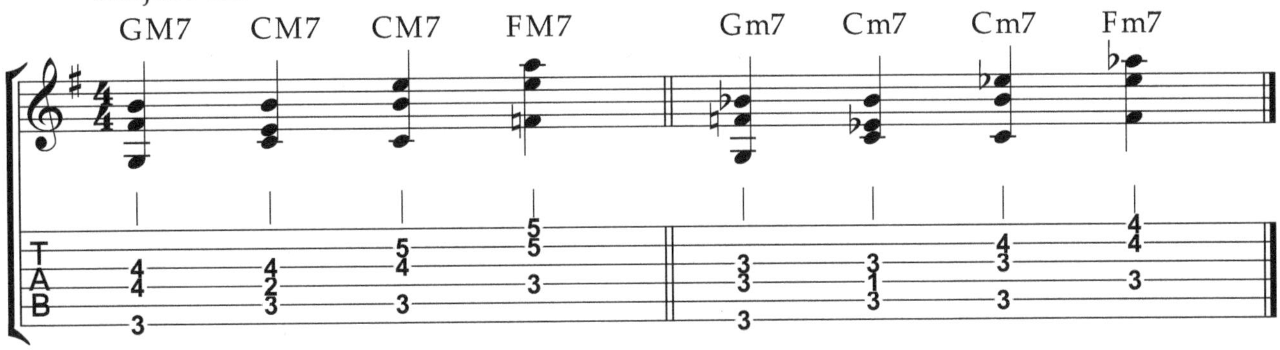

Dominant 7ths

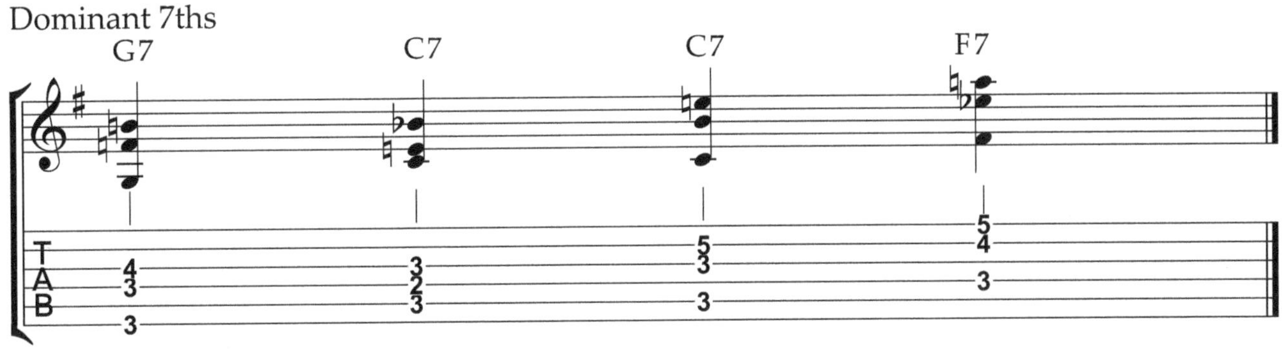

Another approach

Root on the 6th string, third on the 3rd string — Root on the 5th string, third on the 4th string

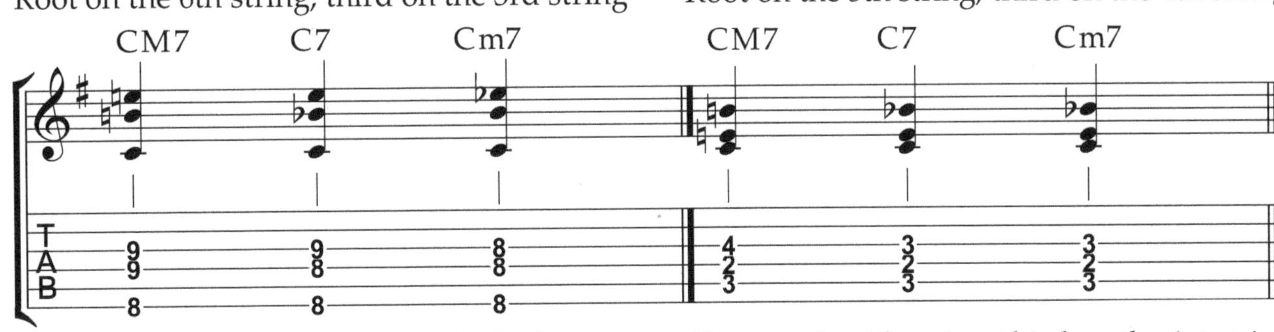

Root on the 5th string, third on the 2nd string — Root on the 4th string, third on the 1st string

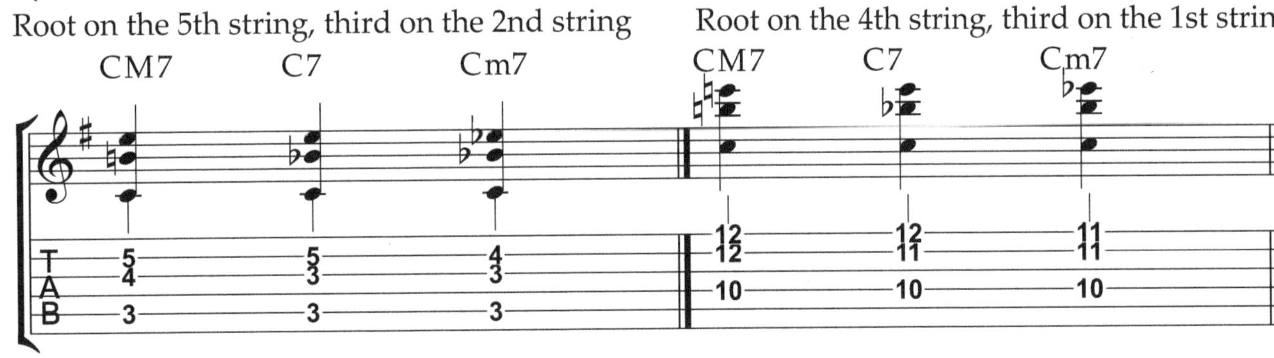

Exercises

Root on the 6th string, third on the 3rd string

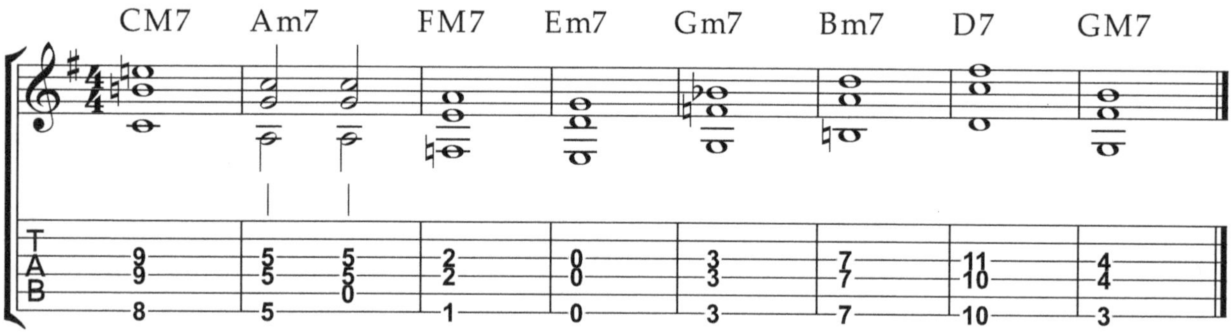

Root on the 5th string, third on the 4th string

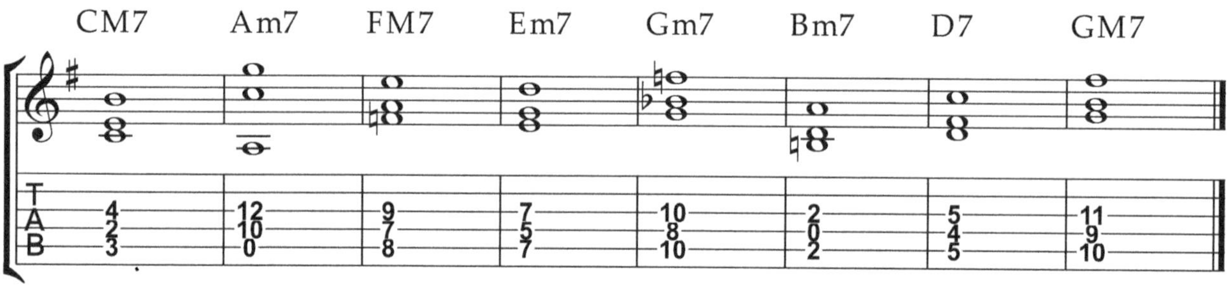

Root on the 5th string, third on the 2nd string

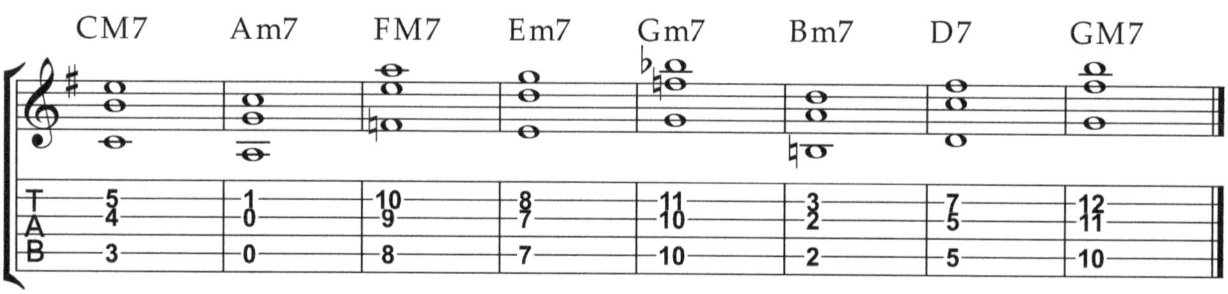

Root on the 4th string, third on the 1st string

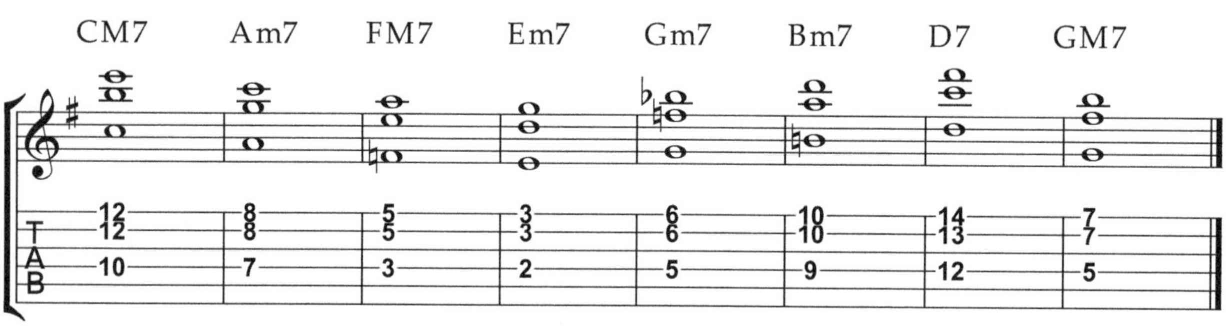

Root on the 6th, 5th and 4th string

Example 1

Track 56

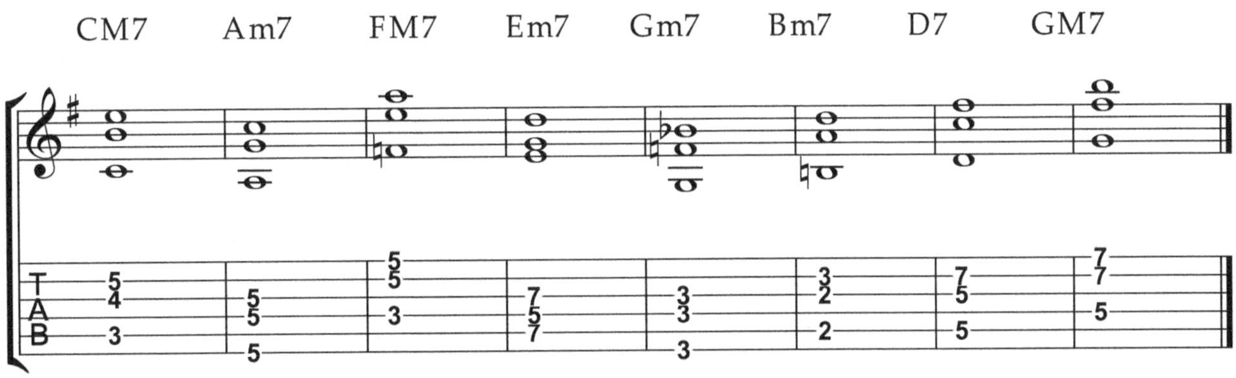

Example 2

Track 57

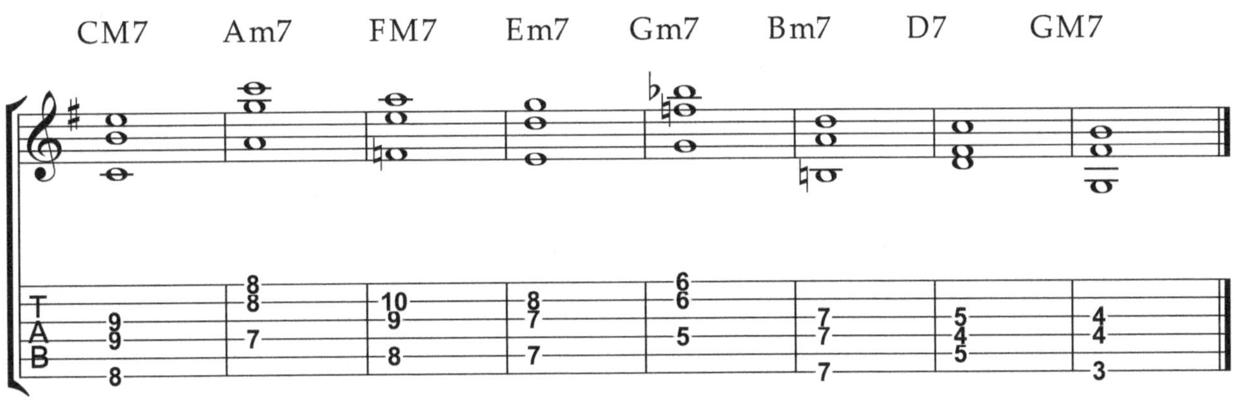

CHAPTER 24

Shell Voicings and Melodic Material

Use arpeggiation, chord parts, add bass lines, a mix of fretted notes and open strings, play dyads (chord note together with any scale note).

Some examples:

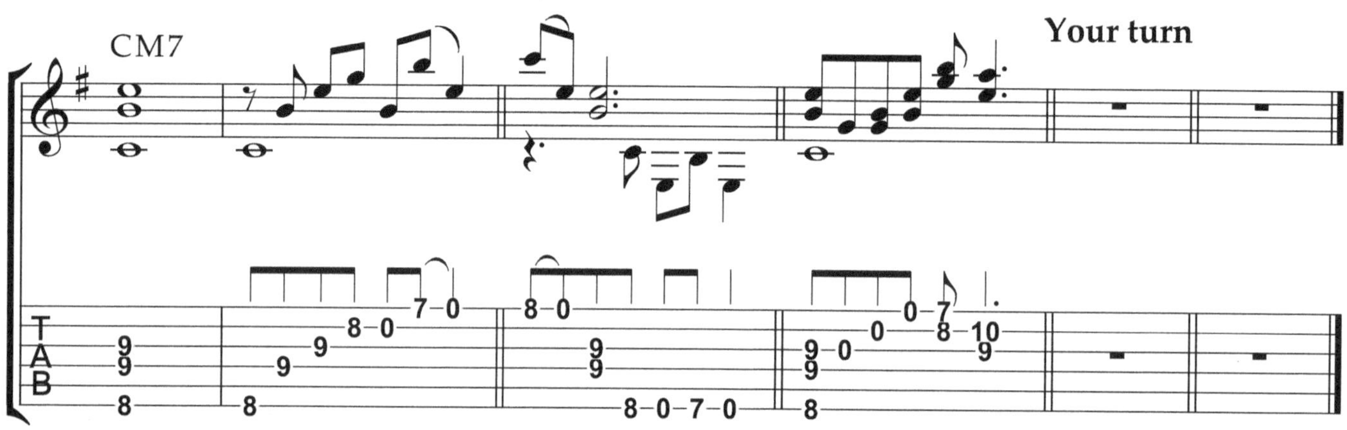

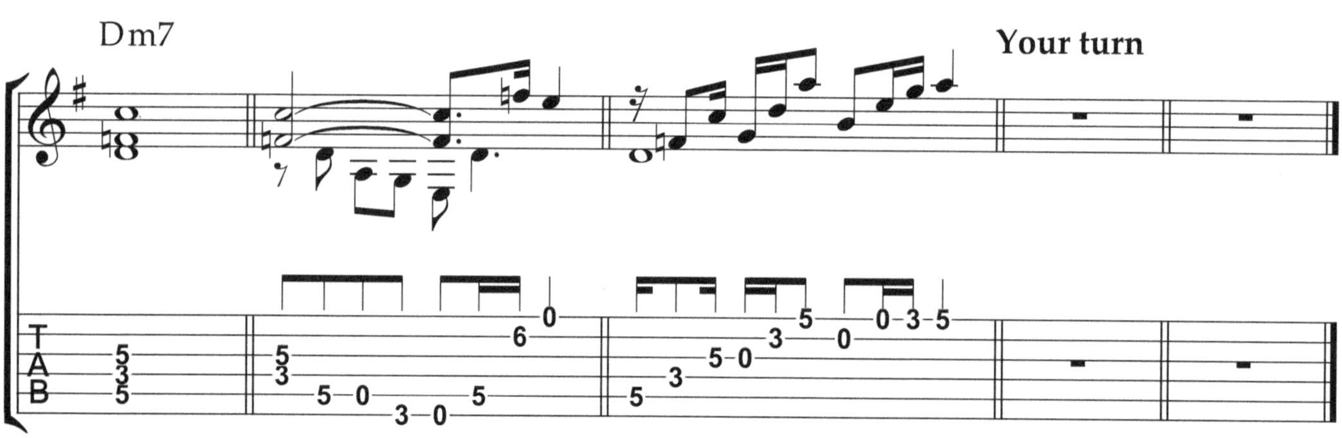

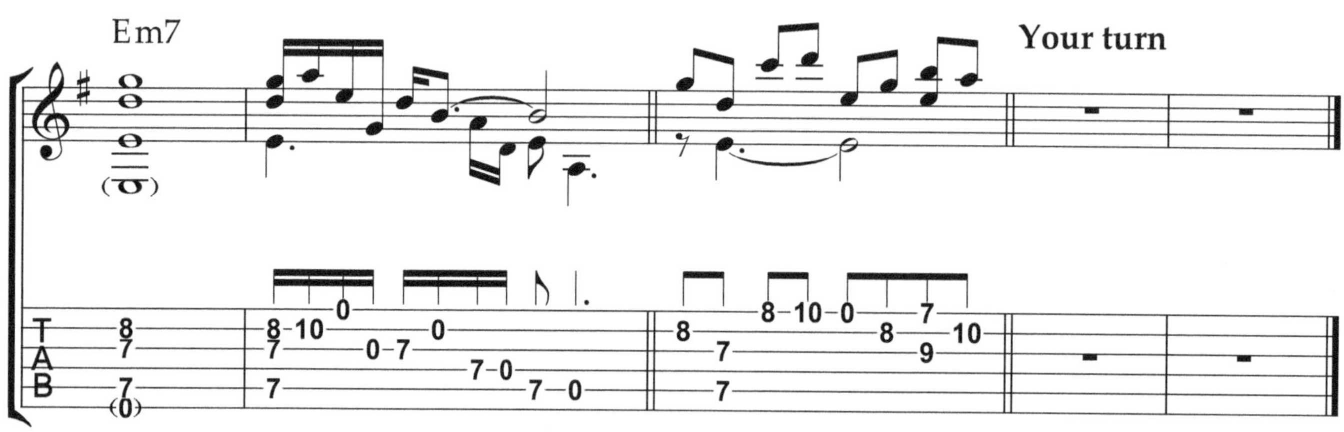

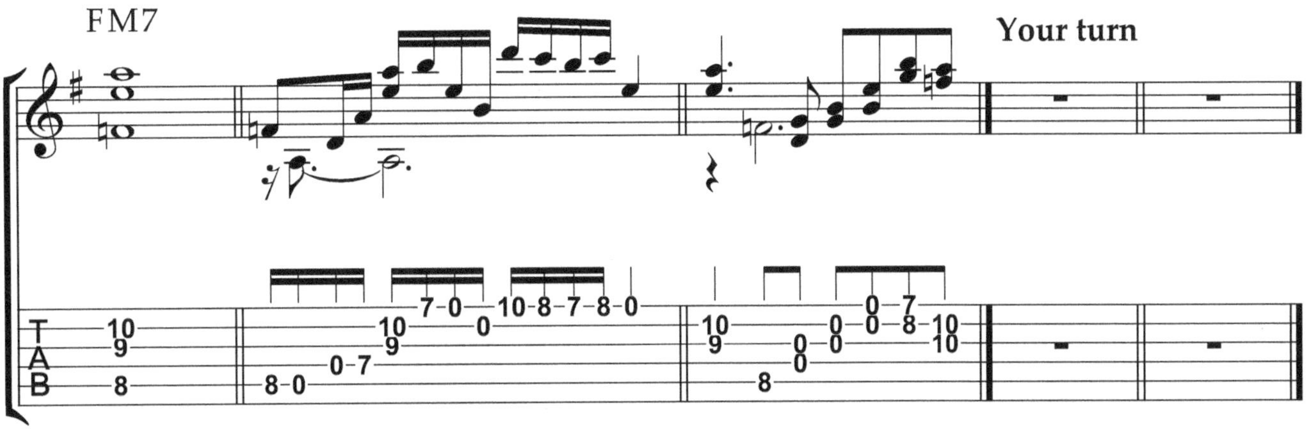
FM7
Your turn

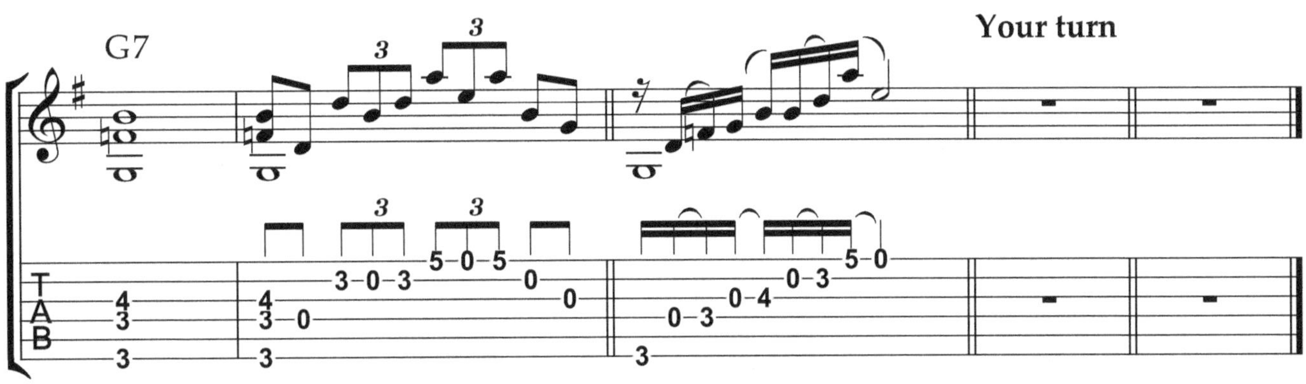
G7
Your turn

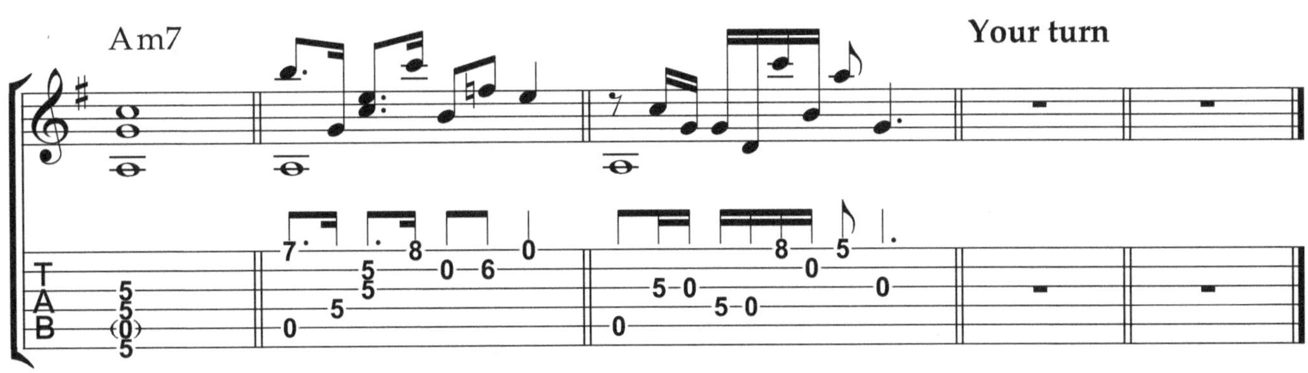
Am7
Your turn

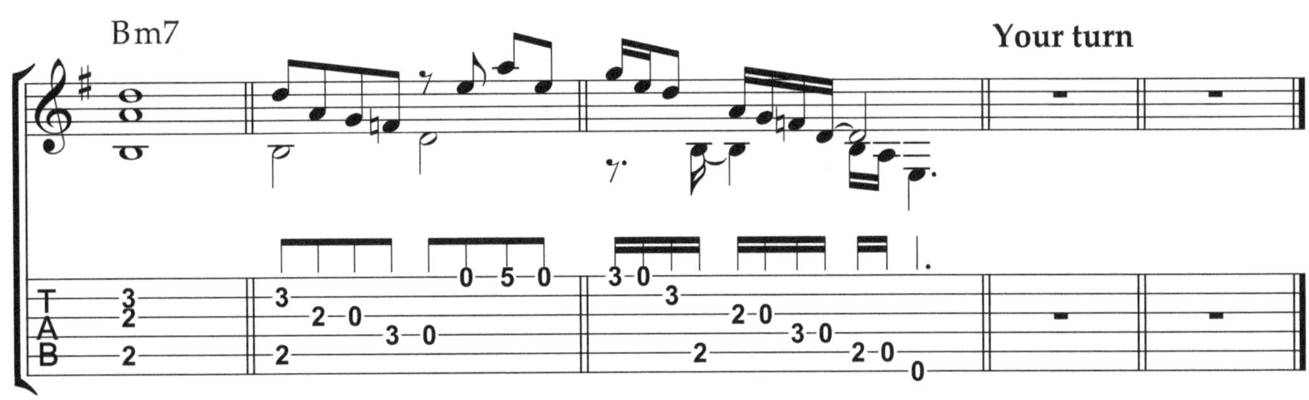
Bm7
Your turn

On a chord progression

Track 58

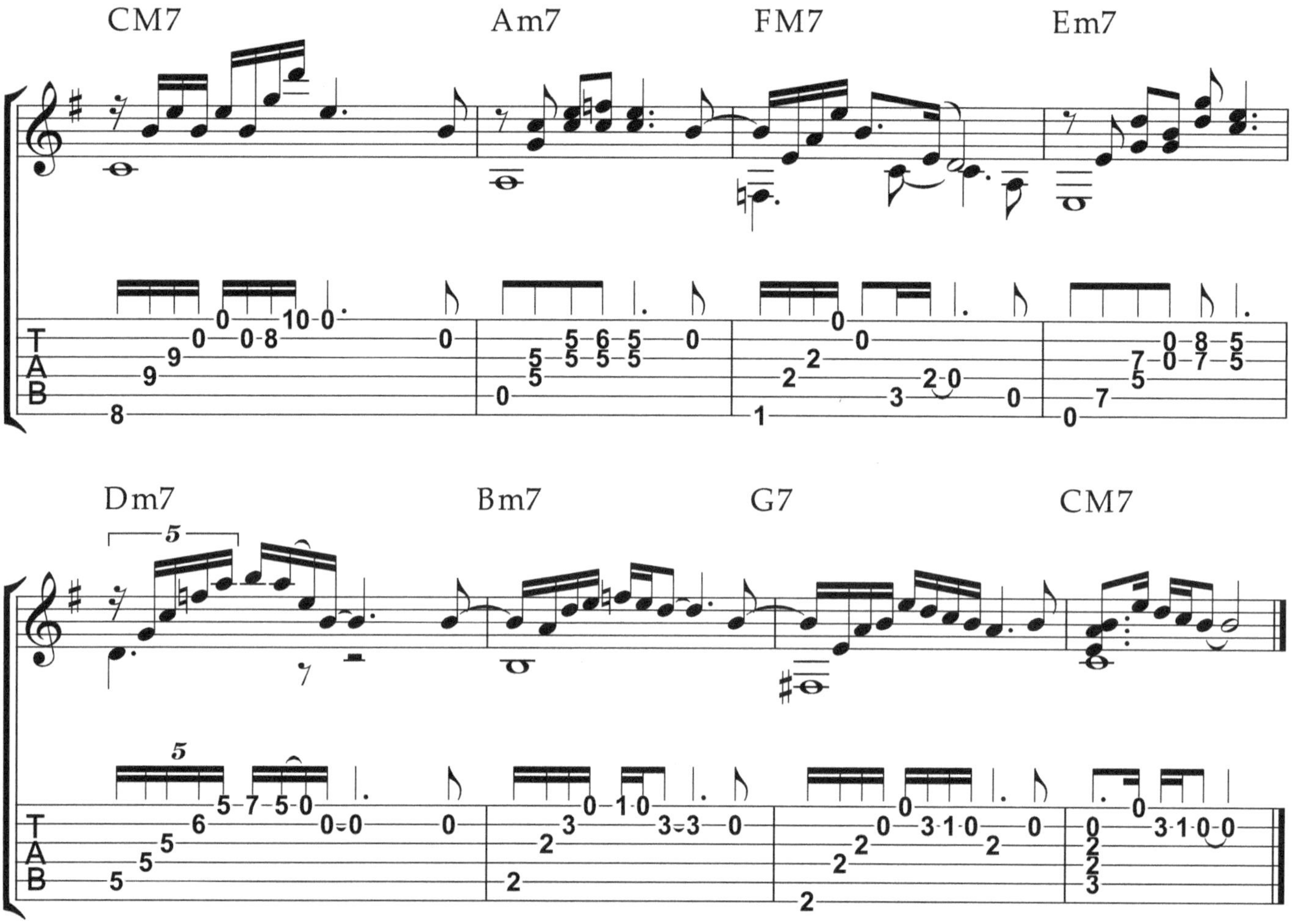

Your turn

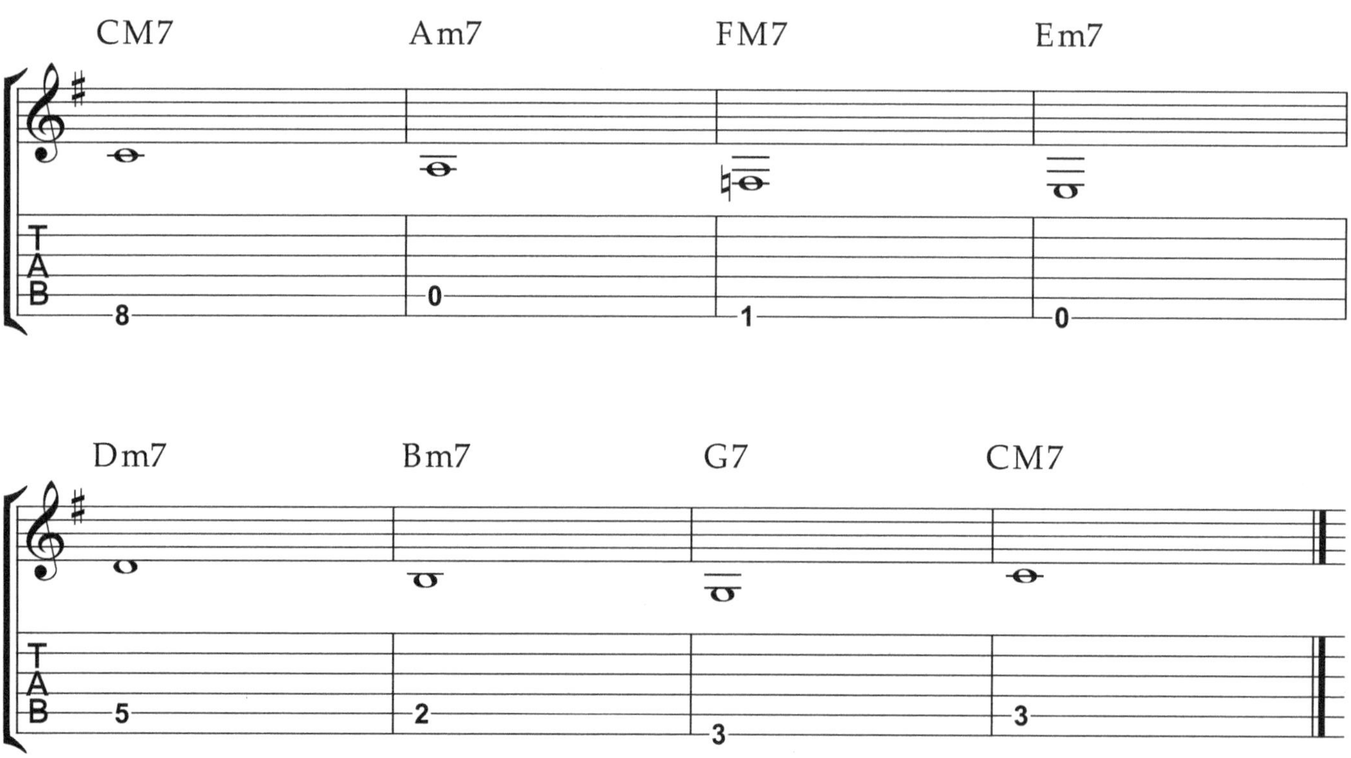

CHAPTER 25

Direct Substitutions on Shell Voicings

Some examples:

On Major Chords

Some direct substitutions. Look for others

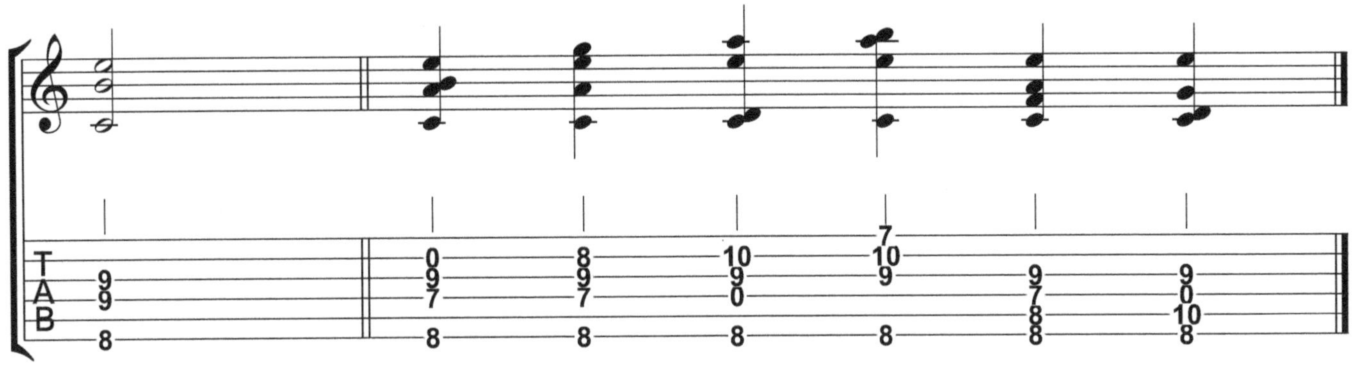

Some direct substitutions. Look for others

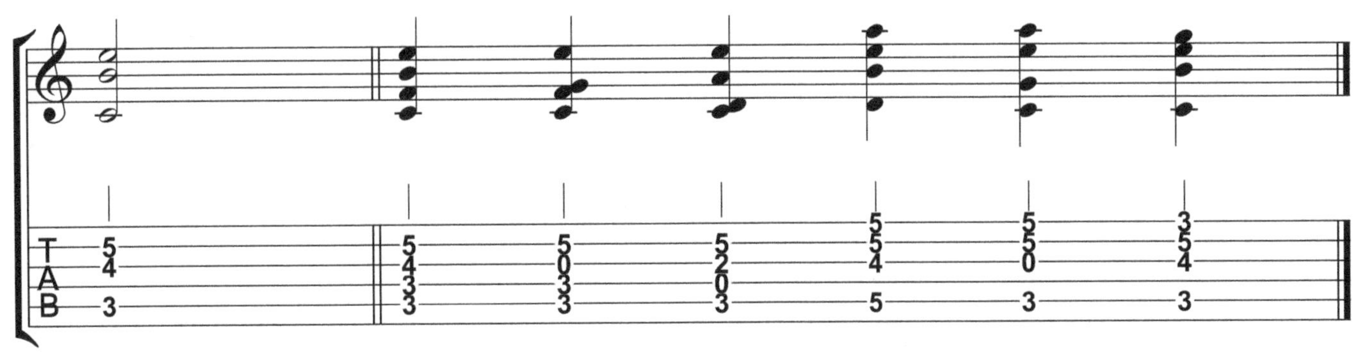

Some direct substitutions. Look for others

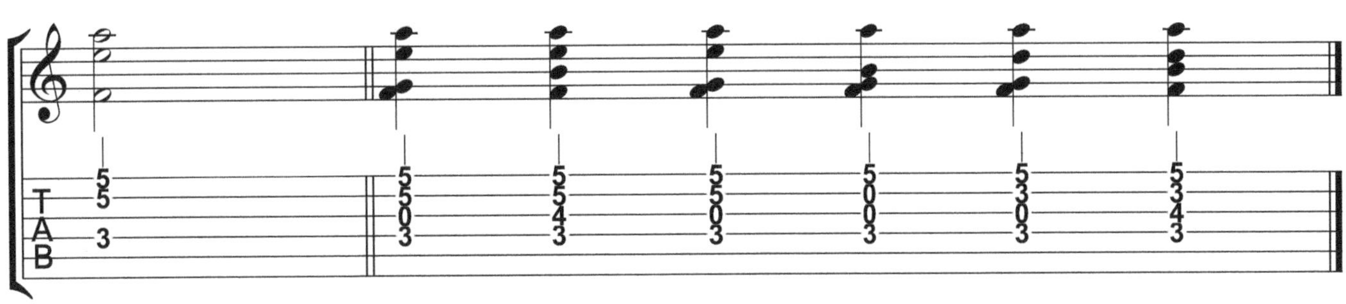

On Minor Chords

Some direct substitutions. Look for others

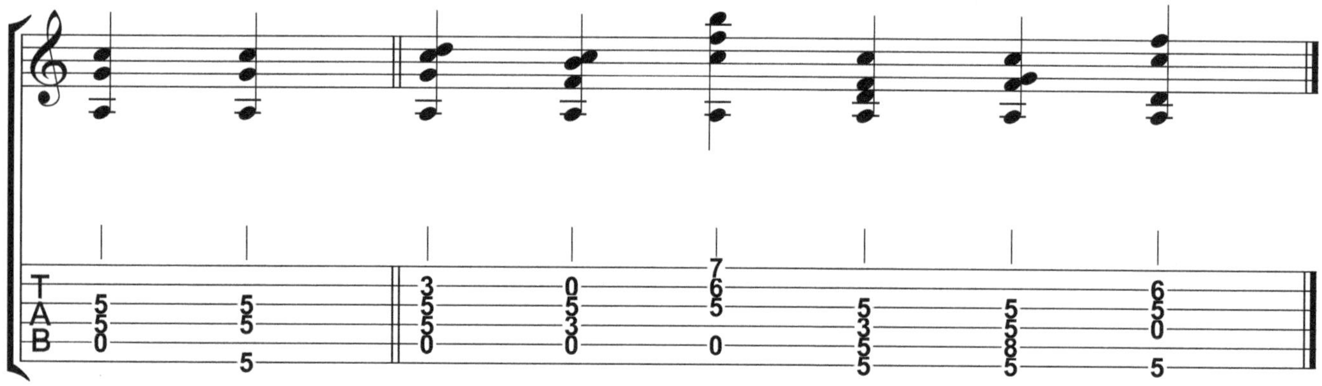

Some direct substitutions. Look for others

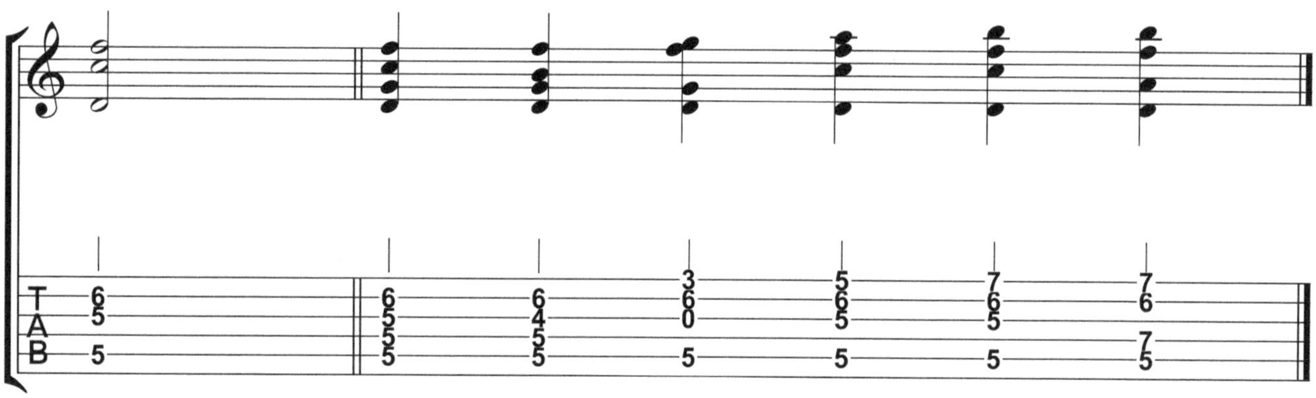

Some direct substitutions. Look for others

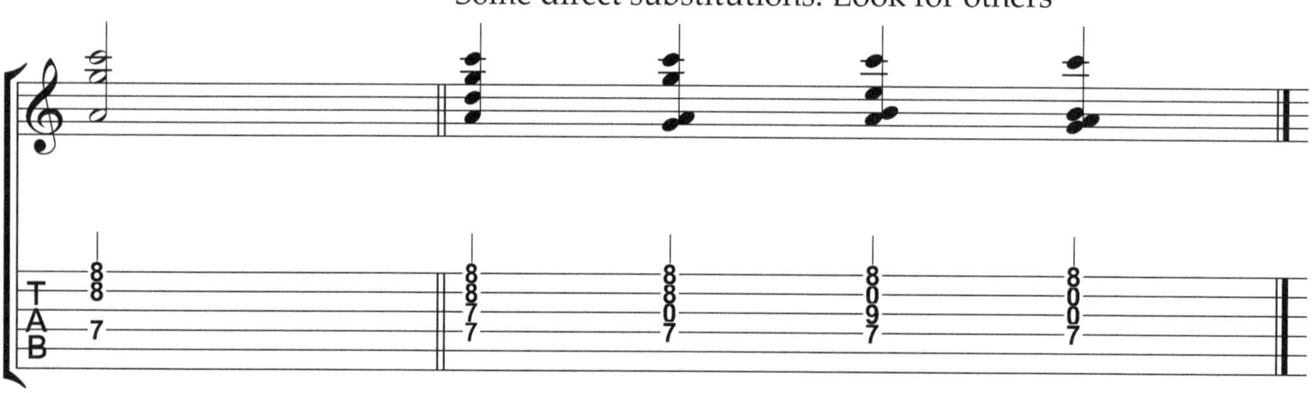

On Dominant7 Chords

Some direct substitutions

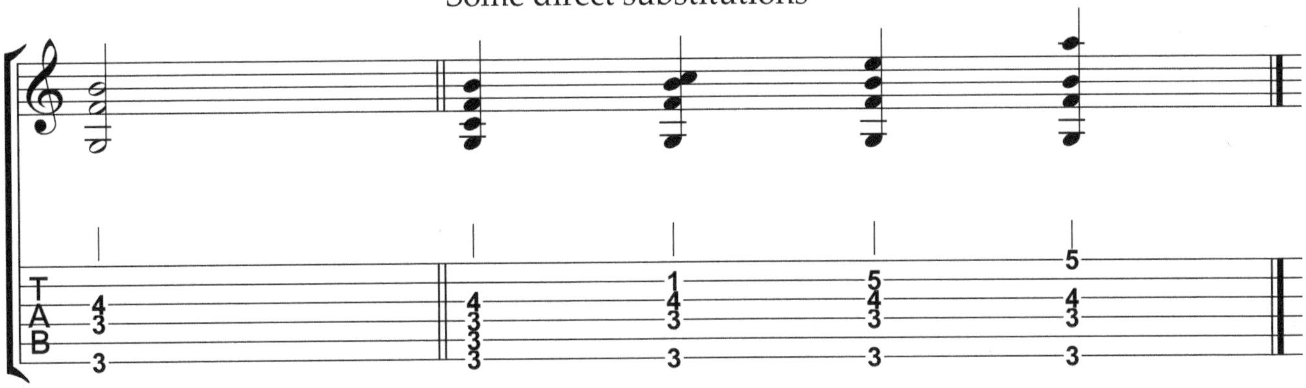

Some direct substitutions

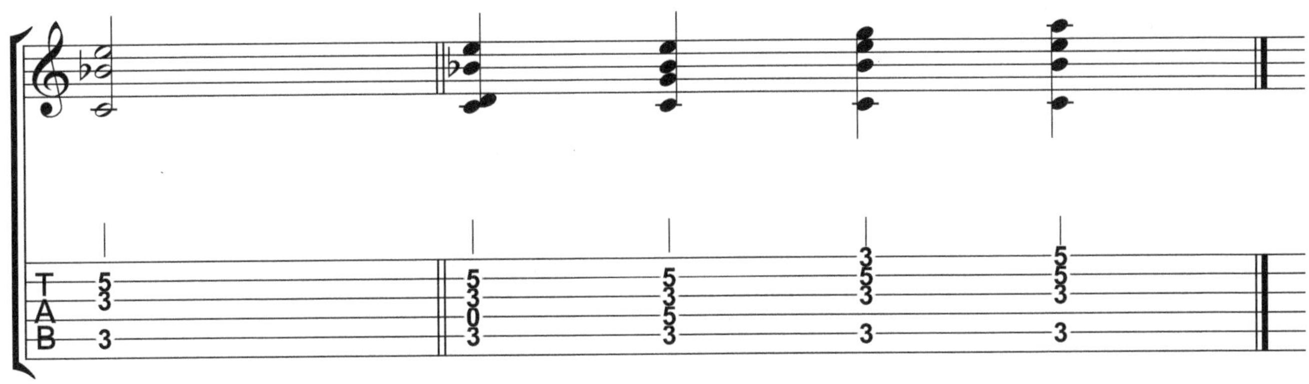

Some direct substitutions

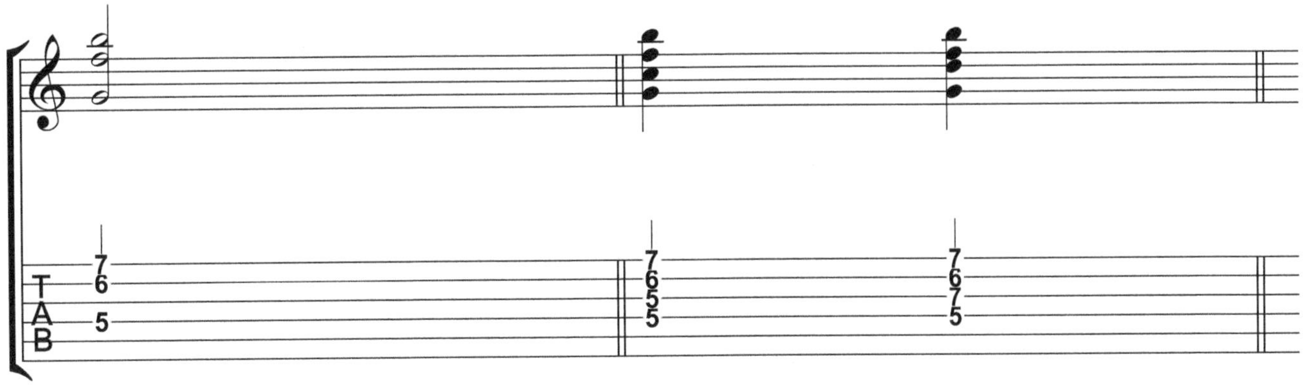

On a chord progression

Example 1

Track 59

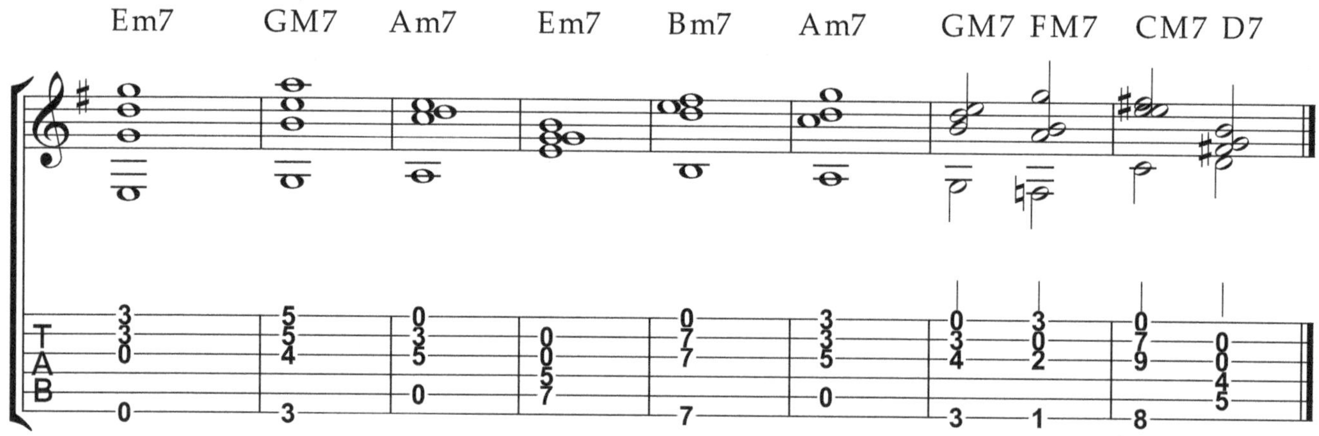

Example 2

Track 60

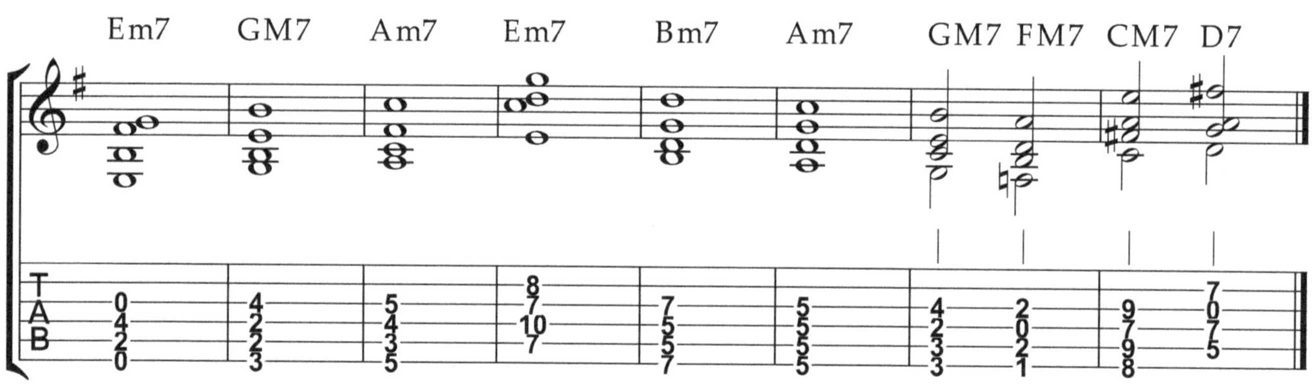

Track 61

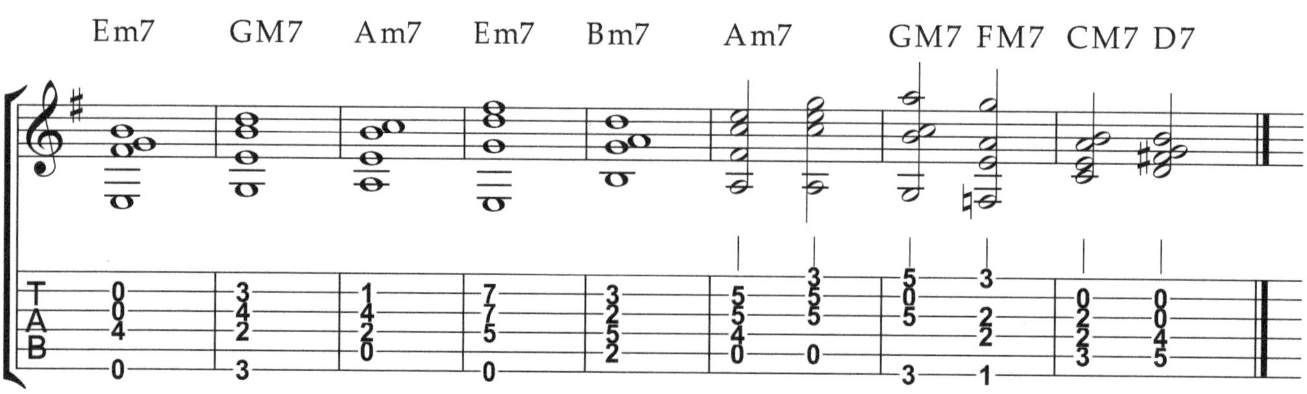

Improvisation on example 3

Track 62

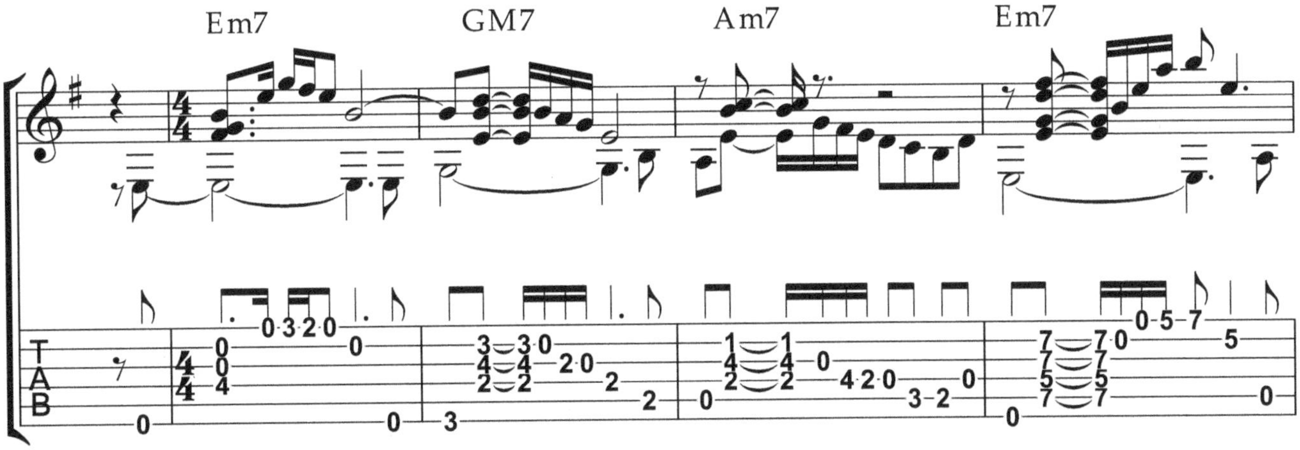

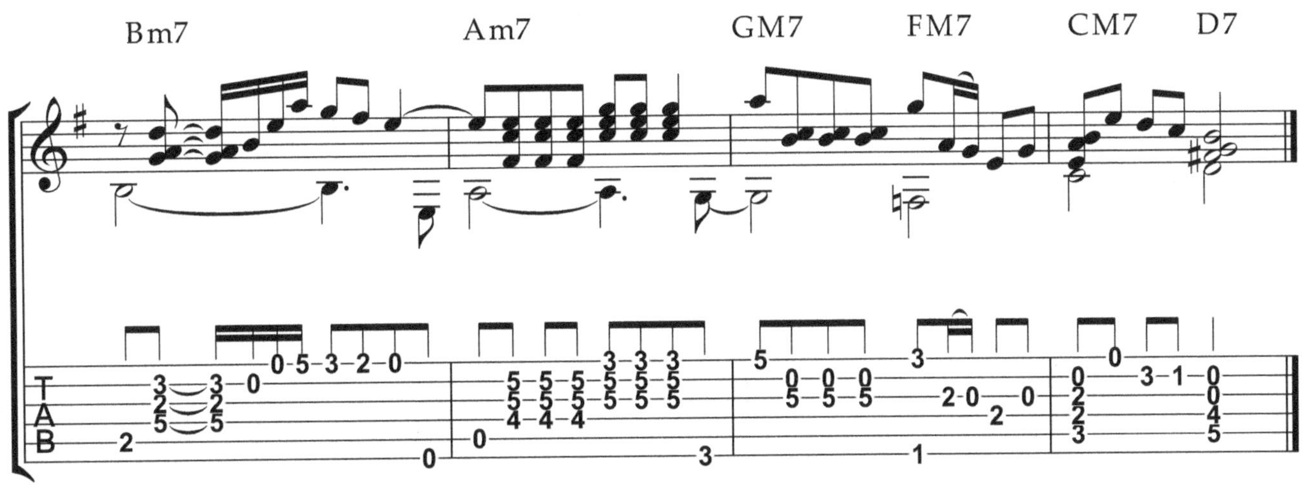

Your turn

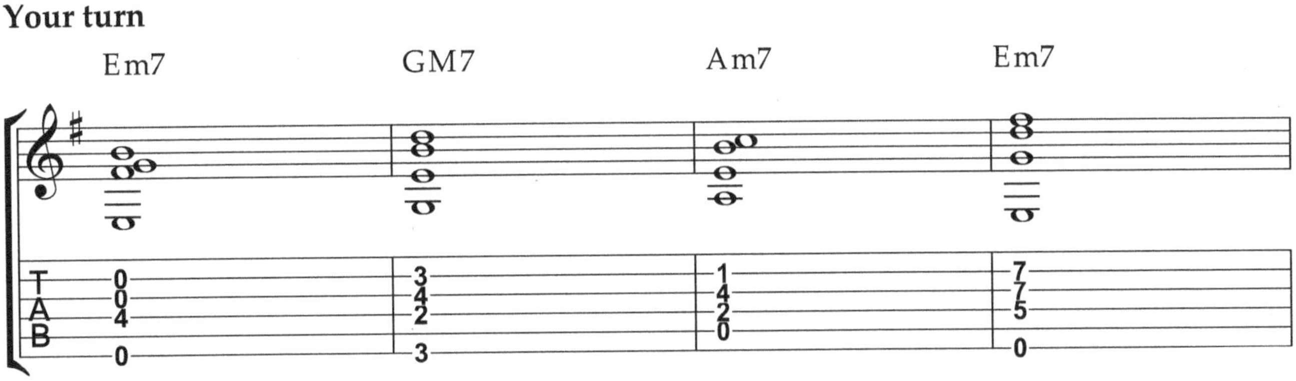

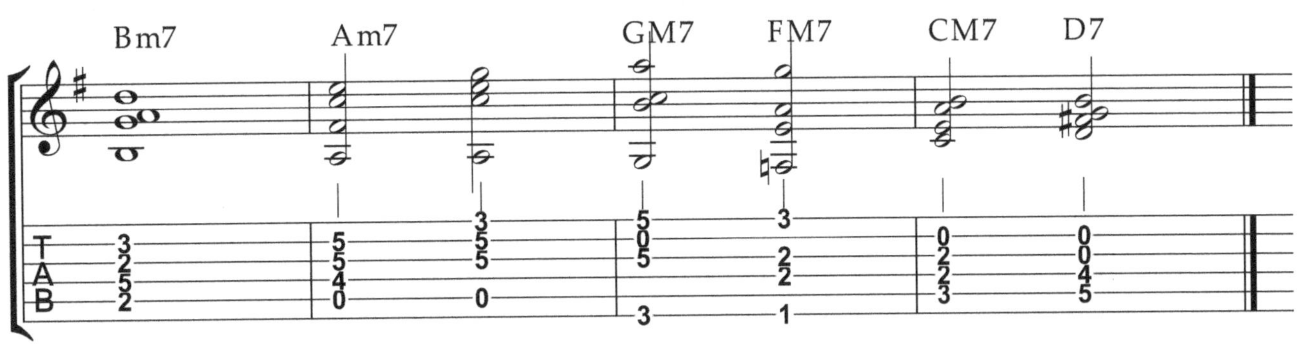

CHAPTER 26

Modern Sounds in Higher Positions

♭5 ♯5 --) lower or raise the 5th a half step (1 fret)
mM7 --) raise the ♭7 a half step
sus2 sus4 --) replace the 3rd by a 2nd or a 4th
m2 (♭2, ♭9) --) raise the root with a half step

Major chords

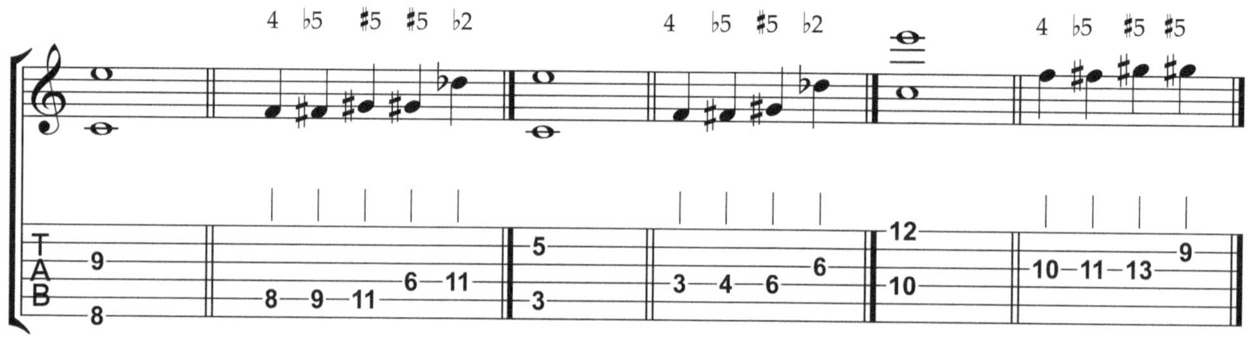

Minor chords

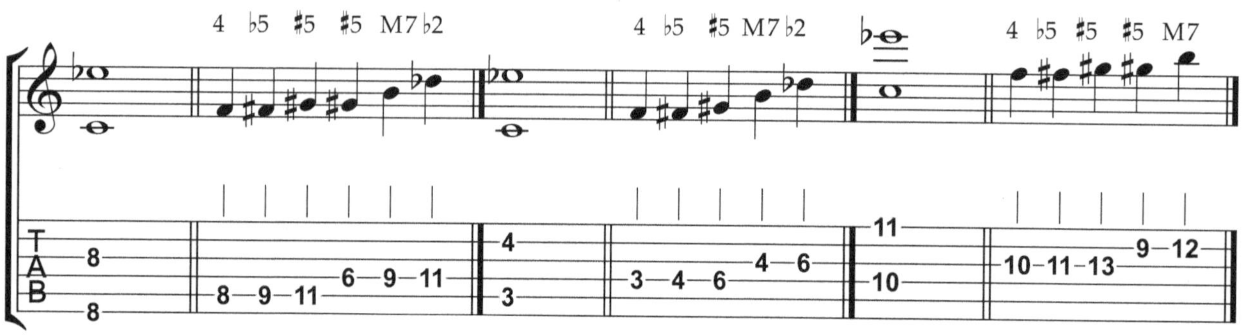

Dominant 7 chords

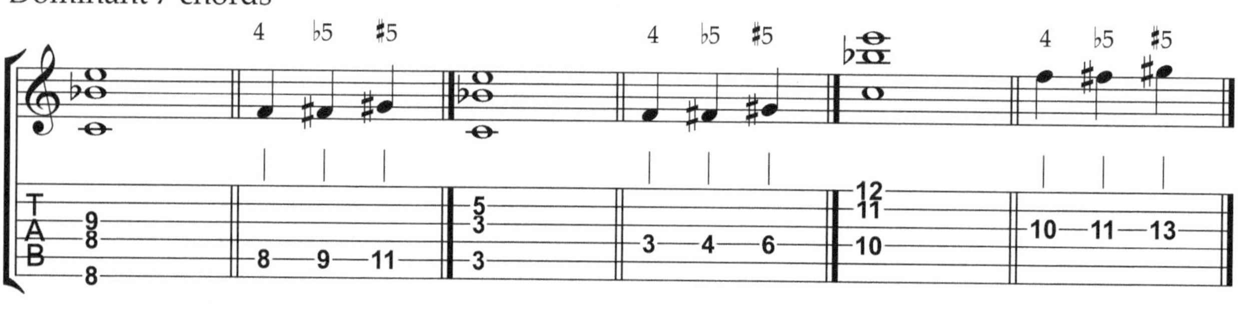

On another place on the fingerboard

Major chords

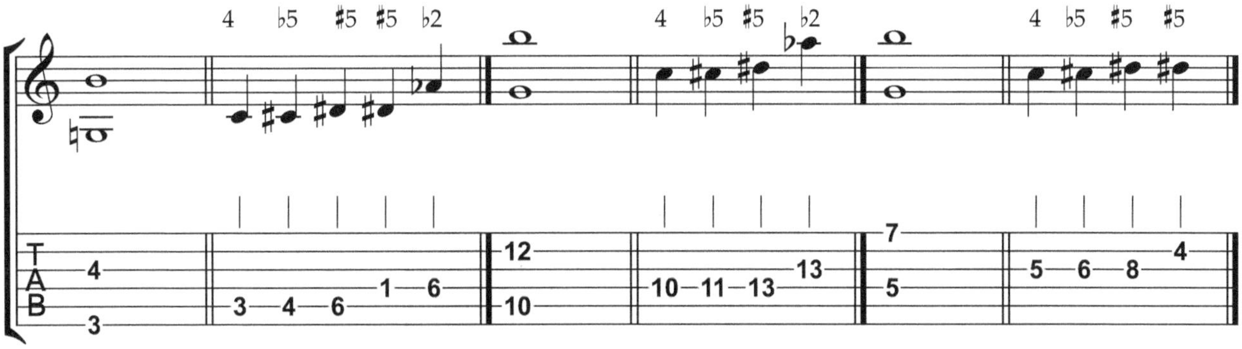

Minor chords

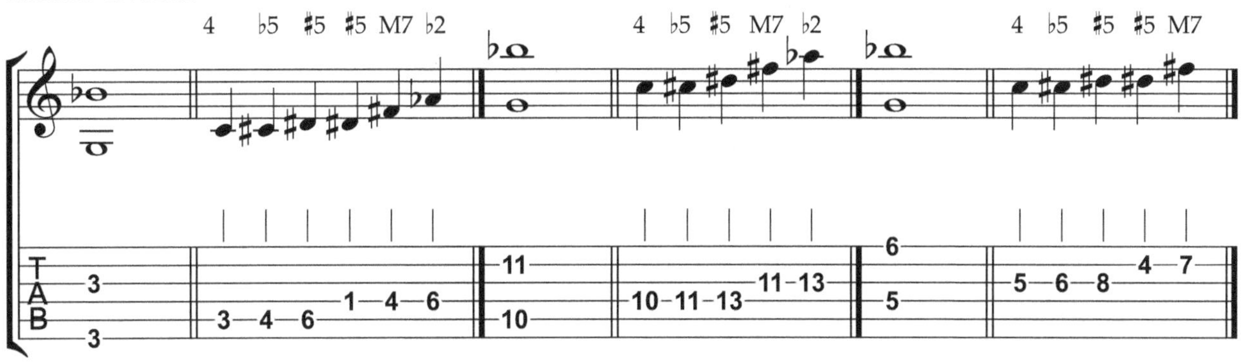

Dominant 7 chords

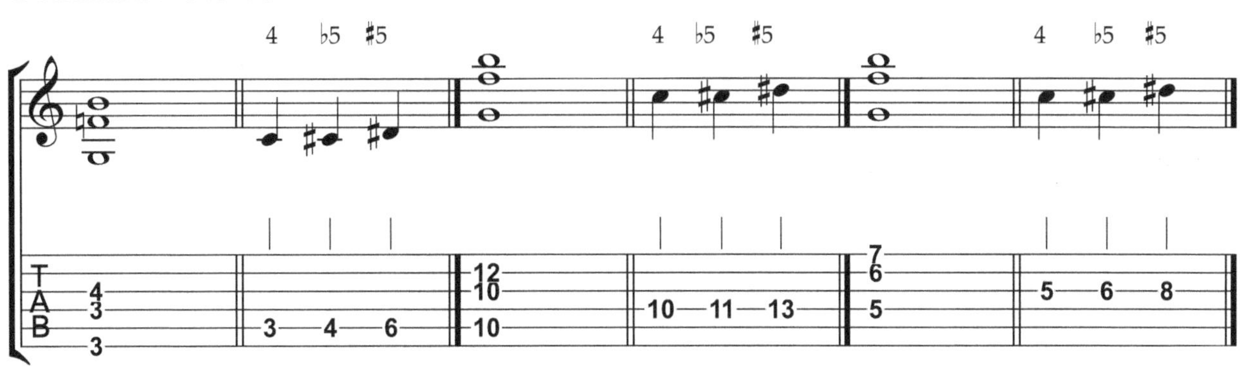

On a chord progression

Track 63

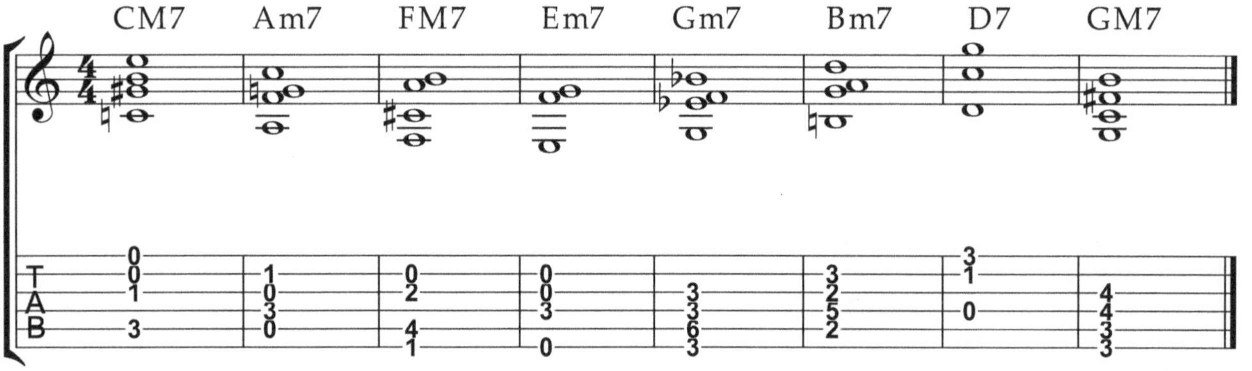

Example

Track 64

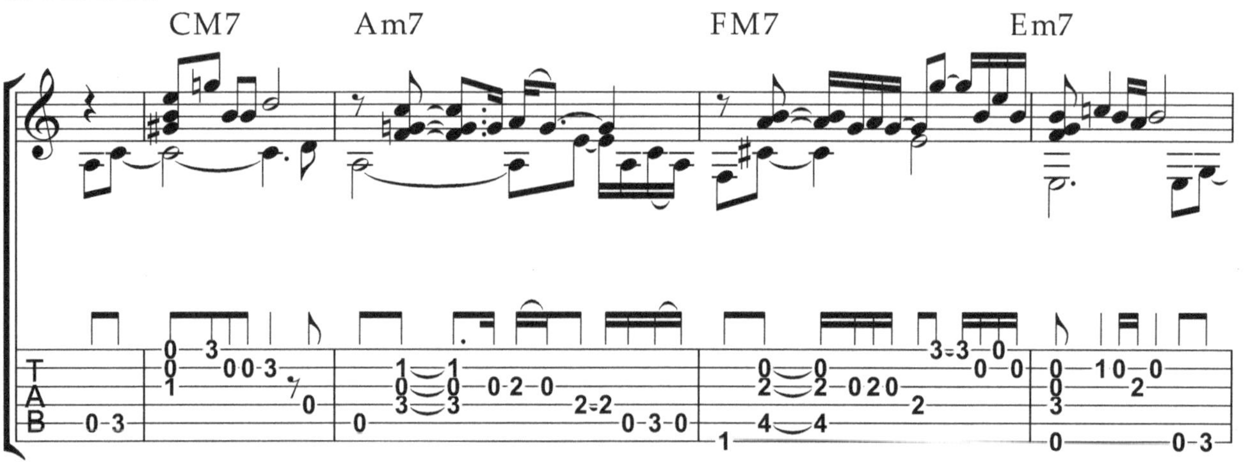

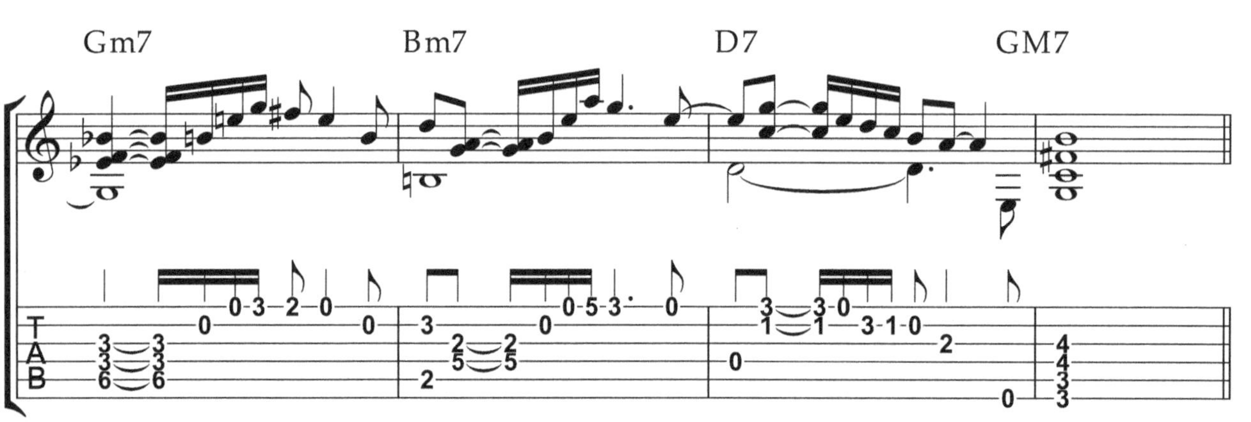

Your turn

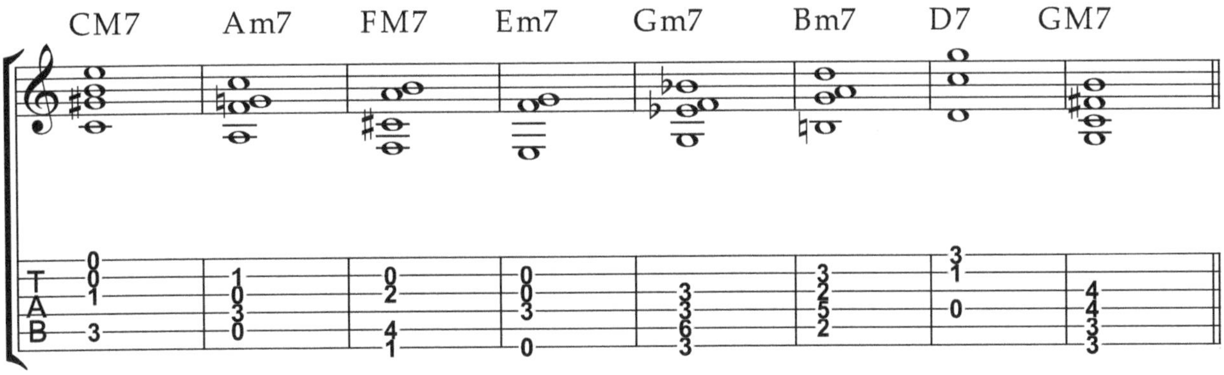

On another chord progression

Track 65

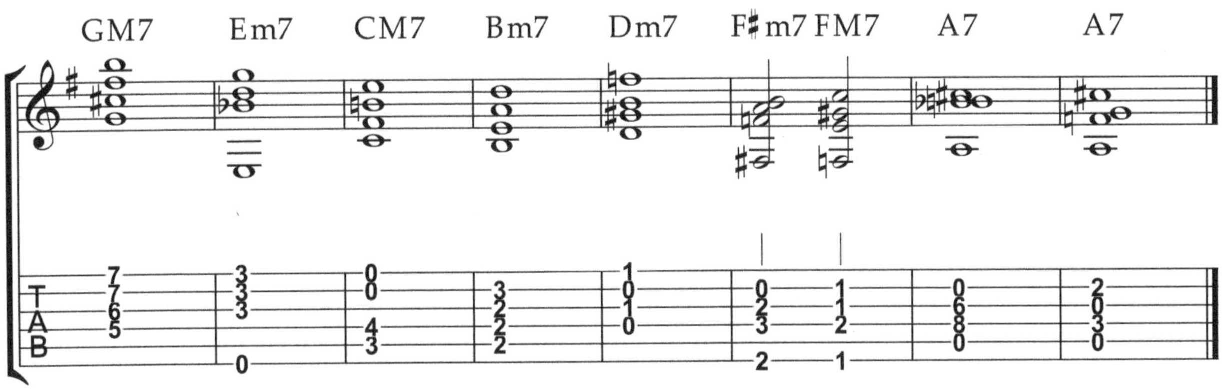

Example

Track 66

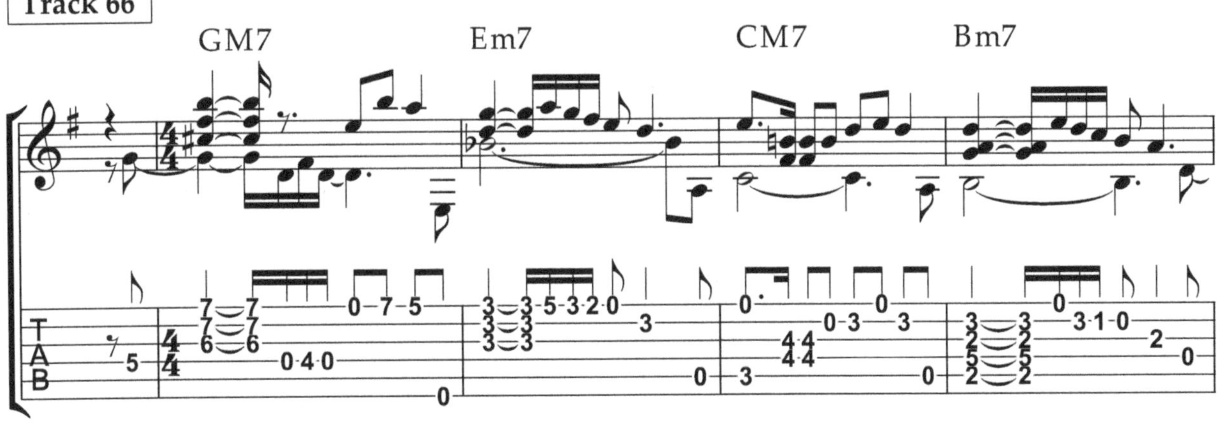

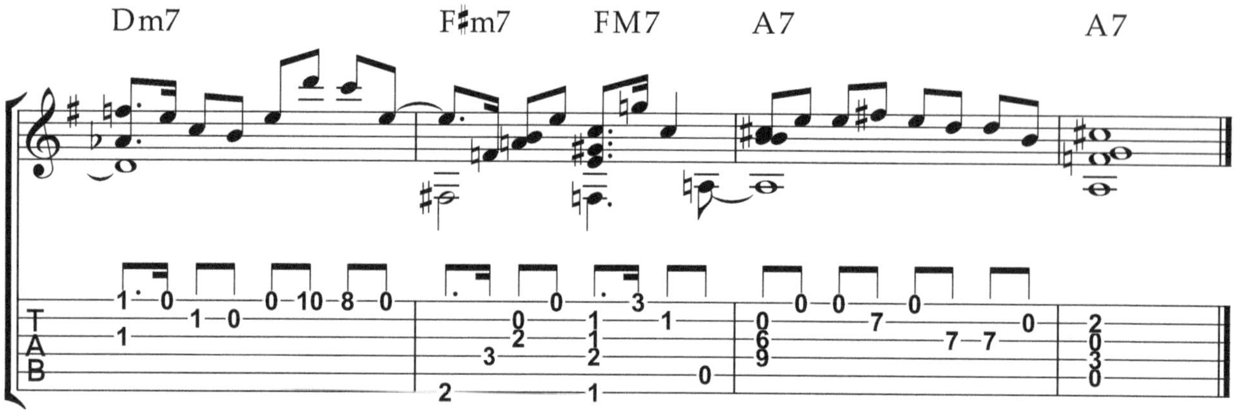

Your turn

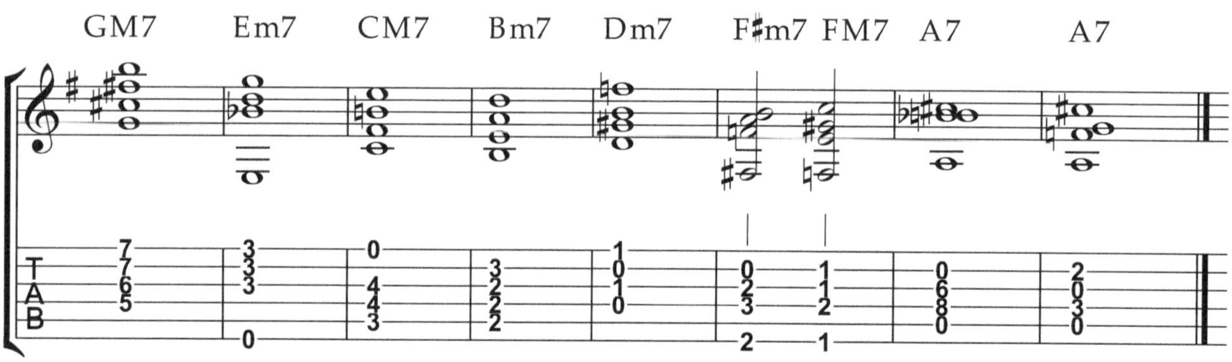

CHAPTER 27

Altered Dominants: ♭5 ♯5 ♭9 ♯9 in the Upper Voice

Root on the 5th string

on C7

9 ♭9 ♯9

C7♭9: C E B♭ D♭

C7♯9: C E B♭ D♯

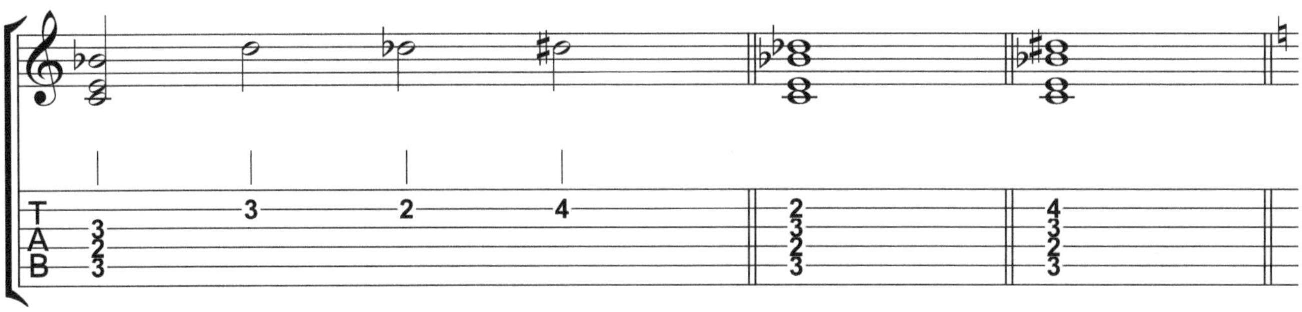

5 ♭5 ♯5

C7♭5: C E B♭ G♭

C7♯5: C E B♭ G♯

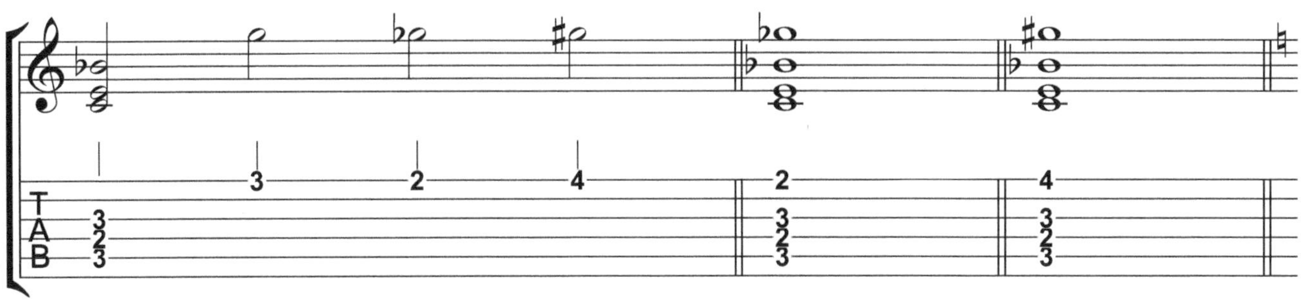

9 ♭9 ♯9

C7♭9: C E B♭ D♭

C7♯9: C E B♭ D♯

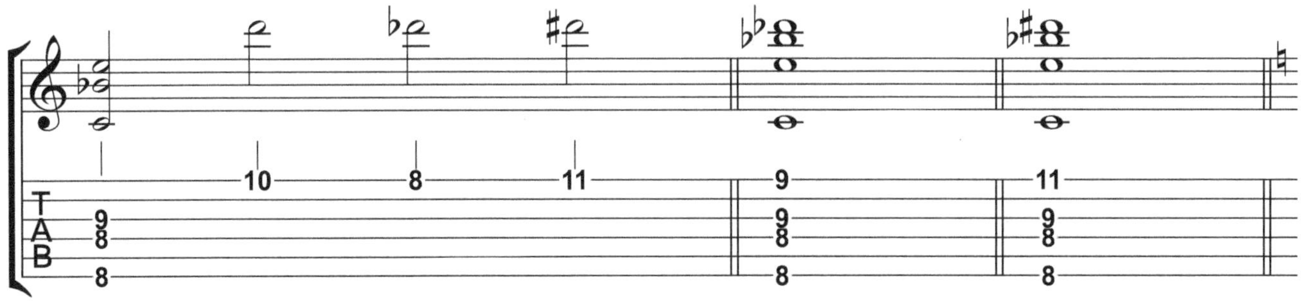

5 ♭5 ♯5

C7♭5:
C E B♭ G♭

C7♯5:
C E B♭ G♯

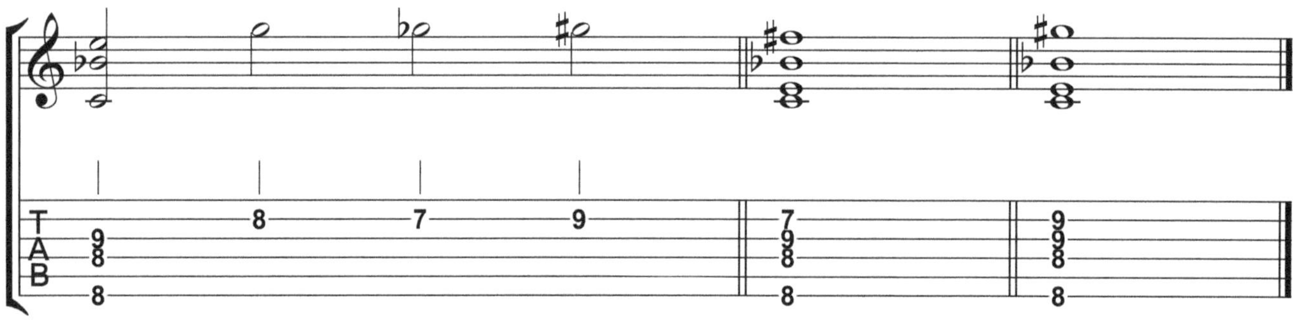

On a chord progression in C Major

Track 67

C7♭9
C D♭ E F G A B♭ C

D7♯9
D E F♯ G A B C D

G7♭9
G A♭ B C D E F G

A7♭9
A B♭ C♯ D E F G A

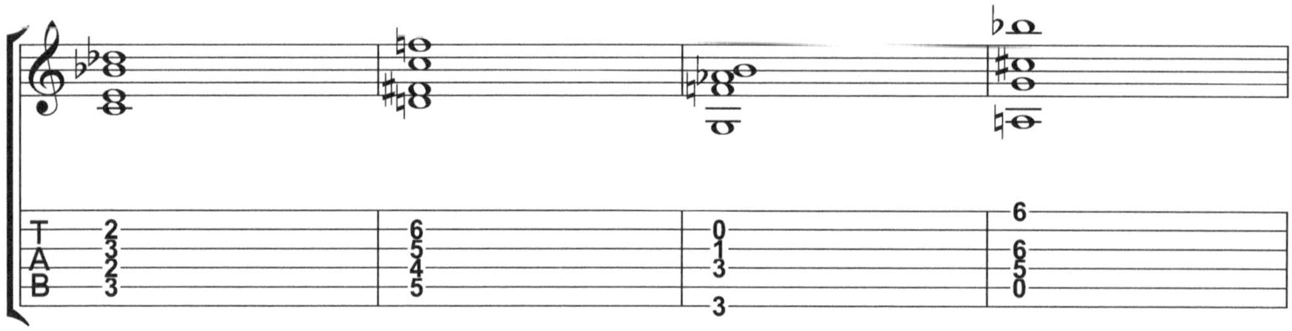

B7♭5
B C D♯ E F G A B

F7♭5
F G A B C D E♭ F

E7♯9 E7♭9 D7♯9 C♯7♭9

A7♭9
A B♭ C♯ D E F G A

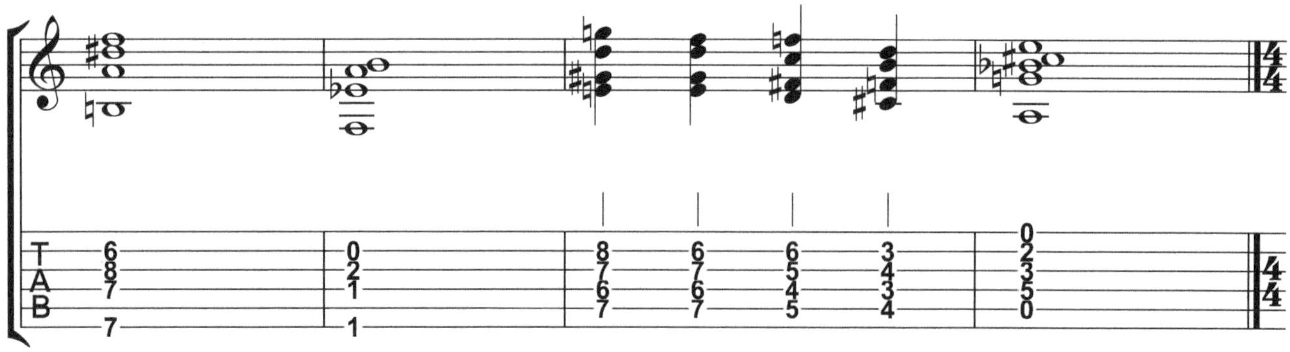

Example

Track 68

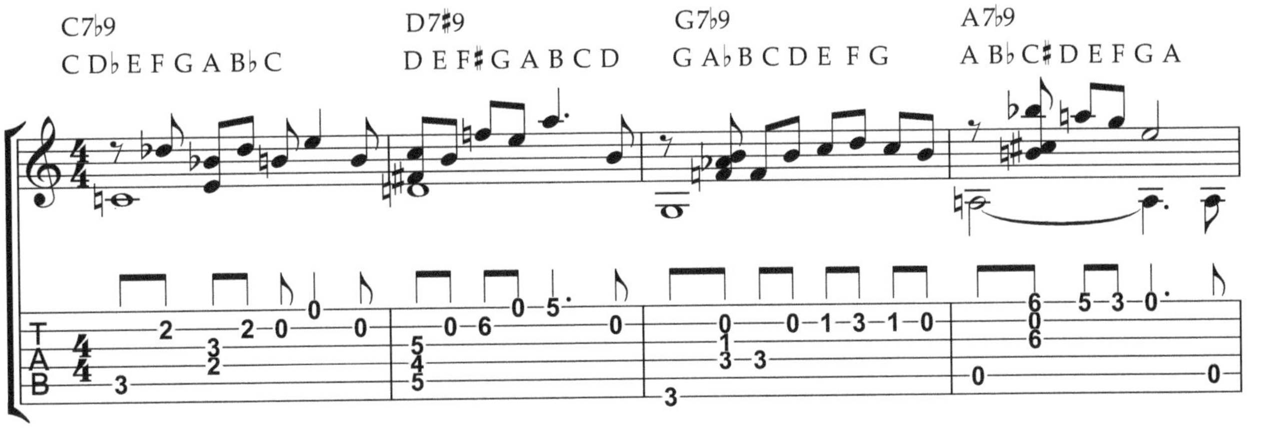

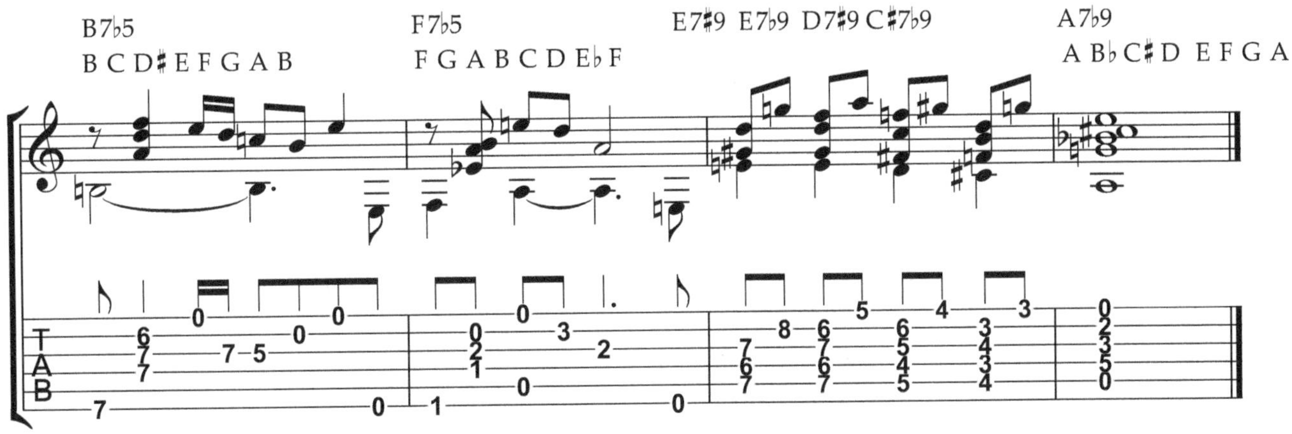

Your turn

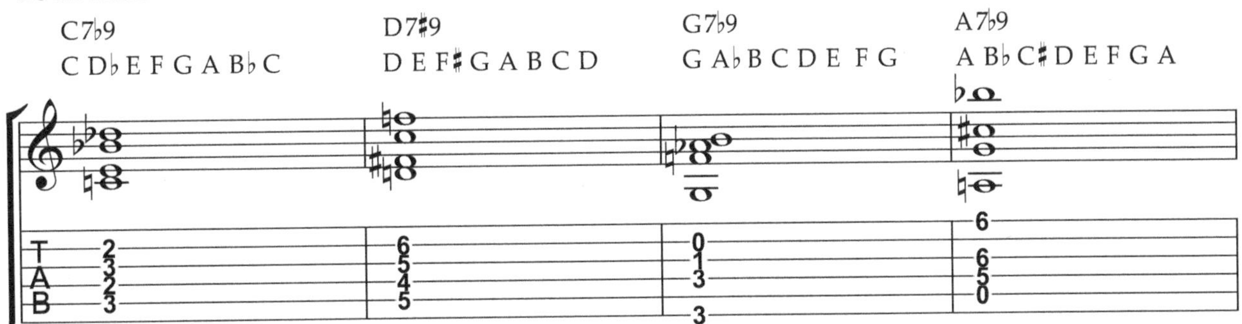

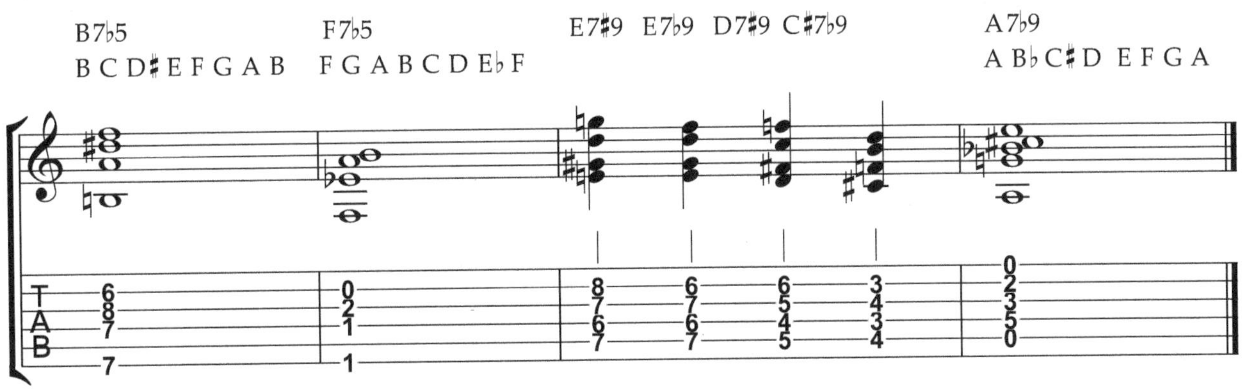

CHAPTER 28

Chord Progressions with Specific Chord Names

Sometimes chord names are very specific. Then it is advisable to figure out the formula and play the chords as suggested.

EmM9 = E G D F♯ (1 ♭3 5 7 9) The 5th is deleted, as it does not contribute to the sense of major or minor.
Bm7sus4 = B D E A (1 ♭3 4 ♭7)
D/F♯ (a **slash chord** such as D/F♯ means that the chord indicated on the left-hand side of the slash is played with the bass note indicated on the right-hand side of the slash. In this example the chord D is played over the bass note A.) (D A/F♯) (1 ♭7/3)
A/B♭ = A C♯ E/B♭ (1 3 5/♭9)
B/C = B D♯ F♯/C (1 3 5/♭2)
Bm/F = B D/F (1 ♭3/♭5)
Am+5: A C♯ F (1 3 ♯5)
Gm/C♯: G B♭ D/C♯ (1 ♭3 5/♭5)

Track 69

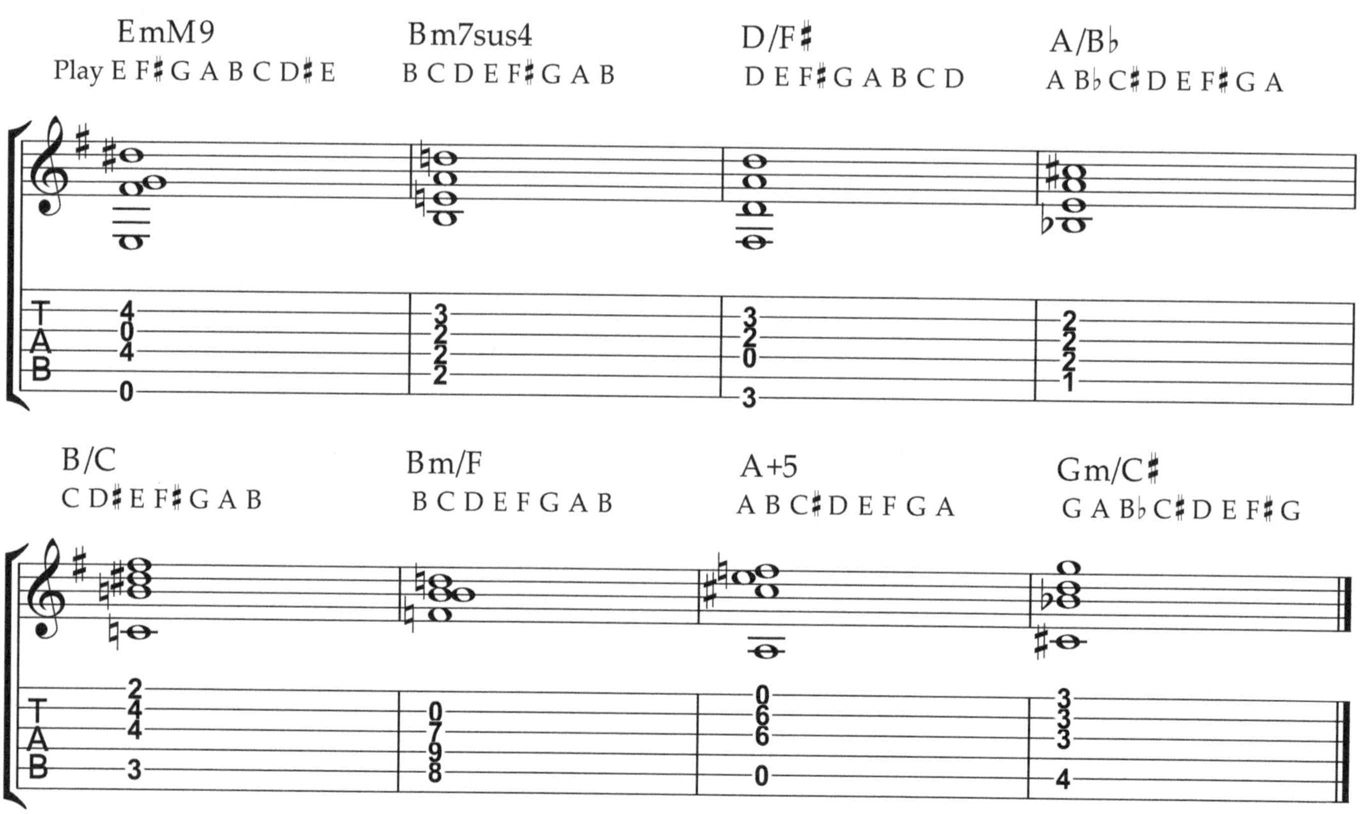

Track 70

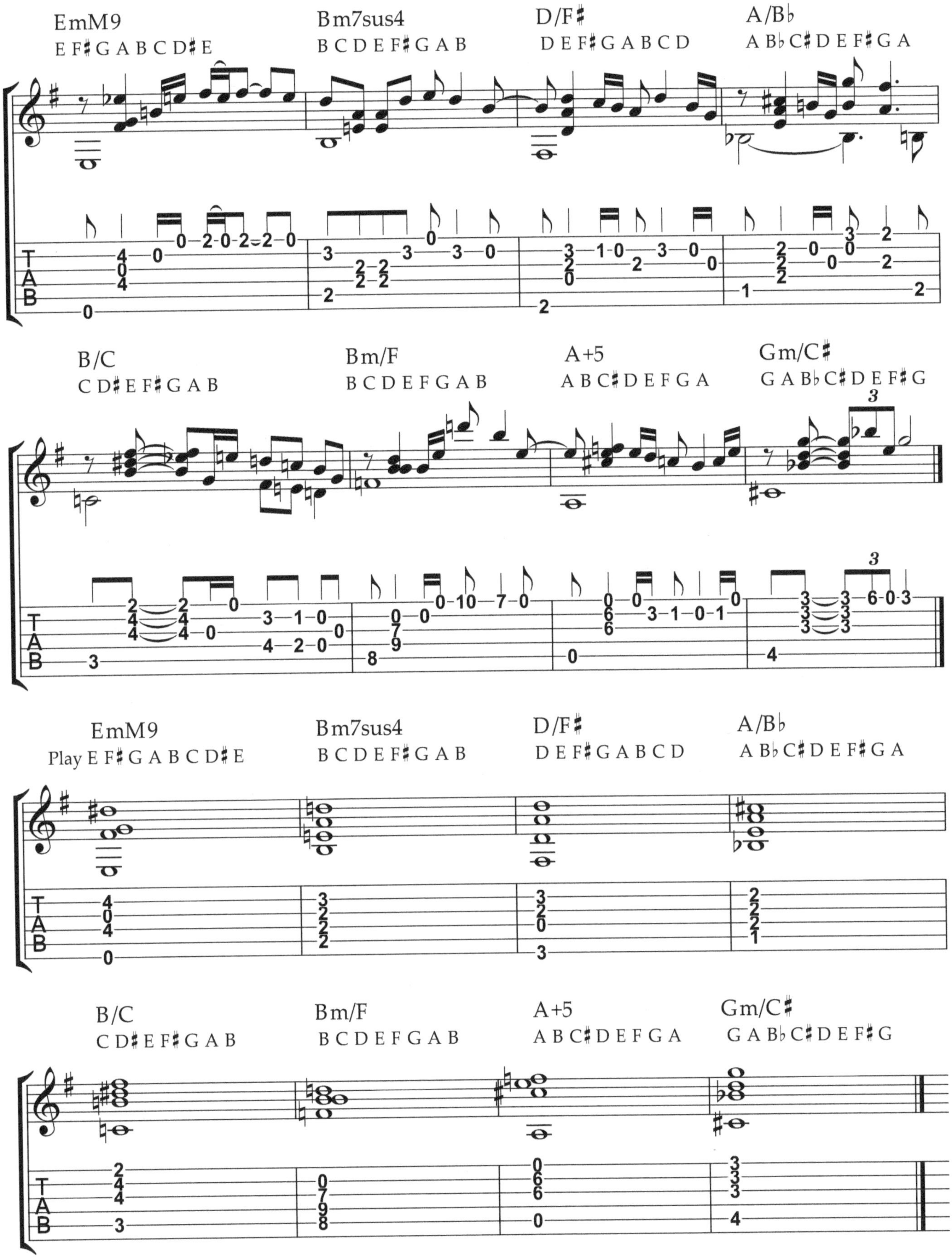
EmM9
E F♯ G A B C D♯ E
Bm7sus4
B C D E F♯ G A B
D/F♯
D E F♯ G A B C D
A/B♭
A B♭ C♯ D E F♯ G A
B/C
C D♯ E F♯ G A B
Bm/F
B C D E F G A B
A+5
A B C♯ D E F G A
Gm/C♯
G A B♭ C♯ D E F♯ G
EmM9
Play E F♯ G A B C D♯ E
Bm7sus4
B C D E F♯ G A B
D/F♯
D E F♯ G A B C D
A/B♭
A B♭ C♯ D E F♯ G A
B/C
C D♯ E F♯ G A B
Bm/F
B C D E F G A B
A+5
A B C♯ D E F G A
Gm/C♯
G A B♭ C♯ D E F♯ G

CHAPTER 29

All Together Now

In the following chord progression, almost every bar focuses on a different approach. From bar 18 on I combine different approaches.
Try to find the following:
1. Single line preceded by the root in the bass (Chapter 2)
2. Melodic line preceded by a dyad based on the root in the bass (Chapter 3)
3. Root-Root (Chapter 4)
4. Adding a middle voice based on scale notes (Chapter 5)
5. Chord arpeggiation (Chapter 8)
6. Chord parts and upper voice movement (Chapter 9)
7. Dyads based on all the scale notes (Chapter 10)
8. Root-third in the bottom voice (Chapter 12)
9. Embellishing the bass line: approach notes (Chapter 13)
10. Embellishing the bass line: a freer approach (Chapter 14)
11. Adding chromatic tones in the melody (Chapter 15)
12. ♭5 and ♯5 in the middle voice (Chapter 16)
13. Major and minor seconds in the middle voice (Chapter 18)
14. Adding an M7 to minor chords in the middle voice (Chapter 17)
15. Sus2 and sus4 chords (Chapter 19)
16. Root and upper voice movement in higher positions (Chapter 20)
17. Root-third: two part playing (Chapter 22)
18. Shell voicings and melodic material (Chapter 24)
19. Direct substitutions and melodic material (Chapter 25)
20. Modern sounds in the middle voice

Track 71

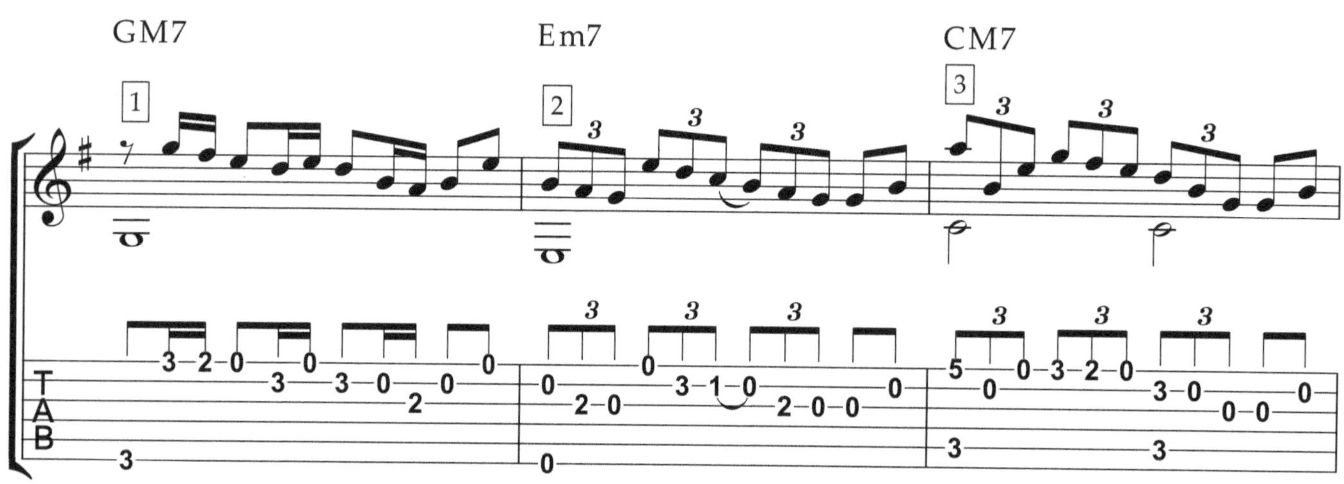

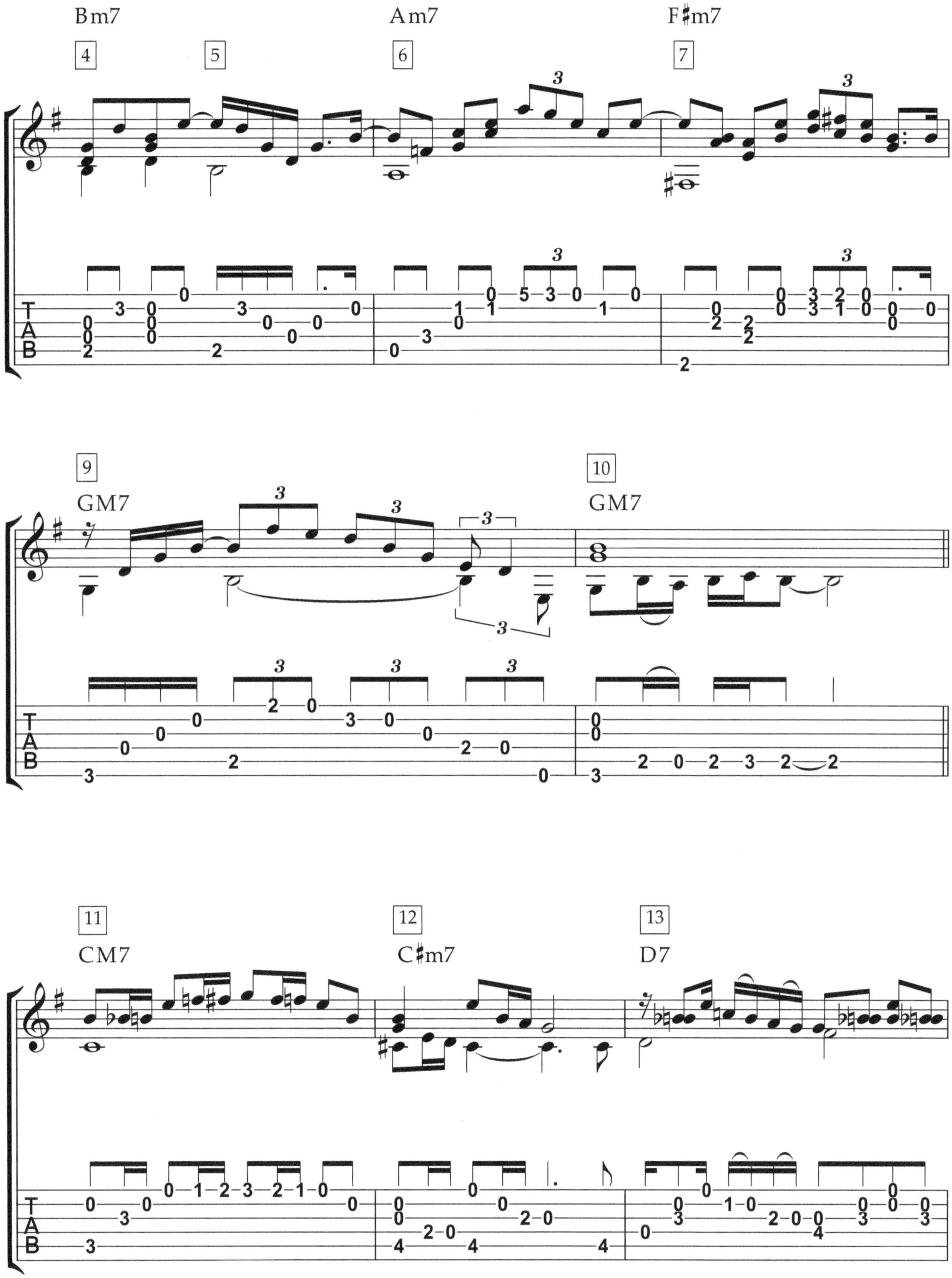
Bm7
4
5
Am7
6
F♯m7
7
9
GM7
10
GM7
11
CM7
12
C♯m7
13
D7

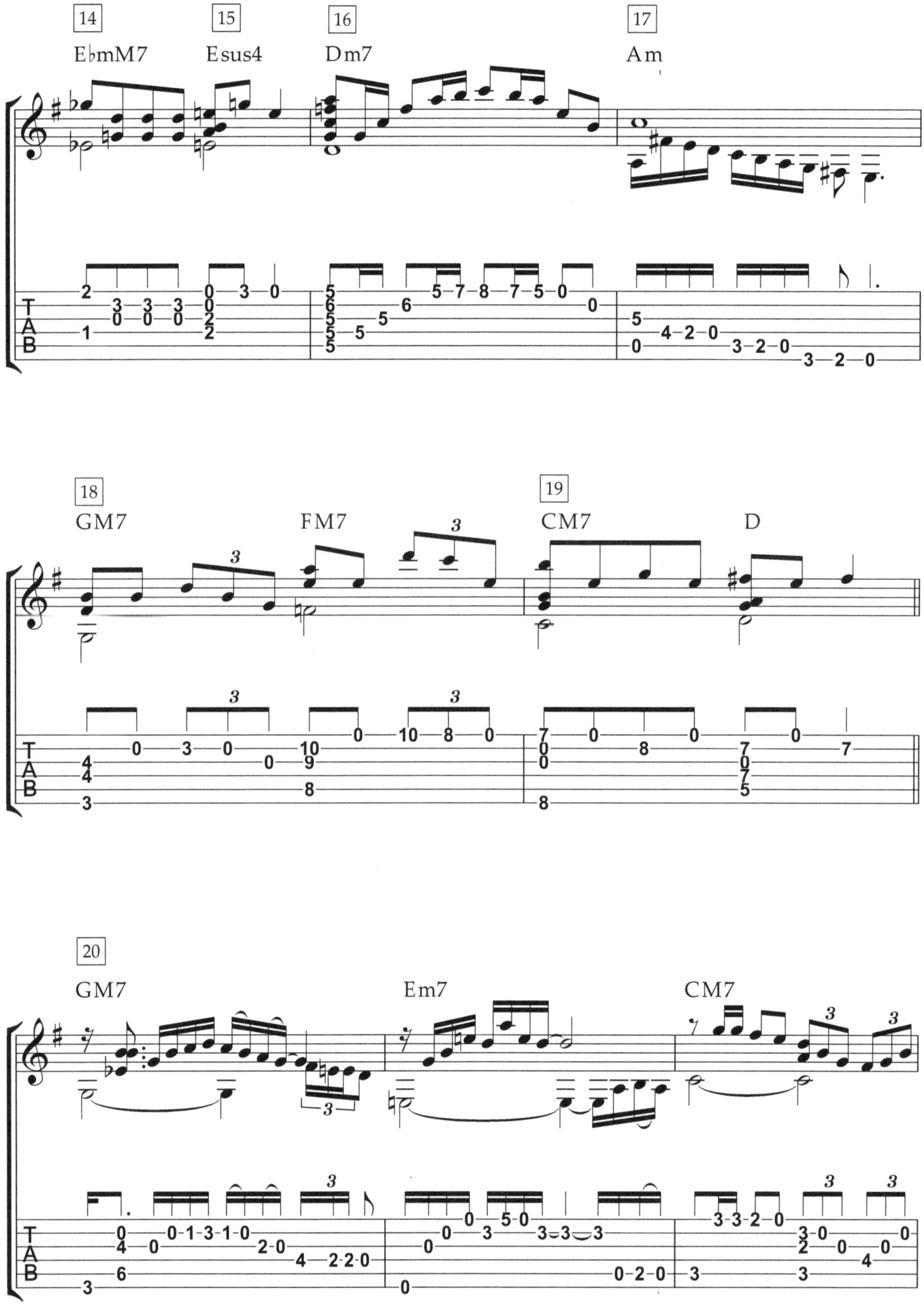
14
E♭mM7
15
Esus4
16
Dm7
17
Am
18
GM7
FM7
19
CM7
D
20
GM7
Em7
CM7

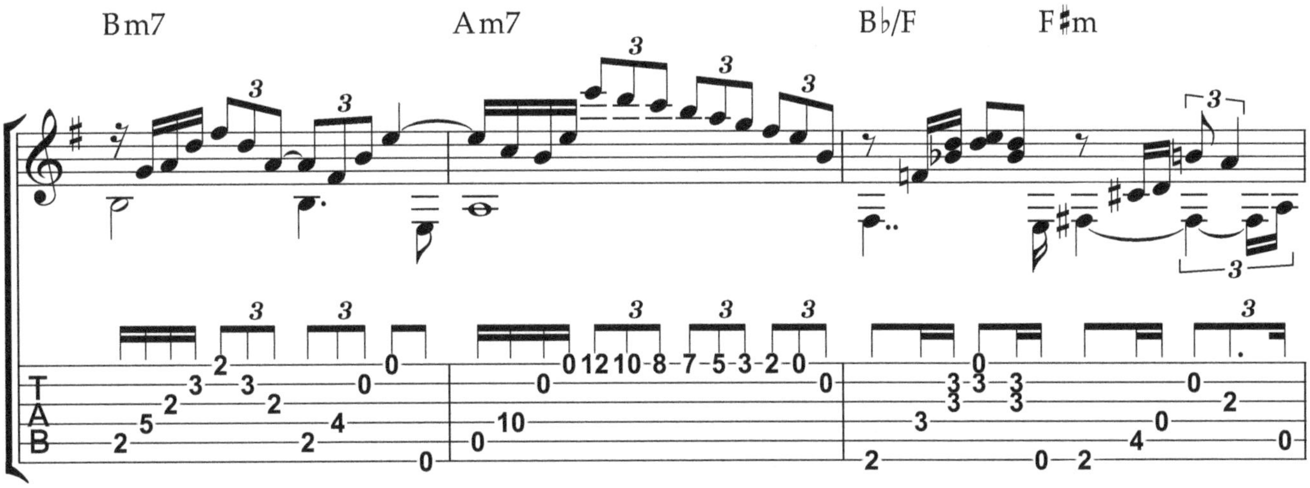
Bm7
Am7
B♭/F
F♯m

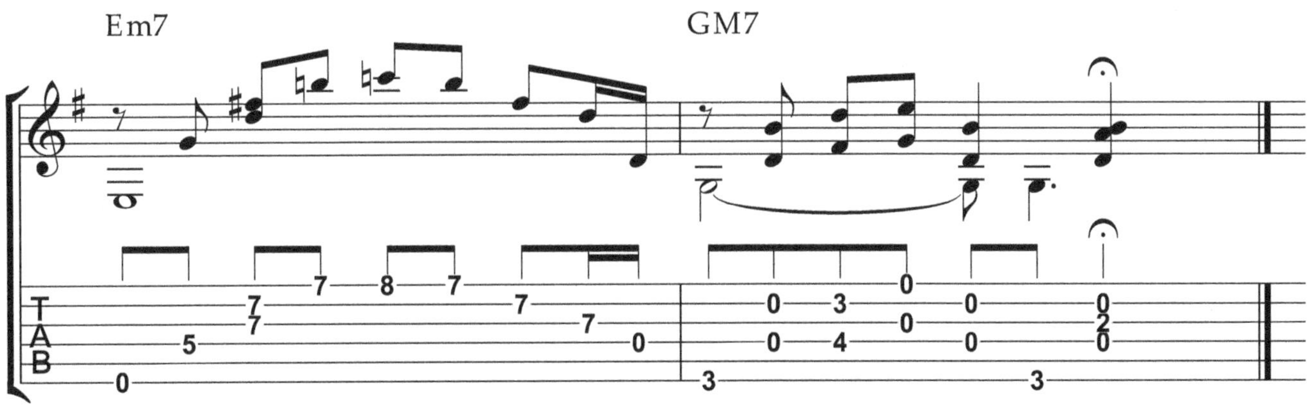
Em7
GM7

Audio Track Listing

Track **Page**

Track	Page

Fingerpicking Blues

Best of Blues Guitar (Sokolow)
Blind Joe Death: The Music of John Fahey (Lardner)
Blues & Jazz for Fingerstyle Guitar (Morone)
Blues and Ragtime Guitar of Rev. Gary Davis
Blues Classics for Acoustic Guitar (Eckels)
Blues Guitar Songbook (Silverman)
Complete Blues Guitar (M. Christiansen)
Duck Baker's Fingerstyle Blues Guitar 101
Fingerpicking Blues and Rock Guitar (Schell)
Fingerpicking Blues Guitar Solos (Grossman)
Fingerstyle Blues Method (Eckels)
Great Blues Solos (Sokolow)
Kentucky Thumbpicking Blues for Guitar (Flint)
Master Anthology of Blues Guitar Solos Vol. 1 (Multiple Authors)
Mel Bay Guitar University Fingerstyle Curriculum: Best Blues Solos (Multiple Authors)
Mississippi Delta Blues Fingerstyle Solos Made Easy (McCabe)
The Guitar of Robert Johnson (Mann)
You Can Teach Yourself Blues Guitar (M. Christiansen)

Celtic Fingerpicking

Celtic Back-Up (C. Smith)
Celtic Crossing (Coulter)
Celtic Guitar Encyclopedia (Weiser)
Complete Celtic Fingerstyle Guitar (Grossman/D. Baker/McMeen)
Deluxe Anthology of O'Carolan Music for Fingerstyle Guitar (Grossman/Renbourn)
Easy Celtic Solos for Fingerstyle Guitar (Crowley)
Encyclopedia of Irish and American Fiddle Tunes (D. Baker)
Irish and Scottish Airs and Ballads for Acoustic Guitar (Brennan)
Islands: Guitar Interpretations of Celtic Music (Hinchliffe)
Mel Bay Guitar University Fingerstyle Curriculum: Best Celtic Solos (Multiple Authors)
Music of the British Isles for Acoustic Guitar (Bellizzi)
Northumbrian and Border Folk Songs (Brennan)
O'Carolan Guitar Arrangements (Stevens)
Pat Kirtley: Irish Guitar
Steve Baughman's Celtic Guitar Method
Traditional Breton Dance Tunes - Fest Breizh (Surette)

Fingerpicking Guitar Technique

Acoustic Fingerstyle Guitar Workshop (Gilewitz)
Fingerpicking Scales (Lolax)
Fingerstyle Guitar Pattern Picking (Ten Broek)
Fingerstyle Technic (W. Bay)
Frailing the Guitar (Baughman)
Play American: Rhythm and Lead Country Guitar (Hartway)
Right-Hand Arpeggio Studies for Acoustic Guitar (Matteson)
Thumbpicking Chord Book (W. Bay)

WWW.MELBAY.COM